PROMETHEA

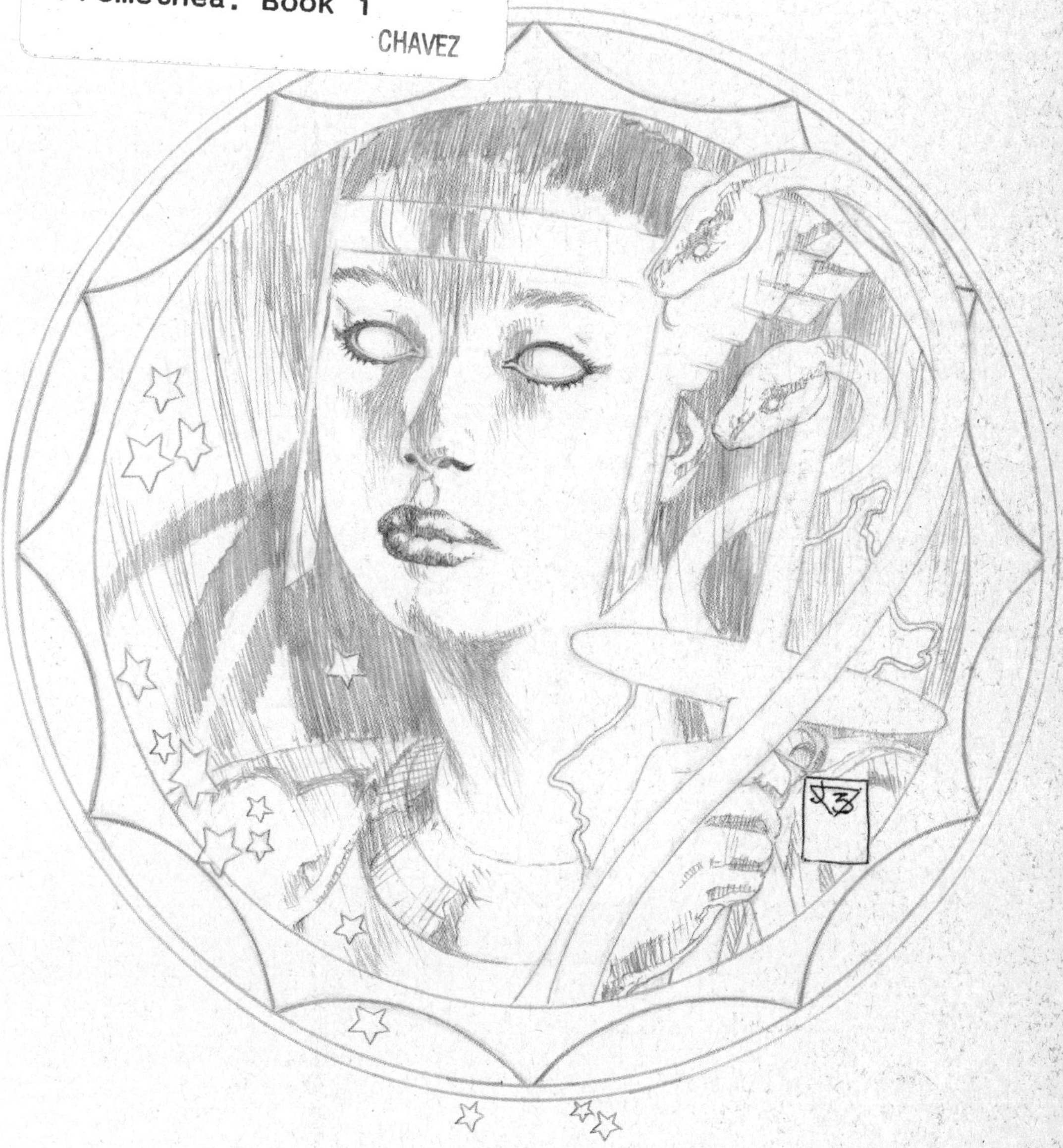

JIM LEE
Editorial Director

JOHN NEE
VP and General Manager

SCOTT DUNBIER
Group Editor
Promethea Editor

ERIC DeSANTIS
JEFF MARIOTTE
Assistant Editors

Front cover dust jacket art by
J.H. Williams III and Jose Villarrubia

Back cover dust jacket art by
J.H. Williams III and Mick Gray

PROMETHEA: BOOK 1 Published by America's Best Comics, LLC. Originally published in single magazine form as PROMETHEA, #1-6. Editorial offices: 7910 Ivanhoe, #438, La Jolla, CA 92037.
Printed in Canada. FIRST PRINTING.

PROMETHEA

COLLECTED EDITION BOOK 1

ALAN MOORE
writer

J.H. WILLIAMS III
penciller

MICK GRAY
inker

ADDITIONAL ART BY
CHARLES
VESS

WILDSTORM FX,
JEROMY COX,
ALEX SINCLAIR,
NICK BELL,
DIGITAL
CHAMELEON
coloring

TODD KLEIN
lettering, logos
and design

Promethea
created by
Alan Moore and
J.H. Williams III

AMERICA'S
BEST COMICS

THE PROMETHEA PUZZLE:
An Adventure in Folklore

"Then to that diamond-beaded glade there came
A pageant throng of sweet imaginings,
Of Faeries, Imps and creatures without name,
A great frenetic bustling of wings.
About their Queen four nymphs-in-waiting stood
Girded in armour, each of beauty rare:
Cowslip, and Flax, and Jenny-in-the-Wood,
And sweet Promethea, with her plaited hair."

With these lines, some fifty stanzas into his epic sentimental fantasy *A Faerie Romance*, New England poet Charlton Sennet (1751-1803) makes his first mention of a character who has since then evolved into a fascinating literary mystery in her own right. Promethea, a handmaiden "with skin like polished betel-wood," is introduced as one of the four handmaidens to the Faerie Queen Titania (a straight crib from *A Midsummer Night's Dream*, to which Sennet originally intended his own poem as a tribute), but within a dozen or so stanzas seems to have completely taken over both the entire poem and the poet's imagination.

What starts out as an idyll with Titania and her faerie entourage at play in some Arcadian backwater of the natural world is quickly sidetracked into a long narrative that details an intense and (for the period) passionate romance between the nymph Promethea and "a mortal shepherd lad, with moon-calf eyes," in whose poetic nature one suspects Sennet intended an extremely flattering depiction of himself. Sennet, from such few descriptions of him as exist, appears as a somewhat unpleasant man whose wife left him abruptly when she learned he had seduced a simple-minded servant girl in their employ. From there the tale becomes more grim and sordid still, although nothing of any substance could ever be proven. Afterward, Sennet would seem to have sunk into a deep depression, ending only with the poet's death from liver failure at the relatively early age of fifty-two years old. All this is a far cry from the moonstruck and sensitive young shepherd/poet that's described in Sennet's narrative, and yet one can't escape the feeling that in the unblemished innocence of his male lead, hopelessly in love with an immortal being from the Land of Faerie, Sennet was describing himself as he *wished* he'd been. His poem, overlong and often plodding in its rhythm, can almost be seen as a protracted and idyllic sexual fantasy in which Sennet sought solace from the bitter circumstances of real life.

The fact that in the first years of the twentieth century both Sennet and his work were in effect unknown makes the next incarnation of Promethea something of a puzzle to the modern literary historian. In 1901, in the Sunday color section of William Randolph Hearst's *New York Clarion*, a comic strip both drawn and written by the artist Margaret Taylor Case commenced a lengthy run that lasted until Case retired in 1920. *Little Margie in Misty Magic Land* was a sometimes saccharine but, more often, genuinely charming and inventive fantasy about a little girl called Margie and her strange adventures in the daydream world of her imagination, the Misty Magic Land of the strip's title. Here, she would encounter fairies, centaurs, ancient gods, and characters from folklore, such as in the memorable extended serial which depicted Margie

helping to depose a Jack who'd grown tyrannical and taken over the enormous Beanstalk-kingdom previously inhabited by giants. Sequences including Margie trapped inside a giantess's sewing basket with its monstrous cotton reels and tape measure showed off Margaret Case's deft ability at conjuring a dreamlike atmosphere by playing with the size and scale of things and made her comic strip a minor legend in its field, still studied by *aficionados* today.

Case claimed that Little Margie was in fact herself as a child, and that the infant's curious adventures (in quaintly-named regions of Misty Magic Land such as The Splendid Strand of Yawn, or Dogworm's Fuming Terrace) were no more than the cartoonist's childhood wanderings in the realm of fancy, transformed almost verbatim into a comic strip. If this is so, then it would seem that Margaret Taylor Case was not aware of the Promethea in Charlton Sennet's poem when she introduced a character of the same name and of a very similar nature to her cast of cartoon players in the fall of 1903. While lost in Baron Fireglove's Chuckling Orchard, Margie is eventually rescued by a brace of characters that would remain her companions for almost the rest of the newspaper strip's duration. These were a benign and often motherly fairy princess named Promethea, and a regrettable comic-relief sidekick named Chinky the Chinese Imp. Chinky, a grotesque and demonic racial caricature complete with pigtail and gibberish dialogue ("Moo foo boo!"), while obviously offensive to contemporary audiences, was hardly out of keeping with the outlook of the times, in which racial minorities were cast, routinely, as degrading comic stooges and buffoons. Chinky can never be said to have developed as a personality during his lengthy tenure in the strip. The same is not true of Promethea.

As Case depicted her, Promethea emerges as a brave, compassionate figure with what at times would seem an almost melancholy air about her. In her earliest appearances, she patiently explains to Little Margie that she's had and lost a daughter of her own, and feels a great attachment to Margie as a direct consequence of this. There is even one sequence, puzzlingly out of character and never subsequently mentioned in any later episode, where Promethea grows angry and resentful of Little Margie's periodic returns to her natural family in the real, waking world: "Don't you think that I'd like to go there with you, now and then? I had a father once myself, you know, when I was a real little girl!" This bewildering outburst is never explained, but it served to indicate the level of complexity and intrigue that Case brought to a supporting character with only a minor role to play.

Promethea's exit from the strip, some several months before Case opted for retirement in May of 1920, is just as striking and as mystifying. Announcing that she's "tired of people and their warlike ways," she says farewell to Margie and embarks, Chinky in tow, upon a journey that she says will lead her to a kingdom of her own. What kingdom this might be is not remarked upon, nor is her statement properly explained, when, in the seventeen years of her stay in *Little Margie* she has seen no warfare and, other than Margie herself, very few examples of what might reasonably be called people. After Promethea's departure, much of the life, imagination and enthusiasm that Case had invested in the work seemed to have departed with her. Six months of pallid and lackluster stories followed before the cartoonist, sensing that the work had lost its magic, put away her brush and pen and settled for a retirement that was comfortable and uneventful.

The Promethea trail grows cold for a few years until the pulp boom of the 1920s, when again we find a character of that name and with certain common traits appearing in a serial narrative. Once more, it would appear as if the various creators who would engineer Promethea's next incarnation did so without knowledge of Charlton Sennet or the background character that had appeared in *Little Margie*, although obviously the latter cannot be entirely ruled out. This Promethea was the lead figure and the heroine of an occasional series of short fantasy novellas that appeared in the acclaimed pulp monthly *Astonishing Stories*, starting in the issue dated February, 1924. Other than in her name and in some details of appearance, this Promethea is very different from her earlier namesakes, being both a fierce and amorous warrior queen constantly fighting to protect her lost fantasy land of Hy Brasil from various devilish and monstrous invaders, all originating in the demon-haunted territories beyond the country's boundaries. In the first published tale, *A Warrior Queen of Hy Brasil*, we find the plucky outlander Promethea as she fights her way up from foot soldier to become the sovereign ruler of the vast and marvelous domain. Credited (as were all subsequent Promethea stories) to Marto Neptura, the tale portrays Promethea as a sexually knowing woman with a string of lovers in her past and a ferocious skill with swords and axes.

In fact, "Marto Neptura" was as nonexistent as Promethea herself, being merely an invented house-pseudonym under which a great number of nameless hack writers churned out what were usually (it must be said) both uninspired and uninspiring potboiler narratives of the "Spicy Fantasy" school. Here follows an example from *Promethea and the Manigators*, the eighth story in the series: "The rivulets of blood on her brown arms were like a scarlet lacework, fitfully illuminated in the staccato and infrequent dazzle of the lightning. With her firm breasts heaving, the beloved Queen of Hy Brasil forced her reptilian antagonist closer and closer to the chasm's edge. His terrifying jaws snapped tight together only inches from her face as, with the muscles standing out on her long, tawny legs, she heaved the alligator-creature into the abyss below." Clearly, the fact that the Promethea tales in *Astonishing* are still remembered fondly and are indeed quite collectible is not based on the literary merit of the stories. It's interesting to observe that both the poet Sennet and the nameless author of the Manigators yarn describe Promethea's skin as tawny.

In actuality, the enduring popularity of Marto Neptura's Promethea had nothing to do with the mythical Mr. Neptura and everything to do with the legendary Grace Brannagh, a pulp cover illustrator with a style that's been compared to near-contemporary Margaret Brundage, who provided painted covers for some fifty issues of *Astonishing*, including all fifteen issues in which the lead story was a new Promethea novella, creating a firm bond in the reader's mind between the artist and the heroine. It hardly comes as a surprise that almost all the articles since written on Promethea in the pulps have focused on Grace Brannagh's contribution, leaving the actual stories and their content virtually ignored. Brannagh's Promethea conceals a number of intriguing elements beneath a pulp veneer. The cover illustrations, in their luminous depictions of the continent of Hy Brasil, portray a world that's hauntingly surreal and alien, with shifting, metamorphic rock formations beneath a swirling

emerald sky that could never have possibly existed on our world, for all that the interior narratives insist that "Hy Brasil" is a real continent in Earth's primordial past. It turns out that the continent of Hy Brasil *was* once considered to be real, and is indeed depicted on the shipping maps of only a few hundred years ago. In many ways it would seem to correspond to Paradise or even Fairyland. Celtic mythology names Hy Brasil as *Tir na Nog*, the Faerie kingdom. Oddly, this almost brings us back to Sennet's vision of Promethea as hailing from the realm of fairies and folklore.

In 1938, the publishers responsible for *Astonishing Stories* were bought out by a group called Apex Magazines, who mostly published comic books. Combing through *Astonishing*'s inventory for characters they might successfully transfer, only Promethea seemed to have any possibilities, and so in 1941 the character's fourth incarnation made her debut as lead feature in Apex's *Smashing Comics*, later graduating to her own book, titled simply *Promethea* (1946). This new Promethea, while loosely modeled on the pulp incarnation, was recast as a "science heroine" of the type in which the company specialized. Thus, Promethea now operates in contemporary America, fighting crooks, spies, and the Nazi menace. She has an FBI man as a boyfriend ("Dirk Dangerfield at your service, Princess!"), and only returns to her other-dimensional kingdom of Hy Brasil for occasional adventures. The artist/writer for these stories, working on the strip from 1941 to his tragic, violent death in 1970, was former Classics teacher William Woolcott. Woolcott was an intensely private man who many later feminist critics of comics have applauded (with some reservations) for the genuine female sensibility which he imparted to the character.

Following Woolcott's death, *Promethea* was handed to a young and radical new comics writer, Steven Shelley, for a revamp, ably assisted by a number of comics artists (including a memborable stint by artist P. Craig Russell). The most noticeable change that Shelley brought to Woolcott's character was to change her skin coloring from firmly Caucasian flesh-pink back to the "polished betel-wood" of earlier incarnations. This was almost certainly because, by Shelley's own admission, he was basing his Promethea upon his lovely and vivacious Hispanic wife, Barbara. Shelley brought a great deal of intelligence and fondness for experiment to his depiction of the character, and his death from cancer in the spring of 1996 led to a suspension of the Apex Comics series in a gesture practically unheard-of in the industry. Cynics, of course, were quick to point out the declining sales of the title as the actual motive for its cancellation, as apparently it's well known that books with a female title character have never performed well in the current male-oriented marketplace.

So today, Promethea is in limbo — or perhaps in Misty Magic Land — with her adventures no longer before the public. Given the current popularity of simplistic post-modern characters such as the inexplicably celebrated Weeping Gorilla, perhaps it's simply that times have moved on, and that there is no longer a place for the romantic fantasy and play of the imagination that Promethea represents. We can only hope that she is merely resting in some corner of the Realm of Faerie, or of Hy Brasil, and that in the future, she'll turn up in a new guise, some fresh twist to her puzzling history, a genuine piece of American folklore in action, of poetry in motion.

— Alan Moore

CHAPTER ONE

A small voice pleads in the desert,
A dread shadow laughs in the city,
A desperate student writes the truth.

Cover art:
Alex Ross (A)
J.H. Williams III
& Mick Gray (B)

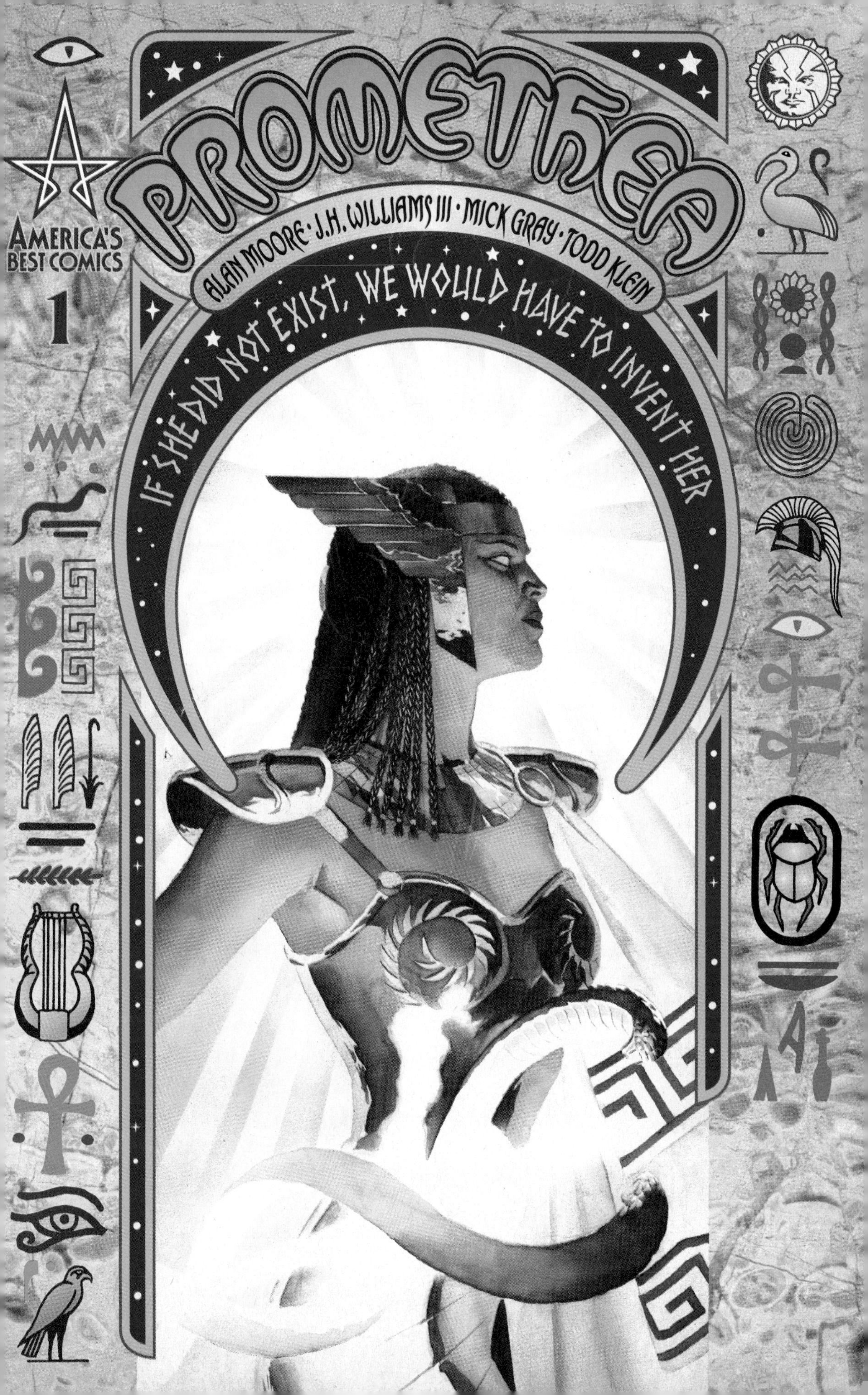
AMERICA'S BEST COMICS
1
PROMETHEA
ALAN MOORE · J.H. WILLIAMS III · MICK GRAY · TODD KLEIN
IF SHE DID NOT EXIST, WE WOULD HAVE TO INVENT HER

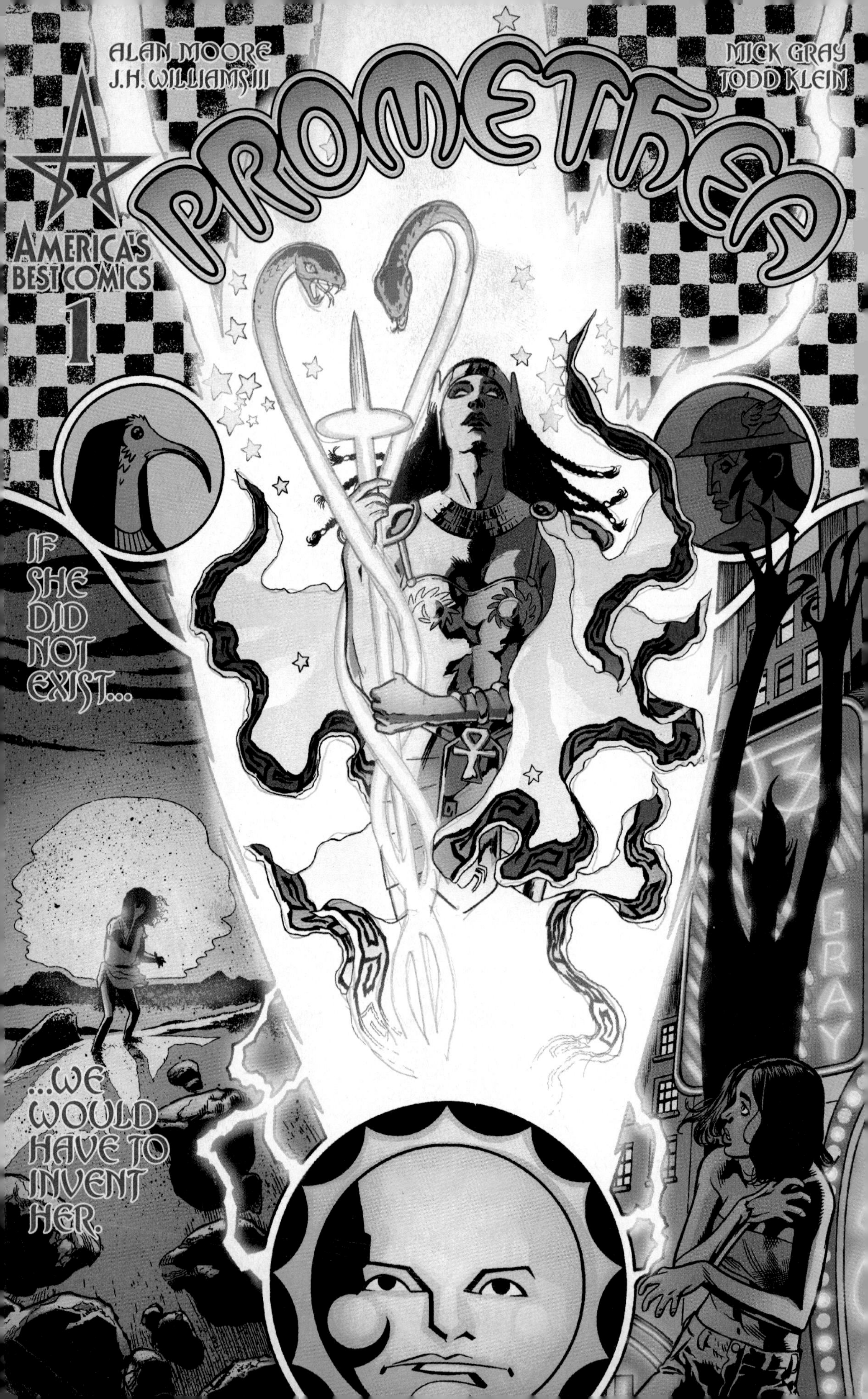
ALAN MOORE
J.H. WILLIAMS III
MICK GRAY
TODD KLEIN
PROMETHEA
AMERICA'S BEST COMICS
1
IF SHE DID NOT EXIST...
...WE WOULD HAVE TO INVENT HER.
GRAY

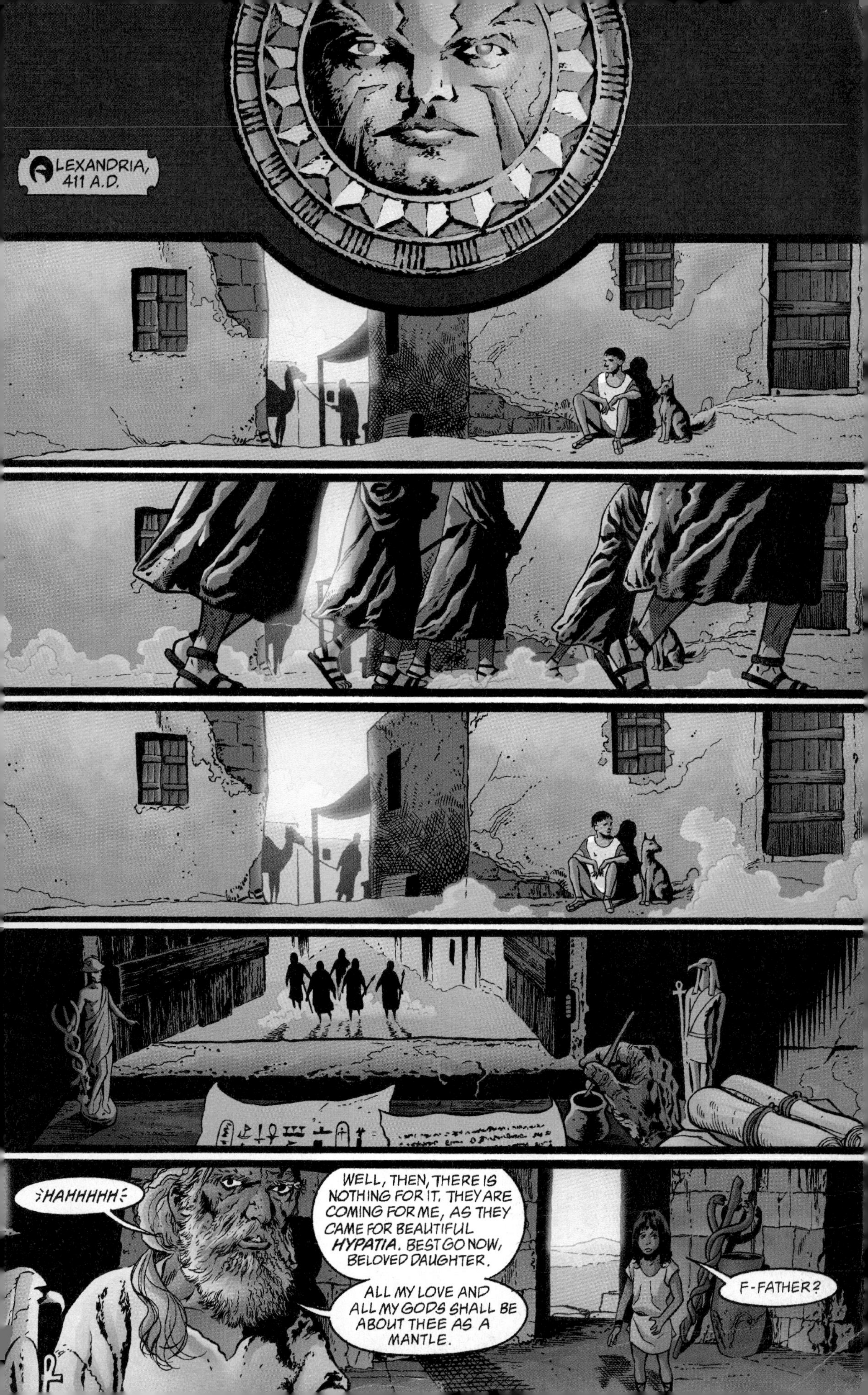
ALEXANDRIA, 411 A.D.
HAHHHHH
WELL, THEN, THERE IS NOTHING FOR IT. THEY ARE COMING FOR ME, AS THEY CAME FOR BEAUTIFUL HYPATIA. BEST GO NOW, BELOVED DAUGHTER.
ALL MY LOVE AND ALL MY GODS SHALL BE ABOUT THEE AS A MANTLE.
F-FATHER?

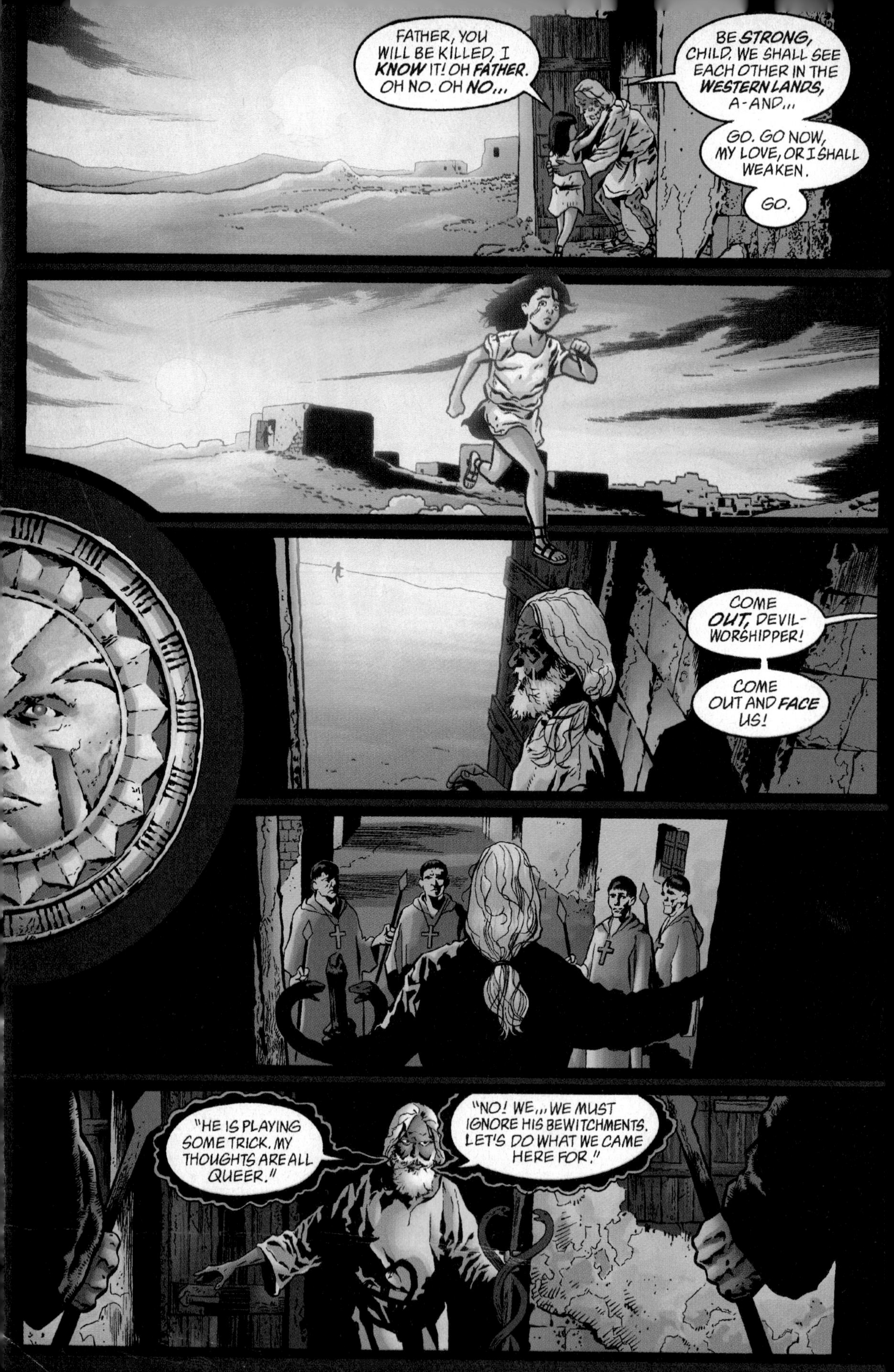
FATHER, YOU WILL BE KILLED, I KNOW IT! OH FATHER. OH NO. OH NO...
BE STRONG, CHILD. WE SHALL SEE EACH OTHER IN THE WESTERN LANDS, A-AND...
GO. GO NOW, MY LOVE, OR I SHALL WEAKEN.
GO.
COME OUT, DEVIL-WORSHIPPER!
COME OUT AND FACE US!
"HE IS PLAYING SOME TRICK. MY THOUGHTS ARE ALL QUEER."
"NO! WE... WE MUST IGNORE HIS BEWITCHMENTS. LET'S DO WHAT WE CAME HERE FOR."

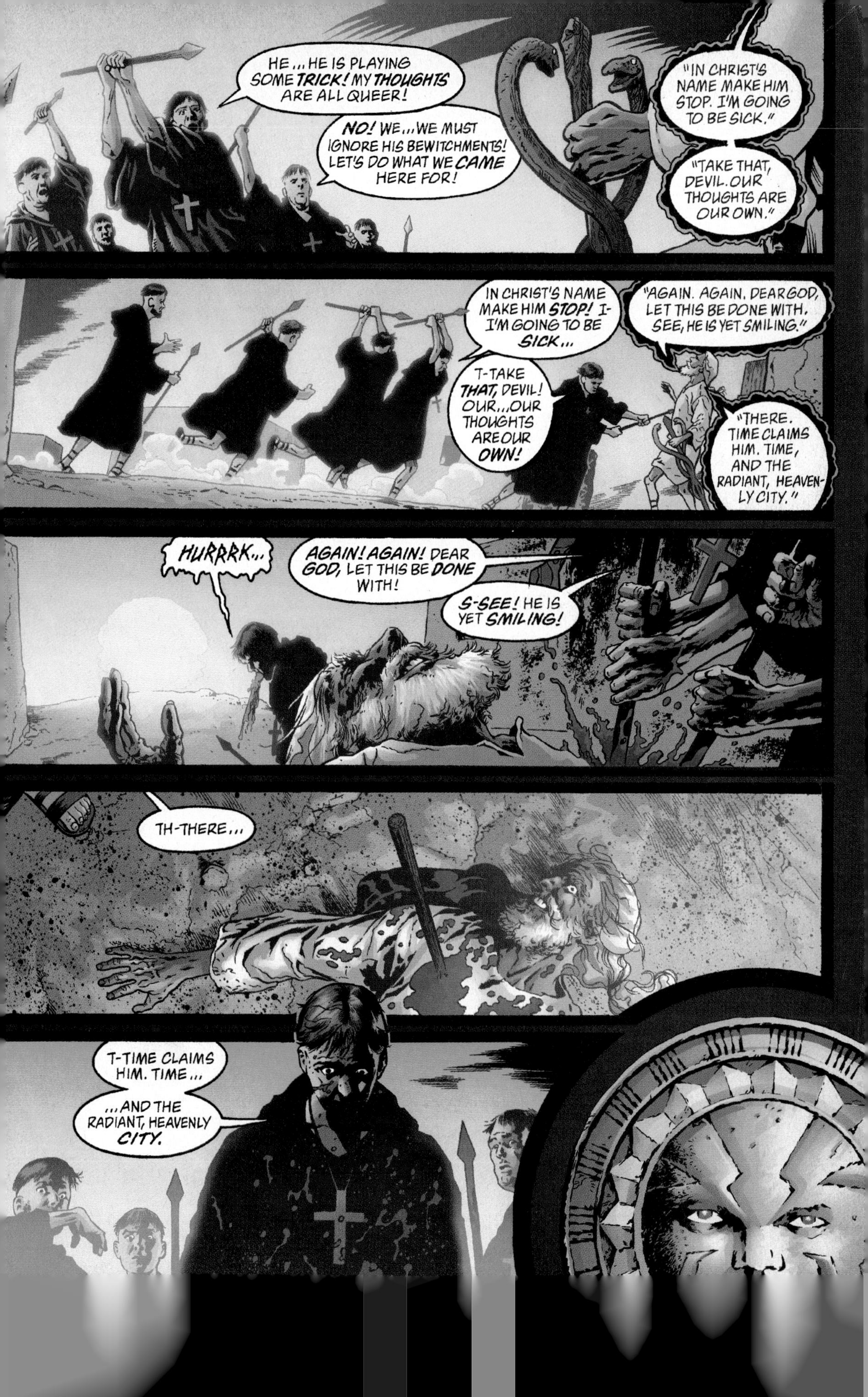
HE... HE IS PLAYING SOME TRICK! MY THOUGHTS ARE ALL QUEER!
NO! WE... WE MUST IGNORE HIS BEWITCHMENTS! LET'S DO WHAT WE CAME HERE FOR!
"IN CHRIST'S NAME MAKE HIM STOP. I'M GOING TO BE SICK."
"TAKE THAT, DEVIL. OUR THOUGHTS ARE OUR OWN."
IN CHRIST'S NAME MAKE HIM STOP! I-I'M GOING TO BE SICK...
"AGAIN. AGAIN. DEAR GOD, LET THIS BE DONE WITH. SEE, HE IS YET SMILING."
T-TAKE THAT, DEVIL! OUR... OUR THOUGHTS ARE OUR OWN!
"THERE. TIME CLAIMS HIM. TIME, AND THE RADIANT, HEAVEN-LY CITY."
HURRRK...
AGAIN! AGAIN! DEAR GOD, LET THIS BE DONE WITH!
S-SEE! HE IS YET SMILING!
TH-THERE...
T-TIME CLAIMS HIM. TIME...
...AND THE RADIANT, HEAVENLY CITY.

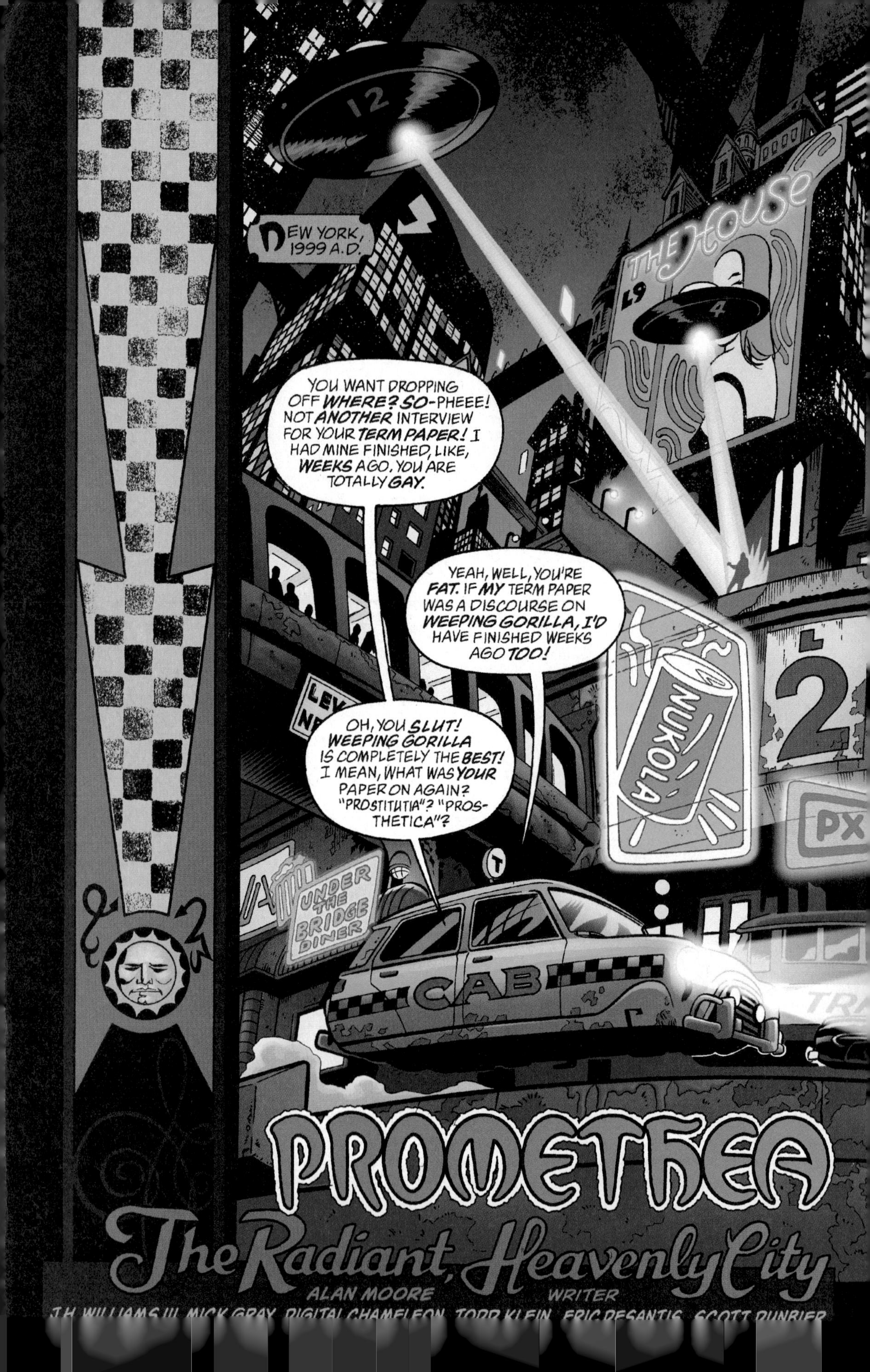
NEW YORK, 1999 A.D.
YOU WANT DROPPING OFF WHERE? SO-PHEEE! NOT ANOTHER INTERVIEW FOR YOUR TERM PAPER! I HAD MINE FINISHED, LIKE, WEEKS AGO. YOU ARE TOTALLY GAY.
YEAH, WELL, YOU'RE FAT. IF MY TERM PAPER WAS A DISCOURSE ON WEEPING GORILLA, I'D HAVE FINISHED WEEKS AGO TOO!
OH, YOU SLUT! WEEPING GORILLA IS COMPLETELY THE BEST! I MEAN, WHAT WAS YOUR PAPER ON AGAIN? "PROSTITUTIA"? "PROSTHETICA"?
THE House
NUKOLA
UNDER THE BRIDGE DINER
CAB
PROMETHEA
The Radiant, Heavenly City
ALAN MOORE WRITER
J.H. WILLIAMS III MICK GRAY DIGITAL CHAMELEON TODD KLEIN ERIC DESANTIS SCOTT DUNBIER

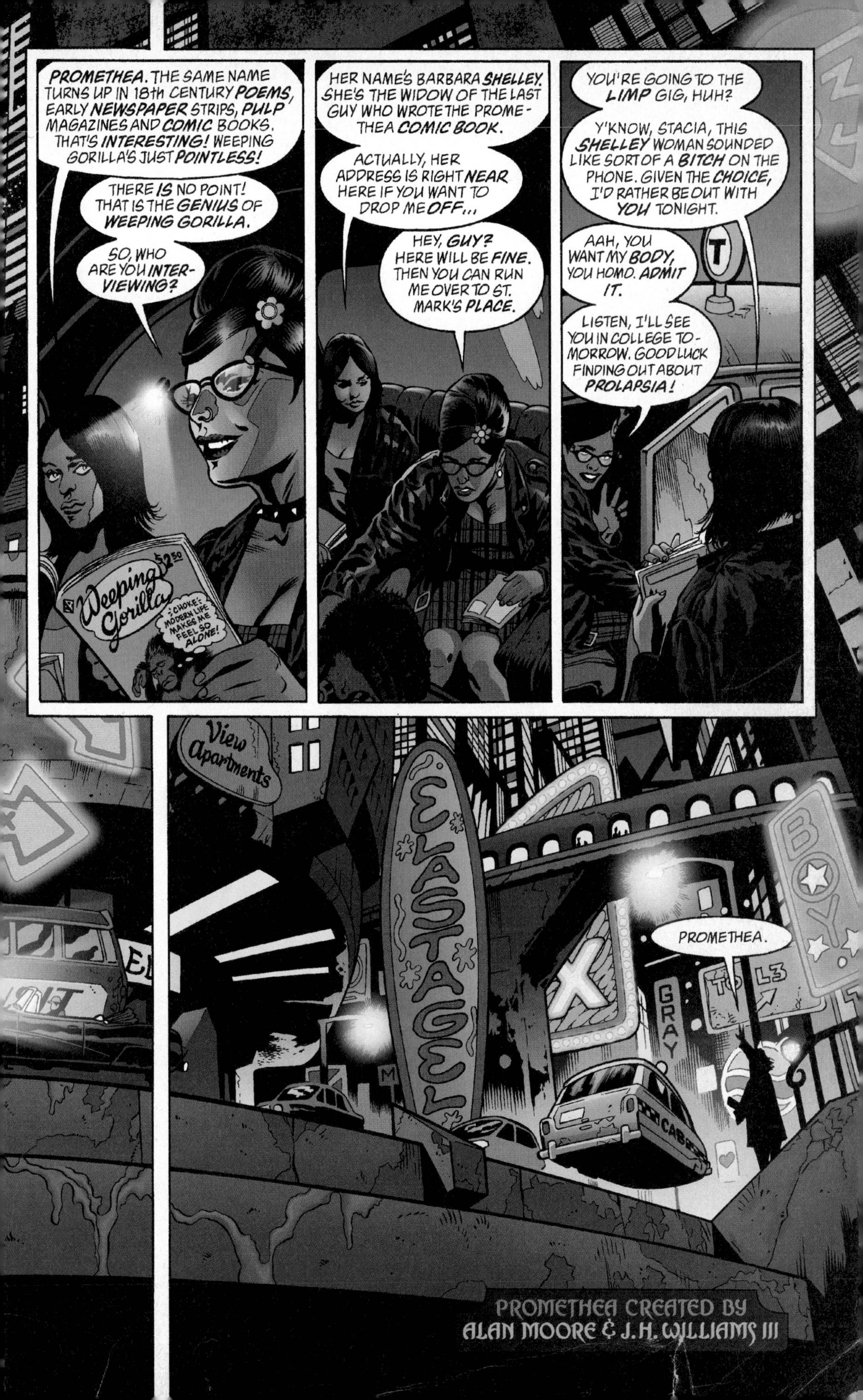
PROMETHEA. THE SAME NAME TURNS UP IN 18th CENTURY POEMS, EARLY NEWSPAPER STRIPS, PULP MAGAZINES AND COMIC BOOKS. THAT'S INTERESTING! WEEPING GORILLA'S JUST POINTLESS!
THERE IS NO POINT! THAT IS THE GENIUS OF WEEPING GORILLA.
SO, WHO ARE YOU INTER-VIEWING?
Weeping Gorilla
$2.50
CHOKE! MODERN LIFE MAKES ME FEEL SO ALONE!
HER NAME'S BARBARA SHELLEY. SHE'S THE WIDOW OF THE LAST GUY WHO WROTE THE PROME-THEA COMIC BOOK.
ACTUALLY, HER ADDRESS IS RIGHT NEAR HERE IF YOU WANT TO DROP ME OFF...
HEY, GUY? HERE WILL BE FINE. THEN YOU CAN RUN ME OVER TO ST. MARK'S PLACE.
YOU'RE GOING TO THE LIMP GIG, HUH?
Y'KNOW, STACIA, THIS SHELLEY WOMAN SOUNDED LIKE SORT OF A BITCH ON THE PHONE. GIVEN THE CHOICE, I'D RATHER BE OUT WITH YOU TONIGHT.
AAH, YOU WANT MY BODY, YOU HOMO. ADMIT IT.
LISTEN, I'LL SEE YOU IN COLLEGE TO-MORROW. GOOD LUCK FINDING OUT ABOUT PROLAPSIA!
T
View Apartments
ELASTAGE
BOY
X
GRAY
CABS
PROMETHEA.
PROMETHEA CREATED BY
ALAN MOORE & J.H. WILLIAMS III

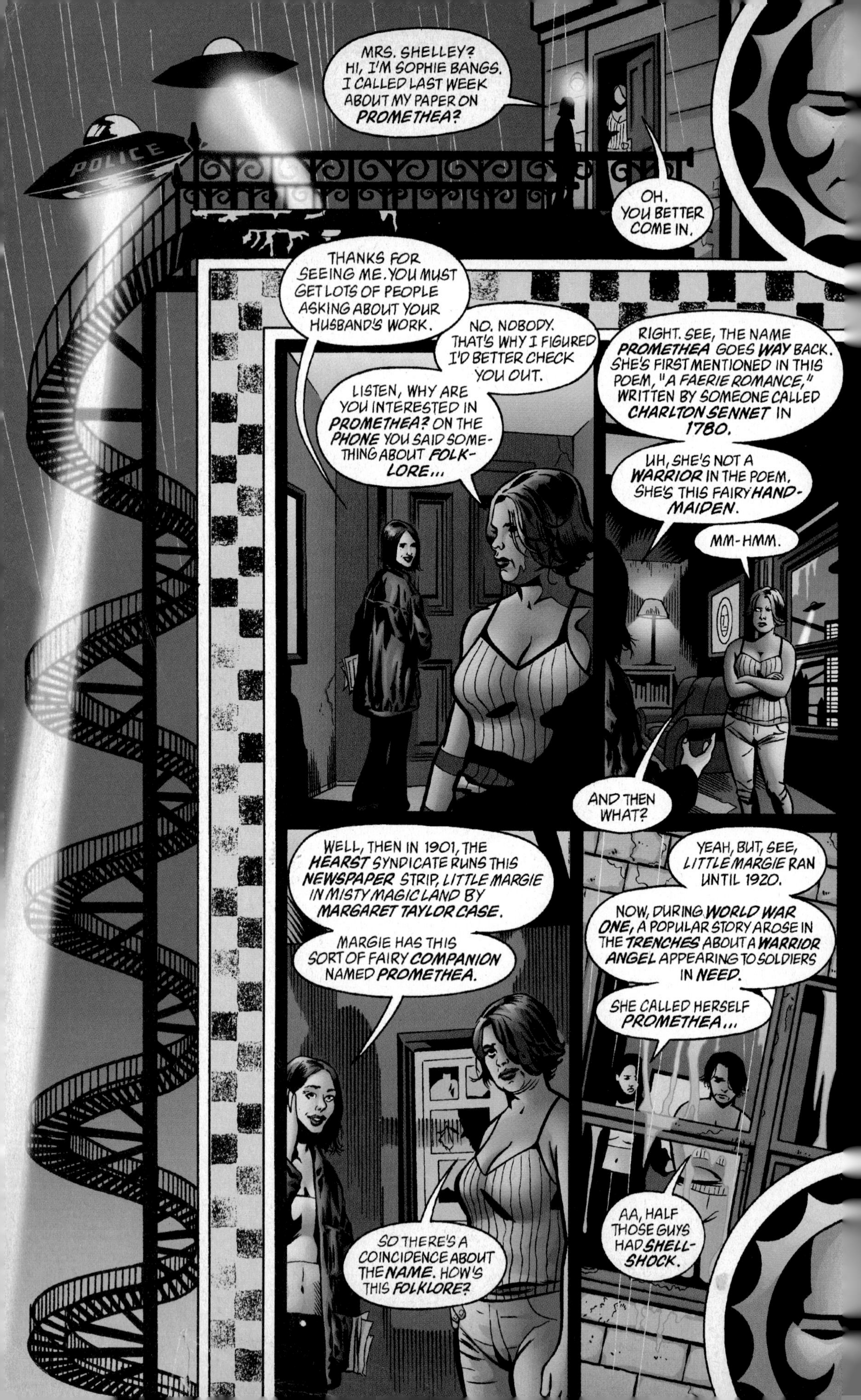
MRS. SHELLEY? HI, I'M SOPHIE BANGS. I CALLED LAST WEEK ABOUT MY PAPER ON PROMETHEA?
OH. YOU BETTER COME IN.
POLICE
THANKS FOR SEEING ME. YOU MUST GET LOTS OF PEOPLE ASKING ABOUT YOUR HUSBAND'S WORK.
NO. NOBODY. THAT'S WHY I FIGURED I'D BETTER CHECK YOU OUT.
LISTEN, WHY ARE YOU INTERESTED IN PROMETHEA? ON THE PHONE YOU SAID SOMETHING ABOUT FOLKLORE...
RIGHT. SEE, THE NAME PROMETHEA GOES WAY BACK. SHE'S FIRST MENTIONED IN THIS POEM, "A FAERIE ROMANCE," WRITTEN BY SOMEONE CALLED CHARLTON SENNET IN 1780.
UH, SHE'S NOT A WARRIOR IN THE POEM. SHE'S THIS FAIRY HANDMAIDEN.
MM-HMM.
AND THEN WHAT?
WELL, THEN IN 1901, THE HEARST SYNDICATE RUNS THIS NEWSPAPER STRIP, LITTLE MARGIE IN MISTY MAGIC LAND BY MARGARET TAYLOR CASE.
MARGIE HAS THIS SORT OF FAIRY COMPANION NAMED PROMETHEA.
SO THERE'S A COINCIDENCE ABOUT THE NAME. HOW'S THIS FOLKLORE?
YEAH, BUT, SEE, LITTLE MARGIE RAN UNTIL 1920.
NOW, DURING WORLD WAR ONE, A POPULAR STORY AROSE IN THE TRENCHES ABOUT A WARRIOR ANGEL APPEARING TO SOLDIERS IN NEED.
SHE CALLED HERSELF PROMETHEA...
AA, HALF THOSE GUYS HAD SHELL-SHOCK.

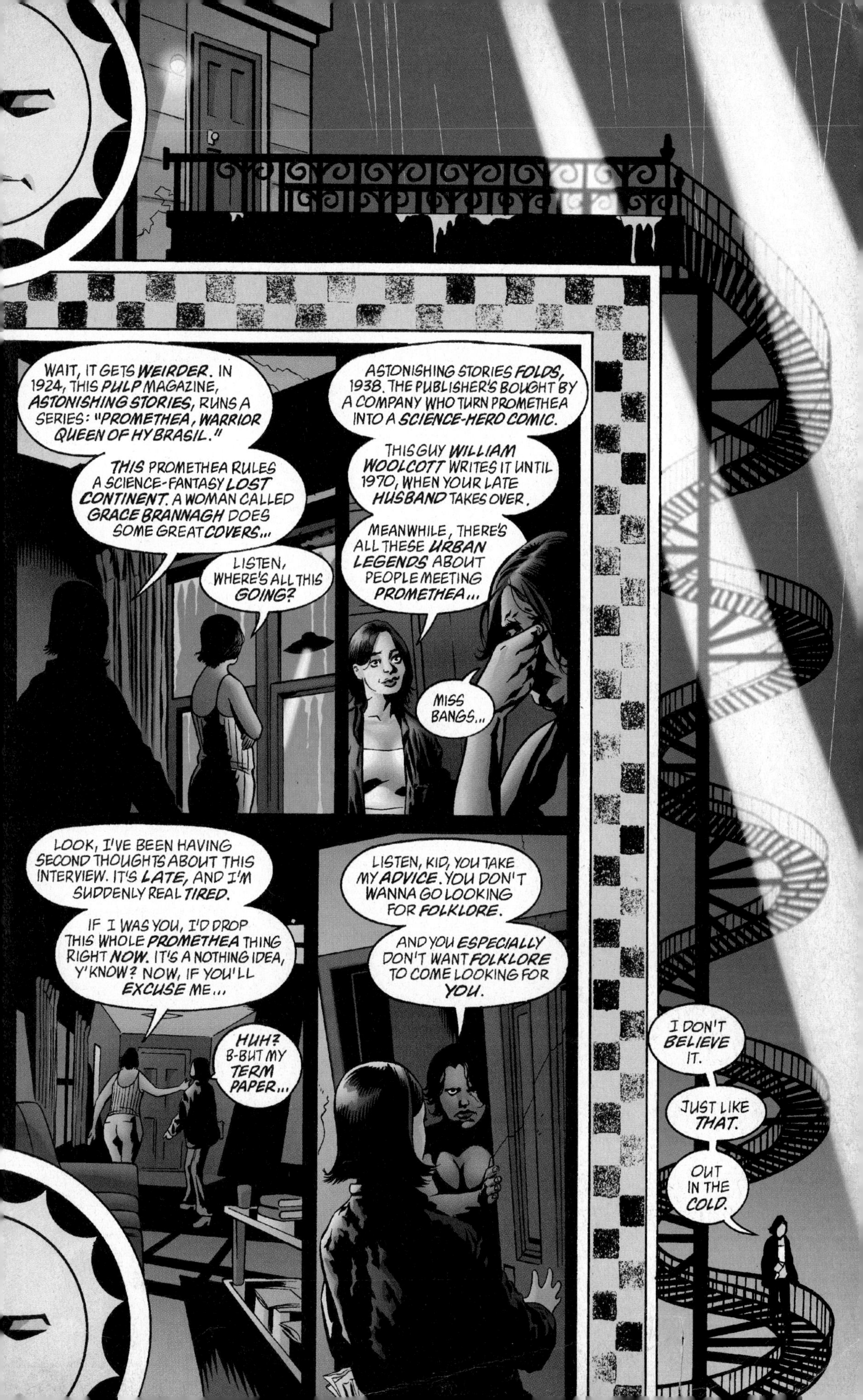
WAIT, IT GETS WEIRDER. IN 1924, THIS PULP MAGAZINE, ASTONISHING STORIES, RUNS A SERIES: "PROMETHEA, WARRIOR QUEEN OF HY BRASIL."
THIS PROMETHEA RULES A SCIENCE-FANTASY LOST CONTINENT. A WOMAN CALLED GRACE BRANNAGH DOES SOME GREAT COVERS...
LISTEN, WHERE'S ALL THIS GOING?
ASTONISHING STORIES FOLDS, 1938. THE PUBLISHER'S BOUGHT BY A COMPANY WHO TURN PROMETHEA INTO A SCIENCE-HERO COMIC.
THIS GUY WILLIAM WOOLCOTT WRITES IT UNTIL 1970, WHEN YOUR LATE HUSBAND TAKES OVER.
MEANWHILE, THERE'S ALL THESE URBAN LEGENDS ABOUT PEOPLE MEETING PROMETHEA...
MISS BANGS...
LOOK, I'VE BEEN HAVING SECOND THOUGHTS ABOUT THIS INTERVIEW. IT'S LATE, AND I'M SUDDENLY REAL TIRED.
IF I WAS YOU, I'D DROP THIS WHOLE PROMETHEA THING RIGHT NOW. IT'S A NOTHING IDEA, Y'KNOW? NOW, IF YOU'LL EXCUSE ME...
HUH? B-BUT MY TERM PAPER...
LISTEN, KID, YOU TAKE MY ADVICE. YOU DON'T WANNA GO LOOKING FOR FOLKLORE.
AND YOU ESPECIALLY DON'T WANT FOLKLORE TO COME LOOKING FOR YOU.
I DON'T BELIEVE IT.
JUST LIKE THAT.
OUT IN THE COLD.

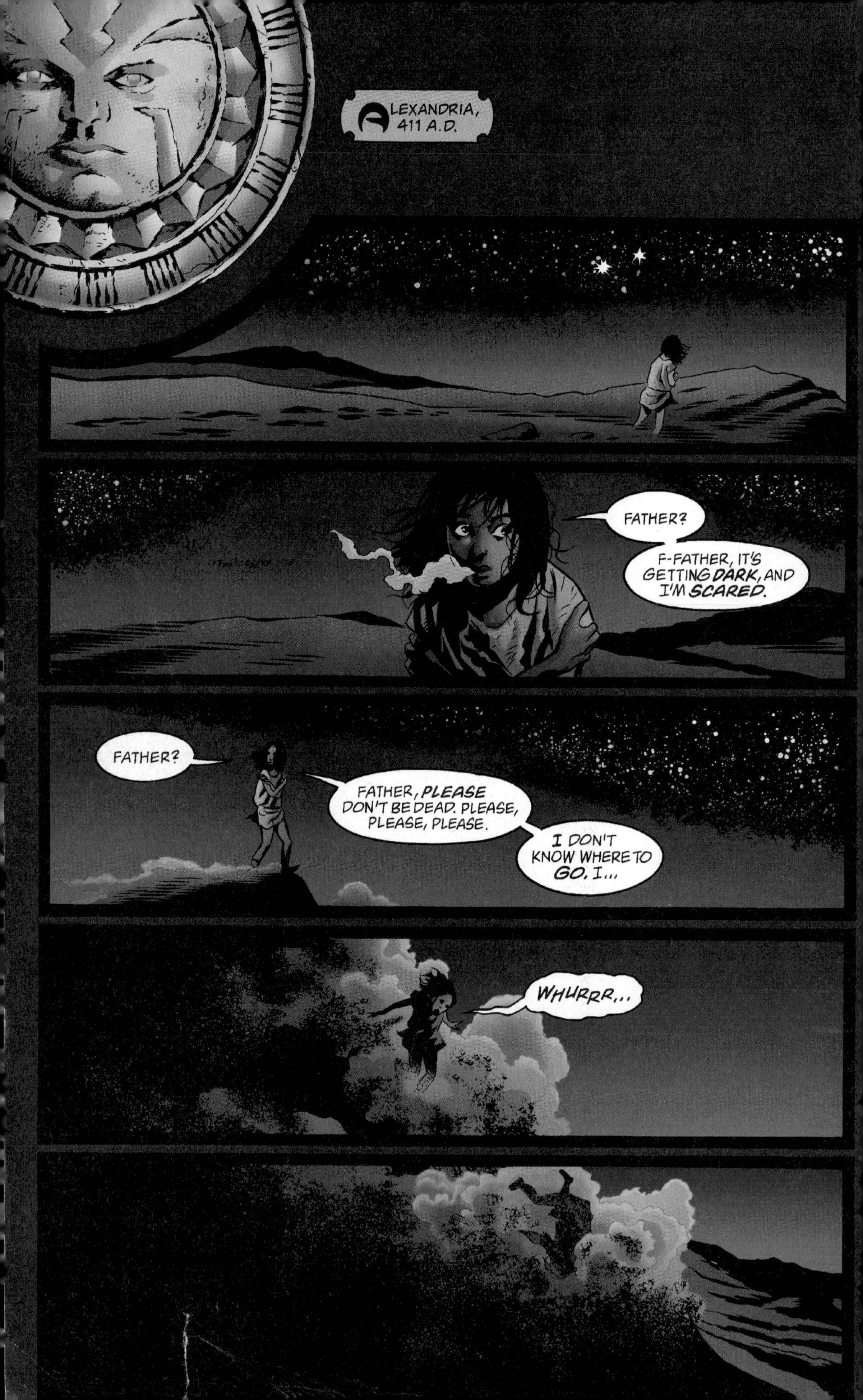
ALEXANDRIA, 411 A.D.
FATHER?
F-FATHER, IT'S GETTING DARK, AND I'M SCARED.
FATHER?
FATHER, PLEASE DON'T BE DEAD. PLEASE, PLEASE, PLEASE.
I DON'T KNOW WHERE TO GO. I...
WHURRR...

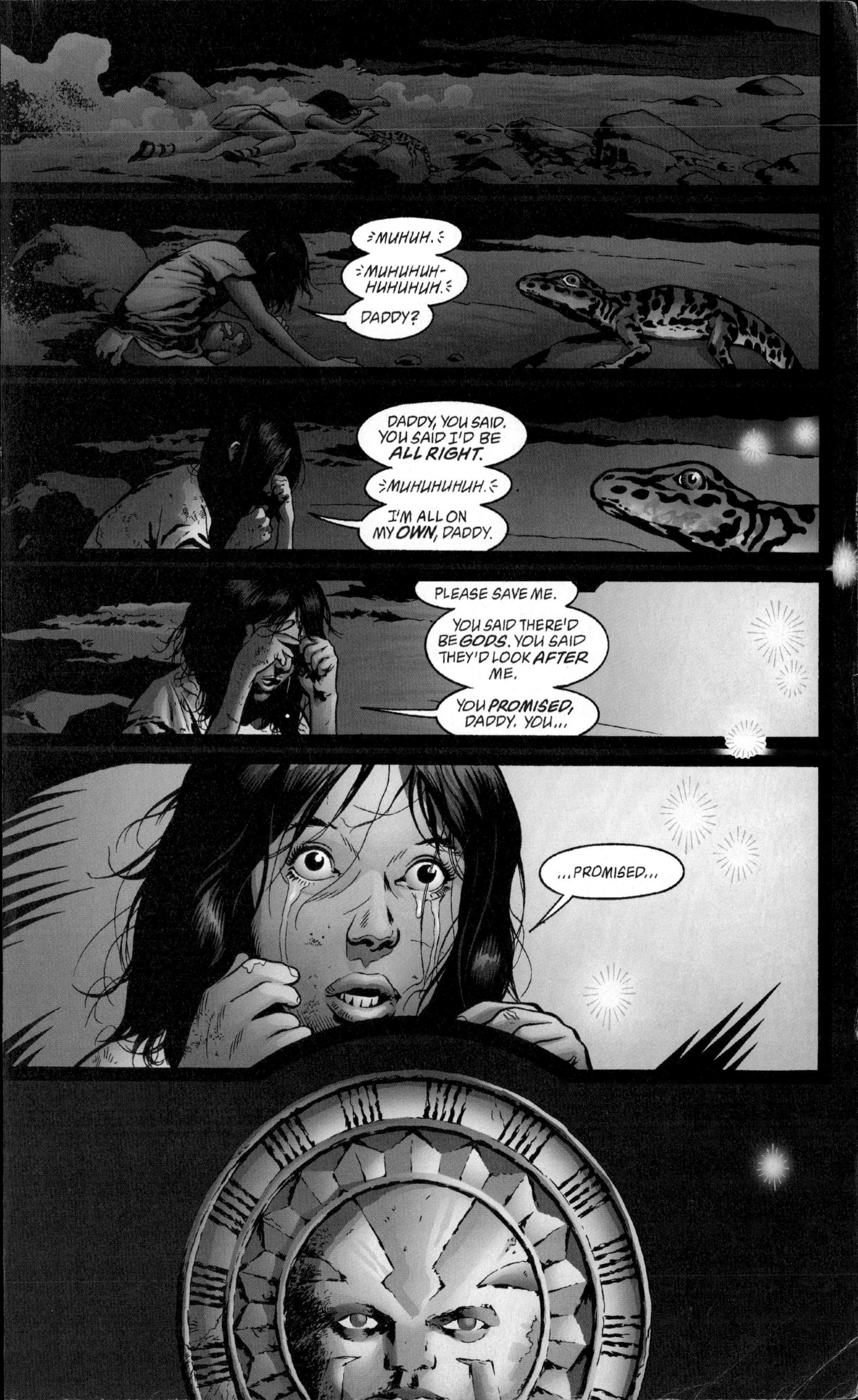

MUHUH.
MUHUHUH-HUHUHUH.
DADDY?
DADDY, YOU SAID. YOU SAID I'D BE ALL RIGHT.
MUHUHUHUH.
I'M ALL ON MY OWN, DADDY.
PLEASE SAVE ME.
YOU SAID THERE'D BE GODS. YOU SAID THEY'D LOOK AFTER ME.
YOU PROMISED, DADDY. YOU...
...PROMISED...

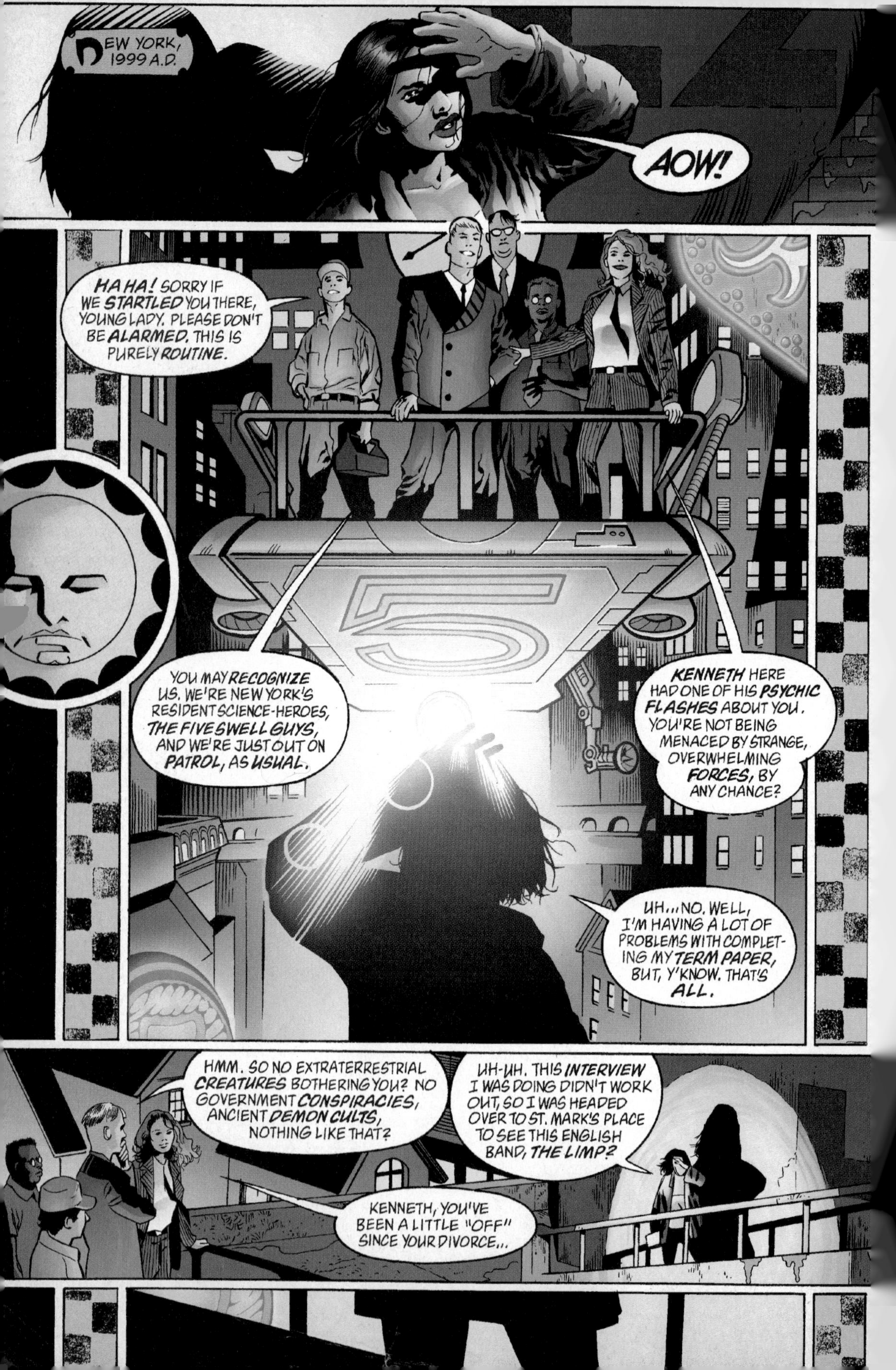
NEW YORK, 1999 A.D.
AOW!
HA HA! SORRY IF WE STARTLED YOU THERE, YOUNG LADY. PLEASE DON'T BE ALARMED. THIS IS PURELY ROUTINE.
YOU MAY RECOGNIZE US. WE'RE NEW YORK'S RESIDENT SCIENCE-HEROES, THE FIVE SWELL GUYS, AND WE'RE JUST OUT ON PATROL, AS USUAL.
KENNETH HERE HAD ONE OF HIS PSYCHIC FLASHES ABOUT YOU. YOU'RE NOT BEING MENACED BY STRANGE, OVERWHELMING FORCES, BY ANY CHANCE?
UH...NO. WELL, I'M HAVING A LOT OF PROBLEMS WITH COMPLETING MY TERM PAPER, BUT, Y'KNOW. THAT'S ALL.
HMM. SO NO EXTRATERRESTRIAL CREATURES BOTHERING YOU? NO GOVERNMENT CONSPIRACIES, ANCIENT DEMON CULTS, NOTHING LIKE THAT?
UH-UH. THIS INTERVIEW I WAS DOING DIDN'T WORK OUT, SO I WAS HEADED OVER TO ST. MARK'S PLACE TO SEE THIS ENGLISH BAND, THE LIMP?
KENNETH, YOU'VE BEEN A LITTLE "OFF" SINCE YOUR DIVORCE...

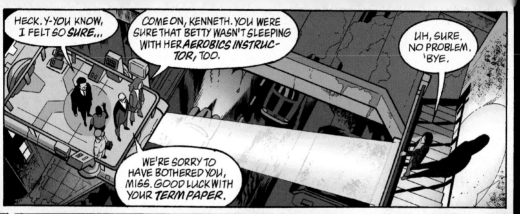

HECK. Y-YOU KNOW, I FELT SO *SURE*...

COME ON, KENNETH. YOU WERE SURE THAT BETTY WASN'T SLEEPING WITH HER *AEROBICS INSTRUCTOR*, TOO.

UH, SURE. NO PROBLEM. 'BYE.

WE'RE SORRY TO HAVE BOTHERED YOU, MISS. GOOD LUCK WITH YOUR *TERM PAPER*.

WOW.

"FIVE SWELL GUYS."

WAIT TILL I TELL *STACIA*.

SHE'LL *HEMORRHAGE*.

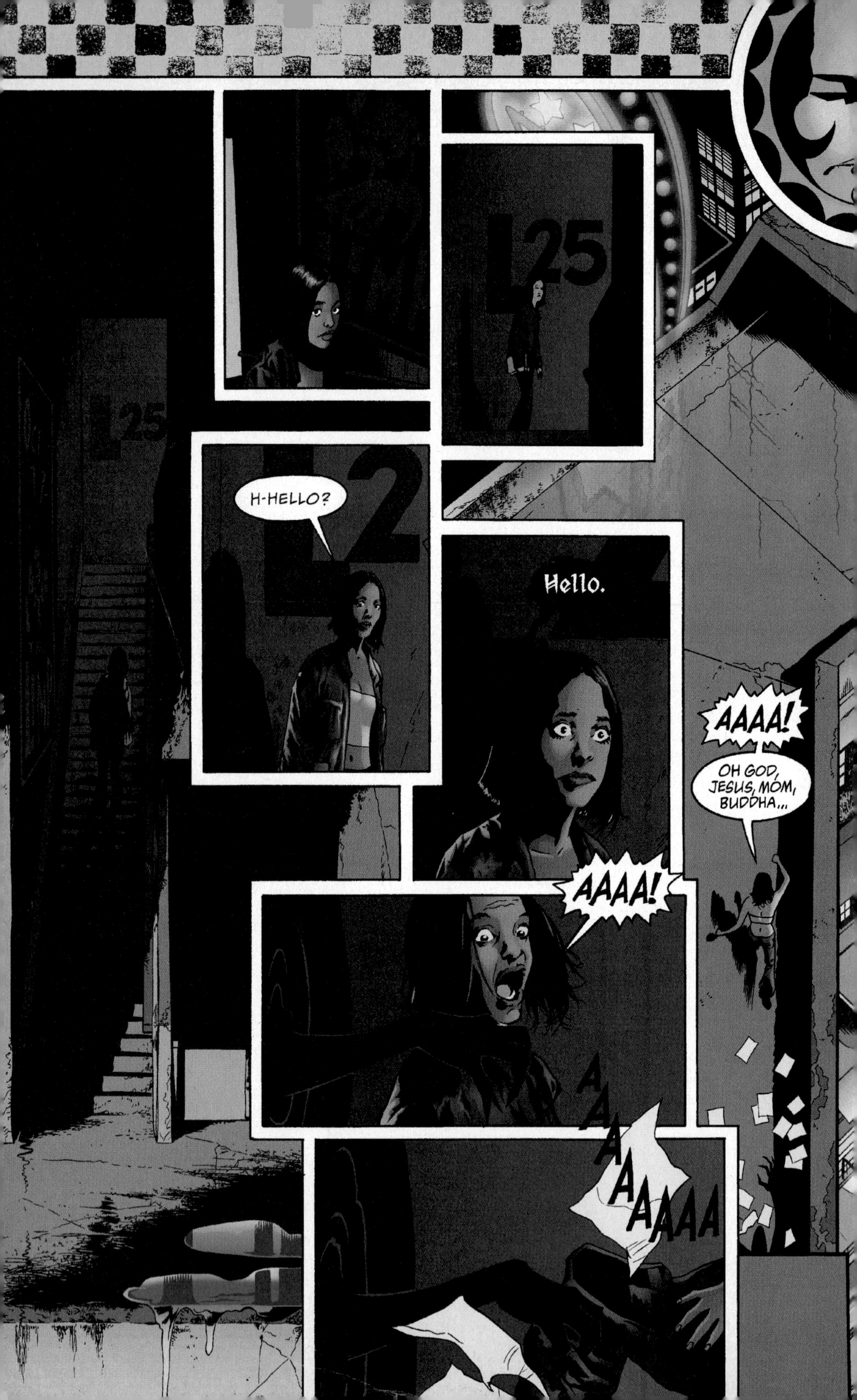

H-HELLO?
Hello.
AAAA!
OH GOD, JESUS, MOM, BUDDHA...
AAAA!
AAAAAAAAA

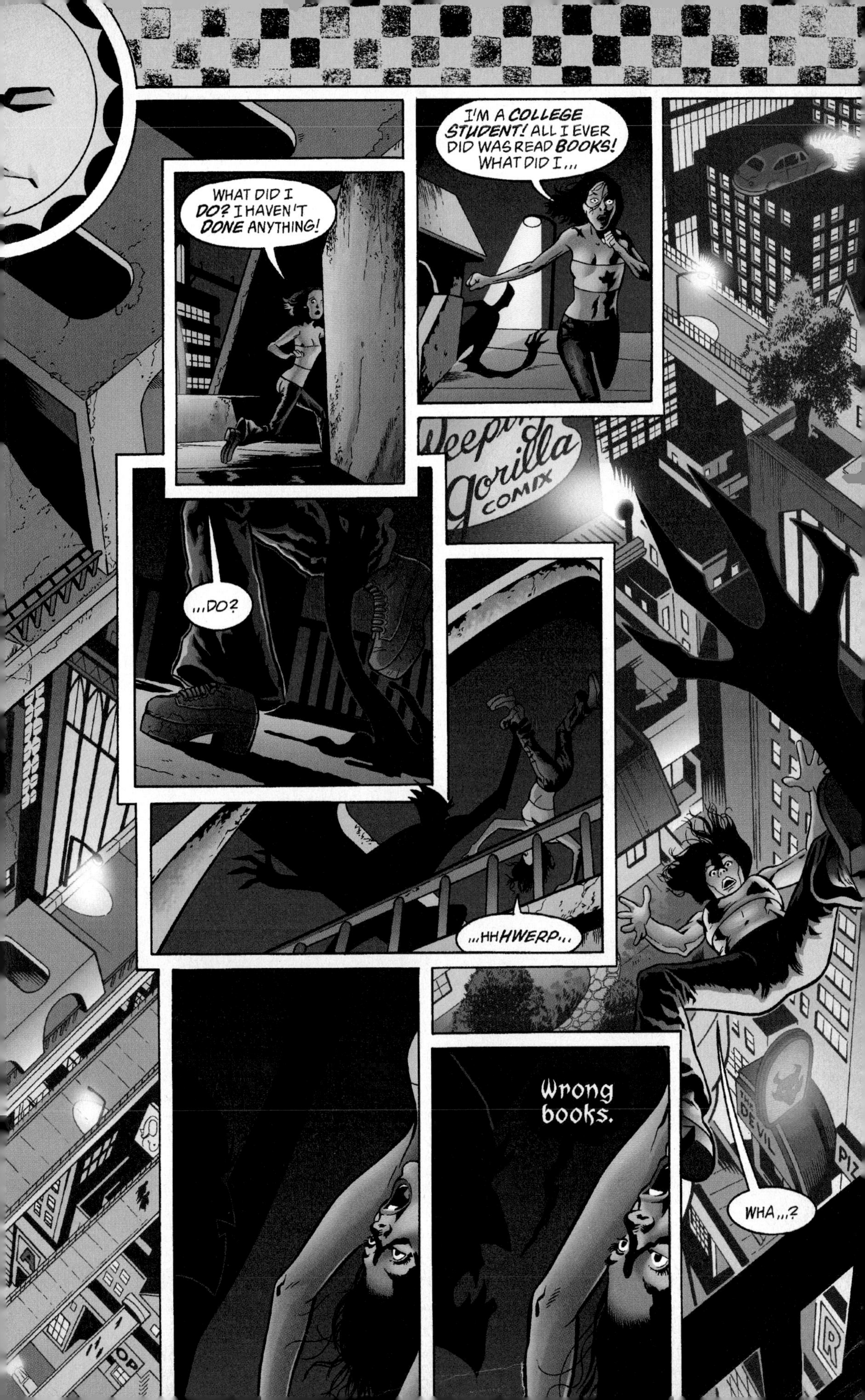
WHAT DID I DO? I HAVEN'T DONE ANYTHING!
I'M A COLLEGE STUDENT! ALL I EVER DID WAS READ BOOKS! WHAT DID I...
...DO?
...HHHWERP...
Wrong books.
WHA...?

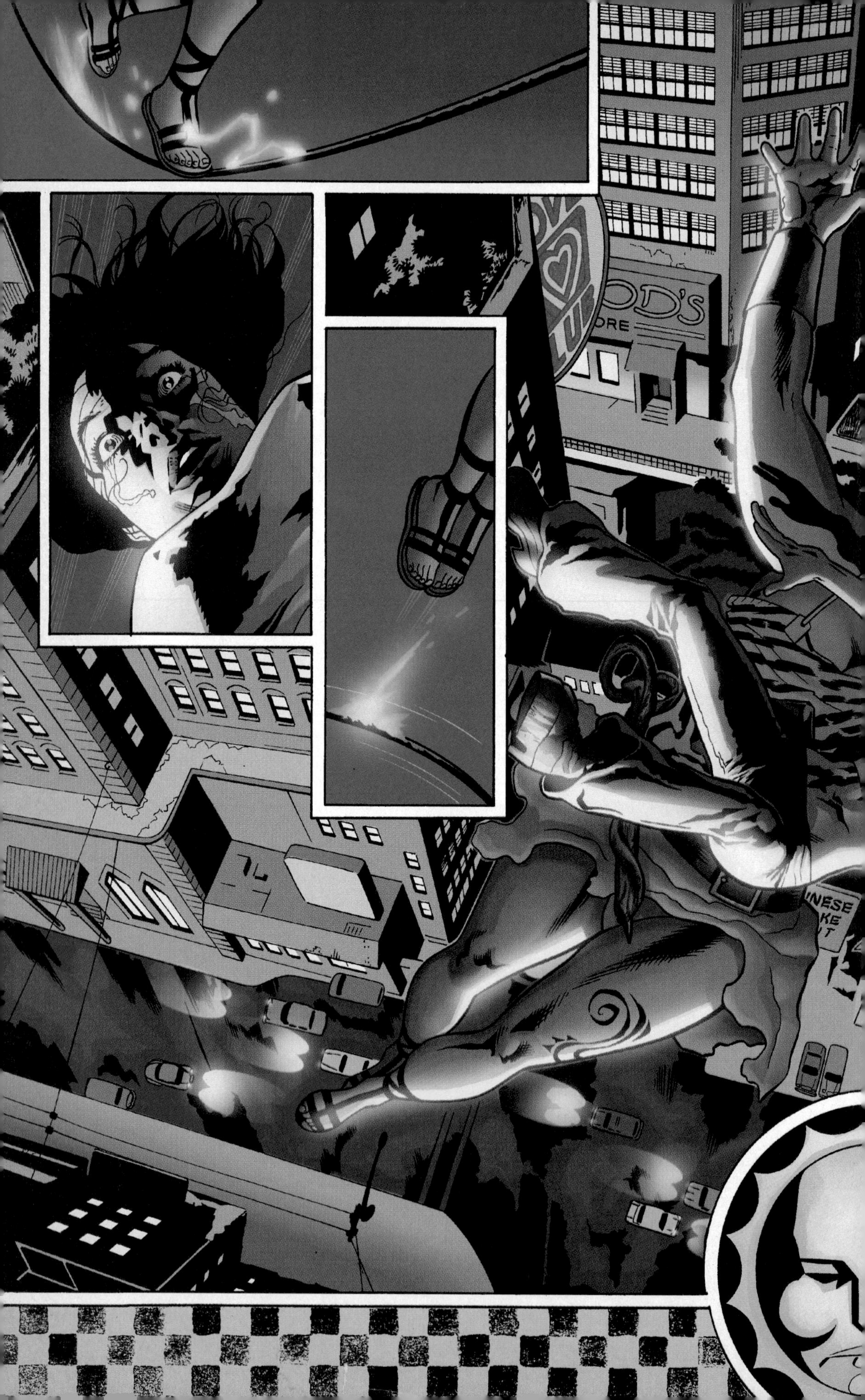

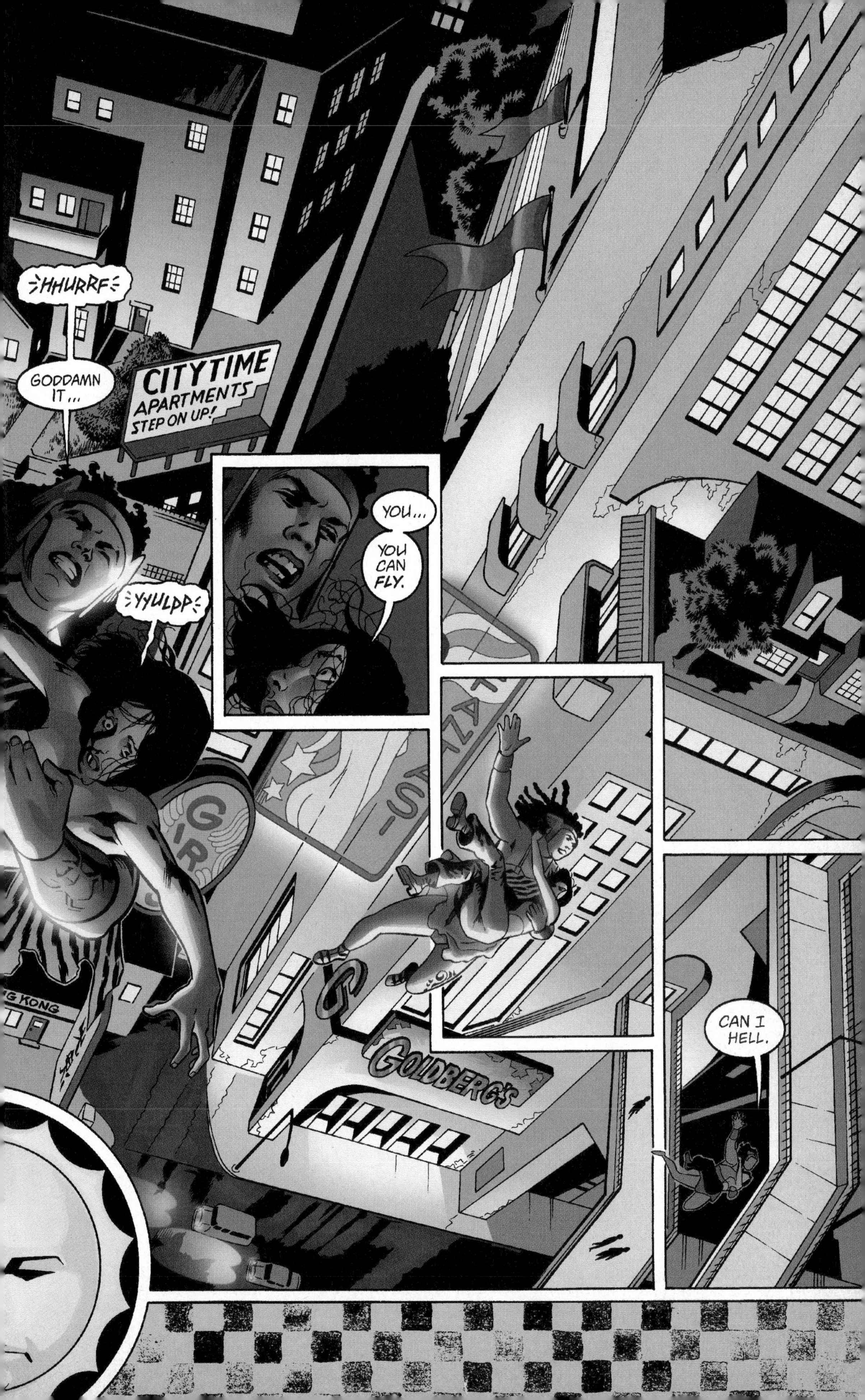
HHURRF
GODDAMN IT...
CITYTIME APARTMENTS STEP ON UP!
YYULPP
YOU...
YOU CAN FLY.
GOLDBERG'S
CAN I HELL.

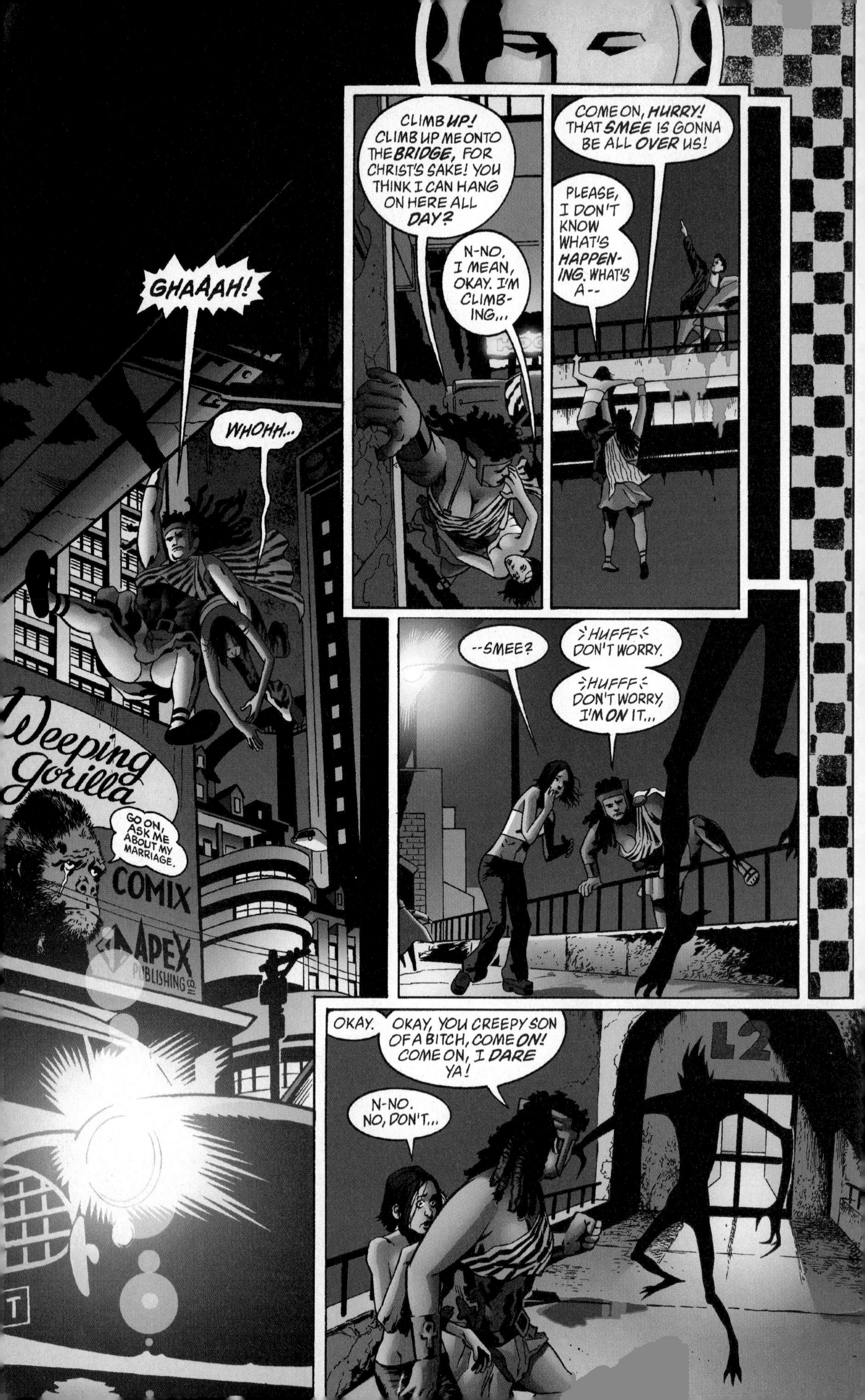
GHAAAH!
WHOHH...
Weeping gorilla
GO ON, ASK ME ABOUT MY MARRIAGE.
COMIX
APEX PUBLISHING CO.
CLIMB UP! CLIMB UP ME ONTO THE BRIDGE, FOR CHRIST'S SAKE! YOU THINK I CAN HANG ON HERE ALL DAY?
N-NO, I MEAN, OKAY. I'M CLIMB-ING...
COME ON, HURRY! THAT SMEE IS GONNA BE ALL OVER US!
PLEASE, I DON'T KNOW WHAT'S HAPPEN-ING. WHAT'S A--
--SMEE?
HUFFF DON'T WORRY.
HUFFF DON'T WORRY, I'M ON IT...
OKAY.
OKAY, YOU CREEPY SON OF A BITCH, COME ON! COME ON, I DARE YA!
N-NO. NO, DON'T...
L2

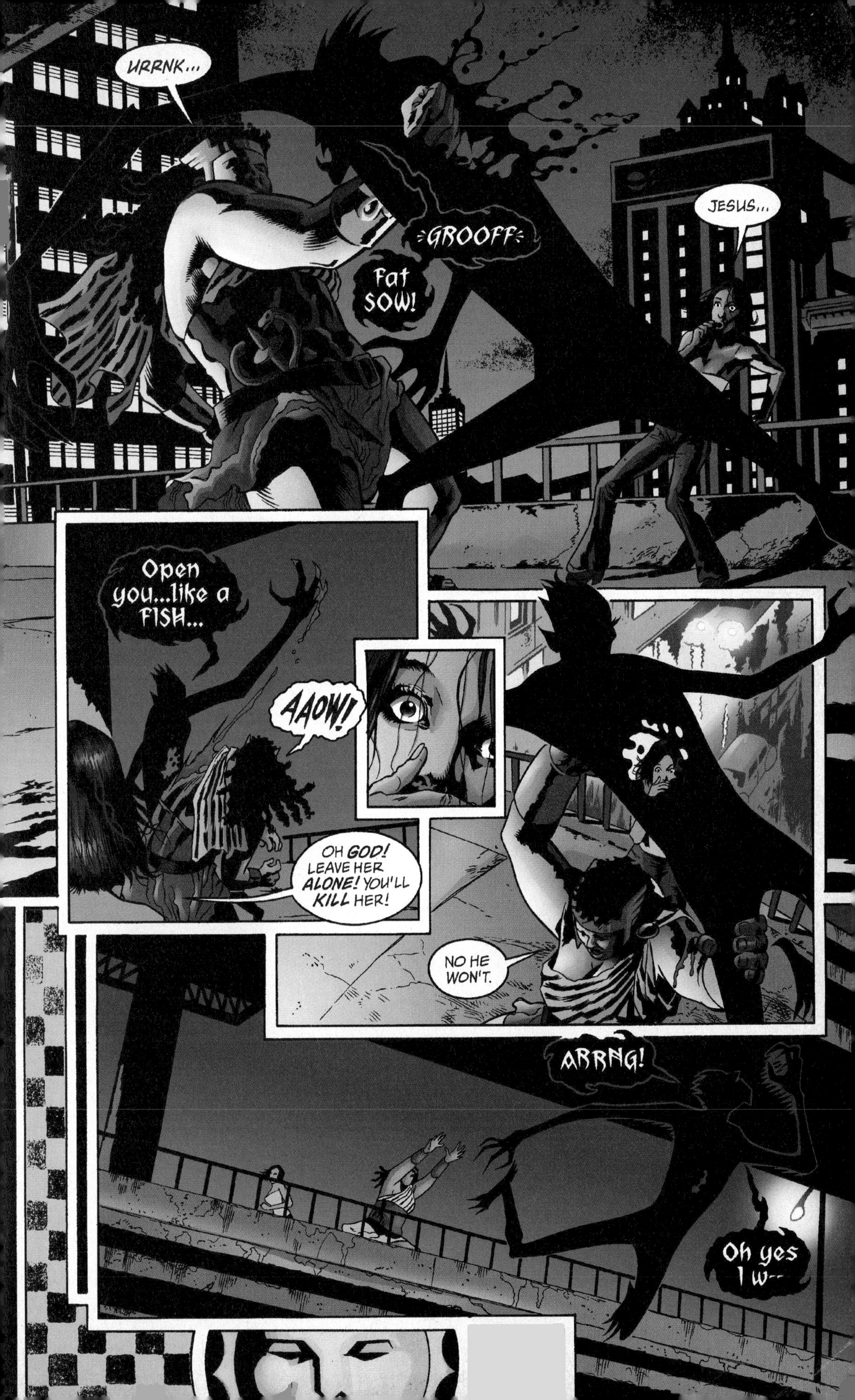
URRNK...
GROOFF
Fat SOW!
JESUS...
Open you...like a FISH...
AAOW!
OH GOD! LEAVE HER ALONE! YOU'LL KILL HER!
NO HE WON'T.
ARRNG!
Oh yes I w--

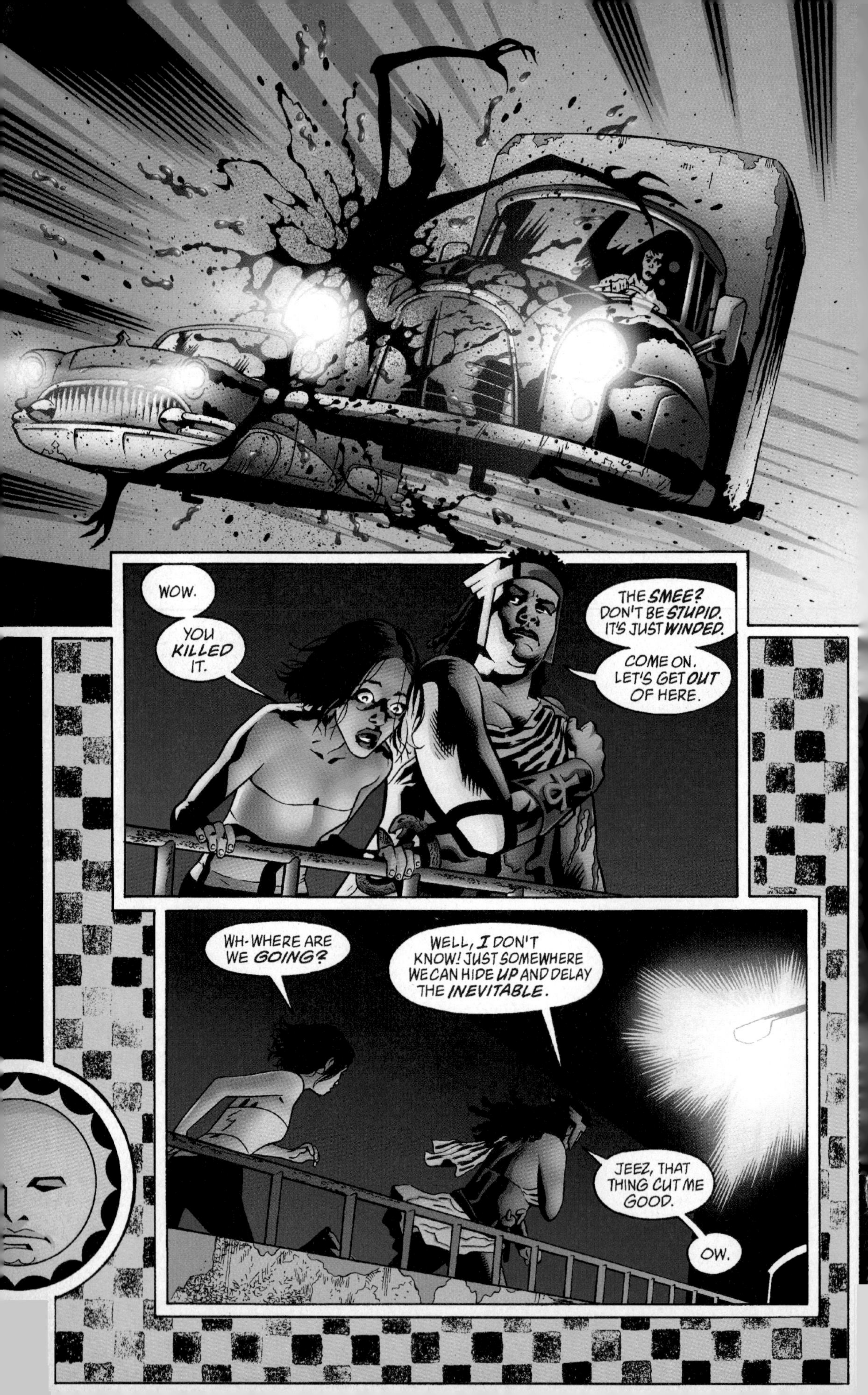

WOW.
YOU KILLED IT.
THE SMEE? DON'T BE STUPID. IT'S JUST WINDED.
COME ON. LET'S GET OUT OF HERE.
WH- WHERE ARE WE GOING?
WELL, I DON'T KNOW! JUST SOMEWHERE WE CAN HIDE UP AND DELAY THE INEVITABLE.
JEEZ, THAT THING CUT ME GOOD.
OW.

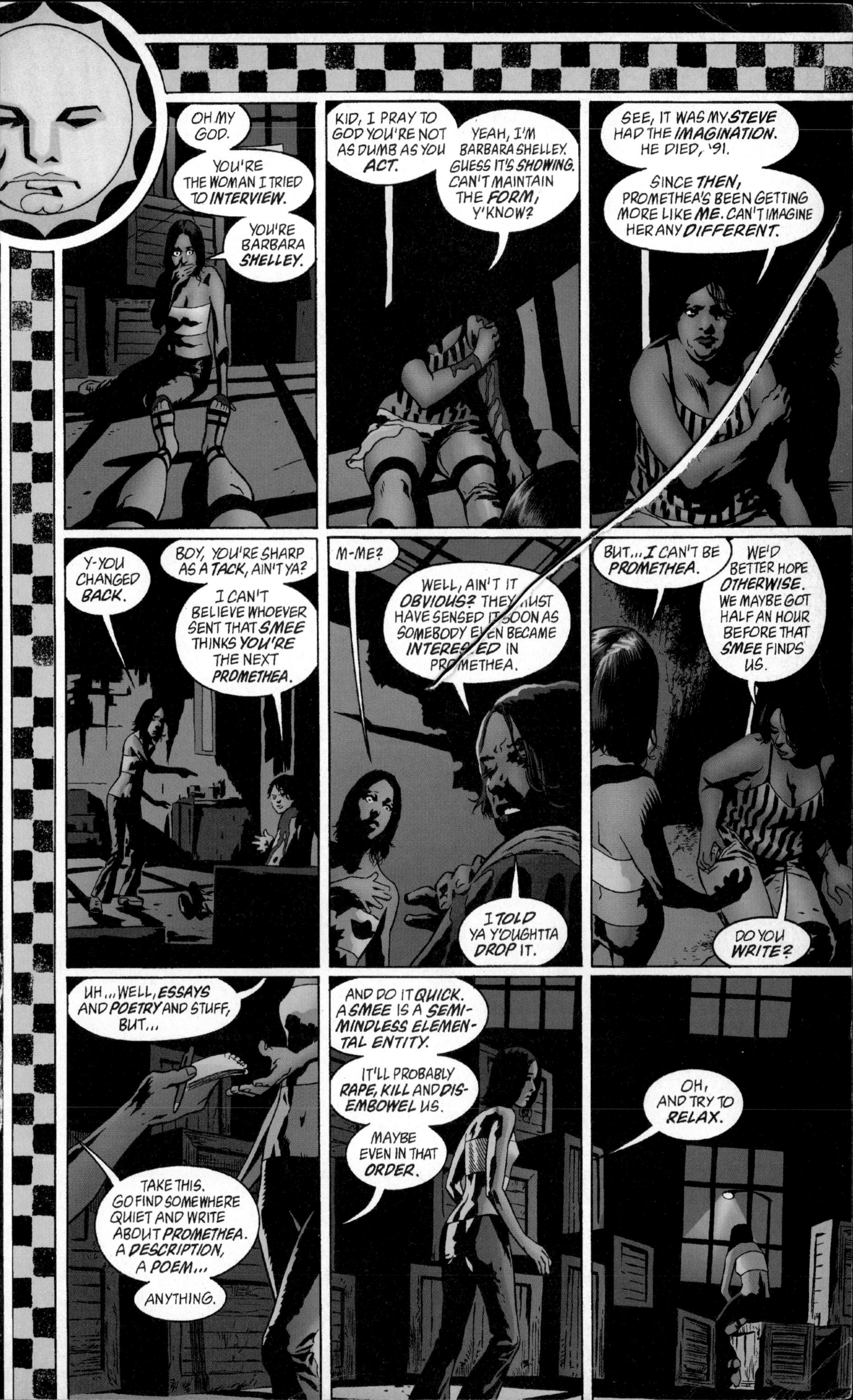
OH MY GOD.
YOU'RE THE WOMAN I TRIED TO INTERVIEW.
YOU'RE BARBARA SHELLEY.
KID, I PRAY TO GOD YOU'RE NOT AS DUMB AS YOU ACT.
YEAH, I'M BARBARA SHELLEY. GUESS IT'S SHOWING. CAN'T MAINTAIN THE FORM, Y'KNOW?
SEE, IT WAS MY STEVE HAD THE IMAGINATION. HE DIED, '91.
SINCE THEN, PROMETHEA'S BEEN GETTING MORE LIKE ME. CAN'T IMAGINE HER ANY DIFFERENT.
Y-YOU CHANGED BACK.
BOY, YOU'RE SHARP AS A TACK, AIN'T YA?
I CAN'T BELIEVE WHOEVER SENT THAT SMEE THINKS YOU'RE THE NEXT PROMETHEA.
M-ME?
WELL, AIN'T IT OBVIOUS? THEY MUST HAVE SENSED IT SOON AS SOMEBODY EVEN BECAME INTERESTED IN PROMETHEA.
I TOLD YA Y'OUGHTTA DROP IT.
BUT... I CAN'T BE PROMETHEA.
WE'D BETTER HOPE OTHERWISE. WE MAYBE GOT HALF AN HOUR BEFORE THAT SMEE FINDS US.
DO YOU WRITE?
UH... WELL, ESSAYS AND POETRY AND STUFF, BUT...
TAKE THIS. GO FIND SOMEWHERE QUIET AND WRITE ABOUT PROMETHEA. A DESCRIPTION, A POEM...
ANYTHING.
AND DO IT QUICK. A SMEE IS A SEMI-MINDLESS ELEMENTAL ENTITY.
IT'LL PROBABLY RAPE, KILL AND DISEMBOWEL US.
MAYBE EVEN IN THAT ORDER.
OH, AND TRY TO RELAX.

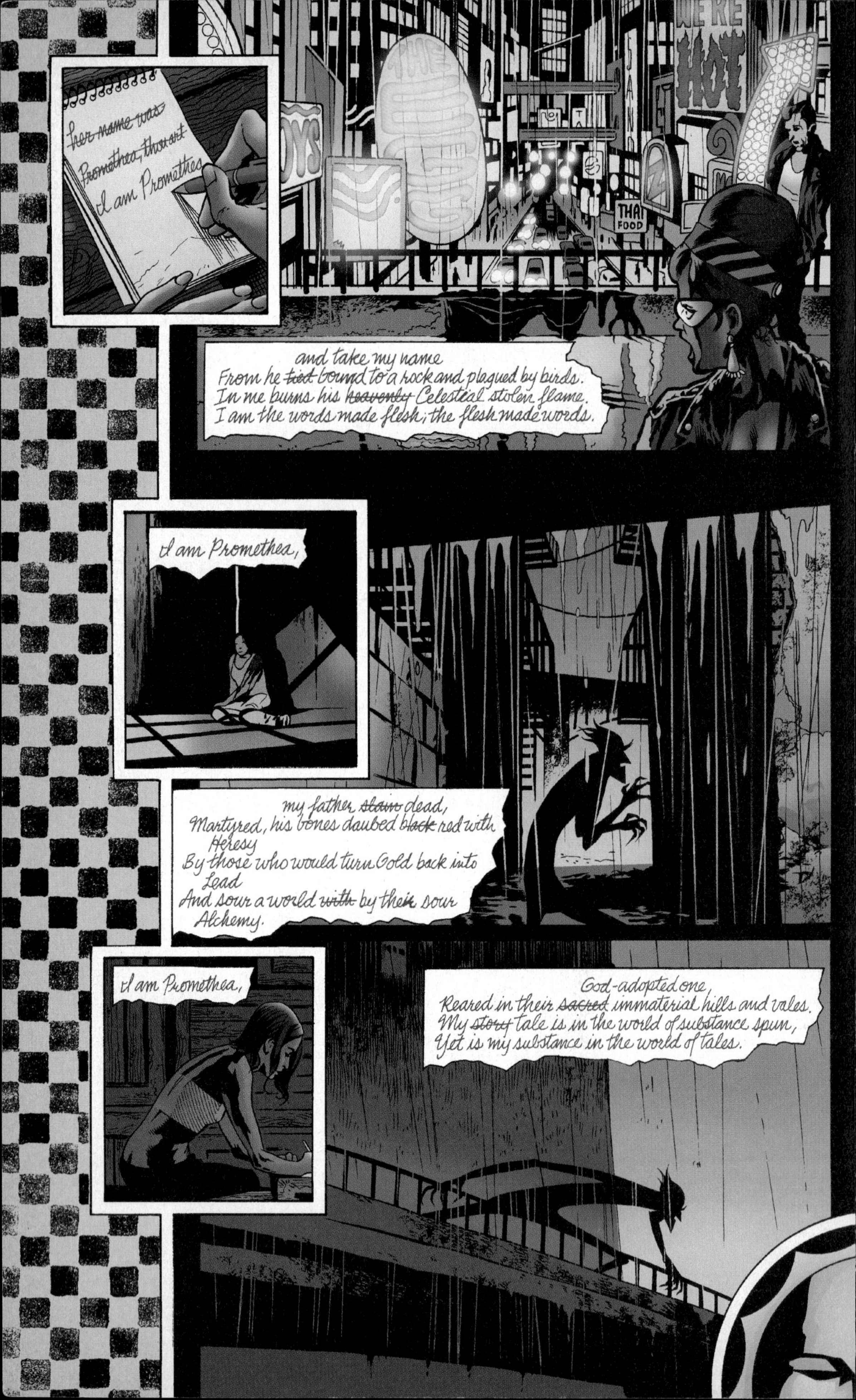
~~her name was~~
~~Promethea, thou art~~
I am Promethea
WE'RE HOT
THE
THAI FOOD
and take my name
From he ~~tied~~ bound to a rock and plagued by birds.
In me burns his ~~heavenly~~ Celestial stolen flame.
I am the words made flesh; the flesh made words.
I am Promethea,
my father ~~slain~~ dead,
Martyred, his bones daubed ~~black~~ red with Heresy
By those who would turn Gold back into Lead
And sour a world ~~with~~ by their sour Alchemy.
I am Promethea,
God-adopted one,
Reared in their ~~sacred~~ immaterial hills and vales.
My ~~story~~ tale is in the world of substance spun,
Yet is my substance in the world of tales.

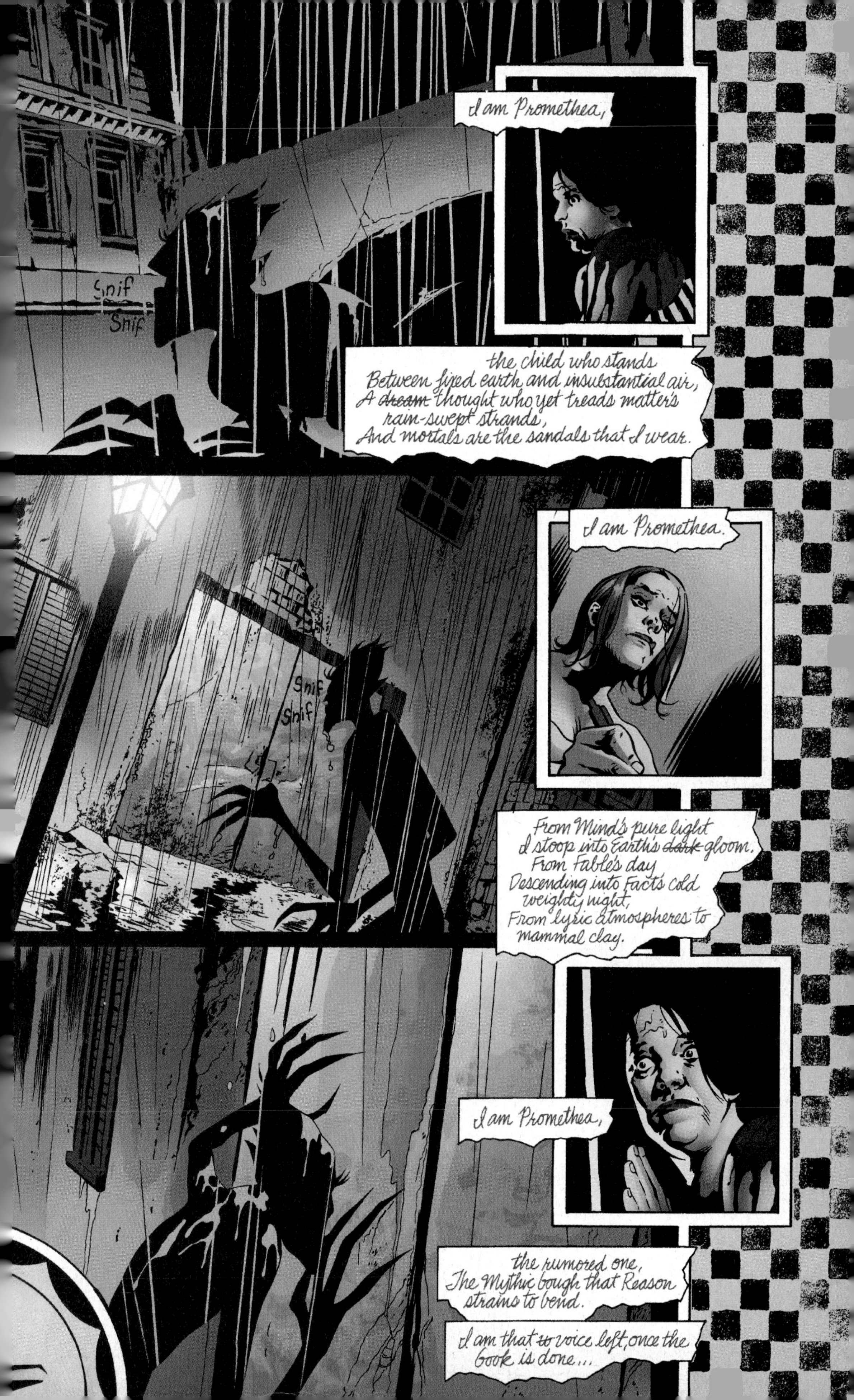
I am Promethea,
Snif
Snif
the child who stands
Between fixed earth and insubstantial air,
A ~~dream~~ thought who yet treads matter's rain-swept strands,
And mortals are the sandals that I wear.
I am Promethea.
Snif
Snif
From Mind's pure light
I stoop into Earth's ~~dark~~ gloom,
From Fable's day
Descending into Fact's cold weighty night,
From lyric atmospheres to mammal clay.
I am Promethea,
the rumored one,
The Mythic bough that Reason strains to bend.
I am that ~~to~~ voice left, once the Book is done...

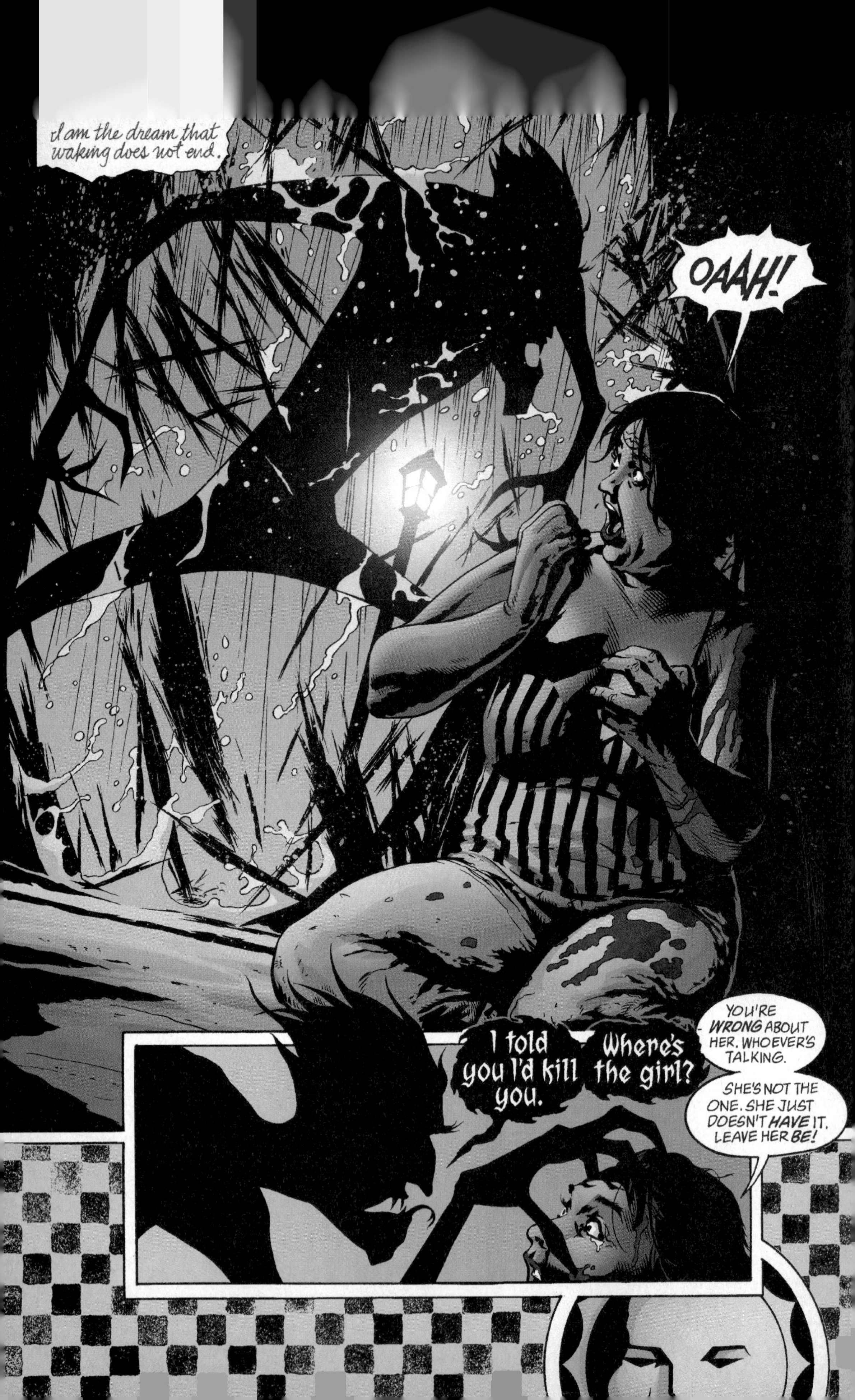
I am the dream that waking does not end.
OAAH!
YOU'RE WRONG ABOUT HER. WHOEVER'S TALKING.
I told you I'd kill you.
Where's the girl?
SHE'S NOT THE ONE. SHE JUST DOESN'T HAVE IT. LEAVE HER BE!

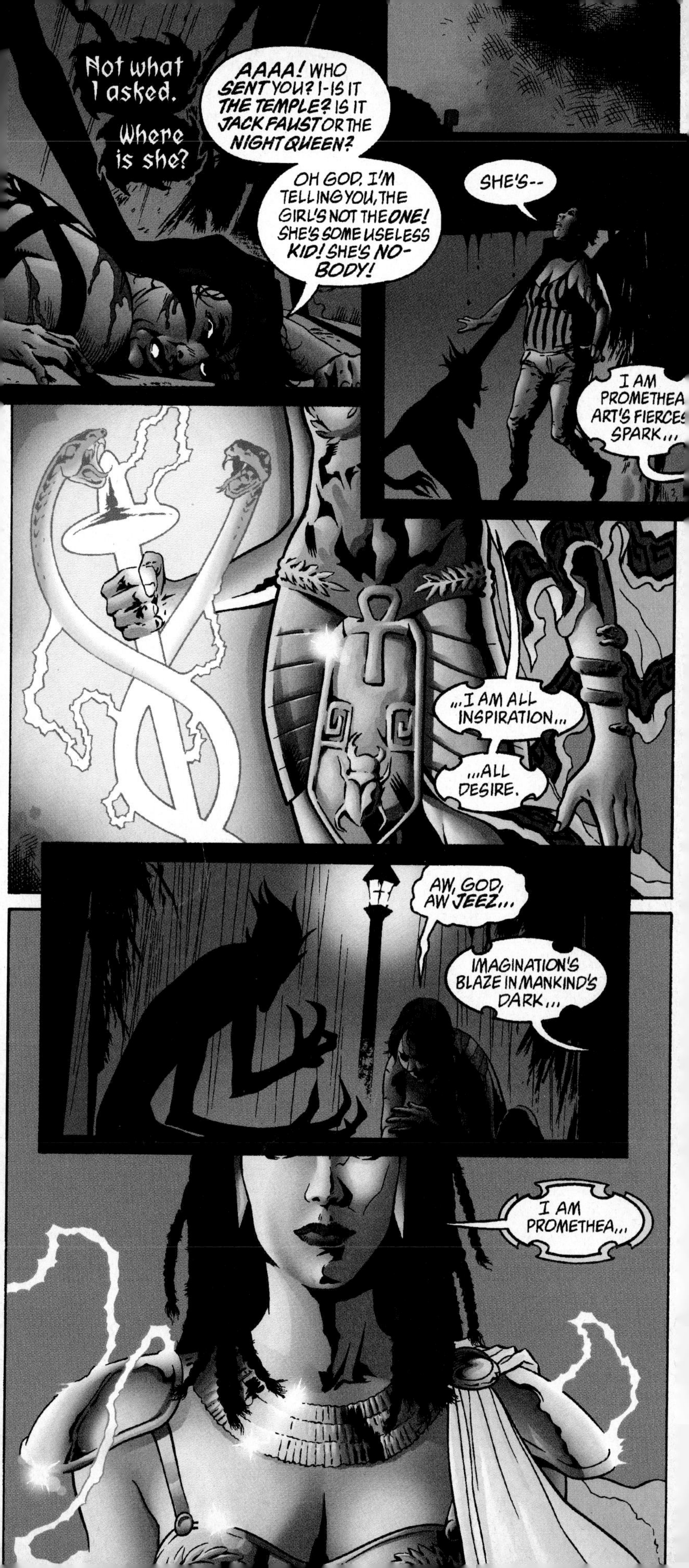
Not what I asked.
Where is she?
AAAA! WHO SENT YOU? I-IS IT THE TEMPLE? IS IT JACK FAUST OR THE NIGHT QUEEN?
OH GOD, I'M TELLING YOU, THE GIRL'S NOT THE ONE! SHE'S SOME USELESS KID! SHE'S NO-BODY!
SHE'S--
I AM PROMETHEA ART'S FIERCES SPARK...
...I AM ALL INSPIRATION...
...ALL DESIRE.
AW, GOD, AW JEEZ...
IMAGINATION'S BLAZE IN MANKIND'S DARK...
I AM PROMETHEA...

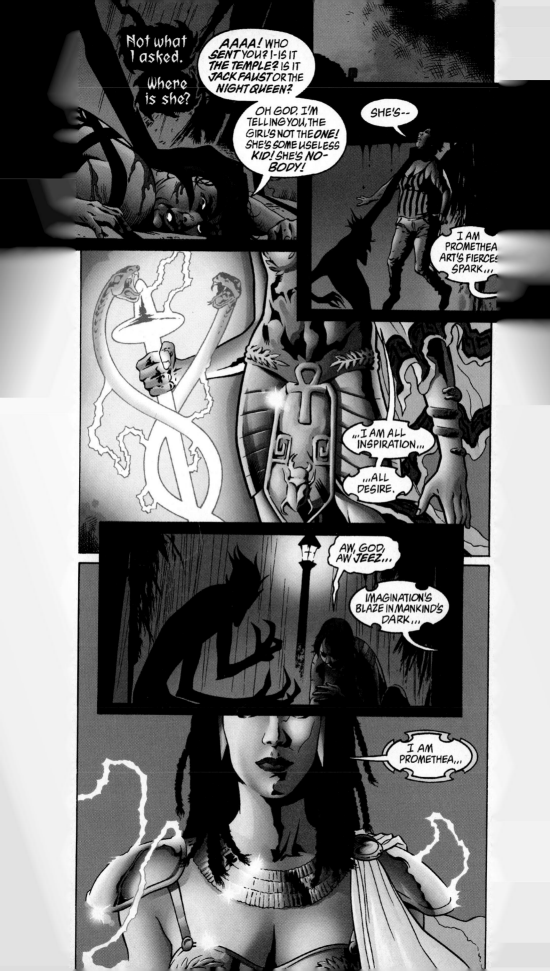

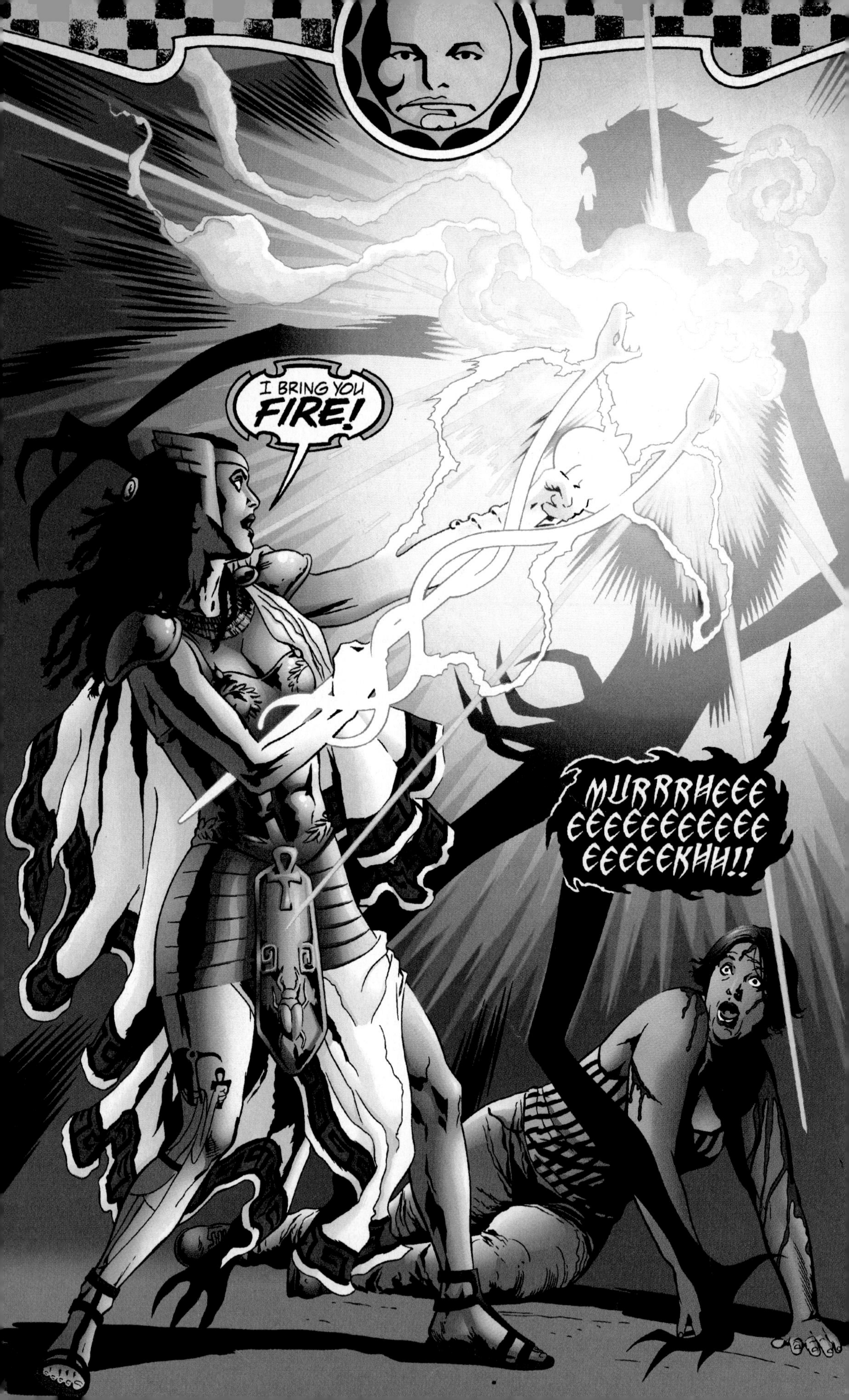

I BRING YOU FIRE!
MURRRHEEE EEEEEEEEEEE EEEEEKHH!!

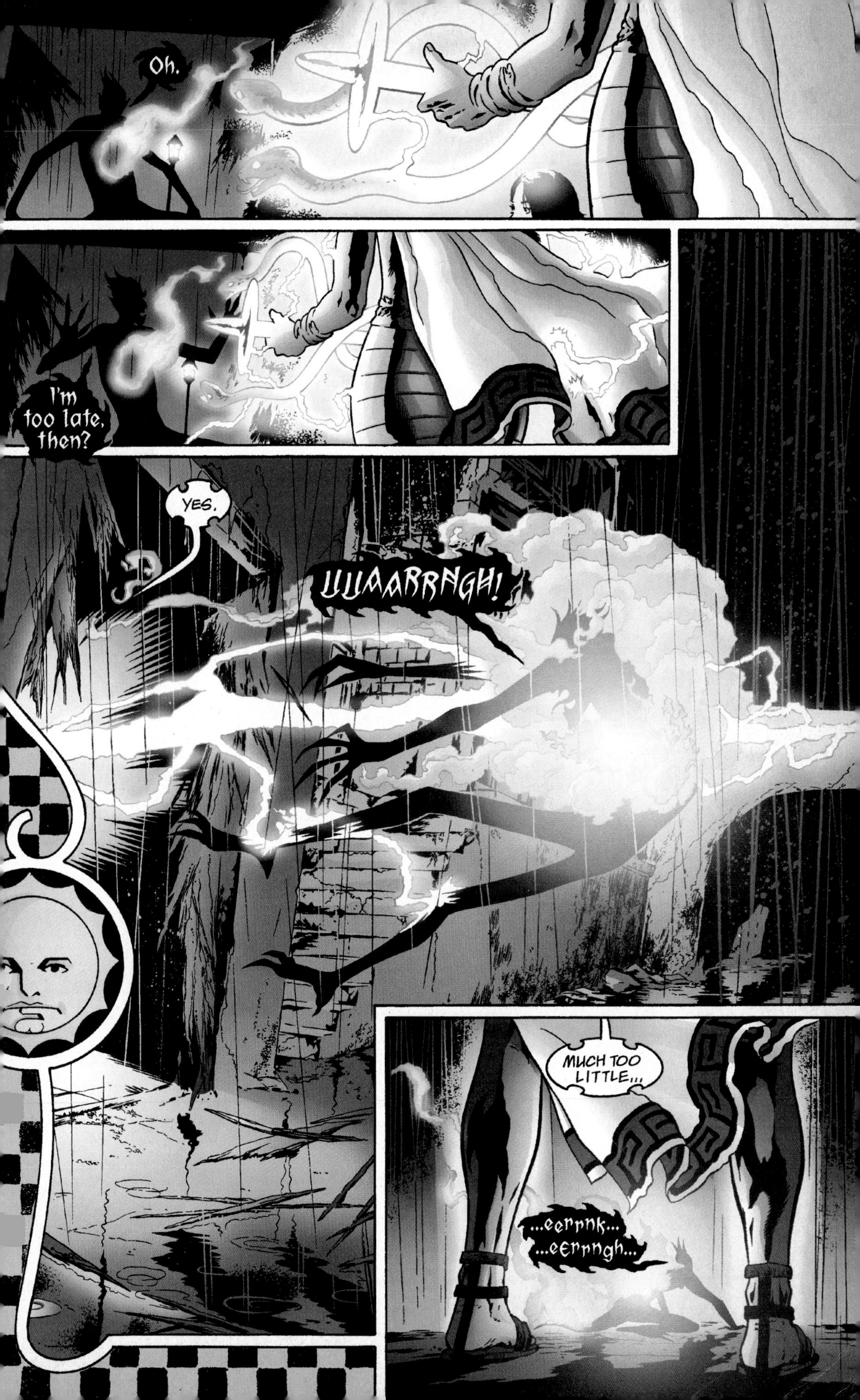
Oh.
I'm too late, then?
YES.
UUAARRRGH!
MUCH TOO LITTLE...
...eernnk...
...eErnngh...

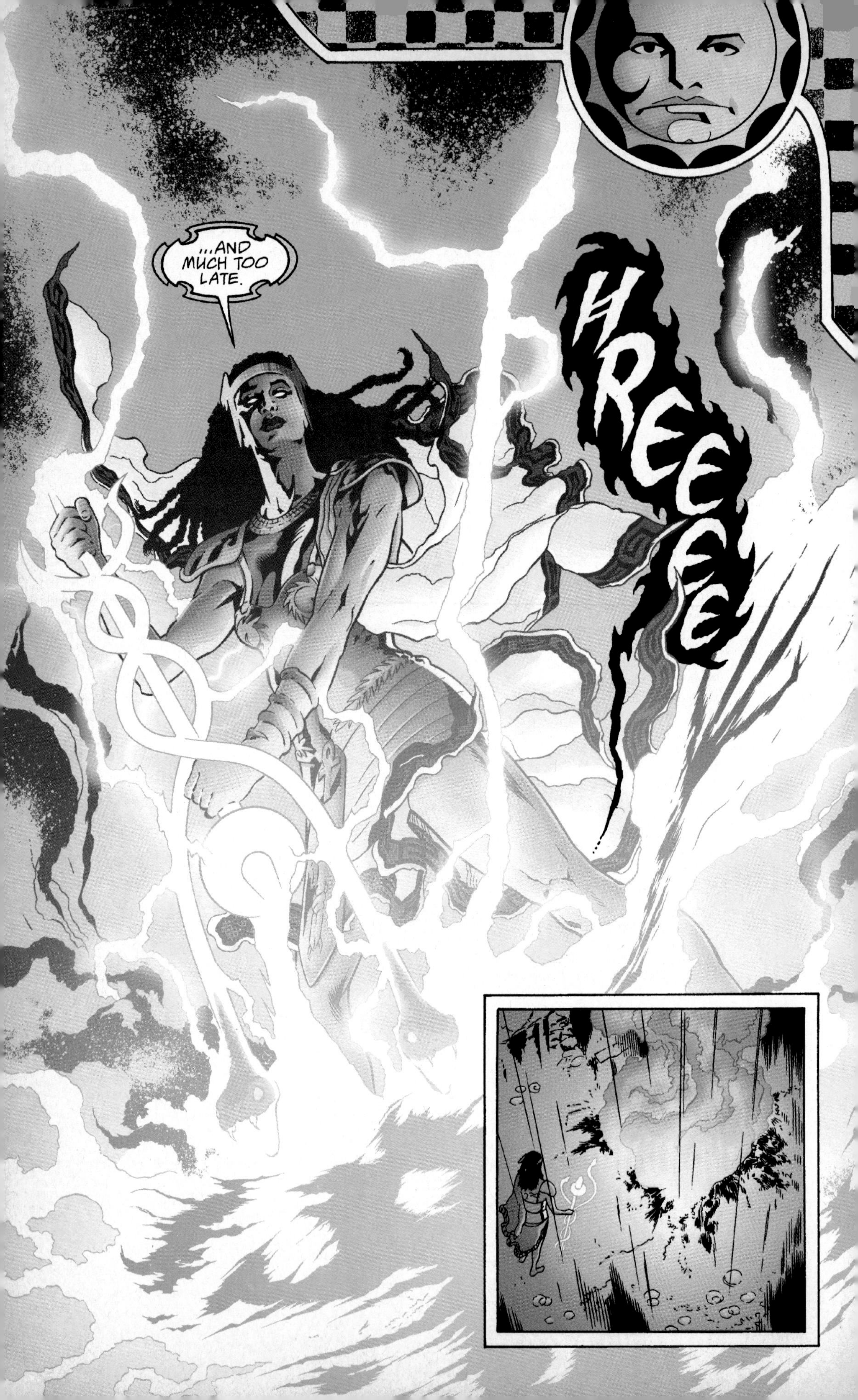
...AND MUCH TOO LATE.
HREEEE

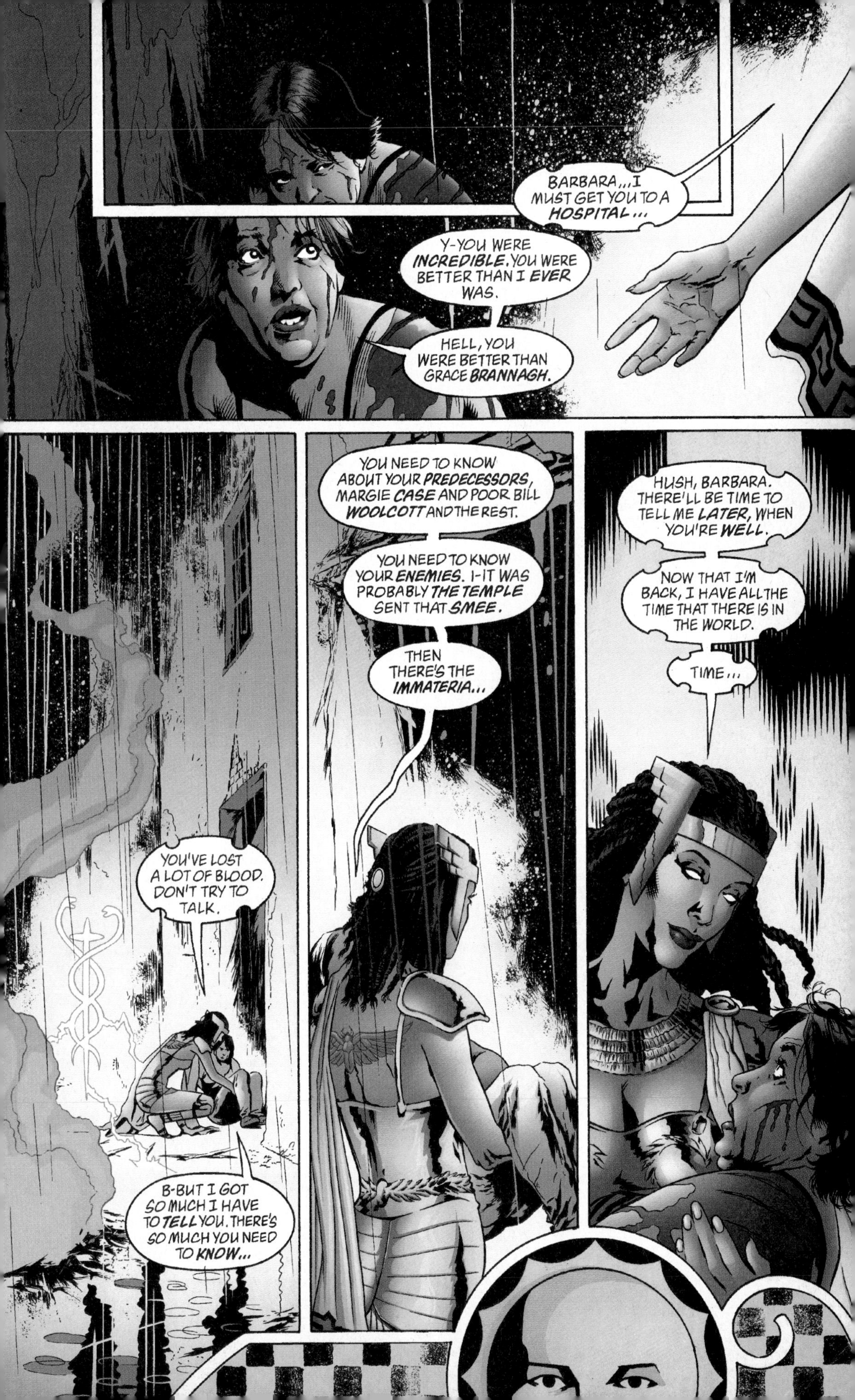
BARBARA...I MUST GET YOU TO A HOSPITAL...
Y-YOU WERE INCREDIBLE. YOU WERE BETTER THAN I EVER WAS.
HELL, YOU WERE BETTER THAN GRACE BRANNAGH.
YOU'VE LOST A LOT OF BLOOD. DON'T TRY TO TALK.
B-BUT I GOT SO MUCH I HAVE TO TELL YOU. THERE'S SO MUCH YOU NEED TO KNOW...
YOU NEED TO KNOW ABOUT YOUR PREDECESSORS, MARGIE CASE AND POOR BILL WOOLCOTT AND THE REST.
YOU NEED TO KNOW YOUR ENEMIES. I-IT WAS PROBABLY THE TEMPLE SENT THAT SMEE.
THEN THERE'S THE IMMATERIA...
HUSH, BARBARA. THERE'LL BE TIME TO TELL ME LATER, WHEN YOU'RE WELL.
NOW THAT I'M BACK, I HAVE ALL THE TIME THAT THERE IS IN THE WORLD.
TIME...

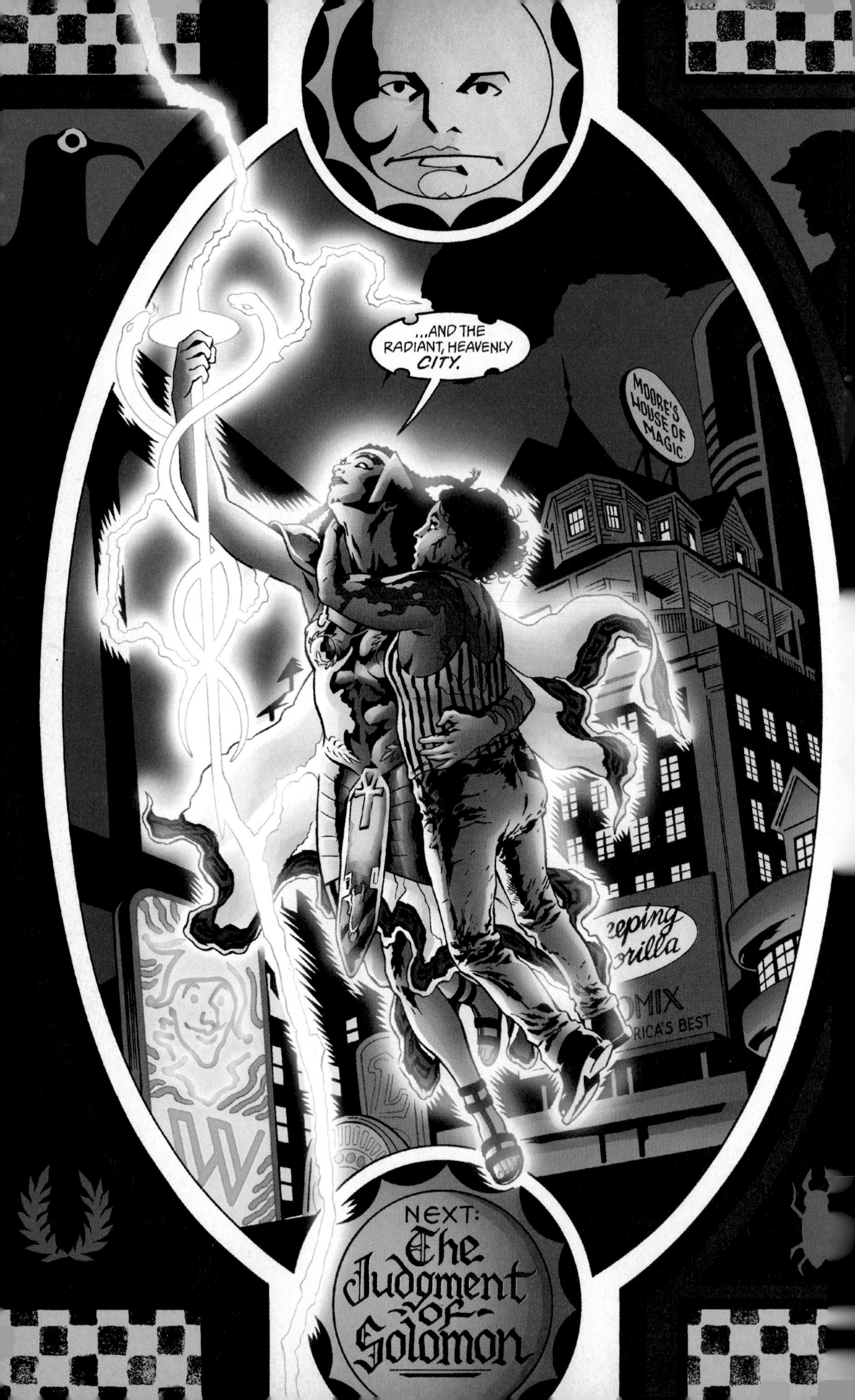
...AND THE RADIANT, HEAVENLY CITY.
MOORE'S HOUSE OF MAGIC.
NEXT: The Judgment of Solomon

CHAPTER TWO

A new champion arises,
A demonic threat is dispatched,
A deadly battle is joined.

Cover art:
J.H. Williams III
& Mick Gray

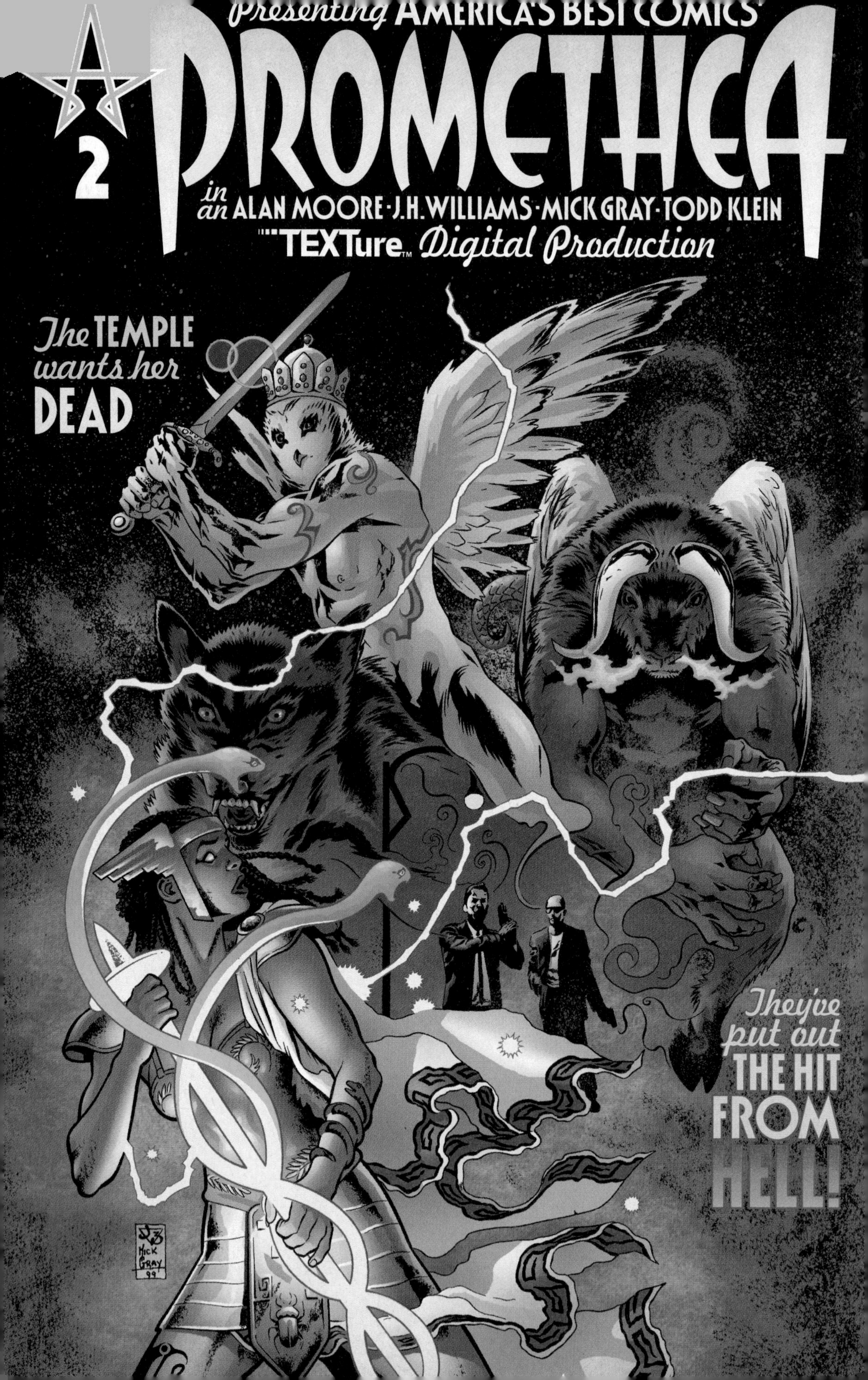
Presenting AMERICA'S BEST COMICS
2
PROMETHEA
in an ALAN MOORE · J.H. WILLIAMS · MICK GRAY · TODD KLEIN
TEXTure™ Digital Production
The TEMPLE wants her DEAD
They've put out THE HIT FROM HELL!
MICK GRAY '99

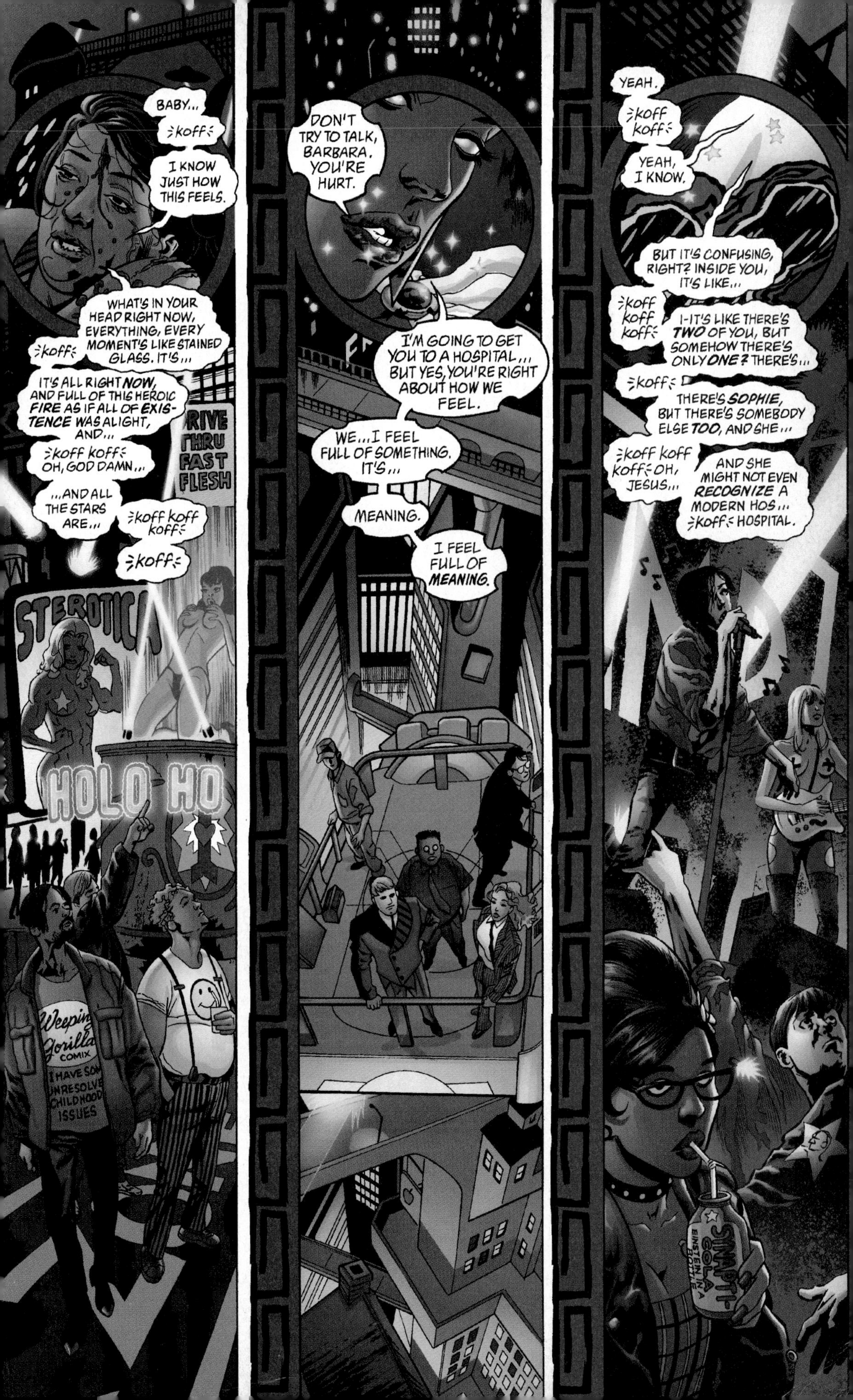
BABY...
koff
I KNOW JUST HOW THIS FEELS.
WHAT'S IN YOUR HEAD RIGHT NOW, EVERYTHING, EVERY MOMENT'S LIKE STAINED GLASS. IT'S...
koff
IT'S ALL RIGHT NOW, AND FULL OF THIS HEROIC FIRE AS IF ALL OF EXISTENCE WAS ALIGHT, AND...
koff koff OH, GOD DAMN...
...AND ALL THE STARS ARE...
koff koff koff
koff
RIVE THRU FAST FLESH
STEROTICA
HOLO HO
Weeping Gorilla COMIX
I HAVE SOM UNRESOLVE CHILDHOOD ISSUES
DON'T TRY TO TALK, BARBARA. YOU'RE HURT.
I'M GOING TO GET YOU TO A HOSPITAL... BUT YES, YOU'RE RIGHT ABOUT HOW WE FEEL.
WE...I FEEL FULL OF SOMETHING. IT'S...
MEANING.
I FEEL FULL OF MEANING.
YEAH.
koff koff
YEAH, I KNOW.
BUT IT'S CONFUSING, RIGHT? INSIDE YOU, IT'S LIKE...
koff koff koff
I-IT'S LIKE THERE'S TWO OF YOU, BUT SOMEHOW THERE'S ONLY ONE? THERE'S...
koff
THERE'S SOPHIE, BUT THERE'S SOMEBODY ELSE TOO, AND SHE...
koff koff koff OH, JESUS...
AND SHE MIGHT NOT EVEN RECOGNIZE A MODERN HOS... koff HOSPITAL.

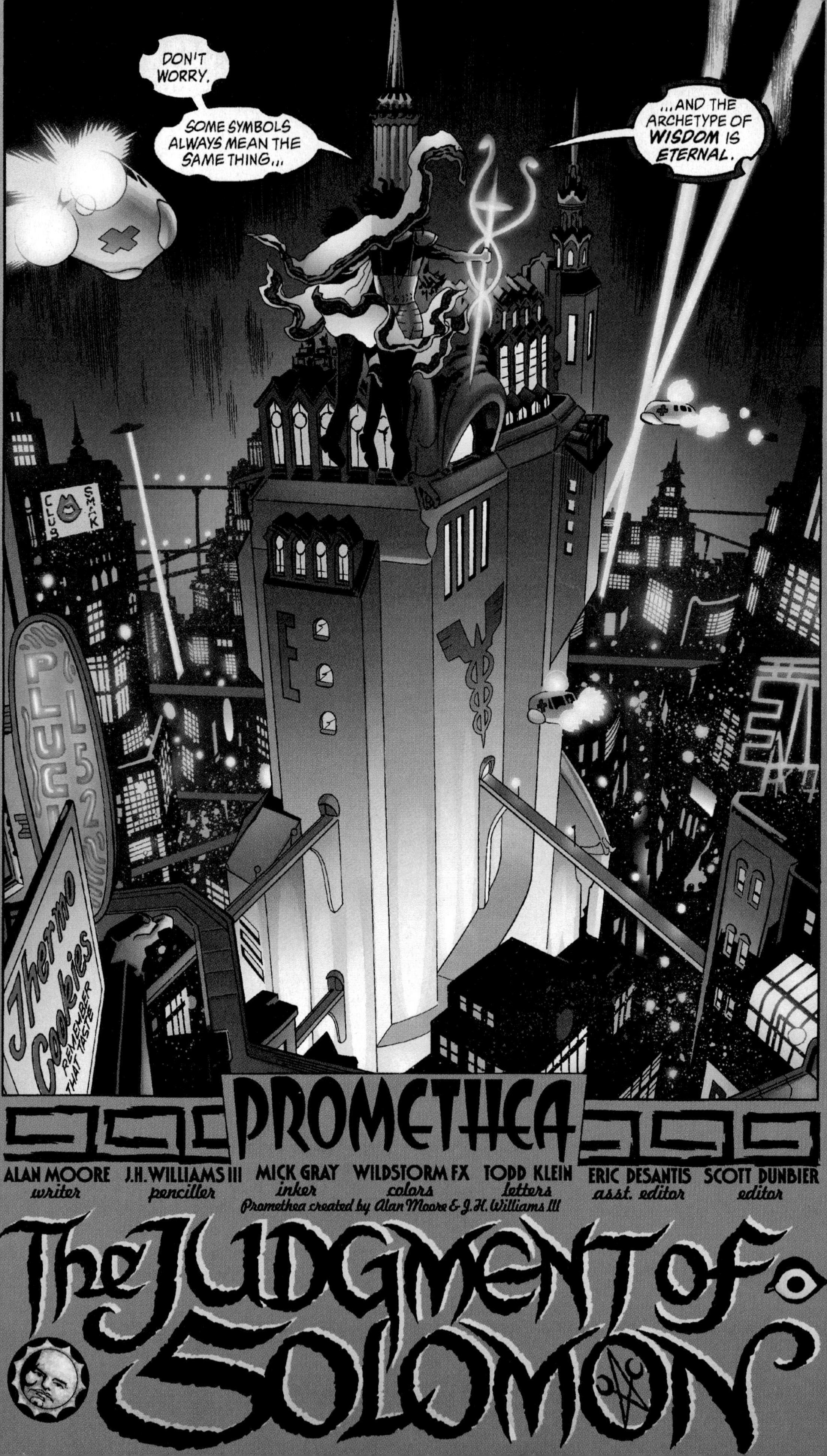
DON'T WORRY.
SOME SYMBOLS ALWAYS MEAN THE SAME THING...
...AND THE ARCHETYPE OF WISDOM IS ETERNAL.
Thermo Cookies
REMEMBER THAT TASTE
PROMETHEA
ALAN MOORE writer
J.H. WILLIAMS III penciller
MICK GRAY inker
WILDSTORM FX colors
TODD KLEIN letters
ERIC DESANTIS asst. editor
SCOTT DUNBIER editor
Promethea created by Alan Moore & J. H. Williams III
The JUDGMENT of SOLOMON

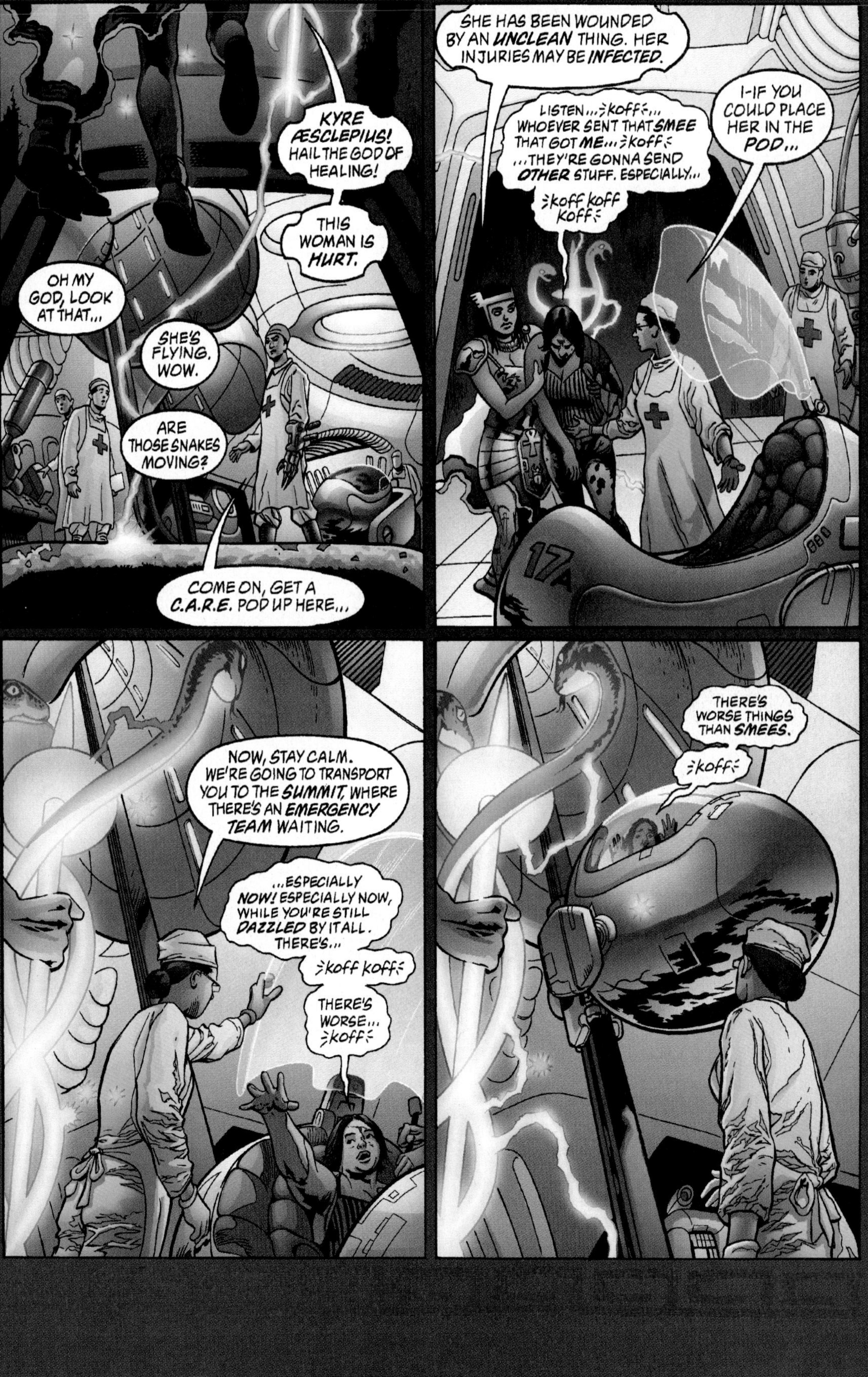
KYRE ÆSCLEPIUS! HAIL THE GOD OF HEALING!
THIS WOMAN IS HURT.
OH MY GOD, LOOK AT THAT...
SHE'S FLYING. WOW.
ARE THOSE SNAKES MOVING?
COME ON, GET A C.A.R.E. POD UP HERE...
SHE HAS BEEN WOUNDED BY AN UNCLEAN THING. HER INJURIES MAY BE INFECTED.
LISTEN... *koff*... WHOEVER SENT THAT SMEE THAT GOT ME... *koff* ...THEY'RE GONNA SEND OTHER STUFF. ESPECIALLY...
koff koff koff
I-IF YOU COULD PLACE HER IN THE POD...
17A
NOW, STAY CALM. WE'RE GOING TO TRANSPORT YOU TO THE SUMMIT, WHERE THERE'S AN EMERGENCY TEAM WAITING.
...ESPECIALLY NOW! ESPECIALLY NOW, WHILE YOU'RE STILL DAZZLED BY IT ALL. THERE'S...
koff koff
THERE'S WORSE... *koff*
THERE'S WORSE THINGS THAN SMEES.
koff

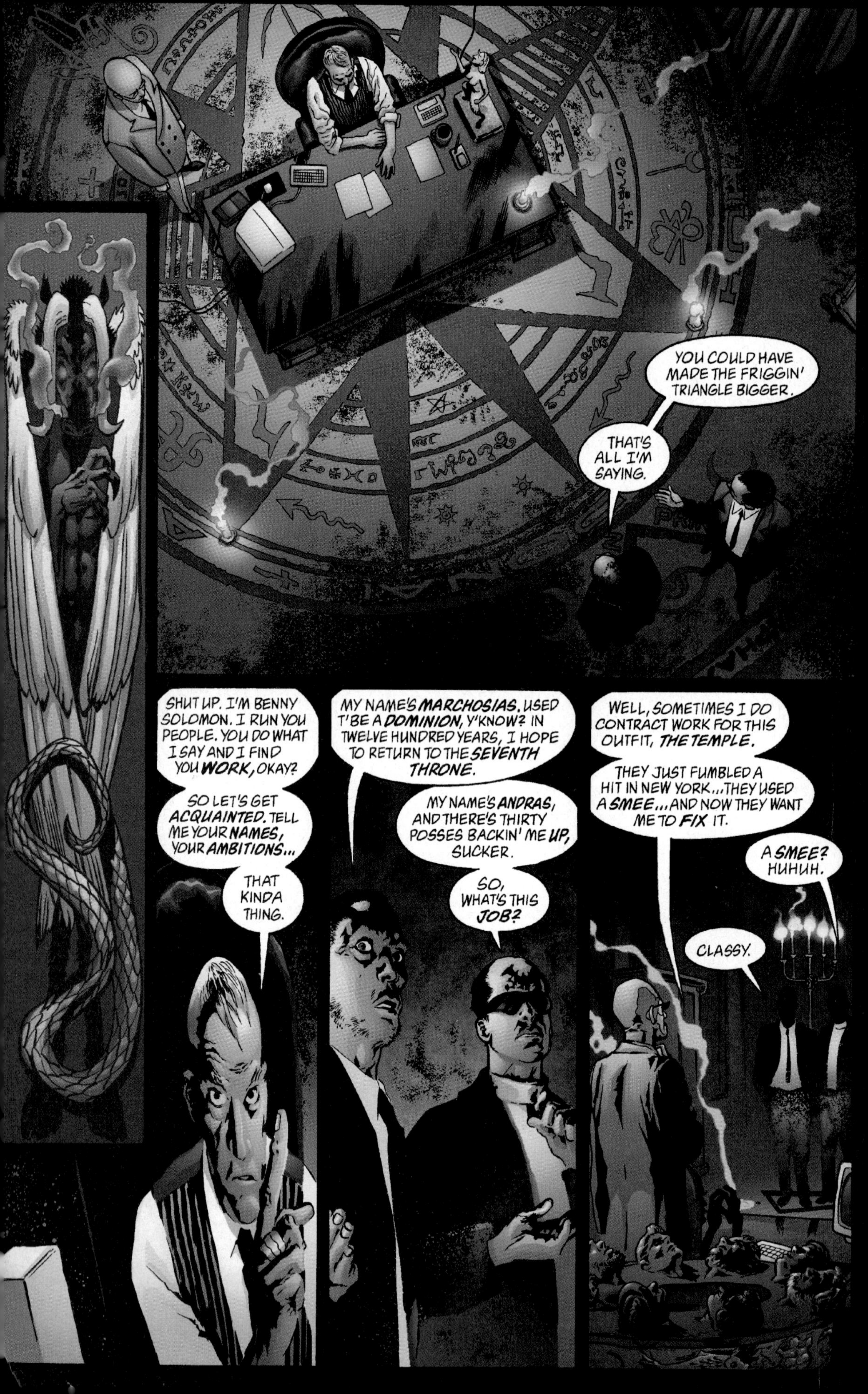
YOU COULD HAVE MADE THE FRIGGIN' TRIANGLE BIGGER.
THAT'S ALL I'M SAYING.
SHUT UP. I'M BENNY SOLOMON. I RUN YOU PEOPLE. YOU DO WHAT I SAY AND I FIND YOU WORK, OKAY?
SO LET'S GET ACQUAINTED. TELL ME YOUR NAMES, YOUR AMBITIONS...
THAT KINDA THING.
MY NAME'S MARCHOSIAS. USED T'BE A DOMINION, Y'KNOW? IN TWELVE HUNDRED YEARS, I HOPE TO RETURN TO THE SEVENTH THRONE.
MY NAME'S ANDRAS, AND THERE'S THIRTY POSSES BACKIN' ME UP, SUCKER.
SO, WHAT'S THIS JOB?
WELL, SOMETIMES I DO CONTRACT WORK FOR THIS OUTFIT, THE TEMPLE.
THEY JUST FUMBLED A HIT IN NEW YORK... THEY USED A SMEE... AND NOW THEY WANT ME TO FIX IT.
A SMEE? HUHUH.
CLASSY.

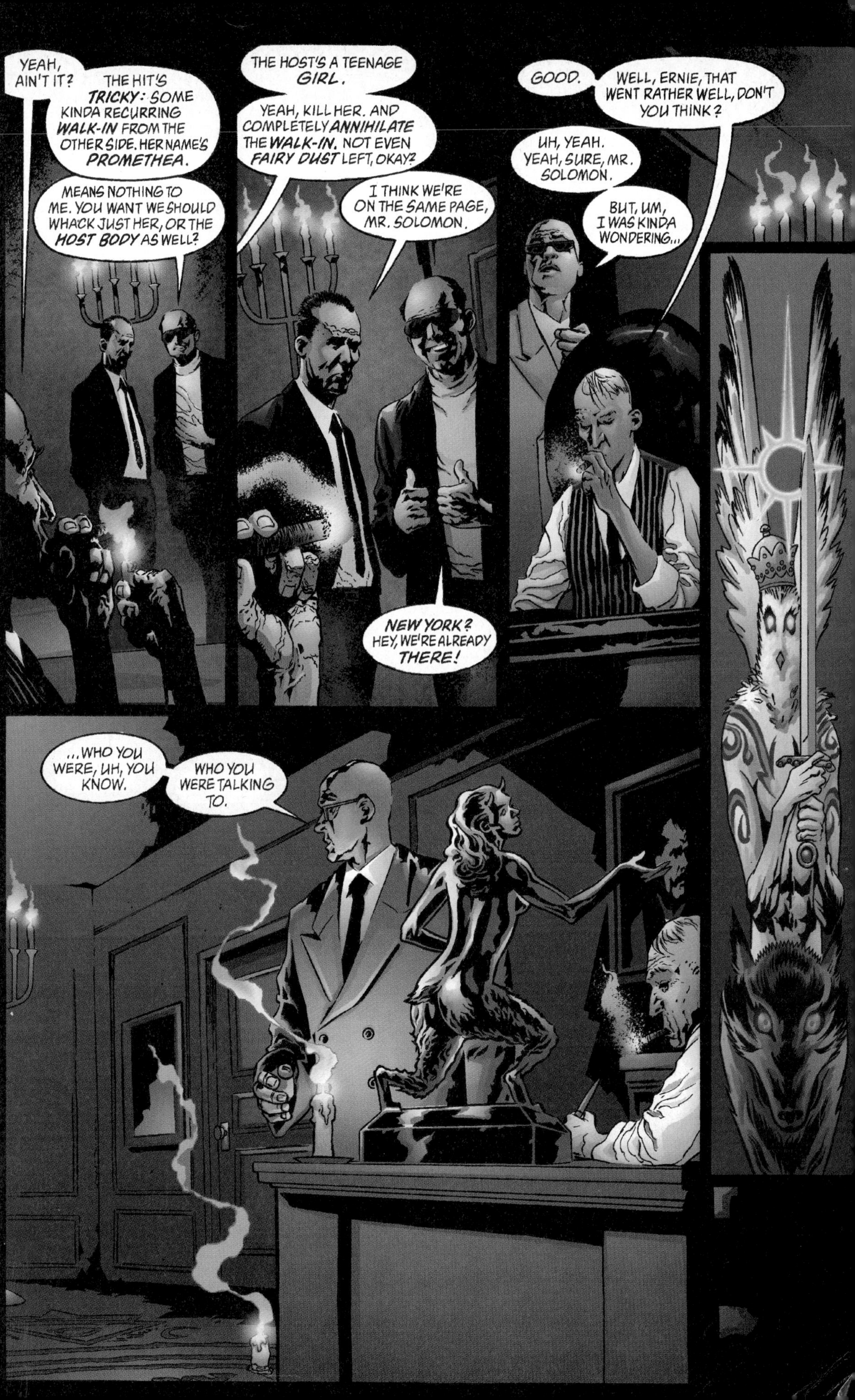

YEAH, AIN'T IT?
THE HIT'S TRICKY: SOME KINDA RECURRING WALK-IN FROM THE OTHER SIDE. HER NAME'S PROMETHEA.
MEANS NOTHING TO ME. YOU WANT WE SHOULD WHACK JUST HER, OR THE HOST BODY AS WELL?
THE HOST'S A TEENAGE GIRL.
YEAH, KILL HER. AND COMPLETELY ANNIHILATE THE WALK-IN. NOT EVEN FAIRY DUST LEFT, OKAY?
I THINK WE'RE ON THE SAME PAGE, MR. SOLOMON.
NEW YORK? HEY, WE'RE ALREADY THERE!
GOOD.
WELL, ERNIE, THAT WENT RATHER WELL, DON'T YOU THINK?
UH, YEAH. YEAH, SURE, MR. SOLOMON.
BUT, UM, I WAS KINDA WONDERING...
...WHO YOU WERE, UH, YOU KNOW.
WHO YOU WERE TALKING TO.

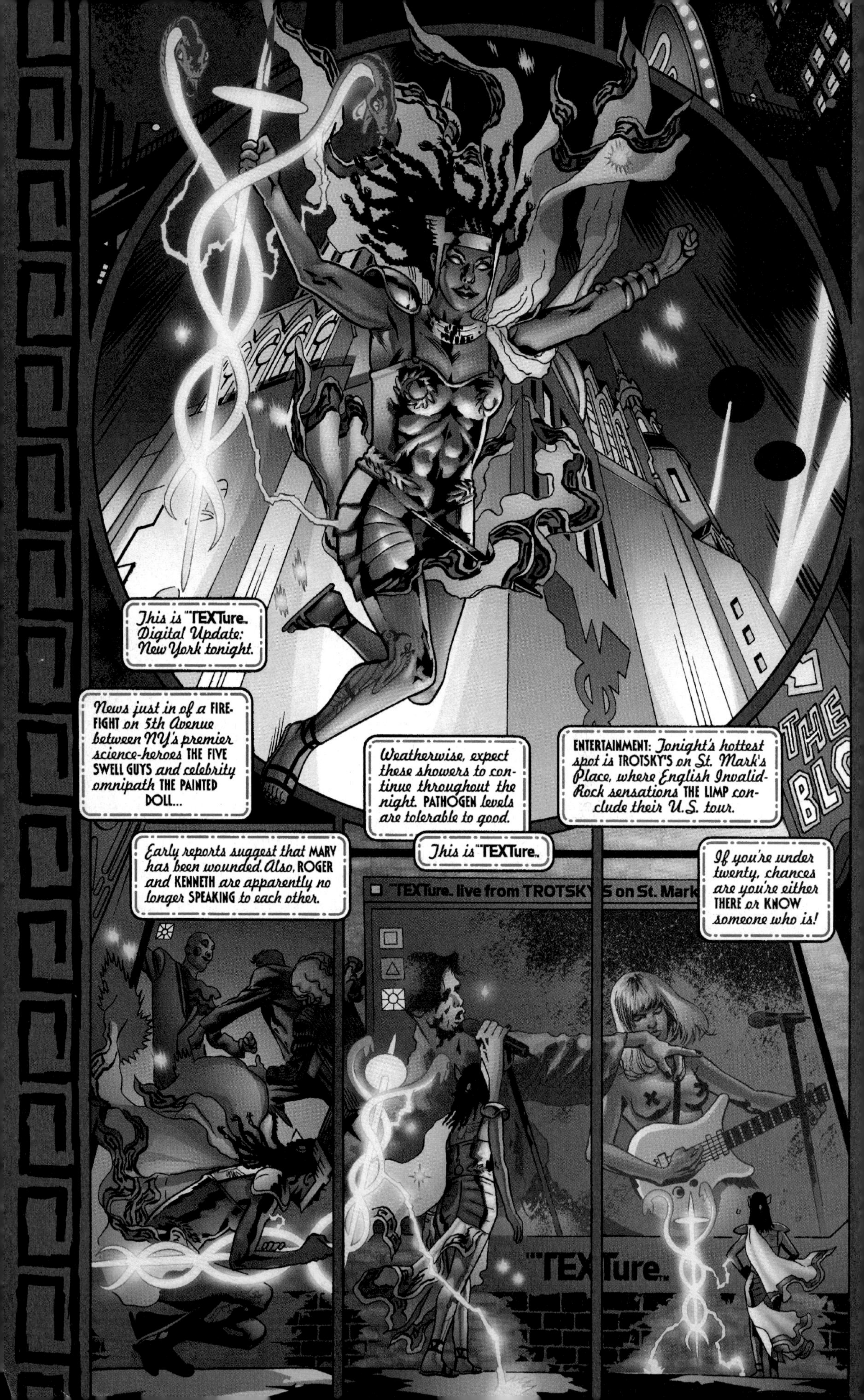
This is "TEXTure. Digital Update: New York tonight.
News just in of a FIRE-FIGHT on 5th Avenue between NY's premier science-heroes THE FIVE SWELL GUYS and celebrity omnipath THE PAINTED DOLL...
Weatherwise, expect these showers to continue throughout the night. PATHOGEN levels are tolerable to good.
ENTERTAINMENT: Tonight's hottest spot is TROTSKY'S on St. Mark's Place, where English Invalid-Rock sensations THE LIMP conclude their U.S. tour.
Early reports suggest that MARV has been wounded. Also, ROGER and KENNETH are apparently no longer SPEAKING to each other.
This is "TEXTure.
If you're under twenty, chances are you're either THERE or KNOW someone who is!
"TEXTure. live from TROTSKY'S on St. Mark
"TEXTure.

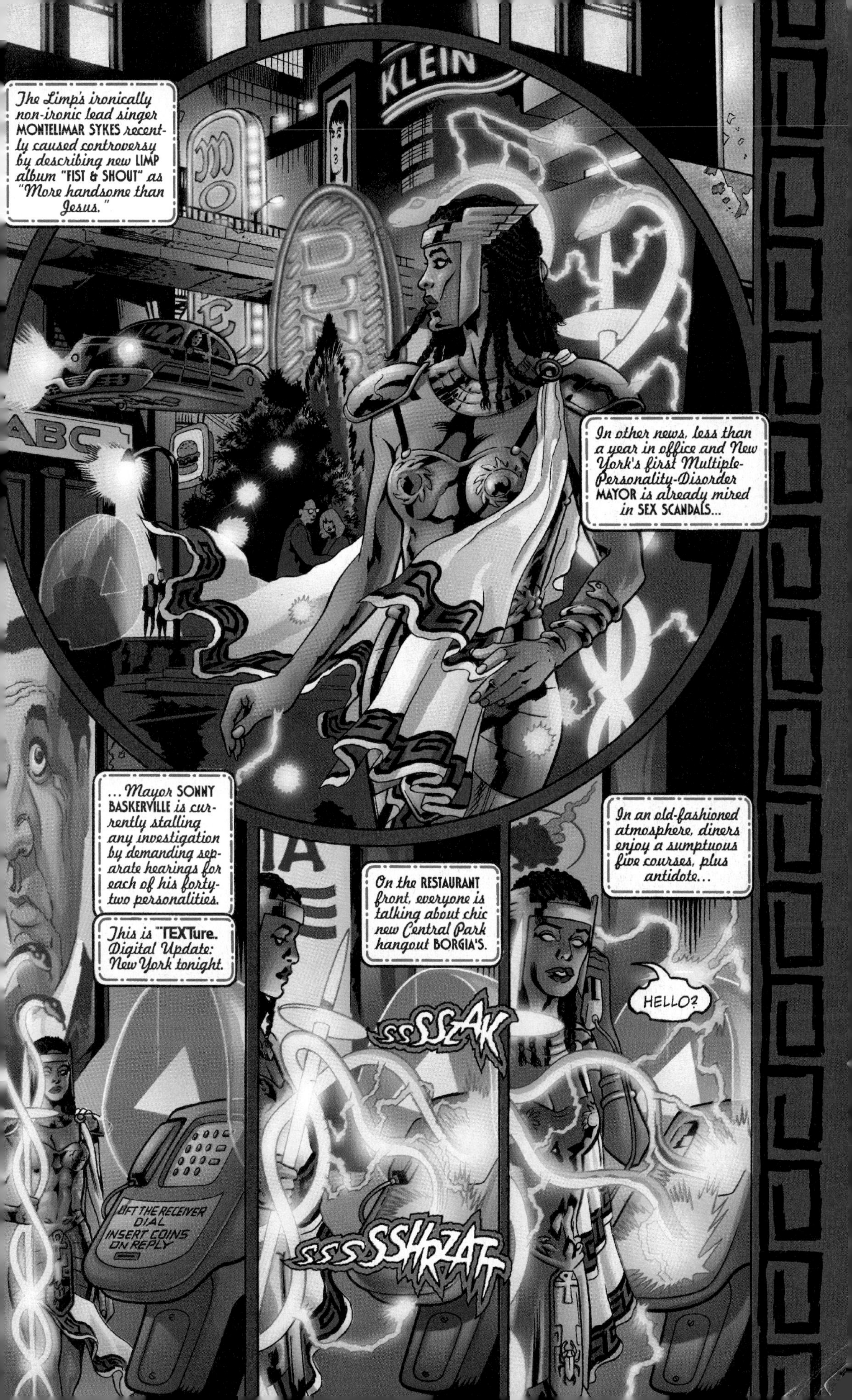

KLEIN
The Limp's ironically non-ironic lead singer MONTELIMAR SYKES recently caused controversy by describing new LIMP album "FIST & SHOUT" as "More handsome than Jesus."
In other news, less than a year in office and New York's first Multiple-Personality-Disorder MAYOR is already mired in SEX SCANDALS...
ABC
...Mayor SONNY BASKERVILLE is currently stalling any investigation by demanding separate hearings for each of his forty-two personalities.
This is "TEXTure. Digital Update: New York tonight.
On the RESTAURANT front, everyone is talking about chic new Central Park hangout BORGIA'S.
In an old-fashioned atmosphere, diners enjoy a sumptuous five courses, plus antidote...
HELLO?
SSSSZAK
LIFT THE RECEIVER
DIAL
INSERT COINS
ON REPLY
SSSSSHRZATT

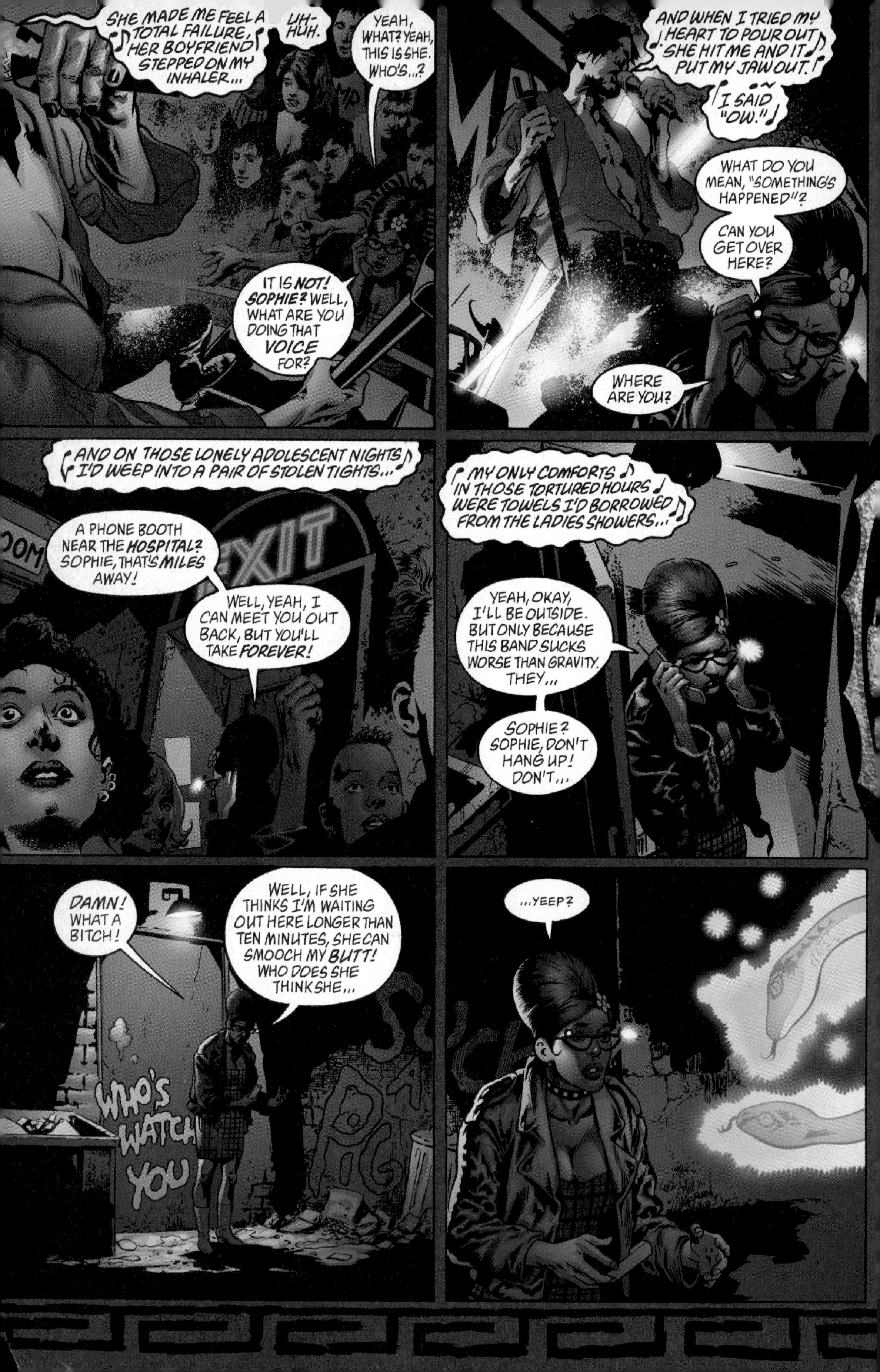
SHE MADE ME FEEL A TOTAL FAILURE, HER BOYFRIEND STEPPED ON MY INHALER...
UH-HUH.
YEAH, WHAT? YEAH, THIS IS SHE. WHO'S...?
IT IS NOT! SOPHIE? WELL, WHAT ARE YOU DOING THAT VOICE FOR?
AND WHEN I TRIED MY HEART TO POUR OUT SHE HIT ME AND IT PUT MY JAW OUT.
I SAID "OW."
WHAT DO YOU MEAN, "SOMETHING'S HAPPENED"?
CAN YOU GET OVER HERE?
WHERE ARE YOU?
AND ON THOSE LONELY ADOLESCENT NIGHTS I'D WEEP INTO A PAIR OF STOLEN TIGHTS...
A PHONE BOOTH NEAR THE HOSPITAL? SOPHIE, THAT'S MILES AWAY!
EXIT
WELL, YEAH, I CAN MEET YOU OUT BACK, BUT YOU'LL TAKE FOREVER!
MY ONLY COMFORTS IN THOSE TORTURED HOURS WERE TOWELS I'D BORROWED FROM THE LADIES SHOWERS...
YEAH, OKAY, I'LL BE OUTSIDE. BUT ONLY BECAUSE THIS BAND SUCKS WORSE THAN GRAVITY. THEY...
SOPHIE? SOPHIE, DON'T HANG UP! DON'T...
DAMN! WHAT A BITCH!
WELL, IF SHE THINKS I'M WAITING OUT HERE LONGER THAN TEN MINUTES, SHE CAN SMOOCH MY BUTT! WHO DOES SHE THINK SHE...
WHO'S WATCH YOU
...YEEP?

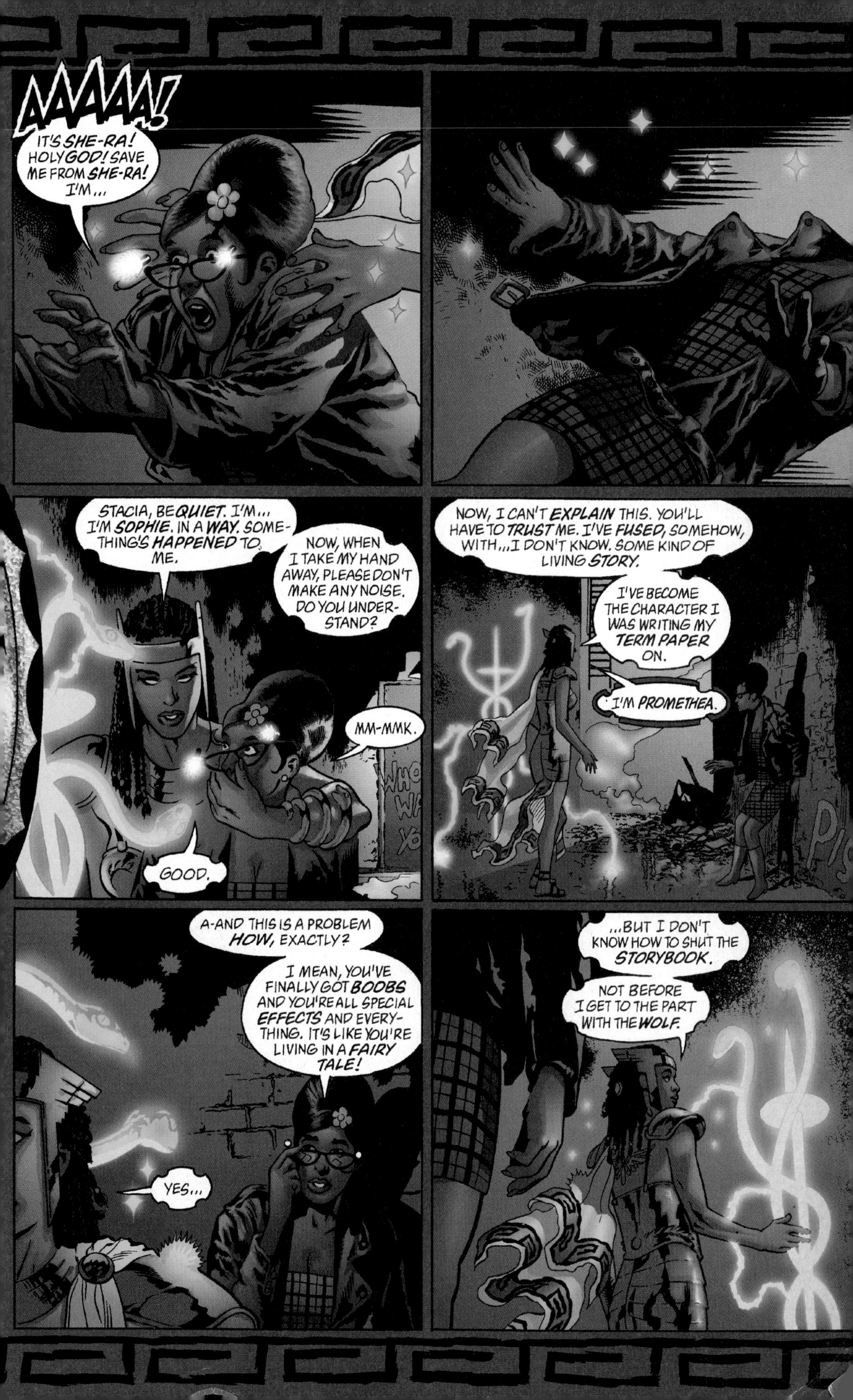
AAAAA!
IT'S SHE-RA! HOLY GOD! SAVE ME FROM SHE-RA! I'M...
STACIA, BE QUIET. I'M... I'M SOPHIE. IN A WAY. SOMETHING'S HAPPENED TO ME.
NOW, WHEN I TAKE MY HAND AWAY, PLEASE DON'T MAKE ANY NOISE. DO YOU UNDERSTAND?
MM-MMK.
GOOD.
NOW, I CAN'T EXPLAIN THIS. YOU'LL HAVE TO TRUST ME. I'VE FUSED, SOMEHOW, WITH... I DON'T KNOW. SOME KIND OF LIVING STORY.
I'VE BECOME THE CHARACTER I WAS WRITING MY TERM PAPER ON.
I'M PROMETHEA.
A-AND THIS IS A PROBLEM HOW, EXACTLY?
I MEAN, YOU'VE FINALLY GOT BOOBS AND YOU'RE ALL SPECIAL EFFECTS AND EVERYTHING. IT'S LIKE YOU'RE LIVING IN A FAIRY TALE!
YES...
...BUT I DON'T KNOW HOW TO SHUT THE STORYBOOK.
NOT BEFORE I GET TO THE PART WITH THE WOLF.

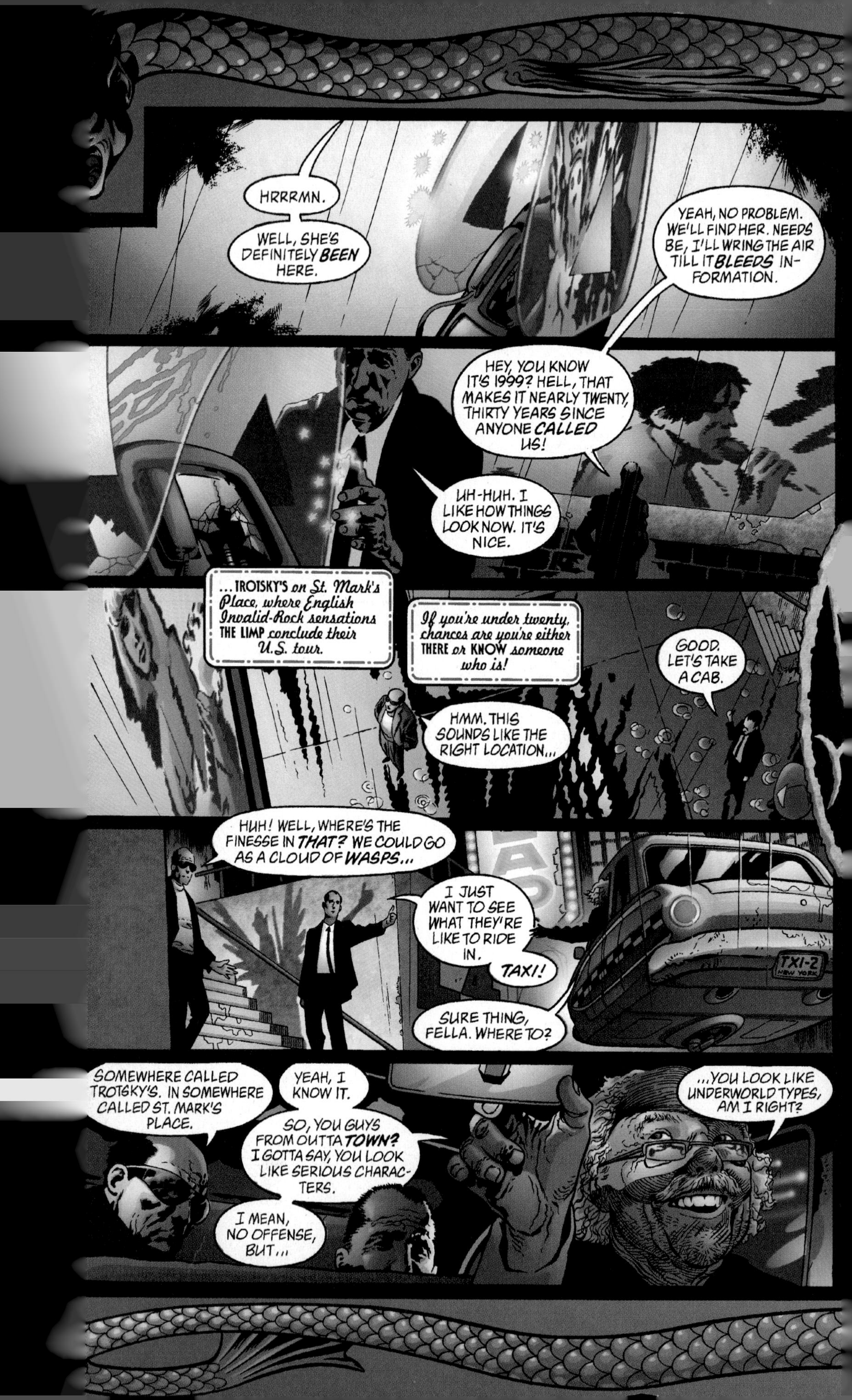
HRRRMN.
WELL, SHE'S DEFINITELY BEEN HERE.
YEAH, NO PROBLEM. WE'LL FIND HER. NEEDS BE, I'LL WRING THE AIR TILL IT BLEEDS IN-FORMATION.
HEY, YOU KNOW IT'S 1999? HELL, THAT MAKES IT NEARLY TWENTY, THIRTY YEARS SINCE ANYONE CALLED US!
UH-HUH. I LIKE HOW THINGS LOOK NOW. IT'S NICE.
...TROTSKY'S on St. Mark's Place, where English Invalid-Rock sensations THE LIMP conclude their U.S. tour.
If you're under twenty, chances are you're either THERE or KNOW someone who is!
HMM. THIS SOUNDS LIKE THE RIGHT LOCATION...
GOOD. LET'S TAKE A CAB.
HUH! WELL, WHERE'S THE FINESSE IN THAT? WE COULD GO AS A CLOUD OF WASPS...
I JUST WANT TO SEE WHAT THEY'RE LIKE TO RIDE IN.
TAXI!
TXI-2 NEW YORK
SURE THING, FELLA. WHERE TO?
SOMEWHERE CALLED TROTSKY'S. IN SOMEWHERE CALLED ST. MARK'S PLACE.
YEAH, I KNOW IT.
SO, YOU GUYS FROM OUTTA TOWN? I GOTTA SAY, YOU LOOK LIKE SERIOUS CHARAC-TERS.
I MEAN, NO OFFENSE, BUT...
...YOU LOOK LIKE UNDERWORLD TYPES, AM I RIGHT?

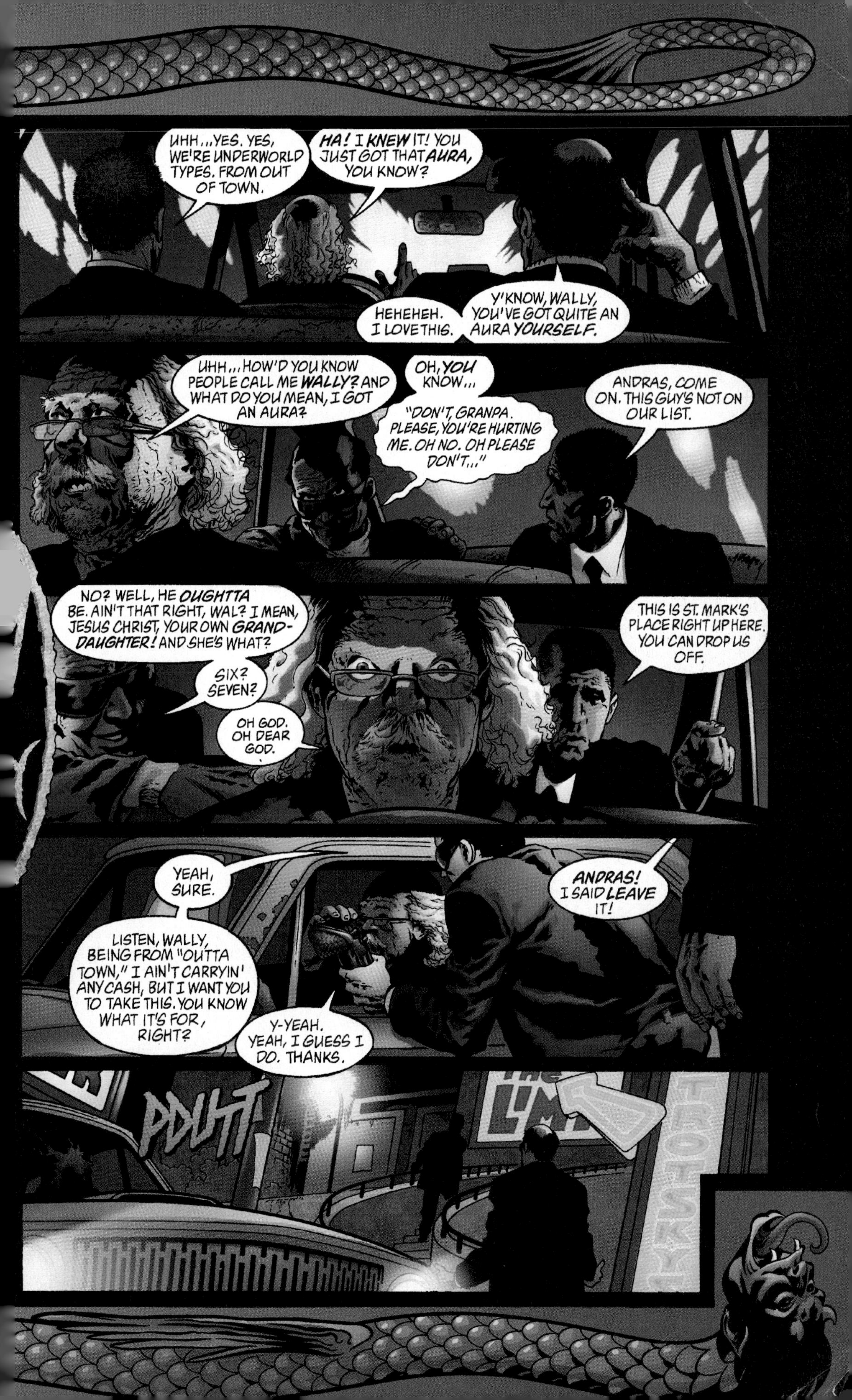

UHH...YES. YES, WE'RE UNDERWORLD TYPES. FROM OUT OF TOWN.
HA! I KNEW IT! YOU JUST GOT THAT AURA, YOU KNOW?
HEHEHEH. I LOVE THIS.
Y'KNOW, WALLY, YOU'VE GOT QUITE AN AURA YOURSELF.
UHH...HOW'D YOU KNOW PEOPLE CALL ME WALLY? AND WHAT DO YOU MEAN, I GOT AN AURA?
OH, YOU KNOW...
"DON'T, GRANPA. PLEASE, YOU'RE HURTING ME. OH NO. OH PLEASE DON'T..."
ANDRAS, COME ON. THIS GUY'S NOT ON OUR LIST.
NO? WELL, HE OUGHTTA BE. AIN'T THAT RIGHT, WAL? I MEAN, JESUS CHRIST, YOUR OWN GRAND-DAUGHTER! AND SHE'S WHAT?
SIX? SEVEN?
OH GOD. OH DEAR GOD.
THIS IS ST. MARK'S PLACE RIGHT UP HERE. YOU CAN DROP US OFF.
YEAH, SURE.
LISTEN, WALLY, BEING FROM "OUTTA TOWN," I AIN'T CARRYIN' ANY CASH, BUT I WANT YOU TO TAKE THIS. YOU KNOW WHAT IT'S FOR, RIGHT?
ANDRAS! I SAID LEAVE IT!
Y-YEAH. YEAH, I GUESS I DO. THANKS.
PDUT
TROTSKY

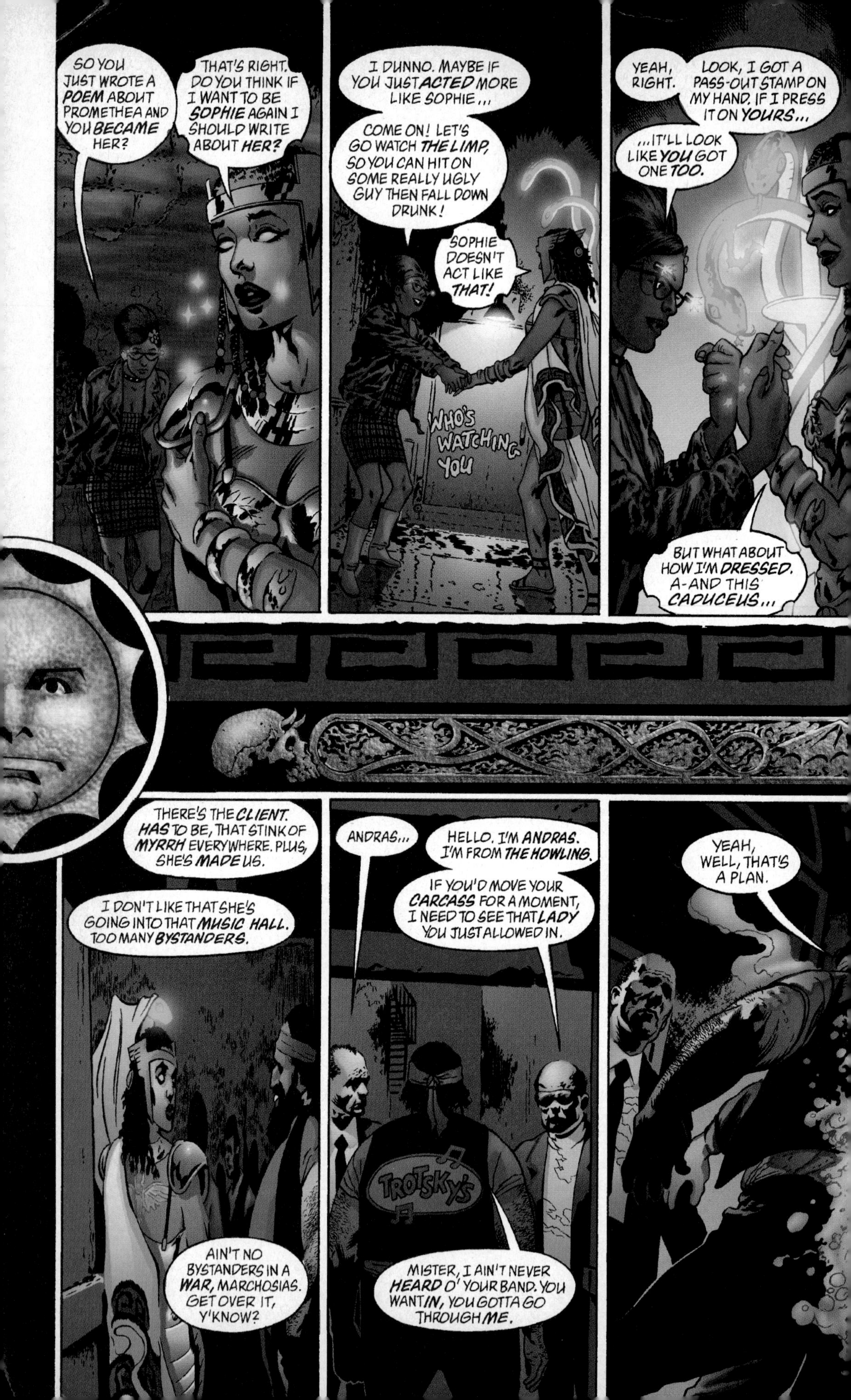
SO YOU JUST WROTE A POEM ABOUT PROMETHEA AND YOU BECAME HER?
THAT'S RIGHT. DO YOU THINK IF I WANT TO BE SOPHIE AGAIN I SHOULD WRITE ABOUT HER?
I DUNNO. MAYBE IF YOU JUST ACTED MORE LIKE SOPHIE...
COME ON! LET'S GO WATCH THE LIMP, SO YOU CAN HIT ON SOME REALLY UGLY GUY THEN FALL DOWN DRUNK!
SOPHIE DOESN'T ACT LIKE THAT!
WHO'S WATCHING YOU
YEAH, RIGHT.
LOOK, I GOT A PASS-OUT STAMP ON MY HAND. IF I PRESS IT ON YOURS...
...IT'LL LOOK LIKE YOU GOT ONE TOO.
BUT WHAT ABOUT HOW I'M DRESSED. A-AND THIS CADUCEUS...
THERE'S THE CLIENT. HAS TO BE, THAT STINK OF MYRRH EVERYWHERE. PLUS, SHE'S MADE US.
I DON'T LIKE THAT SHE'S GOING INTO THAT MUSIC HALL. TOO MANY BYSTANDERS.
AIN'T NO BYSTANDERS IN A WAR, MARCHOSIAS. GET OVER IT, Y'KNOW?
ANDRAS...
HELLO. I'M ANDRAS. I'M FROM THE HOWLING.
IF YOU'D MOVE YOUR CARCASS FOR A MOMENT, I NEED TO SEE THAT LADY YOU JUST ALLOWED IN.
TROTSKY'S
MISTER, I AIN'T NEVER HEARD O' YOUR BAND. YOU WANT IN, YOU GOTTA GO THROUGH ME.
YEAH, WELL, THAT'S A PLAN.

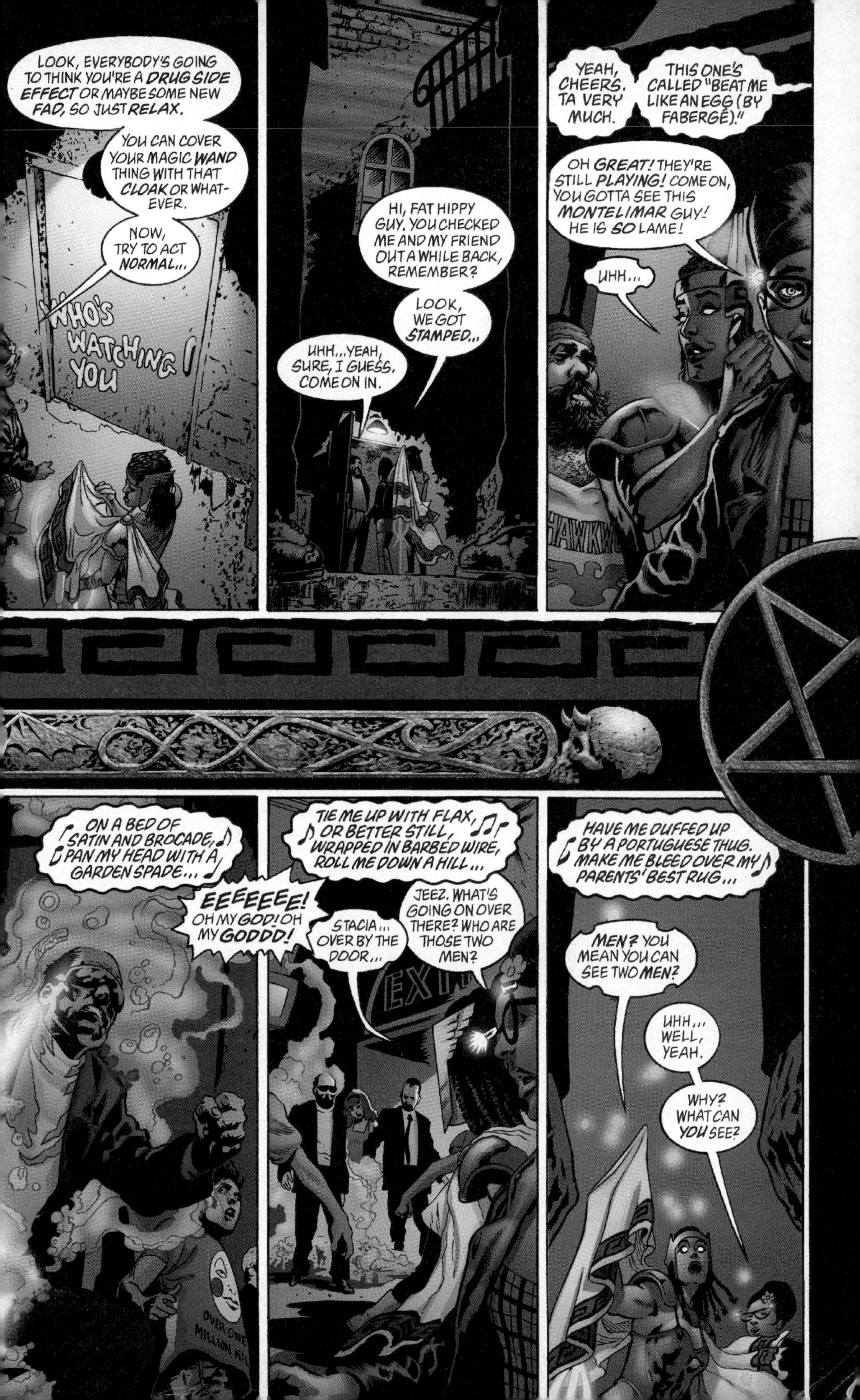
LOOK, EVERYBODY'S GOING TO THINK YOU'RE A DRUG SIDE EFFECT OR MAYBE SOME NEW FAD, SO JUST RELAX.
YOU CAN COVER YOUR MAGIC WAND THING WITH THAT CLOAK OR WHATEVER.
NOW, TRY TO ACT NORMAL...
WHO'S WATCHING YOU
HI, FAT HIPPY GUY. YOU CHECKED ME AND MY FRIEND OUT A WHILE BACK, REMEMBER?
LOOK, WE GOT STAMPED...
UHH...YEAH, SURE, I GUESS. COME ON IN.
YEAH, CHEERS. TA VERY MUCH.
THIS ONE'S CALLED "BEAT ME LIKE AN EGG (BY FABERGÉ)."
OH GREAT! THEY'RE STILL PLAYING! COME ON, YOU GOTTA SEE THIS MONTELIMAR GUY! HE IS SO LAME!
UHH...
HAWKW
ON A BED OF SATIN AND BROCADE, PAN MY HEAD WITH A GARDEN SPADE...
EEEEEEE! OH MY GOD! OH MY GODDD!
TIE ME UP WITH FLAX, OR BETTER STILL, WRAPPED IN BARBED WIRE, ROLL ME DOWN A HILL...
STACIA... OVER BY THE DOOR...
JEEZ. WHAT'S GOING ON OVER THERE? WHO ARE THOSE TWO MEN?
HAVE ME DUFFED UP BY A PORTUGUESE THUG. MAKE ME BLEED OVER MY PARENTS' BEST RUG...
MEN? YOU MEAN YOU CAN SEE TWO MEN?
UHH... WELL, YEAH.
WHY? WHAT CAN YOU SEE?

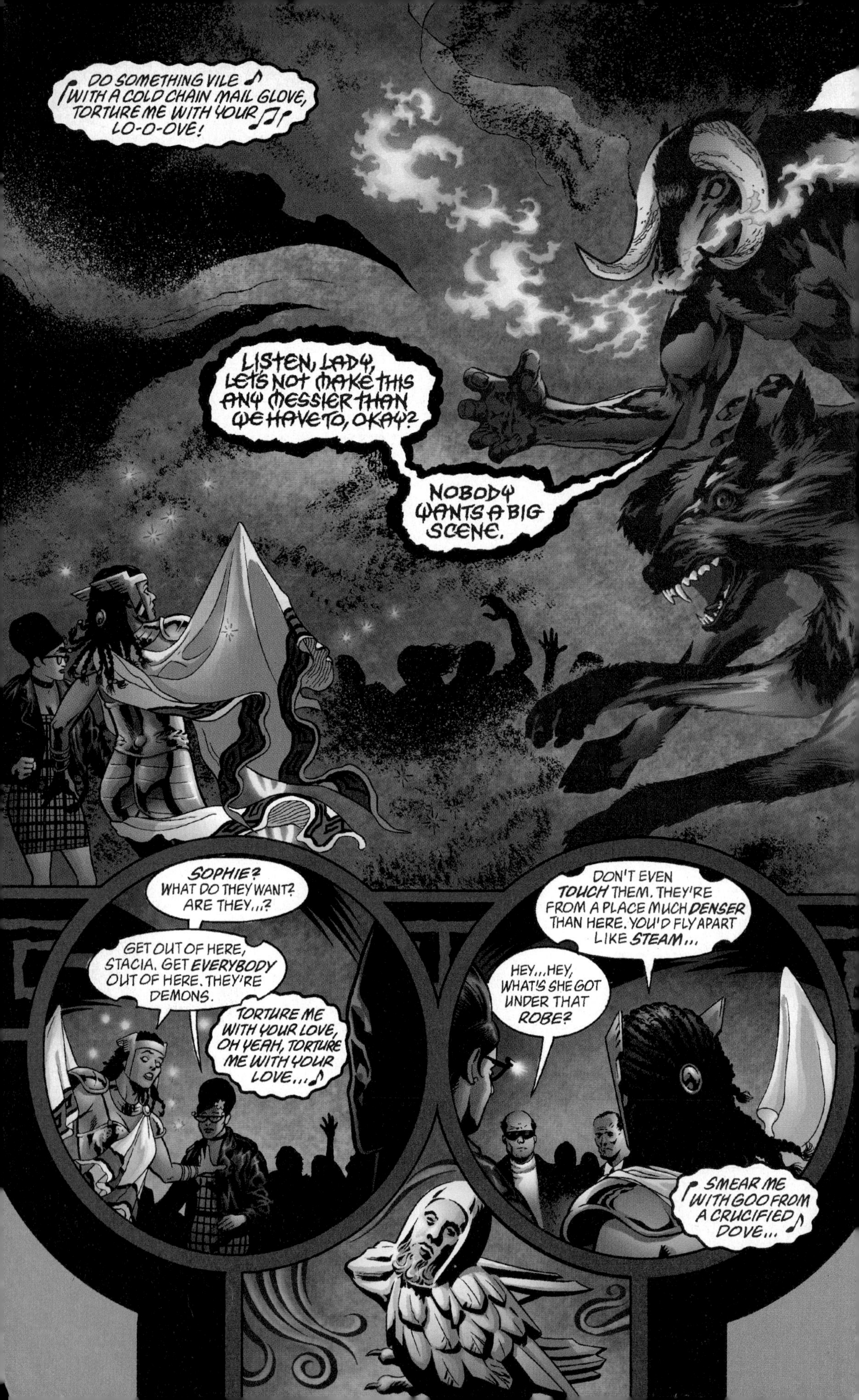
DO SOMETHING VILE WITH A COLD CHAIN MAIL GLOVE, TORTURE ME WITH YOUR LO-O-OVE!
LISTEN, LADY, LET'S NOT MAKE THIS ANY MESSIER THAN WE HAVE TO, OKAY?
NOBODY WANTS A BIG SCENE.
SOPHIE? WHAT DO THEY WANT? ARE THEY...?
GET OUT OF HERE, STACIA. GET EVERYBODY OUT OF HERE. THEY'RE DEMONS.
TORTURE ME WITH YOUR LOVE, OH YEAH, TORTURE ME WITH YOUR LOVE...
DON'T EVEN TOUCH THEM. THEY'RE FROM A PLACE MUCH DENSER THAN HERE. YOU'D FLY APART LIKE STEAM...
HEY...HEY, WHAT'S SHE GOT UNDER THAT ROBE?
SMEAR ME WITH GOO FROM A CRUCIFIED DOVE...

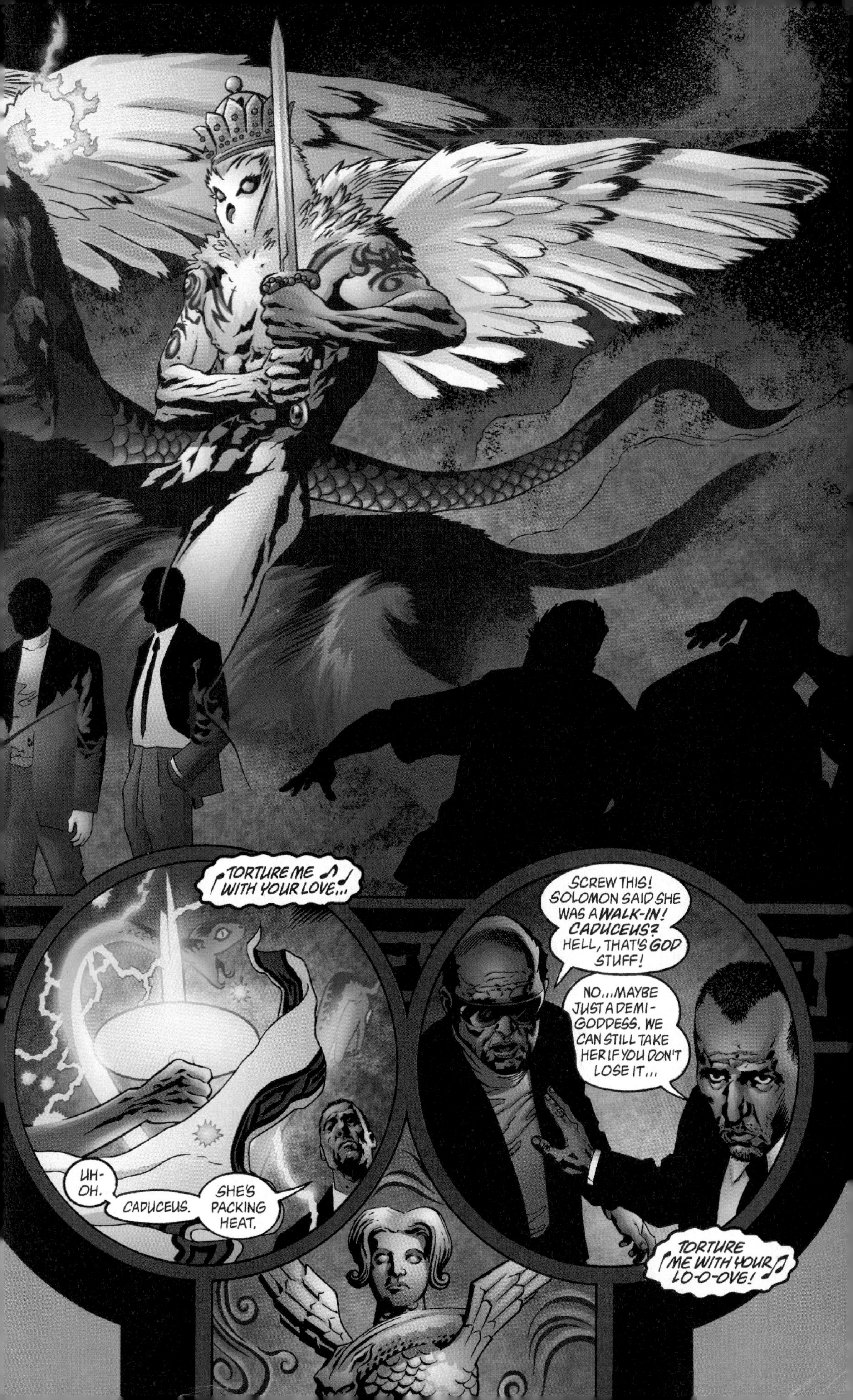
TORTURE ME WITH YOUR LOVE...
UH-OH.
CADUCEUS.
SHE'S PACKING HEAT.
SCREW THIS! SOLOMON SAID SHE WAS A WALK-IN! CADUCEUS? HELL, THAT'S GOD STUFF!
NO...MAYBE JUST A DEMI-GODDESS. WE CAN STILL TAKE HER IF YOU DON'T LOSE IT...
TORTURE ME WITH YOUR LO-O-OVE!

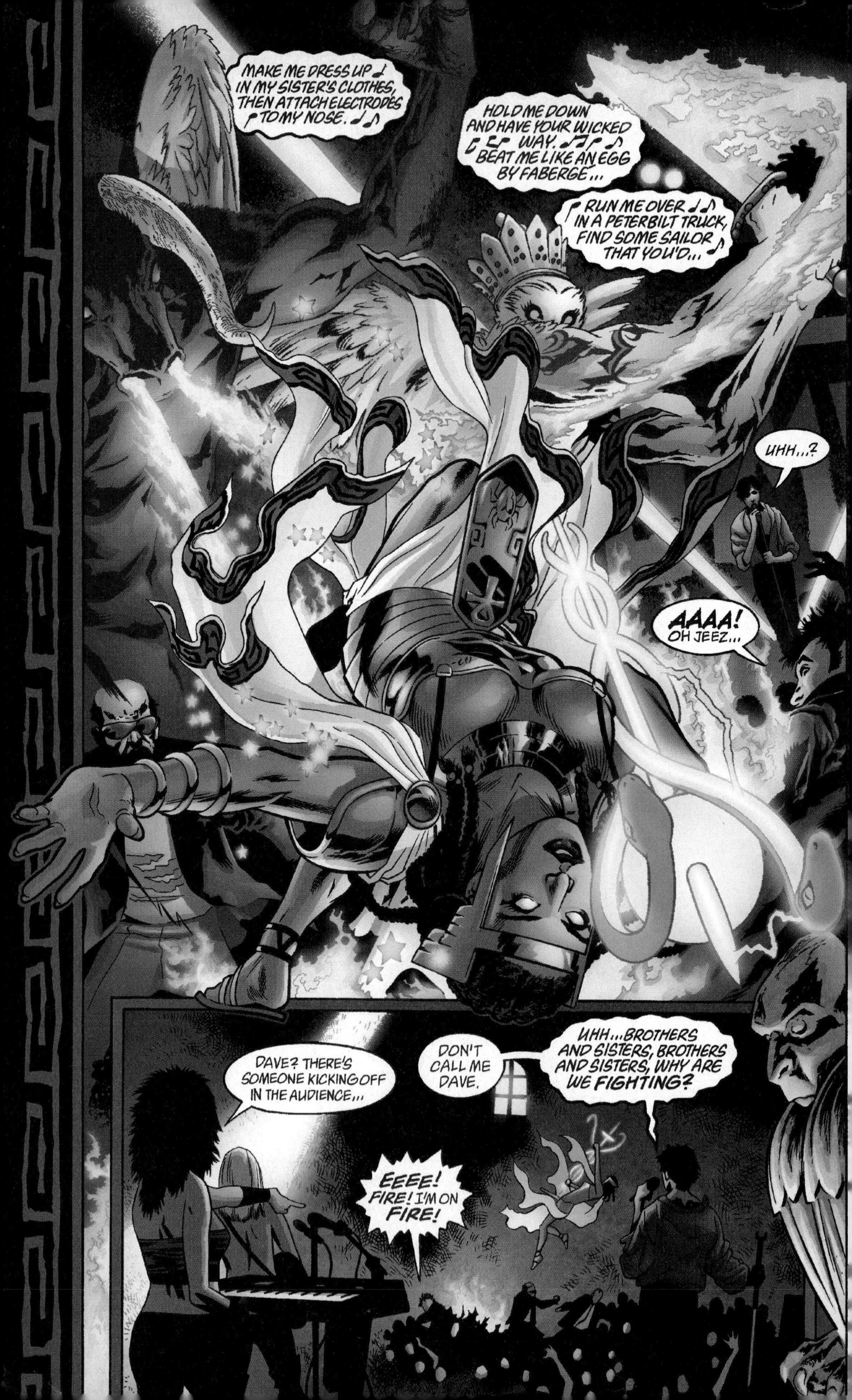
MAKE ME DRESS UP IN MY SISTER'S CLOTHES, THEN ATTACH ELECTRODES TO MY NOSE.
HOLD ME DOWN AND HAVE YOUR WICKED WAY. BEAT ME LIKE AN EGG BY FABERGE...
RUN ME OVER IN A PETERBILT TRUCK, FIND SOME SAILOR THAT YOU'D...
UHH...?
AAAA! OH JEEZ...
DAVE? THERE'S SOMEONE KICKING OFF IN THE AUDIENCE...
DON'T CALL ME DAVE.
UHH...BROTHERS AND SISTERS, BROTHERS AND SISTERS, WHY ARE WE FIGHTING?
EEEE! FIRE! I'M ON FIRE!

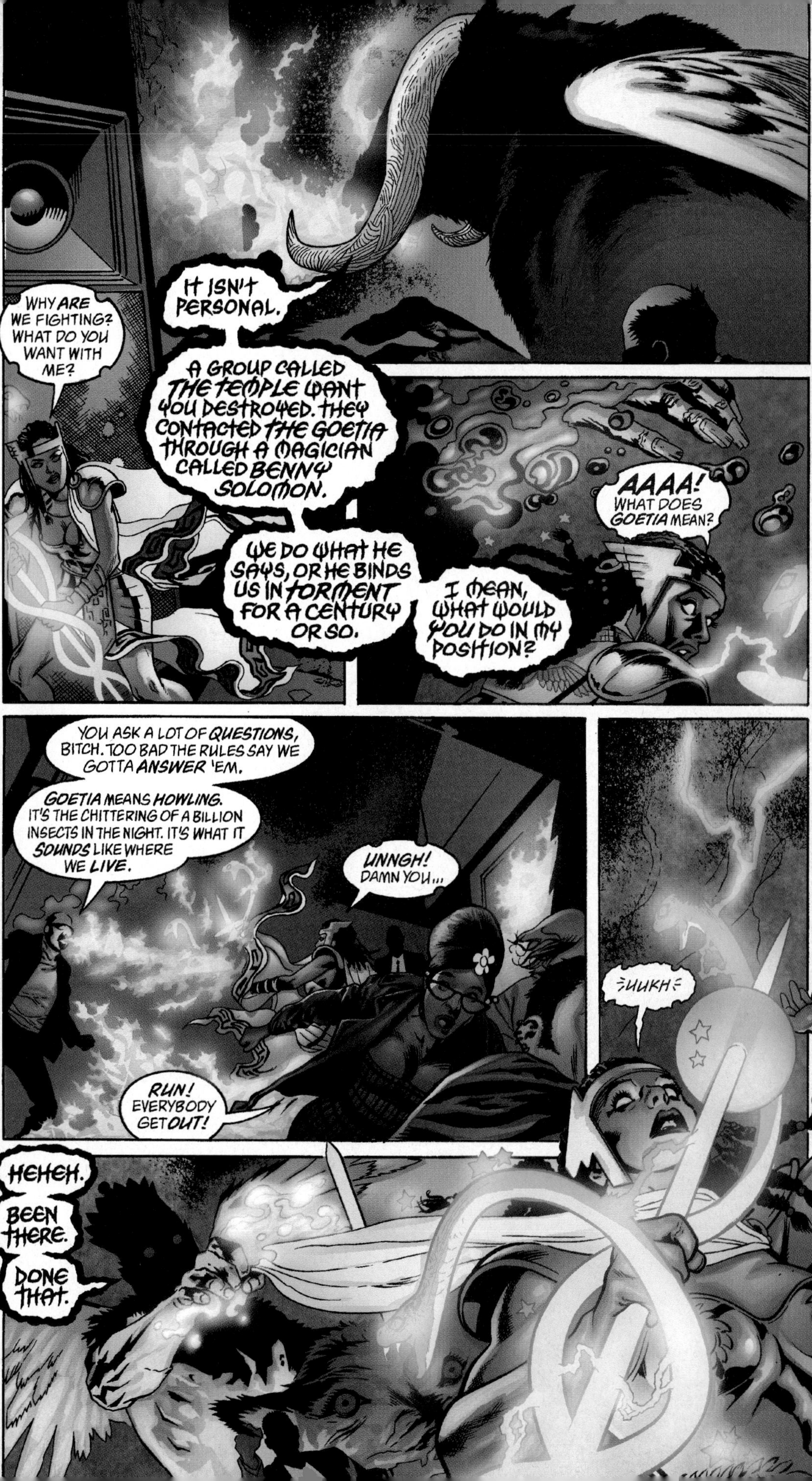
IT ISN'T PERSONAL.
WHY ARE WE FIGHTING? WHAT DO YOU WANT WITH ME?
A GROUP CALLED THE TEMPLE WANT YOU DESTROYED. THEY CONTACTED THE GOETIA THROUGH A MAGICIAN CALLED BENNY SOLOMON.
AAAA! WHAT DOES GOETIA MEAN?
WE DO WHAT HE SAYS, OR HE BINDS US IN TORMENT FOR A CENTURY OR SO.
I MEAN, WHAT WOULD YOU DO IN MY POSITION?
YOU ASK A LOT OF QUESTIONS, BITCH. TOO BAD THE RULES SAY WE GOTTA ANSWER 'EM.
GOETIA MEANS HOWLING. IT'S THE CHITTERING OF A BILLION INSECTS IN THE NIGHT. IT'S WHAT IT SOUNDS LIKE WHERE WE LIVE.
UNNGH! DAMN YOU...
RUN! EVERYBODY GET OUT!
UUKH
HEHEH.
BEEN THERE.
DONE THAT.

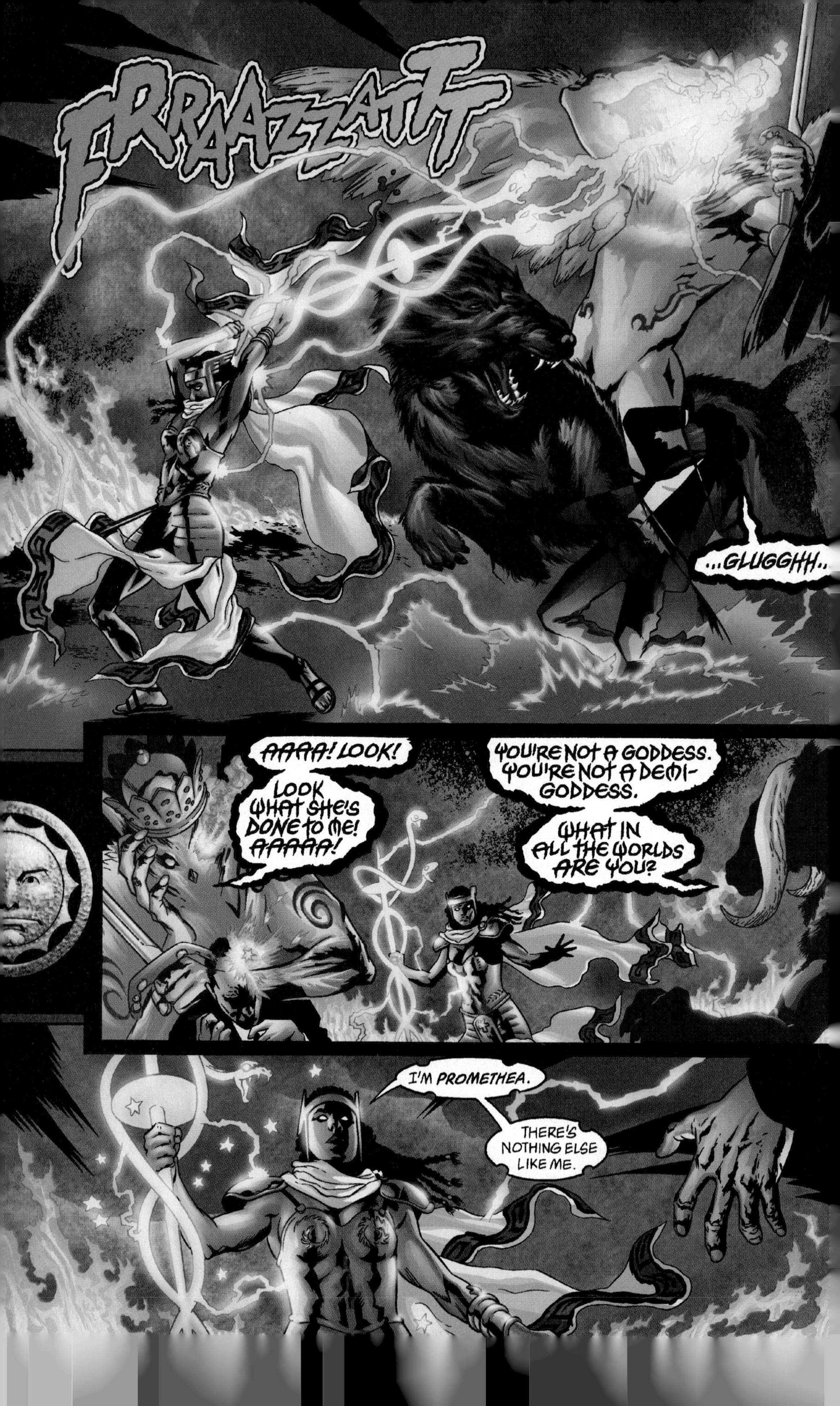
FRRAZZATT
...GLUGGHH...
AAAA! LOOK!
LOOK WHAT SHE'S DONE TO ME! AAAAA!
YOU'RE NOT A GODDESS. YOU'RE NOT A DEMI-GODDESS.
WHAT IN ALL THE WORLDS ARE YOU?
I'M PROMETHEA.
THERE'S NOTHING ELSE LIKE ME.

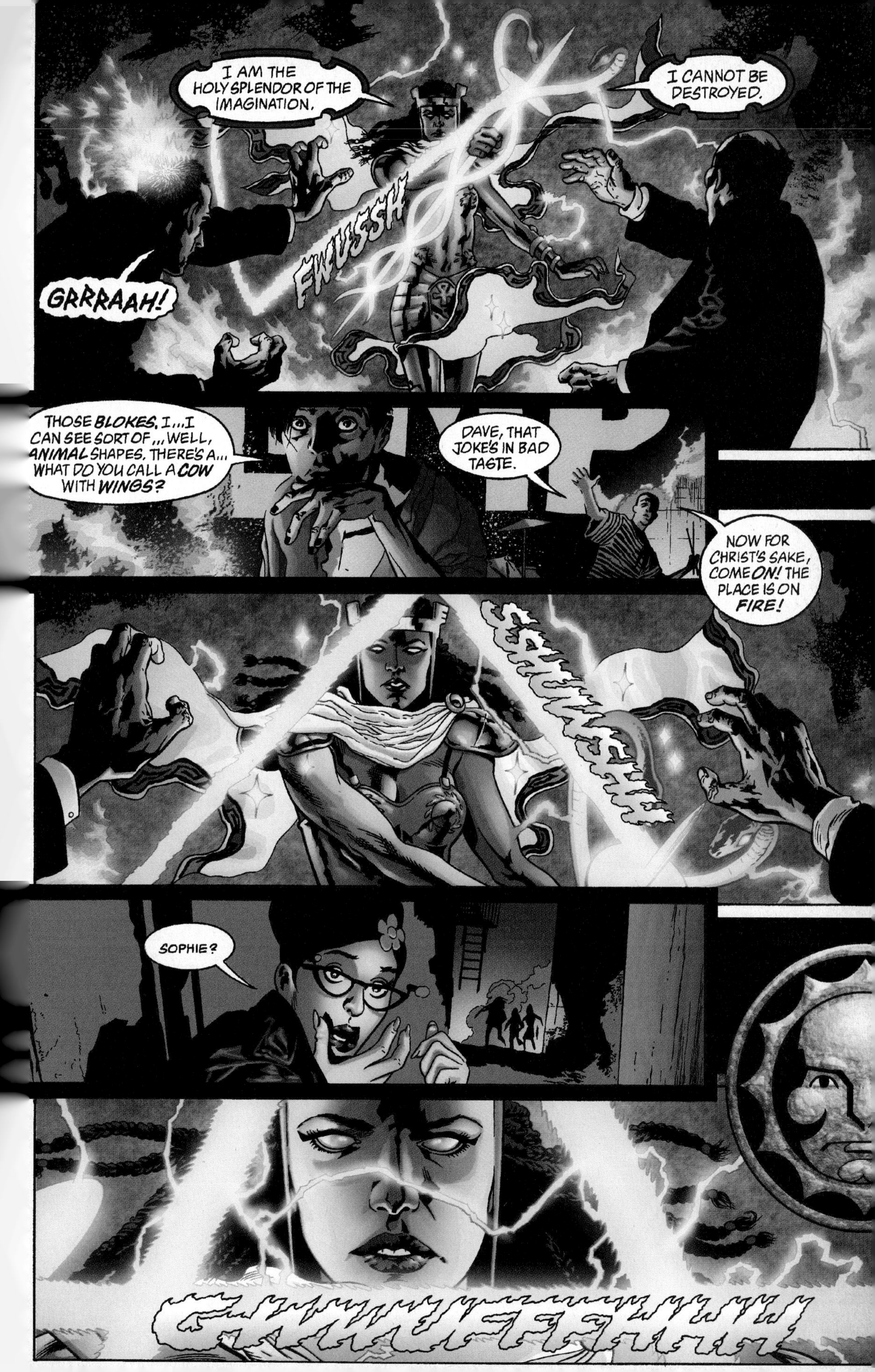

I AM THE HOLY SPLENDOR OF THE IMAGINATION.
I CANNOT BE DESTROYED.
FWUSSH
GRRRAAH!
THOSE BLOKES, I...I CAN SEE SORT OF... WELL, ANIMAL SHAPES. THERE'S A... WHAT DO YOU CALL A COW WITH WINGS?
DAVE, THAT JOKE'S IN BAD TASTE.
NOW FOR CHRIST'S SAKE, COME ON! THE PLACE IS ON FIRE!
SPLUNSH
SOPHIE?

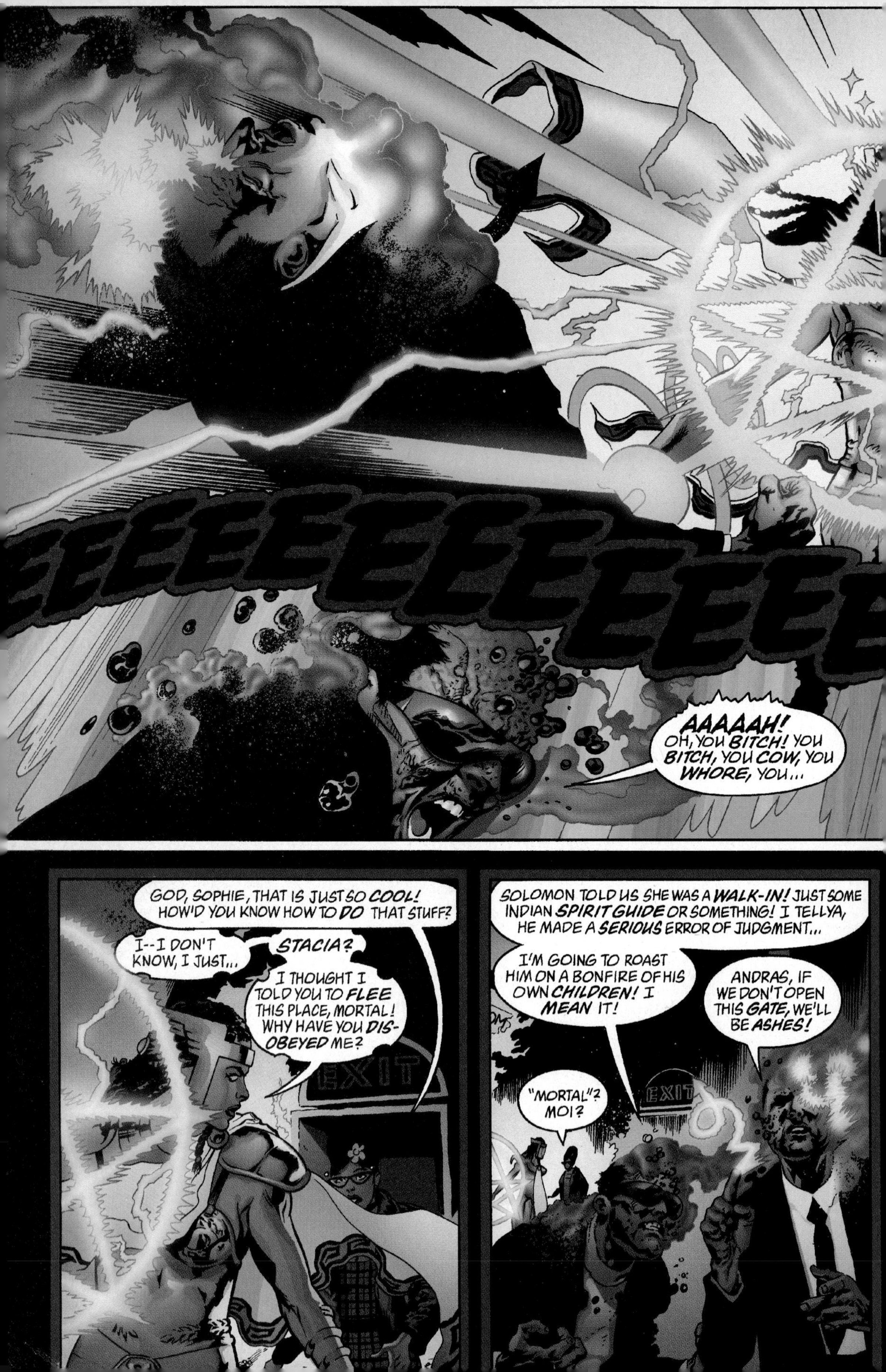
EEEEEEEEEEEEEEEEE
AAAAAH! OH, YOU BITCH! YOU BITCH, YOU COW, YOU WHORE, YOU...
GOD, SOPHIE, THAT IS JUST SO COOL! HOW'D YOU KNOW HOW TO DO THAT STUFF?
I--I DON'T KNOW, I JUST...
STACIA?
I THOUGHT I TOLD YOU TO FLEE THIS PLACE, MORTAL! WHY HAVE YOU DISOBEYED ME?
EXIT
SOLOMON TOLD US SHE WAS A WALK-IN! JUST SOME INDIAN SPIRIT GUIDE OR SOMETHING! I TELLYA, HE MADE A SERIOUS ERROR OF JUDGMENT...
I'M GOING TO ROAST HIM ON A BONFIRE OF HIS OWN CHILDREN! I MEAN IT!
ANDRAS, IF WE DON'T OPEN THIS GATE, WE'LL BE ASHES!
"MORTAL"? MOI?
EXIT

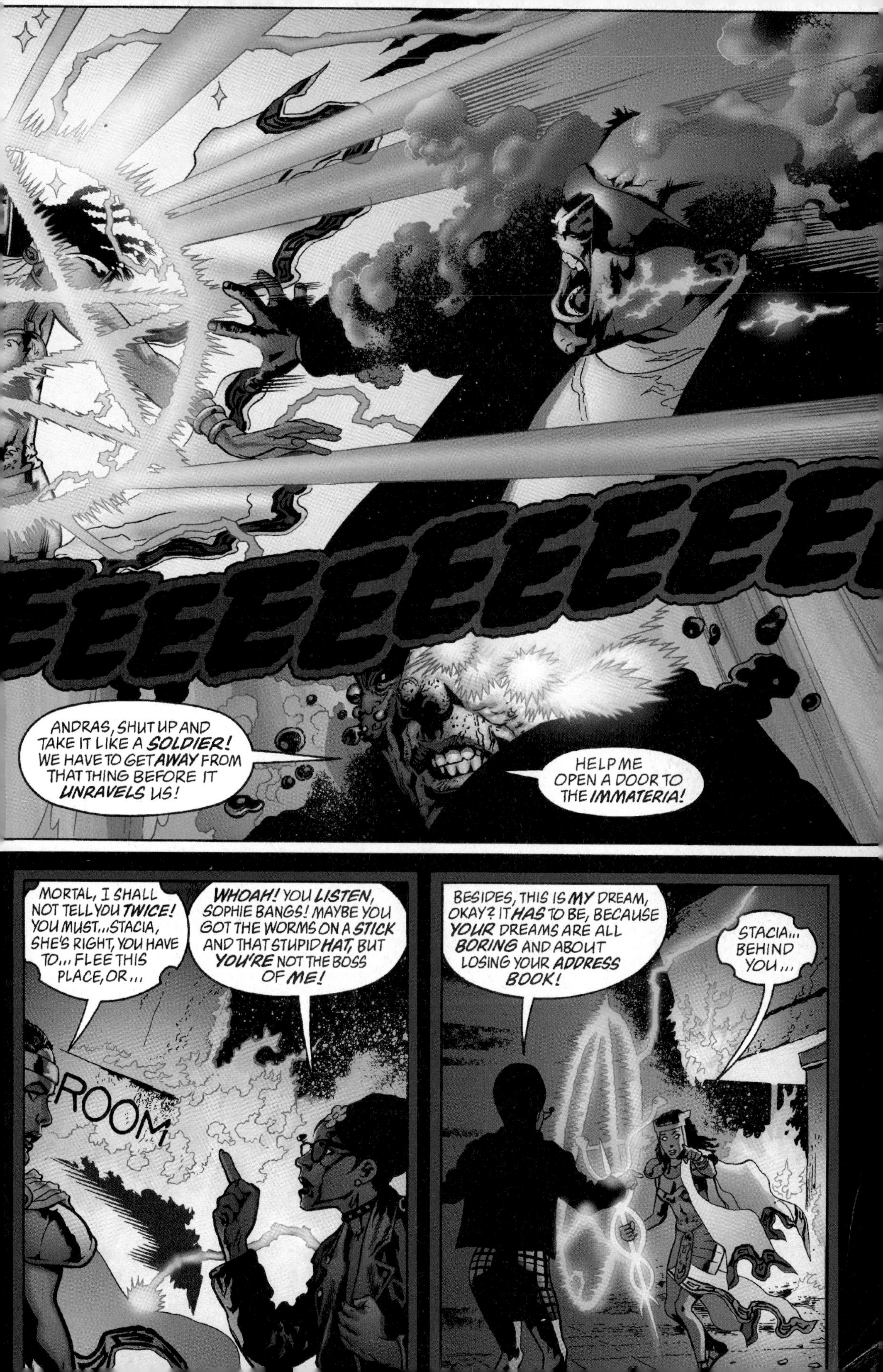
EEEEEEEEEEEEEEE
ANDRAS, SHUT UP AND TAKE IT LIKE A SOLDIER! WE HAVE TO GET AWAY FROM THAT THING BEFORE IT UNRAVELS US!
HELP ME OPEN A DOOR TO THE IMMATERIA!
MORTAL, I SHALL NOT TELL YOU TWICE! YOU MUST...STACIA, SHE'S RIGHT, YOU HAVE TO... FLEE THIS PLACE, OR...
WHOAH! YOU LISTEN, SOPHIE BANGS! MAYBE YOU GOT THE WORMS ON A STICK AND THAT STUPID HAT, BUT YOU'RE NOT THE BOSS OF ME!
ROOM
BESIDES, THIS IS MY DREAM, OKAY? IT HAS TO BE, BECAUSE YOUR DREAMS ARE ALL BORING AND ABOUT LOSING YOUR ADDRESS BOOK!
STACIA... BEHIND YOU...

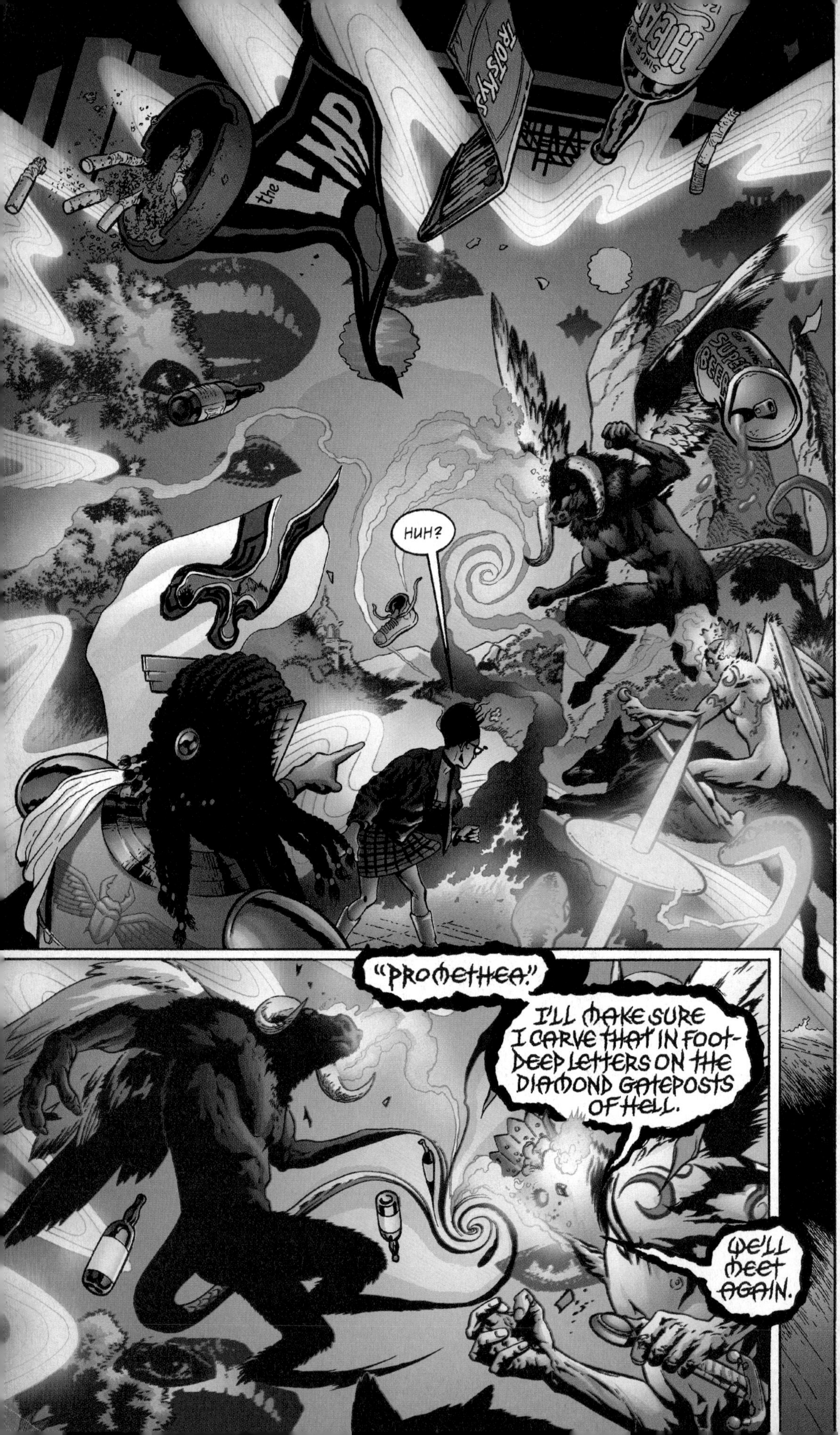

HUH?
"PROMETHEA."
I'LL MAKE SURE I CARVE THAT IN FOOT-DEEP LETTERS ON THE DIAMOND GATEPOSTS OF HELL.
WE'LL MEET AGAIN.

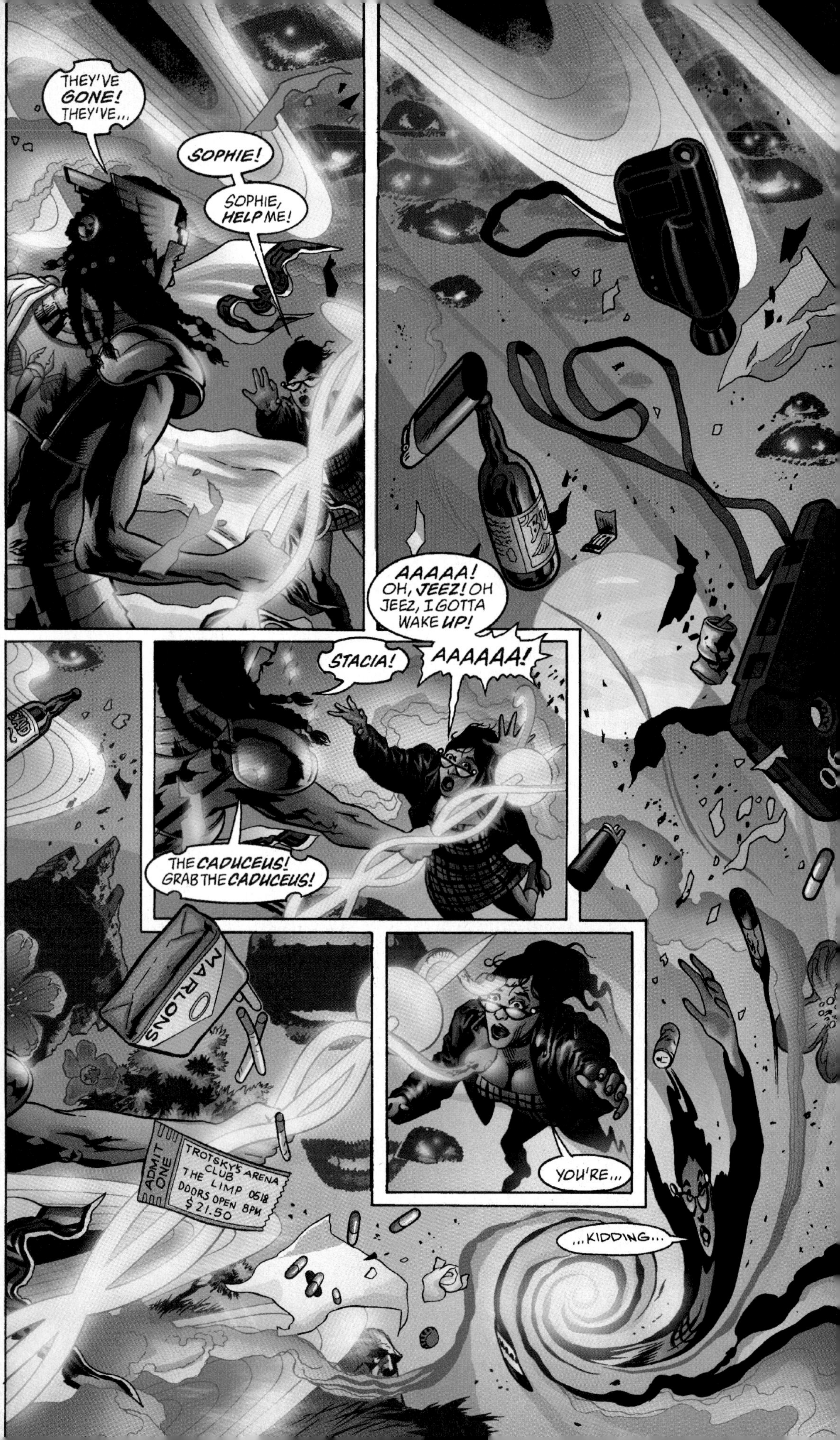

THEY'VE GONE! THEY'VE...
SOPHIE!
SOPHIE, HELP ME!
AAAAA! OH, JEEZ! OH JEEZ, I GOTTA WAKE UP!
STACIA!
AAAAAA!
THE CADUCEUS! GRAB THE CADUCEUS!
MARLONS
ADMIT ONE
TROTSKY'S ARENA CLUB
THE LIMP 0518
DOORS OPEN 8PM
$21.50
YOU'RE...
...KIDDING...

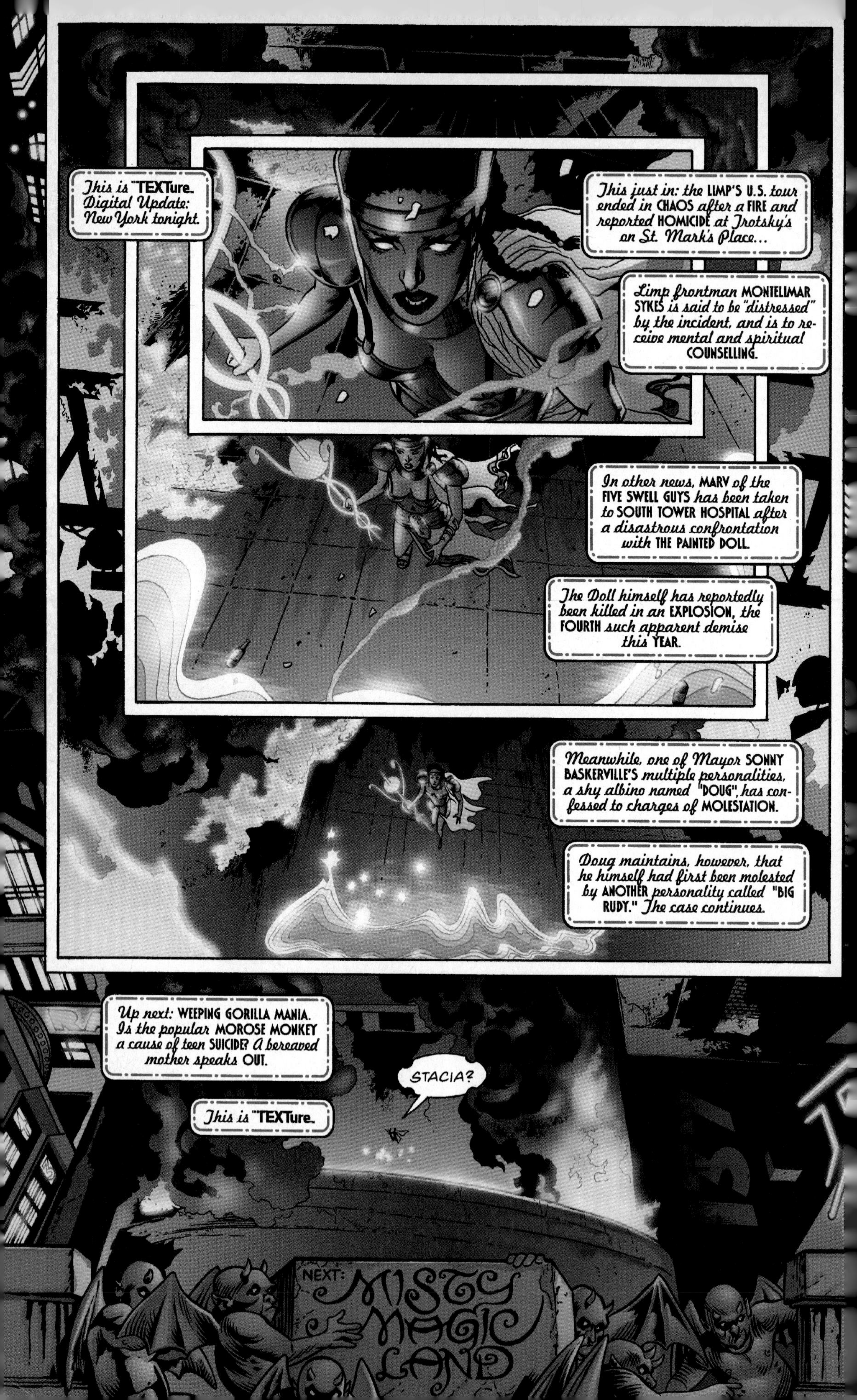
This is "TEXTure. Digital Update: New York tonight.
This just in: the LIMP'S U.S. tour ended in CHAOS after a FIRE and reported HOMICIDE at Trotsky's on St. Mark's Place...
Limp frontman MONTELIMAR SYKES is said to be "distressed" by the incident, and is to receive mental and spiritual COUNSELLING.
In other news, MARV of the FIVE SWELL GUYS has been taken to SOUTH TOWER HOSPITAL after a disastrous confrontation with THE PAINTED DOLL.
The Doll himself has reportedly been killed in an EXPLOSION, the FOURTH such apparent demise this YEAR.
Meanwhile, one of Mayor SONNY BASKERVILLE'S multiple personalities, a shy albino named "DOUG", has confessed to charges of MOLESTATION.
Doug maintains, however, that he himself had first been molested by ANOTHER personality called "BIG RUDY." The case continues.
Up next: WEEPING GORILLA MANIA. Is the popular MOROSE MONKEY a cause of teen SUICIDE? A bereaved mother speaks OUT.
STACIA?
This is "TEXTure.
NEXT: MISTY MAGIC LAND

CHAPTER THREE

A mentor lies wounded,
A friend lost, endangered,
A new world is unveiled.

Cover art:
J.H. Williams III
& Mick Gray

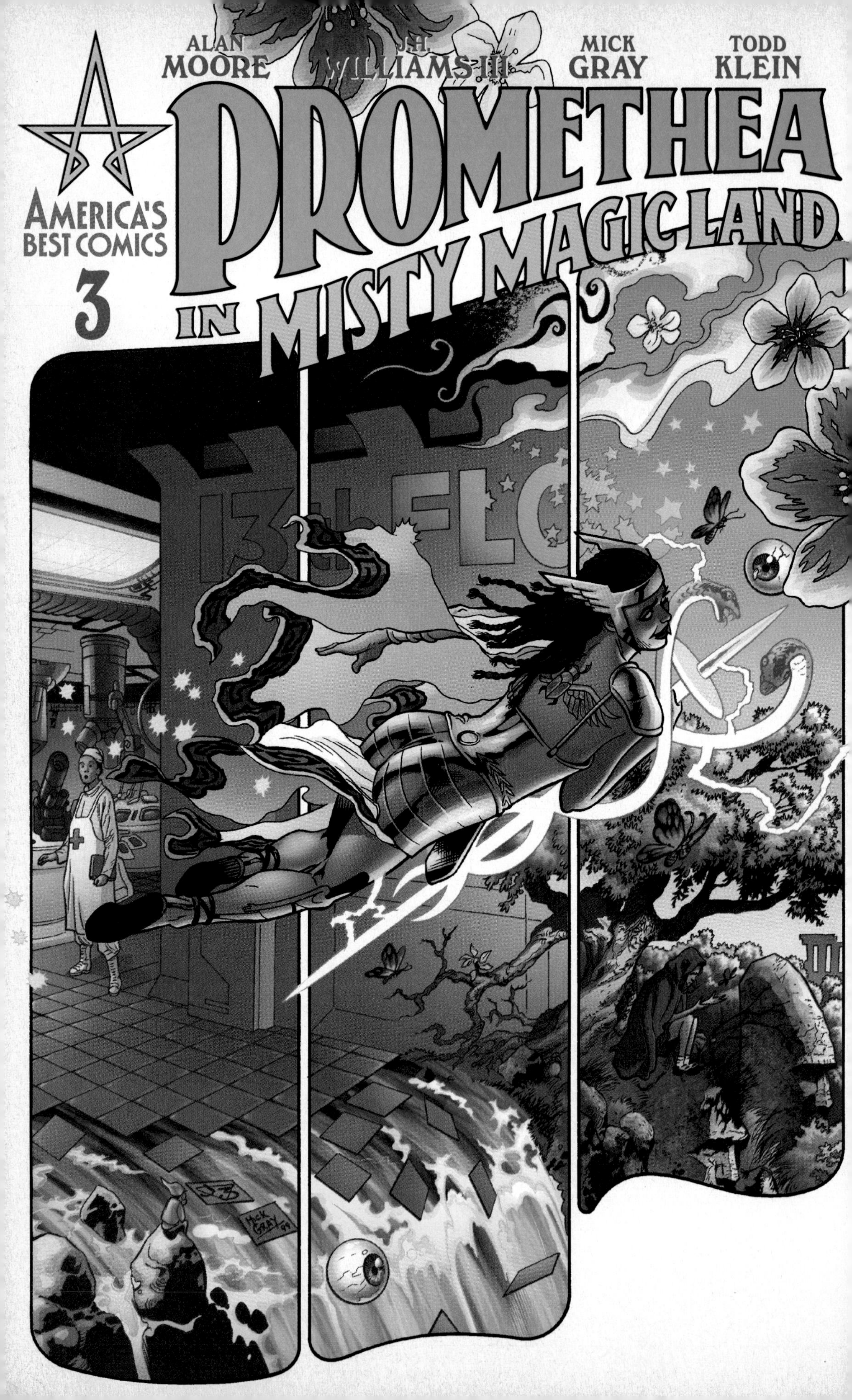
ALAN MOORE
J.H. WILLIAMS III
MICK GRAY
TODD KLEIN
AMERICA'S BEST COMICS
3
PROMETHEA
IN MISTY MAGIC LAND

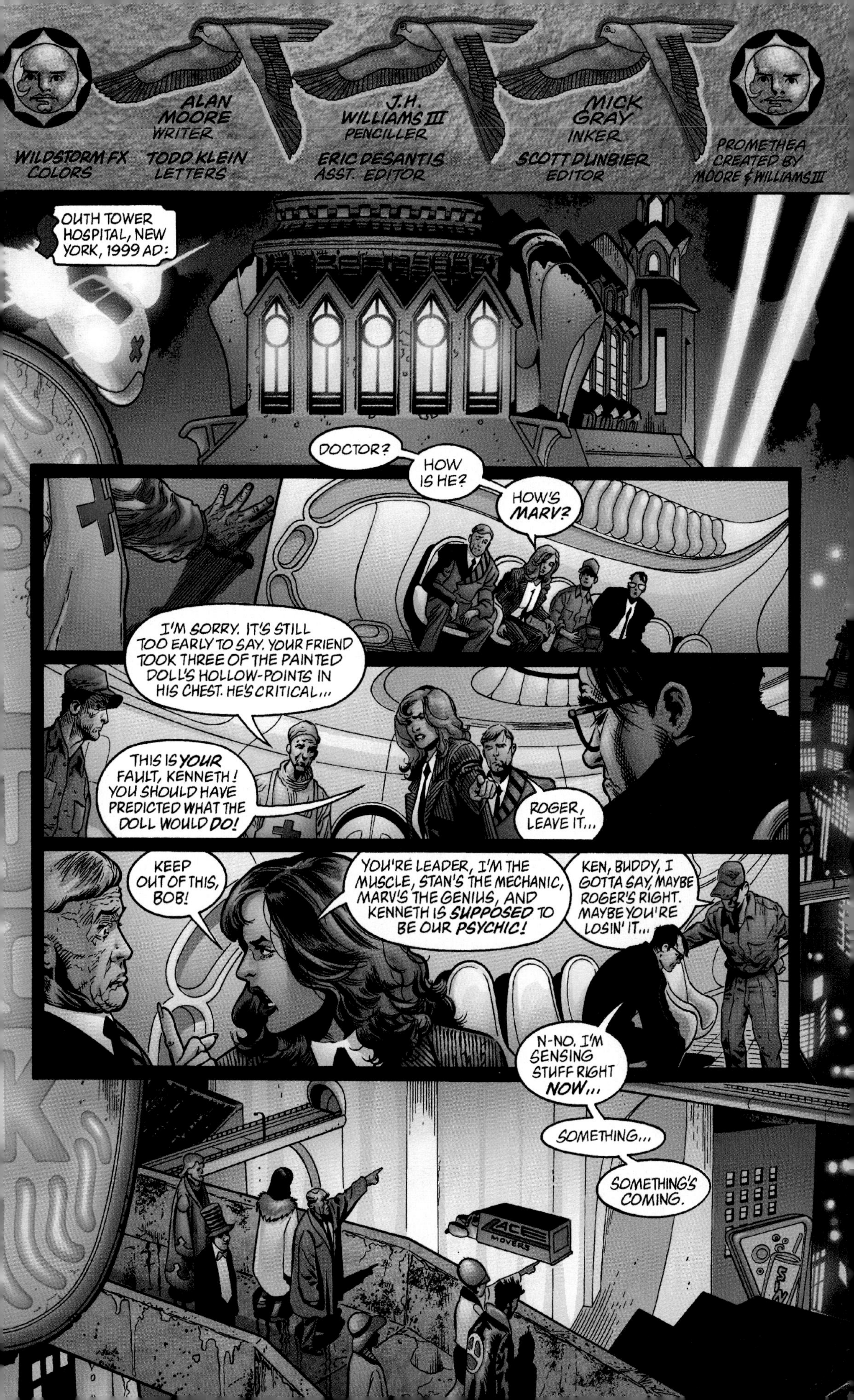

ALAN MOORE WRITER
J.H. WILLIAMS III PENCILLER
MICK GRAY INKER
WILDSTORM FX COLORS
TODD KLEIN LETTERS
ERIC DESANTIS ASST. EDITOR
SCOTT DUNBIER EDITOR
PROMETHEA CREATED BY MOORE & WILLIAMS III
SOUTH TOWER HOSPITAL, NEW YORK, 1999 AD:
DOCTOR?
HOW IS HE?
HOW'S MARV?
I'M SORRY. IT'S STILL TOO EARLY TO SAY. YOUR FRIEND TOOK THREE OF THE PAINTED DOLL'S HOLLOW-POINTS IN HIS CHEST. HE'S CRITICAL...
THIS IS YOUR FAULT, KENNETH! YOU SHOULD HAVE PREDICTED WHAT THE DOLL WOULD DO!
ROGER, LEAVE IT...
KEEP OUT OF THIS, BOB!
YOU'RE LEADER, I'M THE MUSCLE, STAN'S THE MECHANIC, MARV'S THE GENIUS, AND KENNETH IS SUPPOSED TO BE OUR PSYCHIC!
KEN, BUDDY, I GOTTA SAY, MAYBE ROGER'S RIGHT. MAYBE YOU'RE LOSIN' IT...
N-NO. I'M SENSING STUFF RIGHT NOW...
SOMETHING...
SOMETHING'S COMING.
ACE MOVERS

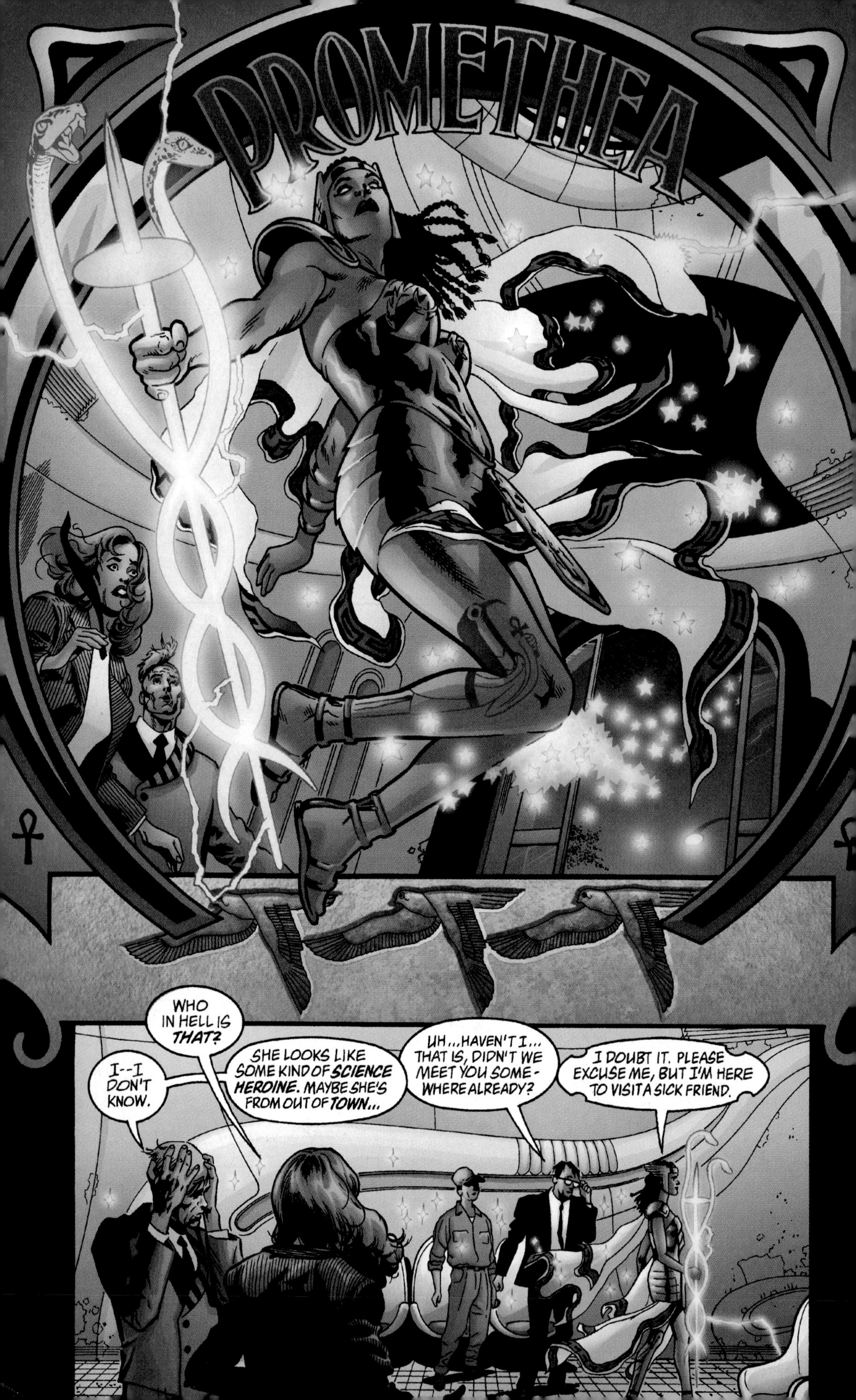
PROMETHEA
WHO IN HELL IS THAT?
I--I DON'T KNOW.
SHE LOOKS LIKE SOME KIND OF SCIENCE HEROINE. MAYBE SHE'S FROM OUT OF TOWN...
UH...HAVEN'T I... THAT IS, DIDN'T WE MEET YOU SOME-WHERE ALREADY?
I DOUBT IT. PLEASE EXCUSE ME, BUT I'M HERE TO VISIT A SICK FRIEND.

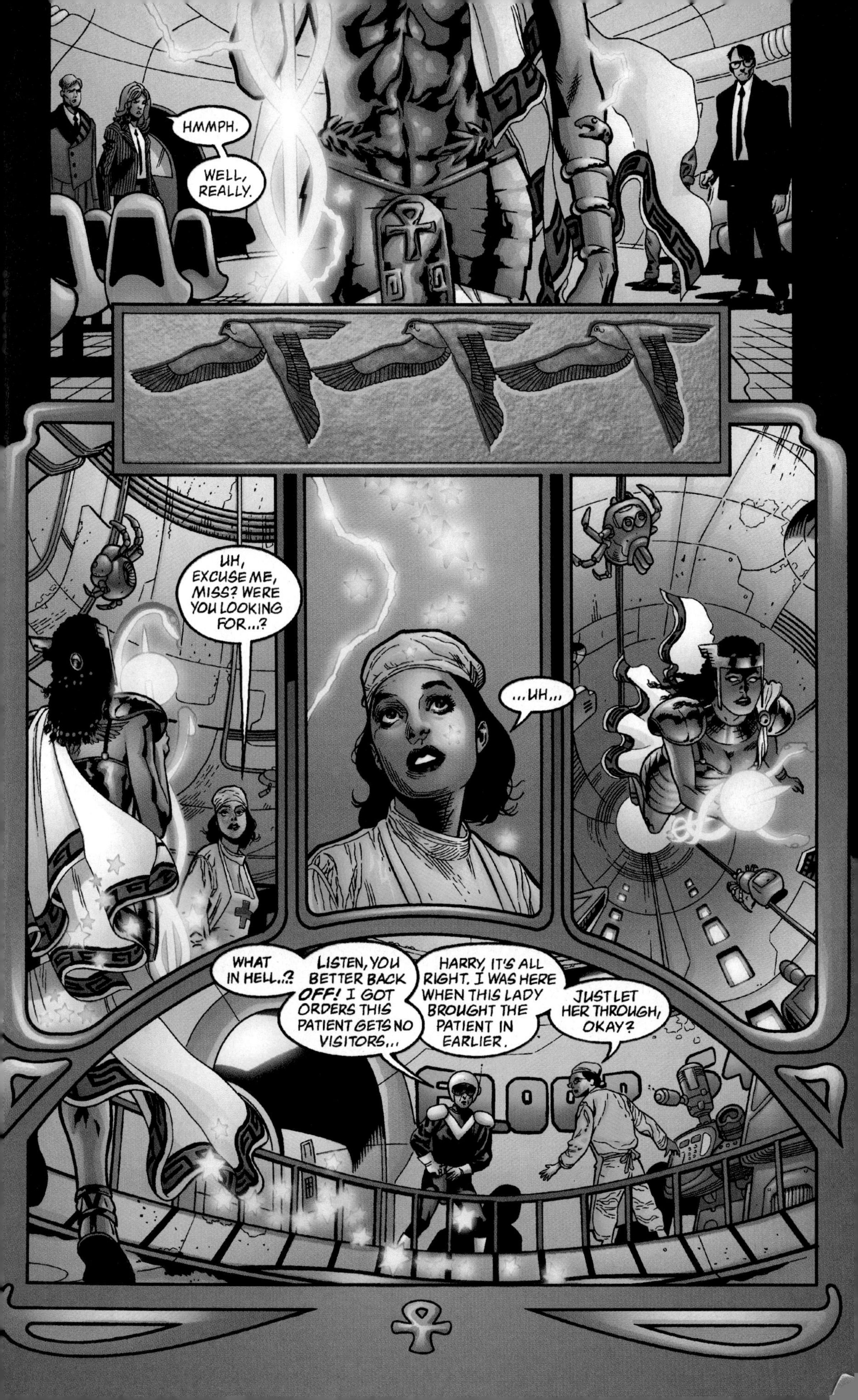
HMMPH.
WELL, REALLY.
UH, EXCUSE ME, MISS? WERE YOU LOOKING FOR...?
...UH...
WHAT IN HELL..?
LISTEN, YOU BETTER BACK OFF! I GOT ORDERS THIS PATIENT GETS NO VISITORS...
HARRY, IT'S ALL RIGHT. I WAS HERE WHEN THIS LADY BROUGHT THE PATIENT IN EARLIER.
JUST LET HER THROUGH, OKAY?

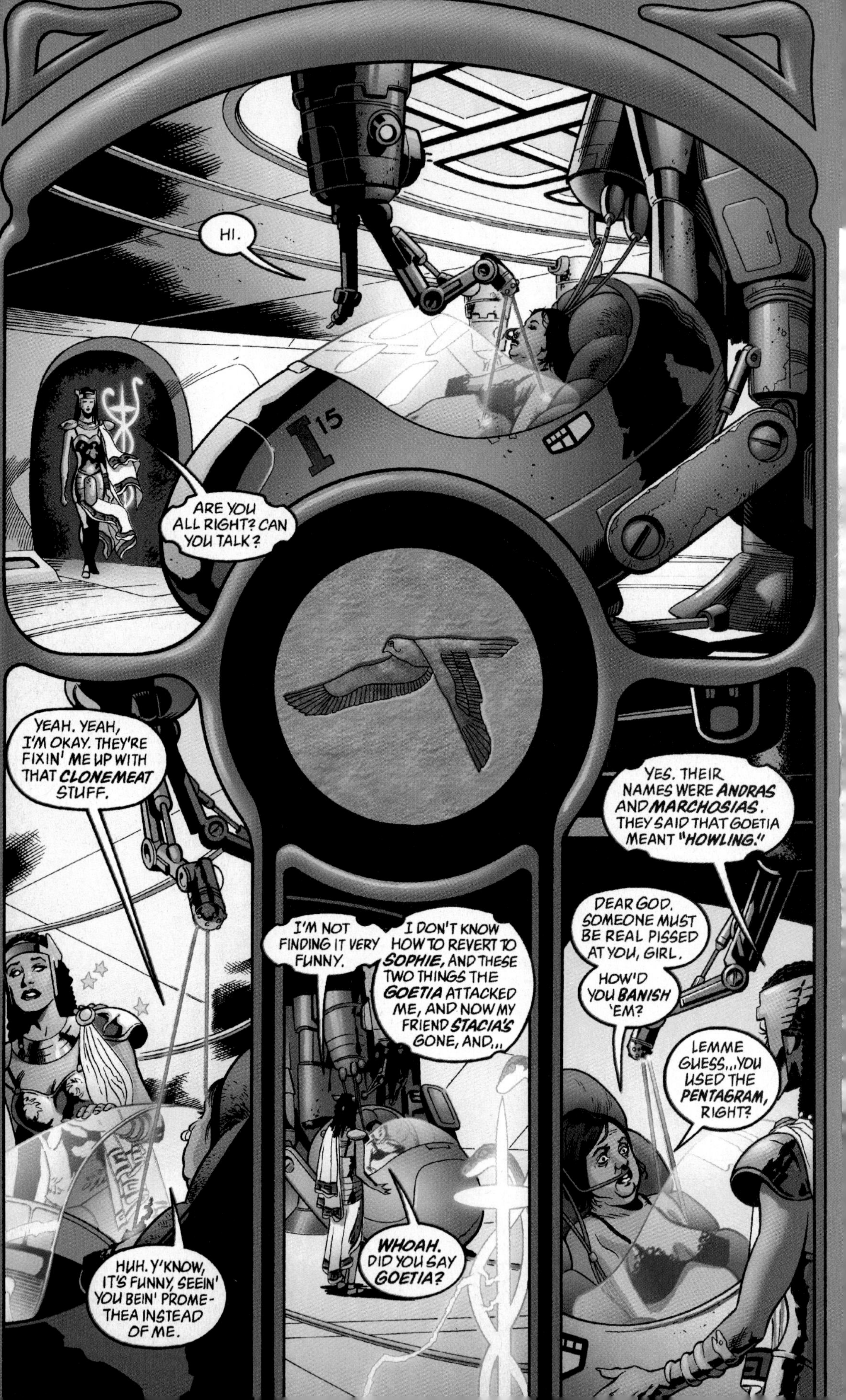
HI.
ARE YOU ALL RIGHT? CAN YOU TALK?
YEAH. YEAH, I'M OKAY. THEY'RE FIXIN' ME UP WITH THAT **CLONEMEAT** STUFF.
HUH. Y'KNOW, IT'S FUNNY, SEEIN' YOU BEIN' PROMETHEA INSTEAD OF ME.
I'M NOT FINDING IT VERY FUNNY.
I DON'T KNOW HOW TO REVERT TO **SOPHIE**, AND THESE TWO THINGS THE **GOETIA** ATTACKED ME, AND NOW MY FRIEND **STACIA'S** GONE, AND...
WHOAH. DID YOU SAY **GOETIA**?
YES. THEIR NAMES WERE **ANDRAS** AND **MARCHOSIAS**. THEY SAID THAT GOETIA MEANT "**HOWLING.**"
DEAR GOD. SOMEONE MUST BE REAL PISSED AT YOU, GIRL.
HOW'D YOU **BANISH** 'EM?
LEMME GUESS... YOU USED THE **PENTAGRAM**, RIGHT?

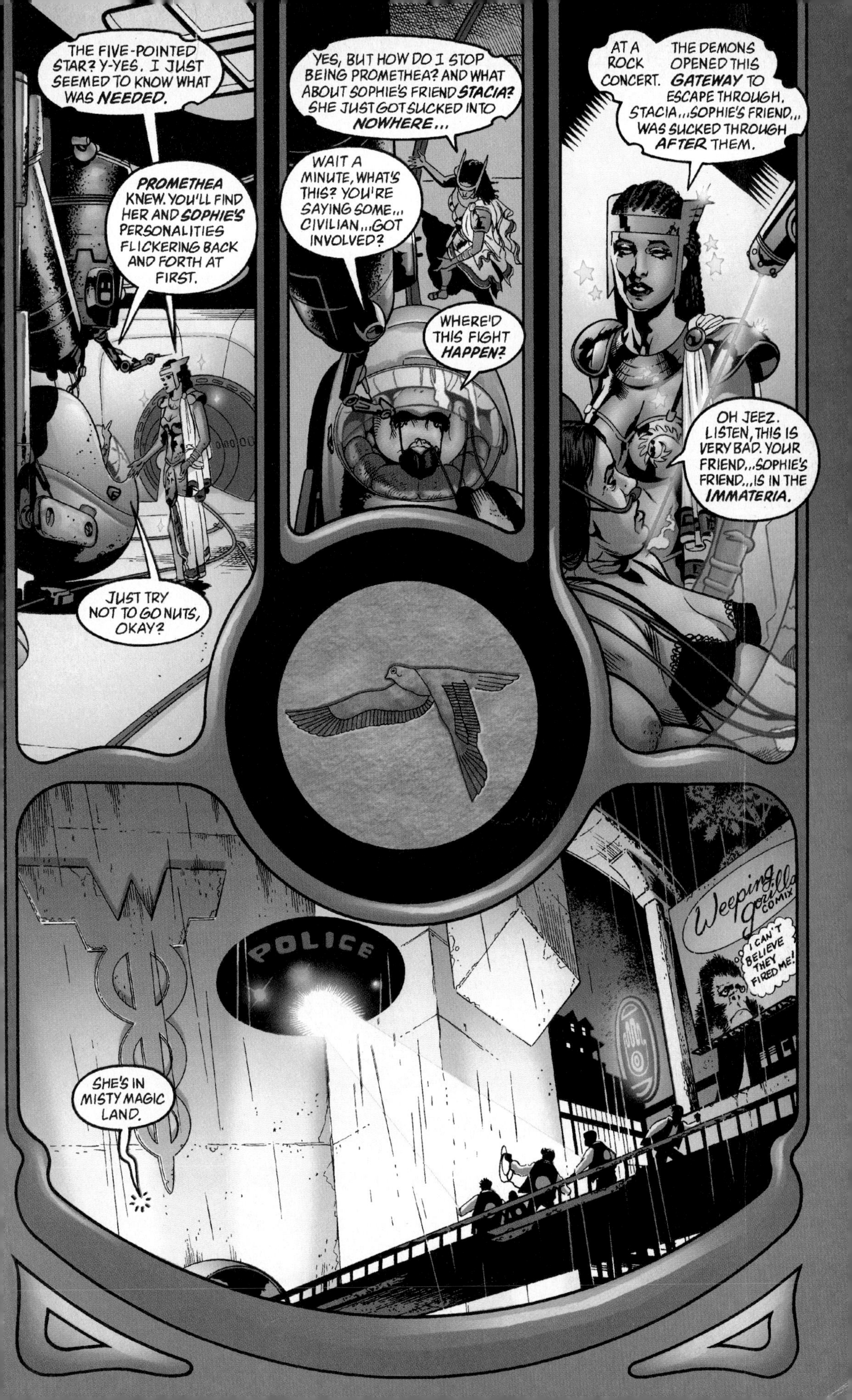

THE FIVE-POINTED STAR? Y-YES. I JUST SEEMED TO KNOW WHAT WAS NEEDED.
PROMETHEA KNEW. YOU'LL FIND HER AND SOPHIE'S PERSONALITIES FLICKERING BACK AND FORTH AT FIRST.
JUST TRY NOT TO GO NUTS, OKAY?
YES, BUT HOW DO I STOP BEING PROMETHEA? AND WHAT ABOUT SOPHIE'S FRIEND STACIA? SHE JUST GOT SUCKED INTO NOWHERE...
WAIT A MINUTE, WHAT'S THIS? YOU'RE SAYING SOME... CIVILIAN...GOT INVOLVED?
WHERE'D THIS FIGHT HAPPEN?
AT A ROCK CONCERT.
THE DEMONS OPENED THIS GATEWAY TO ESCAPE THROUGH. STACIA...SOPHIE'S FRIEND... WAS SUCKED THROUGH AFTER THEM.
OH JEEZ. LISTEN, THIS IS VERY BAD. YOUR FRIEND...SOPHIE'S FRIEND...IS IN THE IMMATERIA.
POLICE
Weeping gorilla COMIX
I CAN'T BELIEVE THEY FIRED ME!
SHE'S IN MISTY MAGIC LAND.

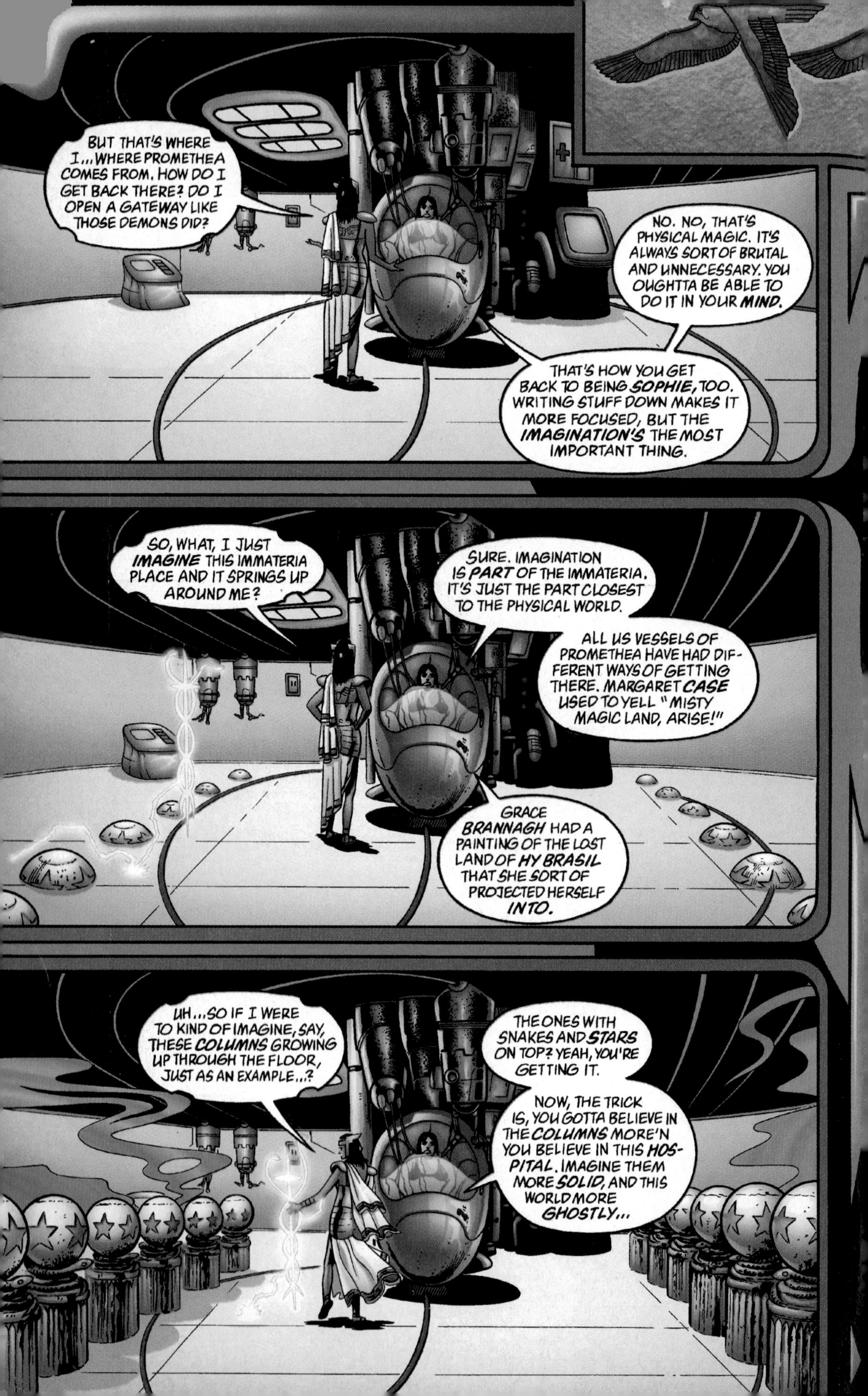
BUT THAT'S WHERE I... WHERE PROMETHEA COMES FROM. HOW DO I GET BACK THERE? DO I OPEN A GATEWAY LIKE THOSE DEMONS DID?
NO. NO, THAT'S PHYSICAL MAGIC. IT'S ALWAYS SORT OF BRUTAL AND UNNECESSARY. YOU OUGHTTA BE ABLE TO DO IT IN YOUR MIND.
THAT'S HOW YOU GET BACK TO BEING SOPHIE, TOO. WRITING STUFF DOWN MAKES IT MORE FOCUSED, BUT THE IMAGINATION'S THE MOST IMPORTANT THING.
SO, WHAT, I JUST IMAGINE THIS IMMATERIA PLACE AND IT SPRINGS UP AROUND ME?
SURE. IMAGINATION IS PART OF THE IMMATERIA. IT'S JUST THE PART CLOSEST TO THE PHYSICAL WORLD.
ALL US VESSELS OF PROMETHEA HAVE HAD DIFFERENT WAYS OF GETTING THERE. MARGARET CASE USED TO YELL "MISTY MAGIC LAND, ARISE!"
GRACE BRANNAGH HAD A PAINTING OF THE LOST LAND OF HY BRASIL THAT SHE SORT OF PROJECTED HERSELF INTO.
UH... SO IF I WERE TO KIND OF IMAGINE, SAY, THESE COLUMNS GROWING UP THROUGH THE FLOOR, JUST AS AN EXAMPLE...?
THE ONES WITH SNAKES AND STARS ON TOP? YEAH, YOU'RE GETTING IT.
NOW, THE TRICK IS, YOU GOTTA BELIEVE IN THE COLUMNS MORE'N YOU BELIEVE IN THIS HOSPITAL. IMAGINE THEM MORE SOLID, AND THIS WORLD MORE GHOSTLY...

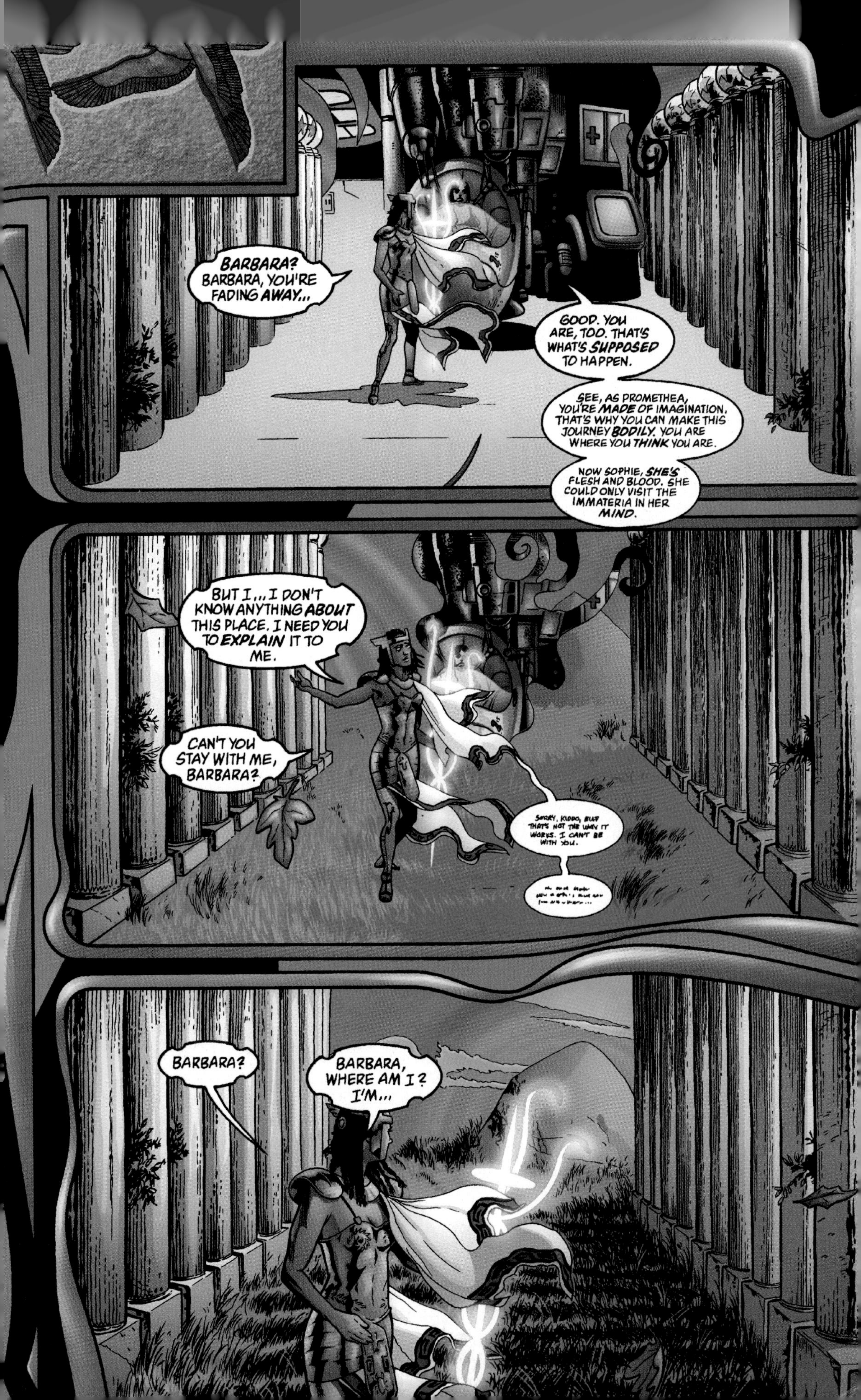
BARBARA? BARBARA, YOU'RE FADING AWAY...
GOOD. YOU ARE, TOO. THAT'S WHAT'S SUPPOSED TO HAPPEN.
SEE, AS PROMETHEA, YOU'RE MADE OF IMAGINATION. THAT'S WHY YOU CAN MAKE THIS JOURNEY BODILY. YOU ARE WHERE YOU THINK YOU ARE.
NOW SOPHIE, SHE'S FLESH AND BLOOD. SHE COULD ONLY VISIT THE IMMATERIA IN HER MIND.
BUT I...I DON'T KNOW ANYTHING ABOUT THIS PLACE. I NEED YOU TO EXPLAIN IT TO ME.
CAN'T YOU STAY WITH ME, BARBARA?
SORRY, KIDDO, BUT THAT'S NOT THE WAY IT WORKS. I CAN'T BE WITH YOU.
BARBARA?
BARBARA, WHERE AM I? I'M...

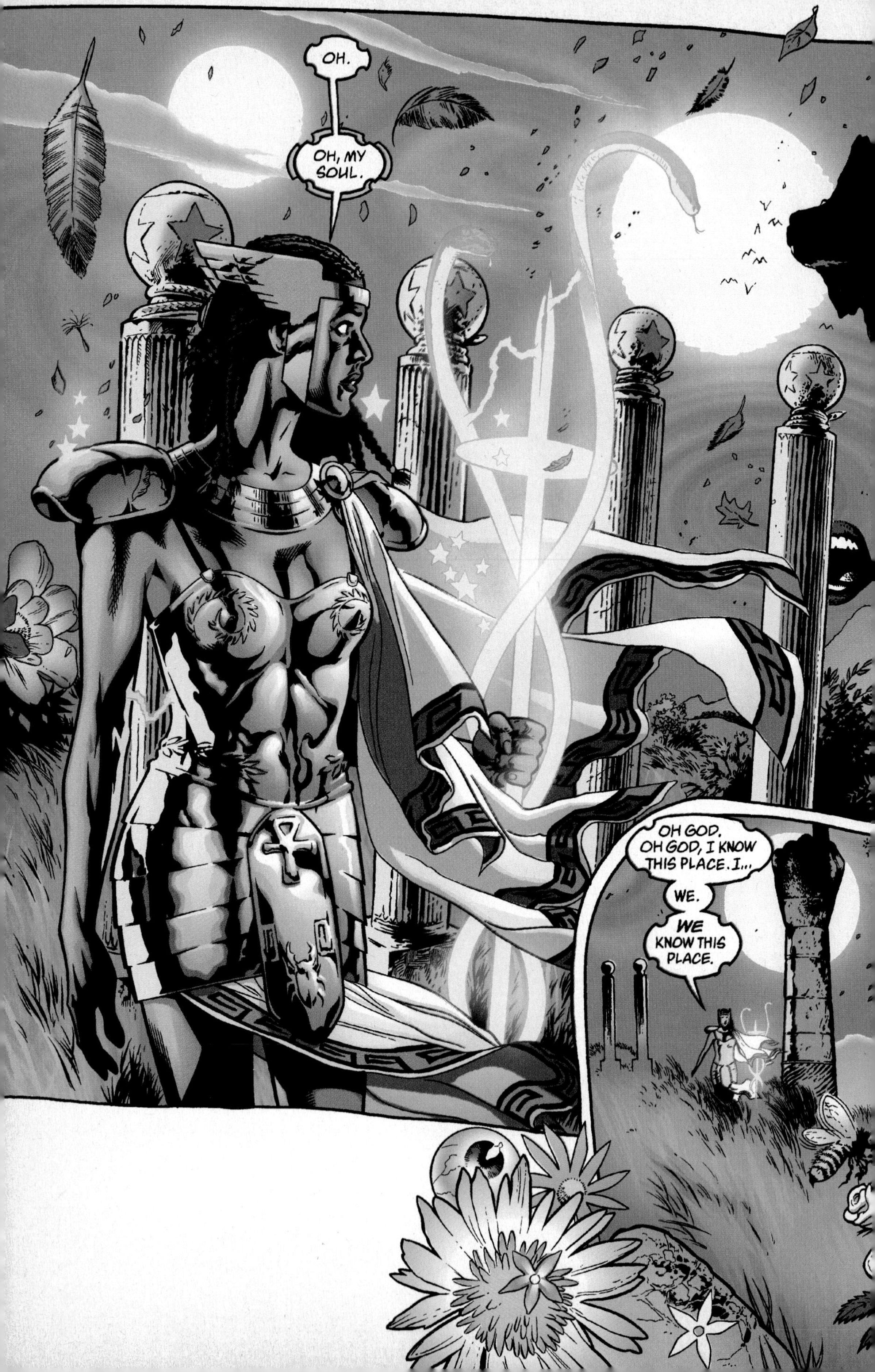
OH.
OH, MY SOUL.
OH GOD. OH GOD, I KNOW THIS PLACE. I...
WE.
WE KNOW THIS PLACE.

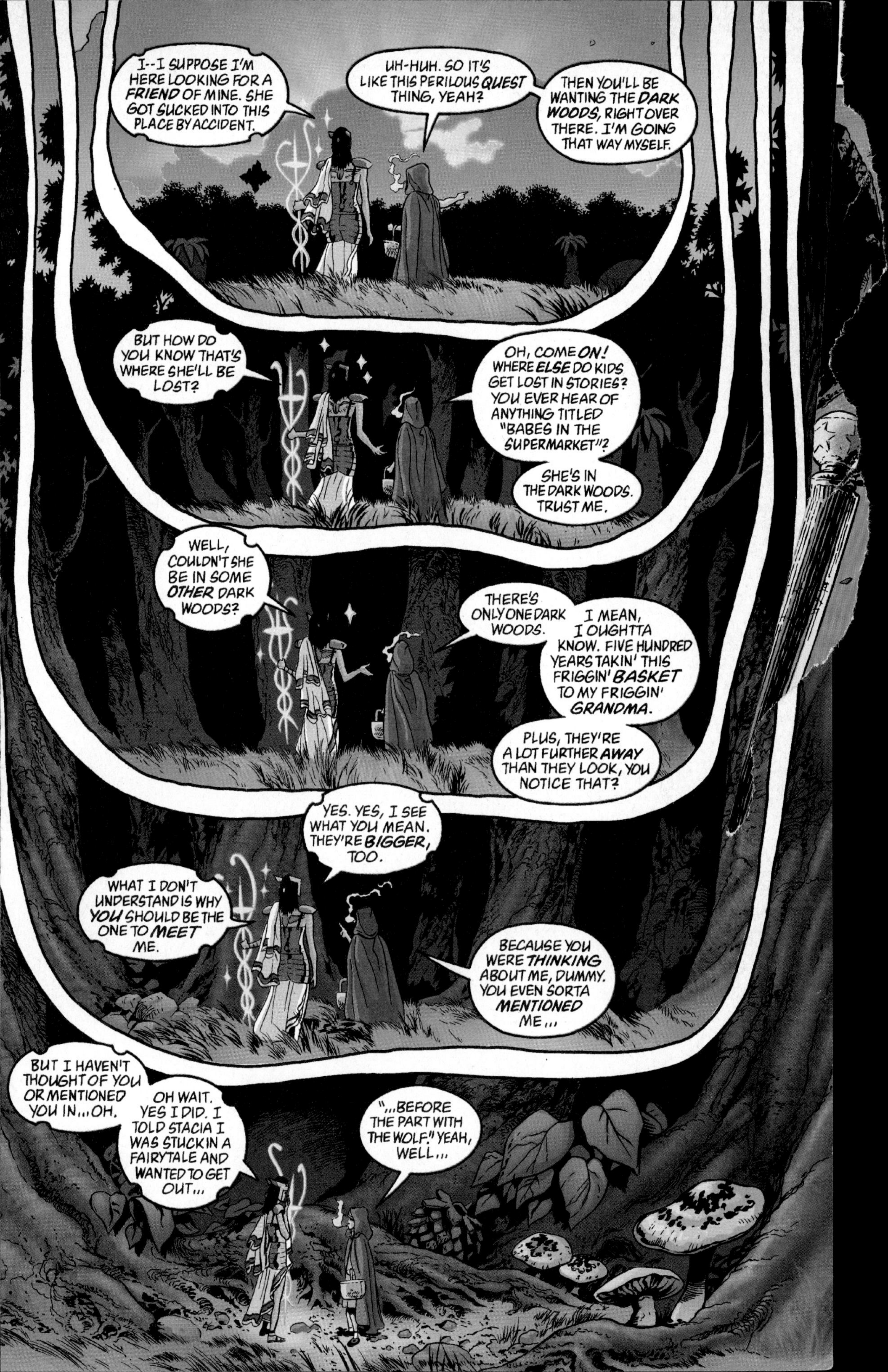

I--I SUPPOSE I'M HERE LOOKING FOR A FRIEND OF MINE. SHE GOT SUCKED INTO THIS PLACE BY ACCIDENT.
UH-HUH. SO IT'S LIKE THIS PERILOUS QUEST THING, YEAH?
THEN YOU'LL BE WANTING THE DARK WOODS, RIGHT OVER THERE. I'M GOING THAT WAY MYSELF.
BUT HOW DO YOU KNOW THAT'S WHERE SHE'LL BE LOST?
OH, COME ON! WHERE ELSE DO KIDS GET LOST IN STORIES? YOU EVER HEAR OF ANYTHING TITLED "BABES IN THE SUPERMARKET"?
SHE'S IN THE DARK WOODS. TRUST ME.
WELL, COULDN'T SHE BE IN SOME OTHER DARK WOODS?
THERE'S ONLY ONE DARK WOODS.
I MEAN, I OUGHTTA KNOW. FIVE HUNDRED YEARS TAKIN' THIS FRIGGIN' BASKET TO MY FRIGGIN' GRANDMA.
PLUS, THEY'RE A LOT FURTHER AWAY THAN THEY LOOK, YOU NOTICE THAT?
YES. YES, I SEE WHAT YOU MEAN. THEY'RE BIGGER, TOO.
WHAT I DON'T UNDERSTAND IS WHY YOU SHOULD BE THE ONE TO MEET ME.
BECAUSE YOU WERE THINKING ABOUT ME, DUMMY. YOU EVEN SORTA MENTIONED ME...
BUT I HAVEN'T THOUGHT OF YOU OR MENTIONED YOU IN... OH.
OH WAIT. YES I DID. I TOLD STACIA I WAS STUCK IN A FAIRYTALE AND WANTED TO GET OUT...
"...BEFORE THE PART WITH THE WOLF." YEAH, WELL...

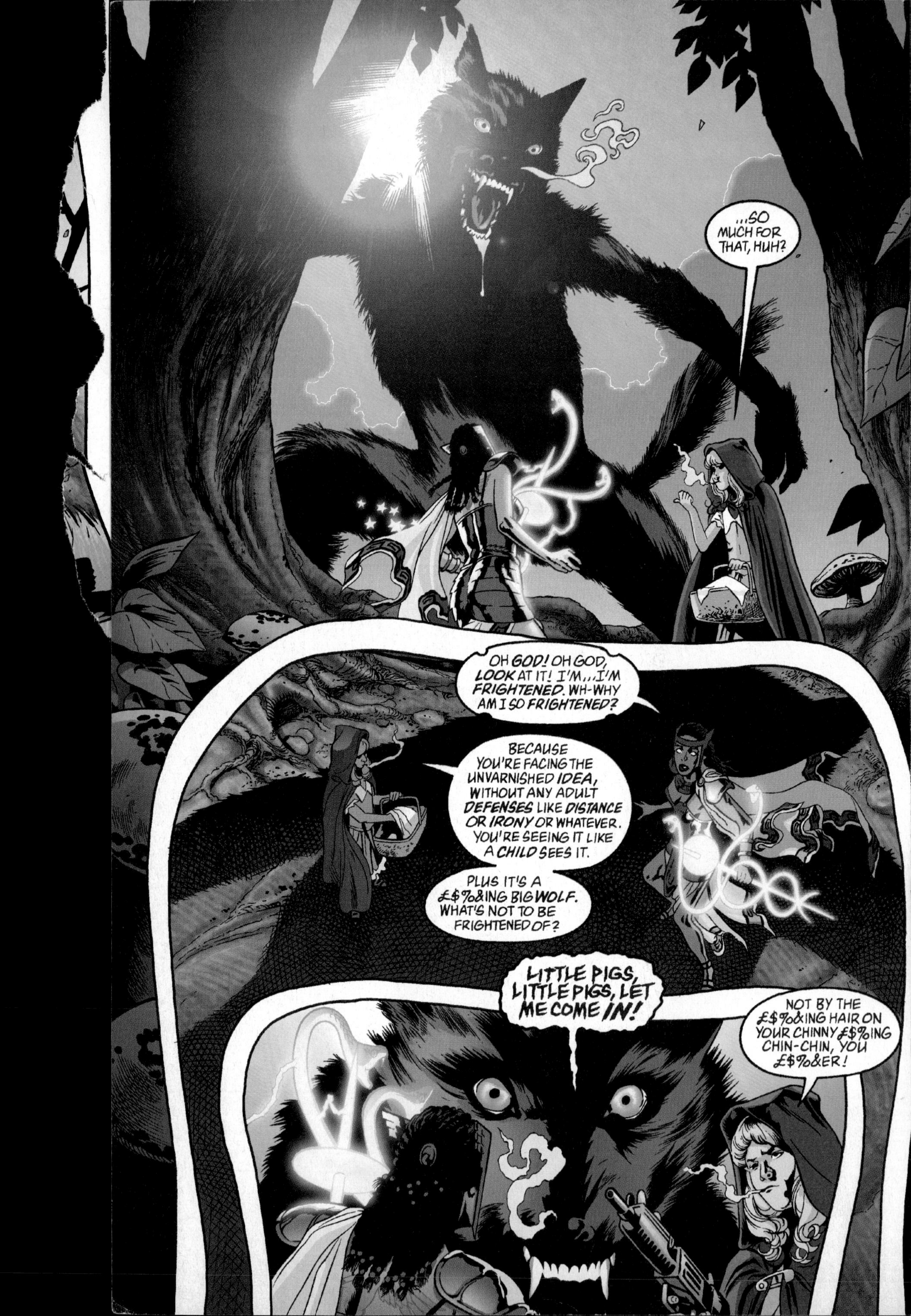

...SO MUCH FOR THAT, HUH?
OH GOD! OH GOD, LOOK AT IT! I'M... I'M FRIGHTENED. WH-WHY AM I SO FRIGHTENED?
BECAUSE YOU'RE FACING THE UNVARNISHED IDEA, WITHOUT ANY ADULT DEFENSES LIKE DISTANCE OR IRONY OR WHATEVER. YOU'RE SEEING IT LIKE A CHILD SEES IT.
PLUS IT'S A £$%&ING BIG WOLF. WHAT'S NOT TO BE FRIGHTENED OF?
LITTLE PIGS, LITTLE PIGS, LET ME COME IN!
NOT BY THE £$%&ING HAIR ON YOUR CHINNY £$%ING CHIN-CHIN, YOU £$%&ER!

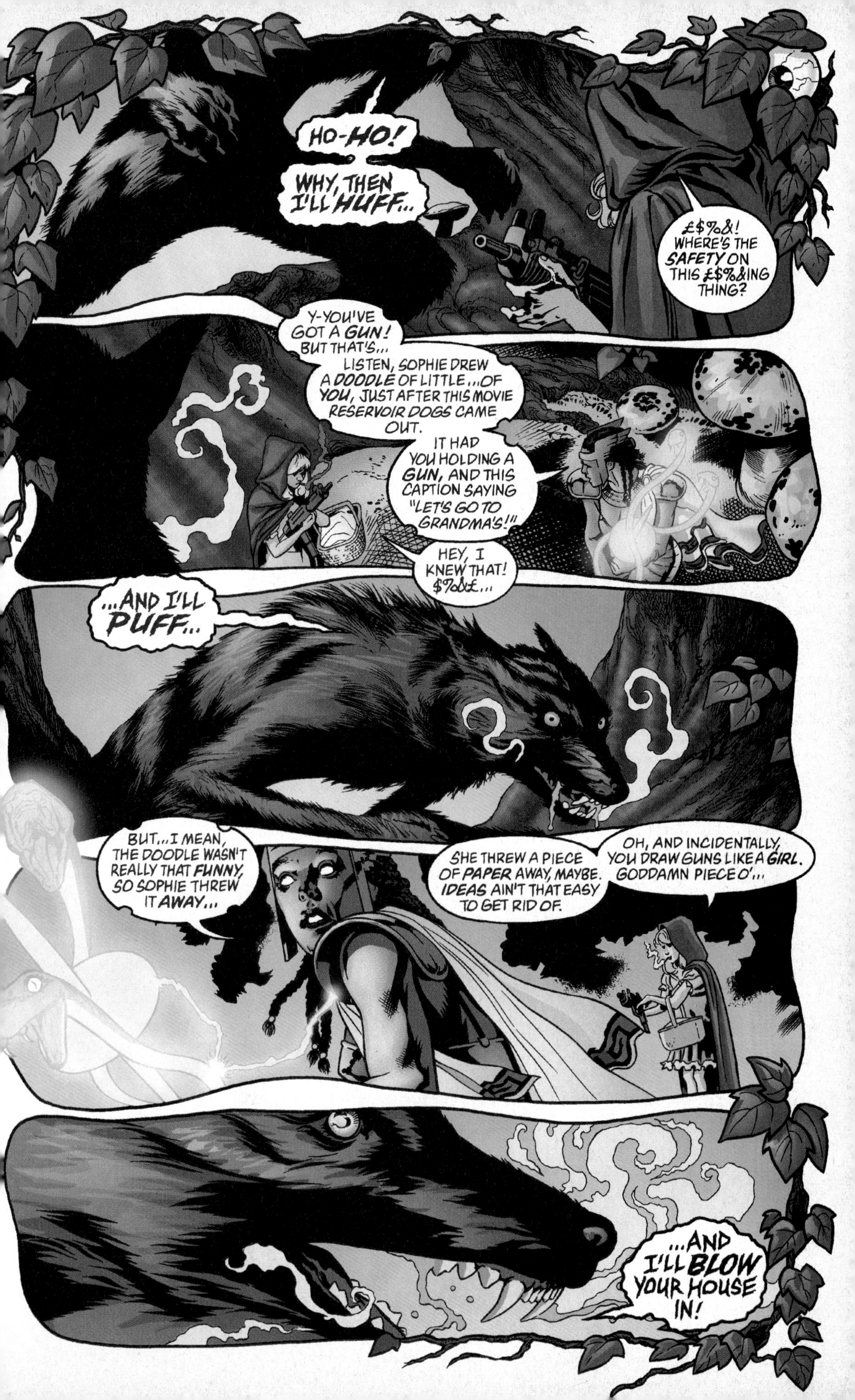

HO-HO!
WHY, THEN I'LL HUFF...
£$%&! WHERE'S THE SAFETY ON THIS £$%&ING THING?
Y-YOU'VE GOT A GUN! BUT THAT'S...
LISTEN, SOPHIE DREW A DOODLE OF LITTLE...OF YOU, JUST AFTER THIS MOVIE RESERVOIR DOGS CAME OUT.
IT HAD YOU HOLDING A GUN, AND THIS CAPTION SAYING "LET'S GO TO GRANDMA'S!"
HEY, I KNEW THAT! $%&£...
...AND I'LL PUFF...
BUT...I MEAN, THE DOODLE WASN'T REALLY THAT FUNNY, SO SOPHIE THREW IT AWAY...
SHE THREW A PIECE OF PAPER AWAY, MAYBE. IDEAS AIN'T THAT EASY TO GET RID OF.
OH, AND INCIDENTALLY, YOU DRAW GUNS LIKE A GIRL. GODDAMN PIECE O'...
...AND I'LL BLOW YOUR HOUSE IN!

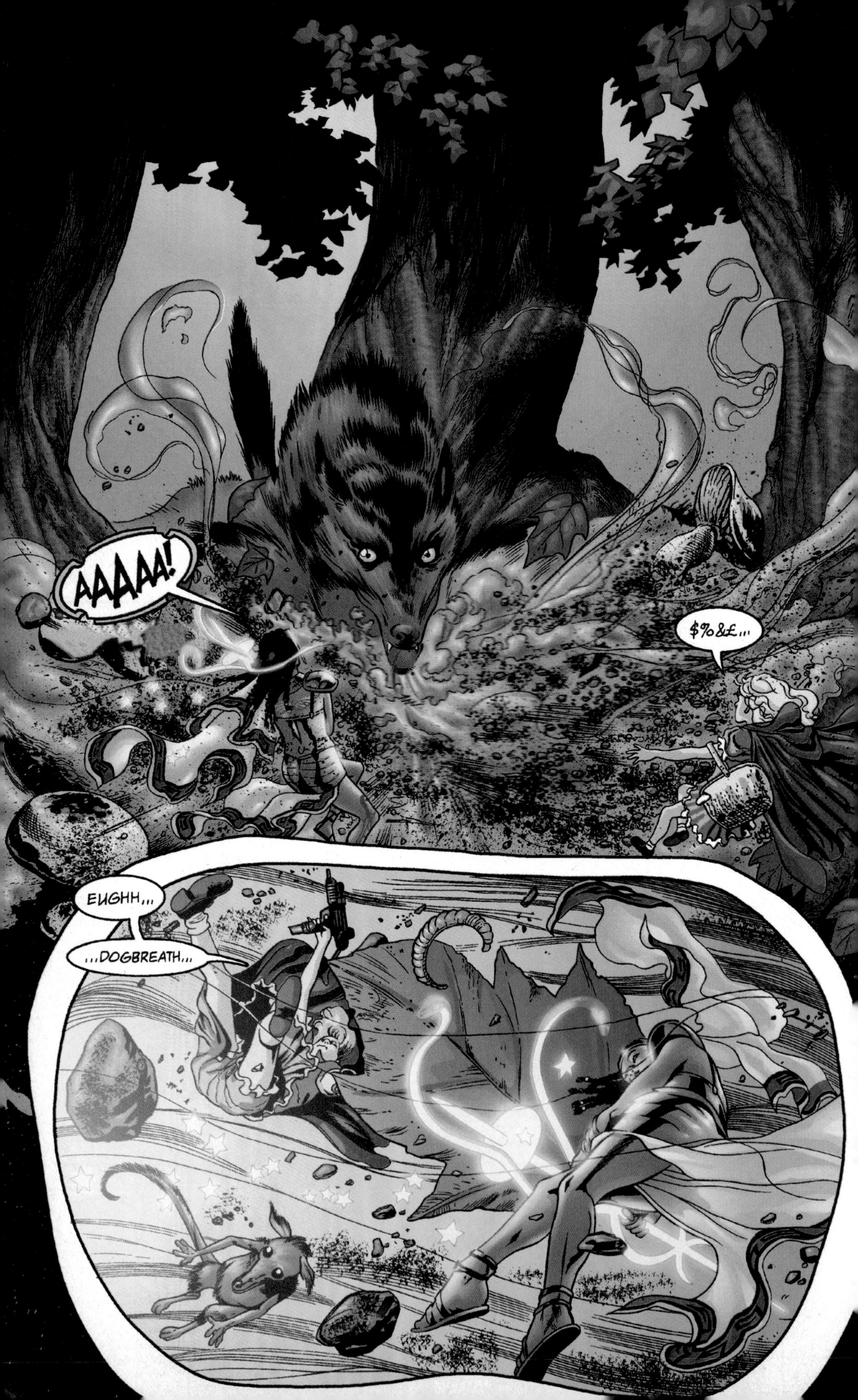
AAAAA!
$%&£...
EUGHH...
...DOGBREATH...

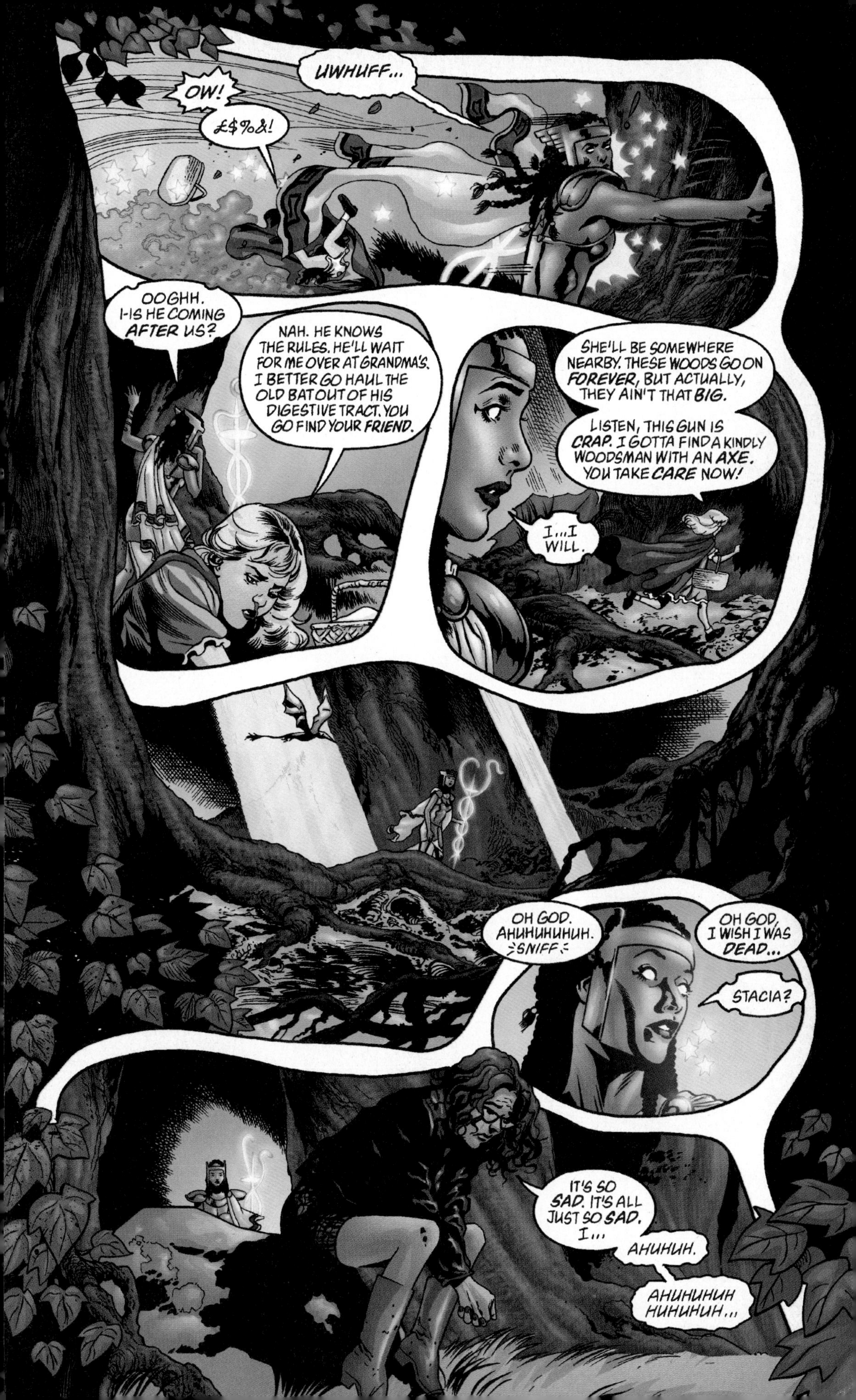
UWHUFF...
OW!
£$%&!
OOGHH. I-IS HE COMING AFTER US?
NAH. HE KNOWS THE RULES. HE'LL WAIT FOR ME OVER AT GRANDMA'S. I BETTER GO HAUL THE OLD BAT OUT OF HIS DIGESTIVE TRACT. YOU GO FIND YOUR FRIEND.
SHE'LL BE SOMEWHERE NEARBY. THESE WOODS GO ON FOREVER, BUT ACTUALLY, THEY AIN'T THAT BIG.
LISTEN, THIS GUN IS CRAP. I GOTTA FIND A KINDLY WOODSMAN WITH AN AXE. YOU TAKE CARE NOW!
I...I WILL.
OH GOD. AHUHUHUHUH. SNIFF
OH GOD, I WISH I WAS DEAD...
STACIA?
IT'S SO SAD. IT'S ALL JUST SO SAD. I...
AHUHUH.
AHUHUHUH HUHUHUH...

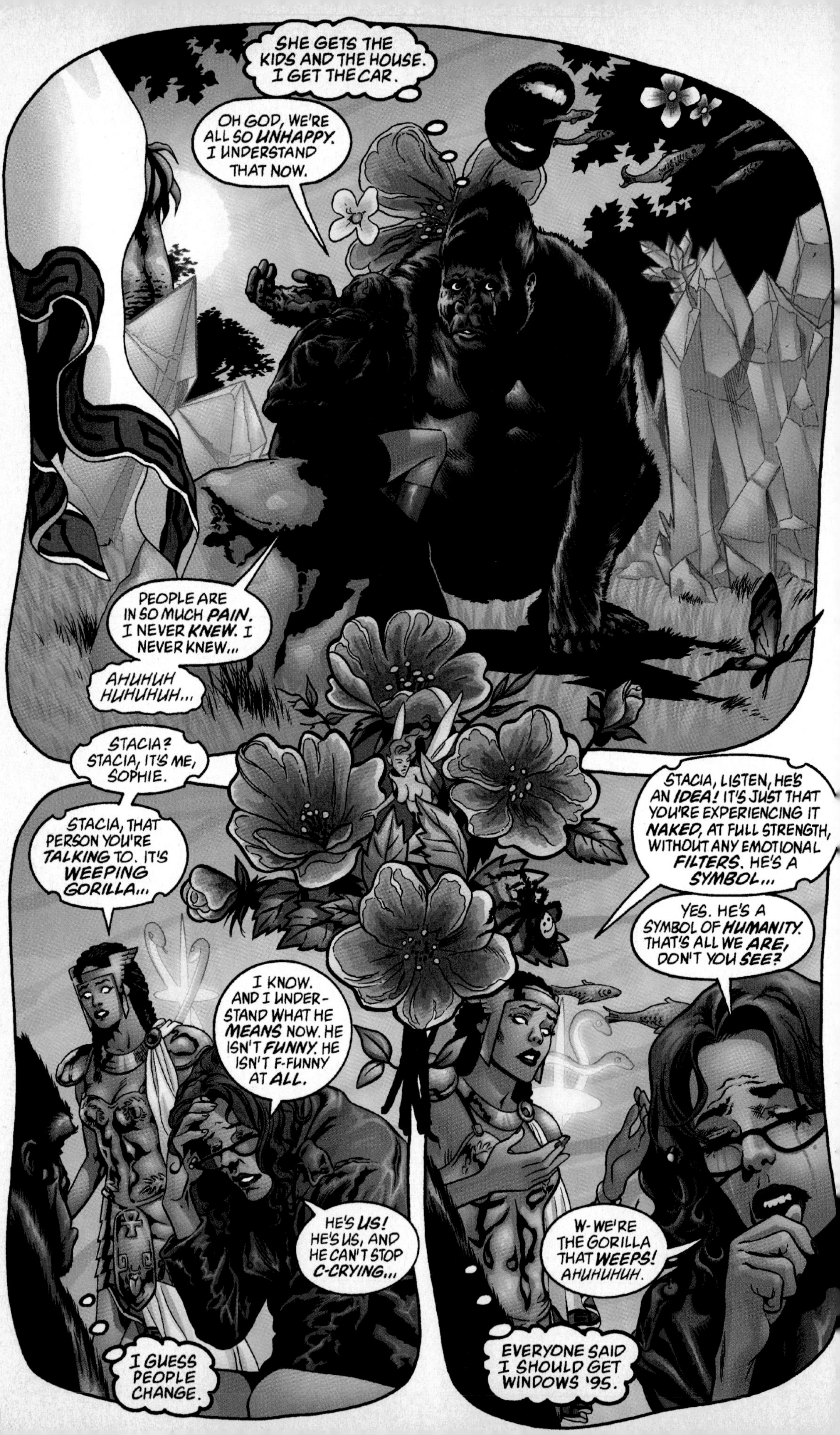
SHE GETS THE KIDS AND THE HOUSE. I GET THE CAR.
OH GOD, WE'RE ALL SO UNHAPPY. I UNDERSTAND THAT NOW.
PEOPLE ARE IN SO MUCH PAIN. I NEVER KNEW. I NEVER KNEW...
AHUHUH HUHUHUH...
STACIA? STACIA, IT'S ME, SOPHIE.
STACIA, THAT PERSON YOU'RE TALKING TO. IT'S WEEPING GORILLA...
I KNOW. AND I UNDERSTAND WHAT HE MEANS NOW. HE ISN'T FUNNY. HE ISN'T F-FUNNY AT ALL.
HE'S US! HE'S US, AND HE CAN'T STOP C-CRYING...
I GUESS PEOPLE CHANGE.
STACIA, LISTEN, HE'S AN IDEA! IT'S JUST THAT YOU'RE EXPERIENCING IT NAKED, AT FULL STRENGTH, WITHOUT ANY EMOTIONAL FILTERS. HE'S A SYMBOL...
YES. HE'S A SYMBOL OF HUMANITY. THAT'S ALL WE ARE, DON'T YOU SEE?
W-WE'RE THE GORILLA THAT WEEPS! AHUHUHUH.
EVERYONE SAID I SHOULD GET WINDOWS '95.

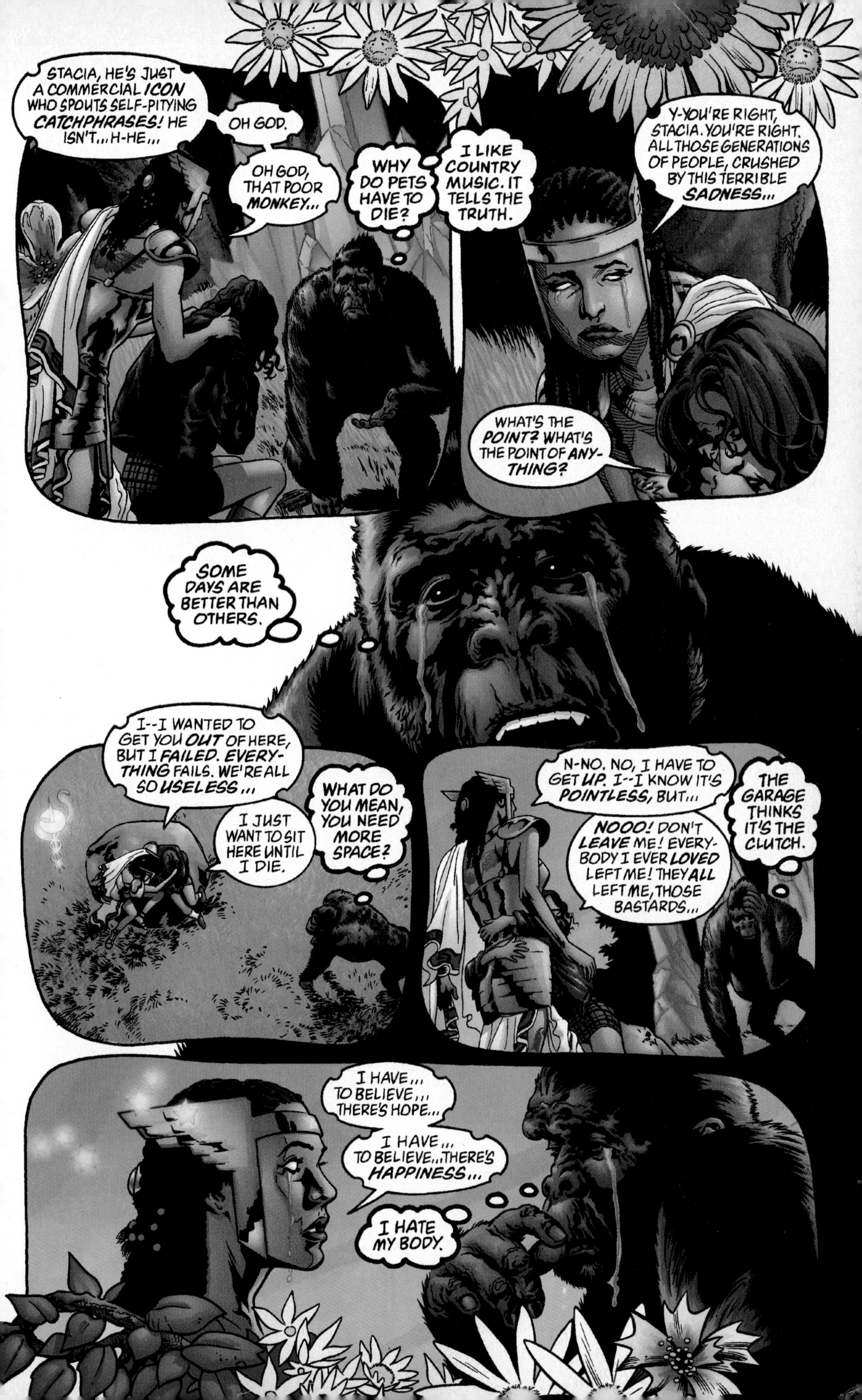

STACIA, HE'S JUST A COMMERCIAL ICON WHO SPOUTS SELF-PITYING CATCHPHRASES! HE ISN'T... H-HE...
OH GOD.
OH GOD, THAT POOR MONKEY...
WHY DO PETS HAVE TO DIE?
I LIKE COUNTRY MUSIC. IT TELLS THE TRUTH.
Y-YOU'RE RIGHT, STACIA. YOU'RE RIGHT. ALL THOSE GENERATIONS OF PEOPLE, CRUSHED BY THIS TERRIBLE SADNESS...
WHAT'S THE POINT? WHAT'S THE POINT OF ANYTHING?
SOME DAYS ARE BETTER THAN OTHERS.
I--I WANTED TO GET YOU OUT OF HERE, BUT I FAILED. EVERYTHING FAILS. WE'RE ALL SO USELESS...
I JUST WANT TO SIT HERE UNTIL I DIE.
WHAT DO YOU MEAN, YOU NEED MORE SPACE?
N-NO. NO, I HAVE TO GET UP. I--I KNOW IT'S POINTLESS, BUT...
THE GARAGE THINKS IT'S THE CLUTCH.
NOOO! DON'T LEAVE ME! EVERYBODY I EVER LOVED LEFT ME! THEY ALL LEFT ME, THOSE BASTARDS...
I HAVE... TO BELIEVE... THERE'S HOPE...
I HAVE... TO BELIEVE... THERE'S HAPPINESS...
I HATE MY BODY.

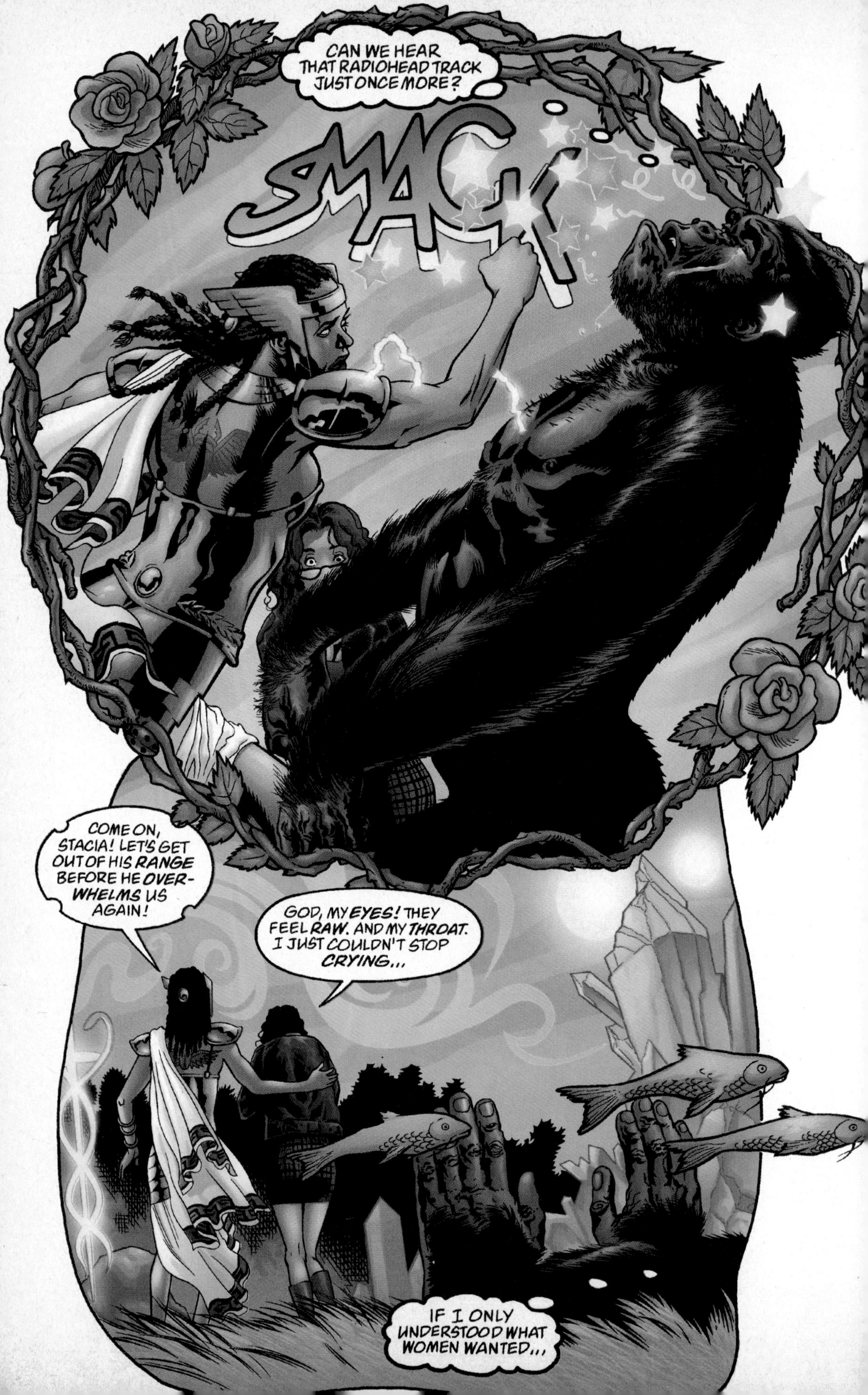
CAN WE HEAR THAT RADIOHEAD TRACK JUST ONCE MORE?
SMACK
COME ON, STACIA! LET'S GET OUT OF HIS RANGE BEFORE HE OVER-WHELMS US AGAIN!
GOD, MY EYES! THEY FEEL RAW. AND MY THROAT. I JUST COULDN'T STOP CRYING...
IF I ONLY UNDERSTOOD WHAT WOMEN WANTED...

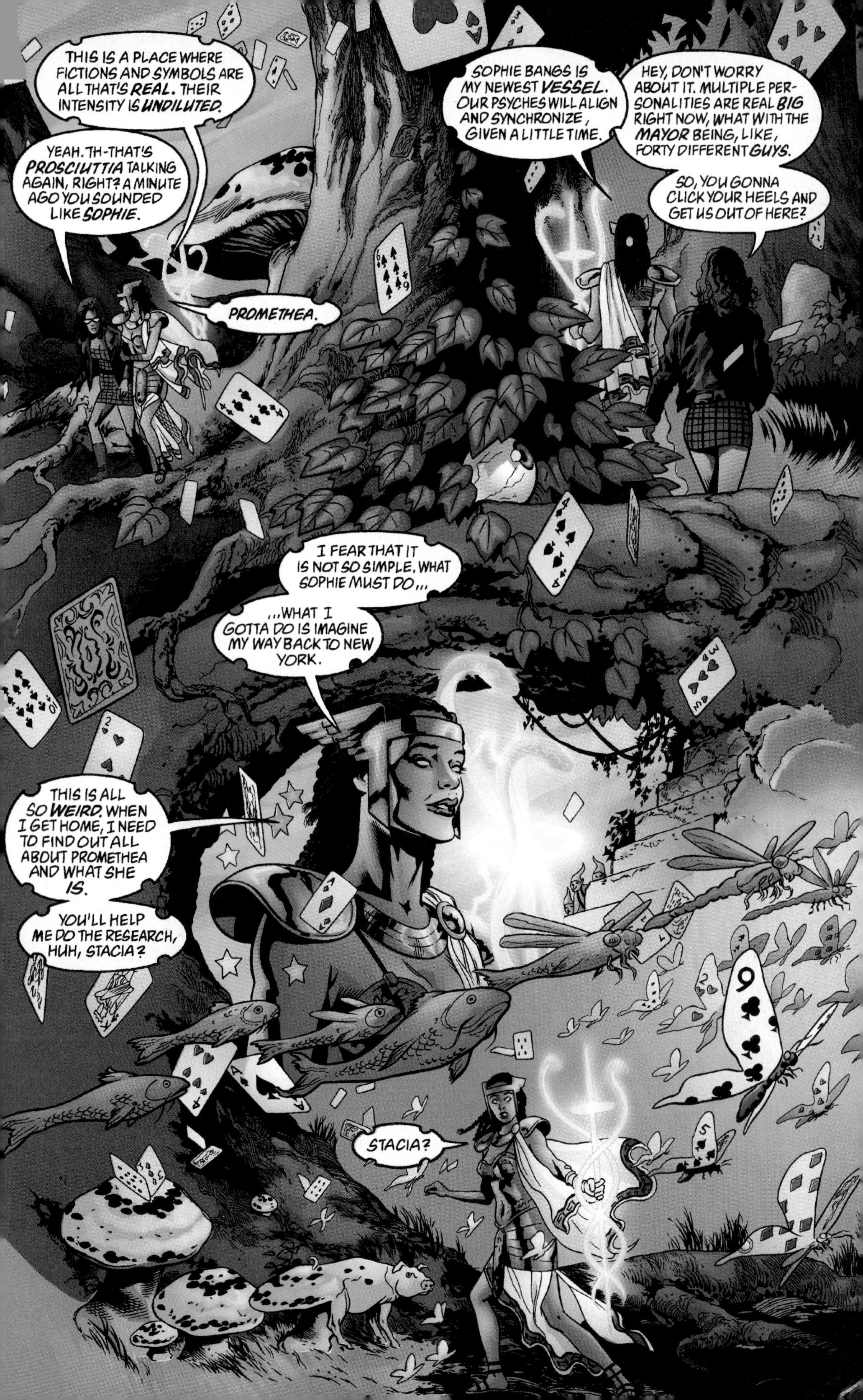
THIS IS A PLACE WHERE FICTIONS AND SYMBOLS ARE ALL THAT'S REAL. THEIR INTENSITY IS UNDILUTED.
YEAH. TH-THAT'S PROSCIUTTIA TALKING AGAIN, RIGHT? A MINUTE AGO YOU SOUNDED LIKE SOPHIE.
PROMETHEA.
SOPHIE BANGS IS MY NEWEST VESSEL. OUR PSYCHES WILL ALIGN AND SYNCHRONIZE, GIVEN A LITTLE TIME.
HEY, DON'T WORRY ABOUT IT. MULTIPLE PERSONALITIES ARE REAL BIG RIGHT NOW, WHAT WITH THE MAYOR BEING, LIKE, FORTY DIFFERENT GUYS.
SO, YOU GONNA CLICK YOUR HEELS AND GET US OUT OF HERE?
I FEAR THAT IT IS NOT SO SIMPLE. WHAT SOPHIE MUST DO...
...WHAT I GOTTA DO IS IMAGINE MY WAY BACK TO NEW YORK.
THIS IS ALL SO WEIRD. WHEN I GET HOME, I NEED TO FIND OUT ALL ABOUT PROMETHEA AND WHAT SHE IS.
YOU'LL HELP ME DO THE RESEARCH, HUH, STACIA?
STACIA?

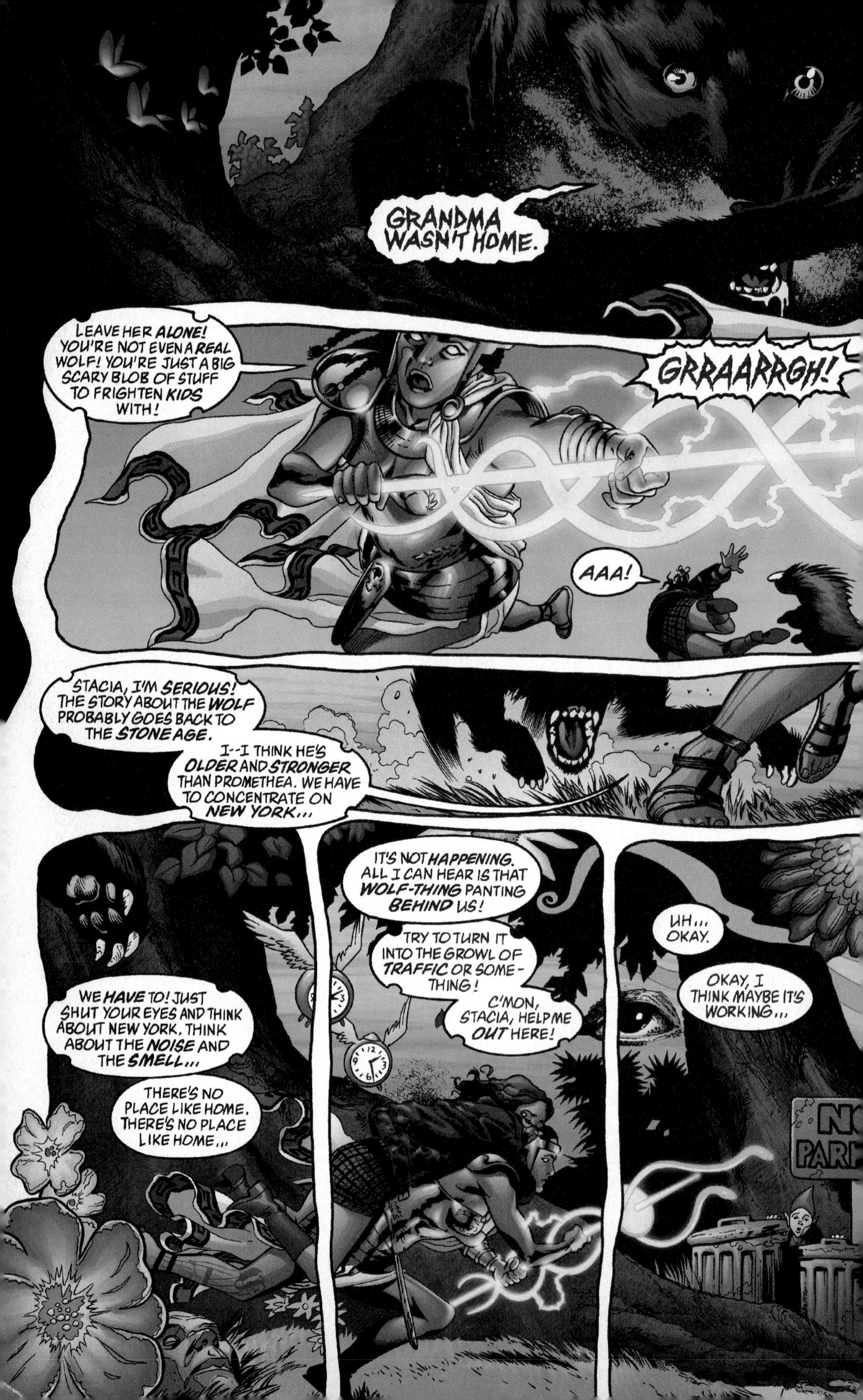
GRANDMA WASN'T HOME.
LEAVE HER ALONE! YOU'RE NOT EVEN A REAL WOLF! YOU'RE JUST A BIG SCARY BLOB OF STUFF TO FRIGHTEN KIDS WITH!
GRRAARRGH!
AAA!
STACIA, I'M SERIOUS! THE STORY ABOUT THE WOLF PROBABLY GOES BACK TO THE STONE AGE.
I--I THINK HE'S OLDER AND STRONGER THAN PROMETHEA. WE HAVE TO CONCENTRATE ON NEW YORK...
WE HAVE TO! JUST SHUT YOUR EYES AND THINK ABOUT NEW YORK. THINK ABOUT THE NOISE AND THE SMELL...
THERE'S NO PLACE LIKE HOME. THERE'S NO PLACE LIKE HOME...
IT'S NOT HAPPENING. ALL I CAN HEAR IS THAT WOLF-THING PANTING BEHIND US!
TRY TO TURN IT INTO THE GROWL OF TRAFFIC OR SOME-THING!
C'MON, STACIA, HELP ME OUT HERE!
UH... OKAY.
OKAY, I THINK MAYBE IT'S WORKING...

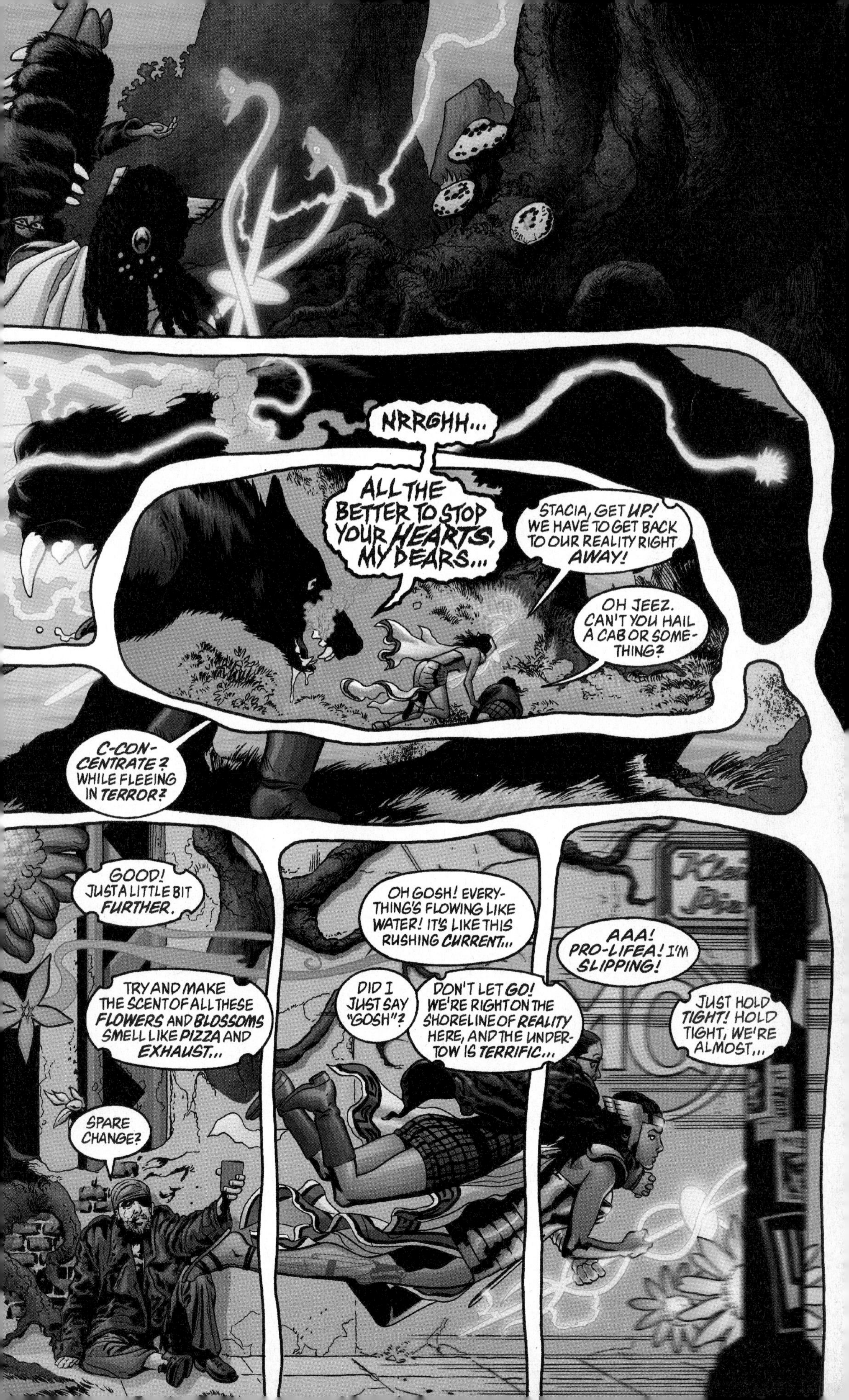
NRRGHH...
ALL THE BETTER TO STOP YOUR HEARTS, MY DEARS...
STACIA, GET UP! WE HAVE TO GET BACK TO OUR REALITY RIGHT AWAY!
OH JEEZ. CAN'T YOU HAIL A CAB OR SOMETHING?
C-CONCENTRATE? WHILE FLEEING IN TERROR?
GOOD! JUST A LITTLE BIT FURTHER.
TRY AND MAKE THE SCENT OF ALL THESE FLOWERS AND BLOSSOMS SMELL LIKE PIZZA AND EXHAUST...
SPARE CHANGE?
OH GOSH! EVERYTHING'S FLOWING LIKE WATER! IT'S LIKE THIS RUSHING CURRENT...
DID I JUST SAY "GOSH"?
DON'T LET GO! WE'RE RIGHT ON THE SHORELINE OF REALITY HERE, AND THE UNDERTOW IS TERRIFIC...
AAA! PRO-LIFEA! I'M SLIPPING!
JUST HOLD TIGHT! HOLD TIGHT, WE'RE ALMOST...

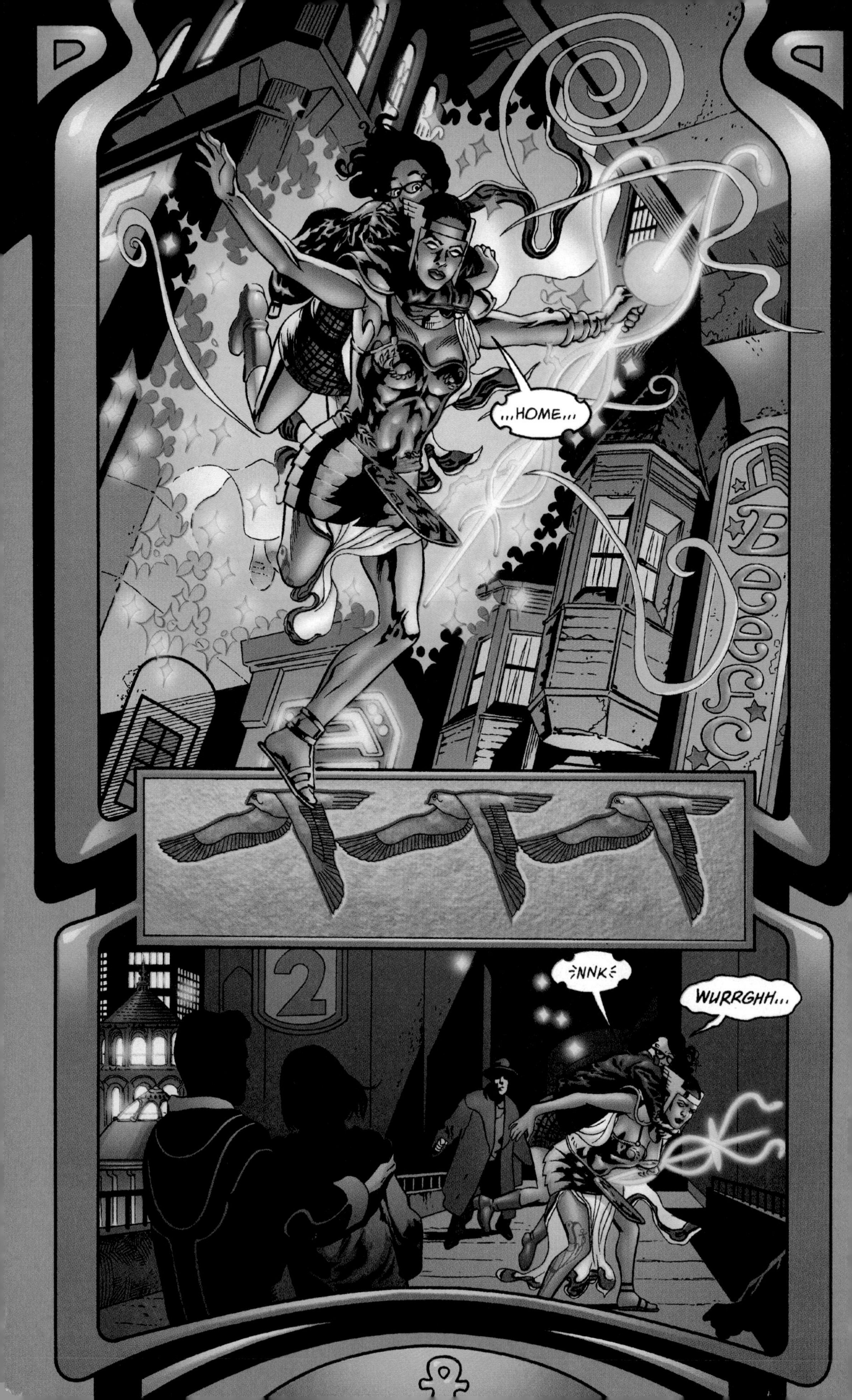
...HOME...
2
NNK
WURRGHH...

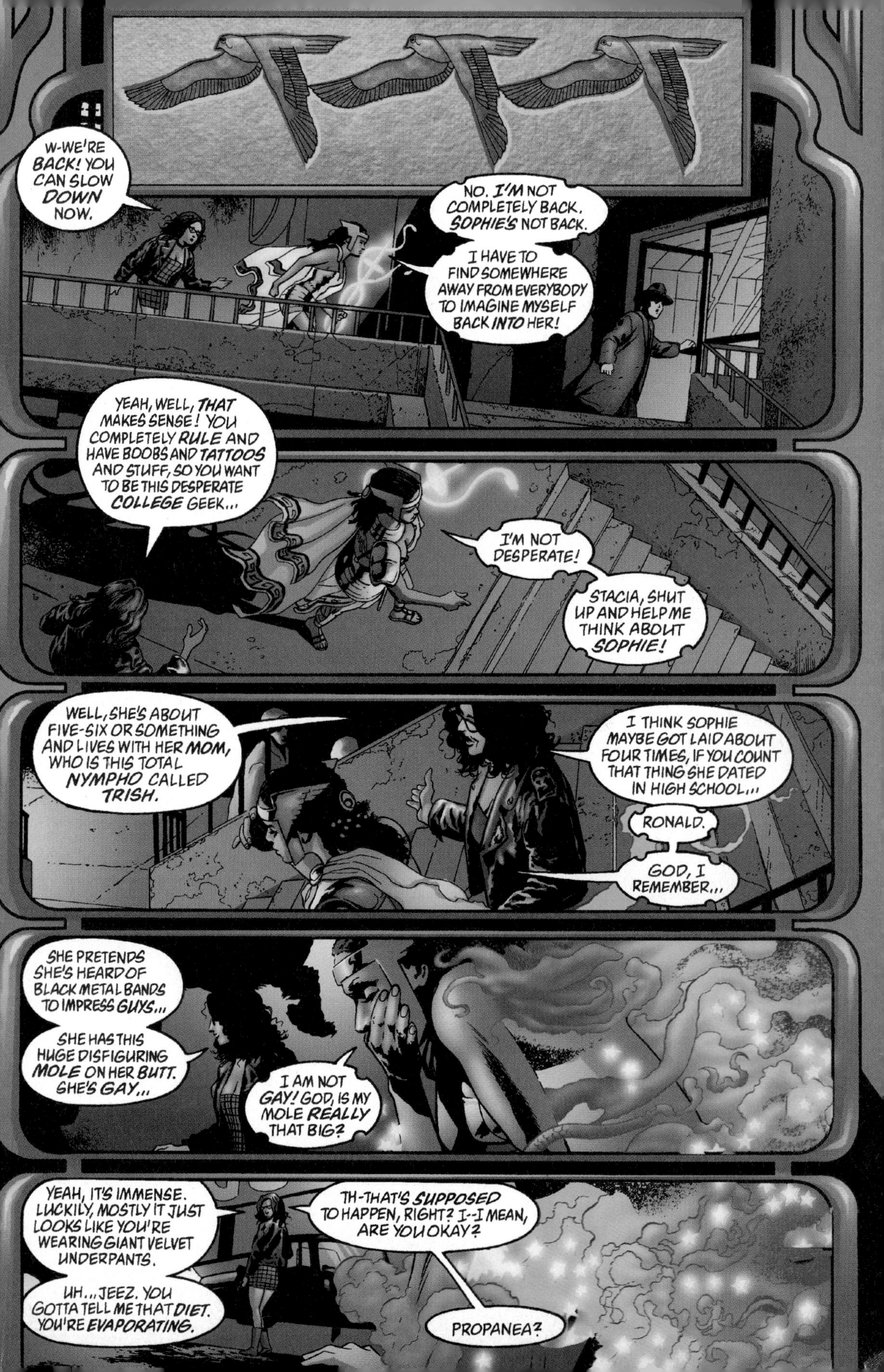

W-WE'RE BACK! YOU CAN SLOW DOWN NOW.
NO. I'M NOT COMPLETELY BACK. SOPHIE'S NOT BACK.
I HAVE TO FIND SOMEWHERE AWAY FROM EVERYBODY TO IMAGINE MYSELF BACK INTO HER!
YEAH, WELL, THAT MAKES SENSE! YOU COMPLETELY RULE AND HAVE BOOBS AND TATTOOS AND STUFF, SO YOU WANT TO BE THIS DESPERATE COLLEGE GEEK...
I'M NOT DESPERATE!
STACIA, SHUT UP AND HELP ME THINK ABOUT SOPHIE!
WELL, SHE'S ABOUT FIVE-SIX OR SOMETHING AND LIVES WITH HER MOM, WHO IS THIS TOTAL NYMPHO CALLED TRISH.
I THINK SOPHIE MAYBE GOT LAID ABOUT FOUR TIMES, IF YOU COUNT THAT THING SHE DATED IN HIGH SCHOOL...
RONALD.
GOD, I REMEMBER...
SHE PRETENDS SHE'S HEARD OF BLACK METAL BANDS TO IMPRESS GUYS...
SHE HAS THIS HUGE DISFIGURING MOLE ON HER BUTT. SHE'S GAY...
I AM NOT GAY! GOD, IS MY MOLE REALLY THAT BIG?
YEAH, IT'S IMMENSE. LUCKILY, MOSTLY IT JUST LOOKS LIKE YOU'RE WEARING GIANT VELVET UNDERPANTS.
TH-THAT'S SUPPOSED TO HAPPEN, RIGHT? I--I MEAN, ARE YOU OKAY?
UH...JEEZ. YOU GOTTA TELL ME THAT DIET. YOU'RE EVAPORATING.
PROPANEA?

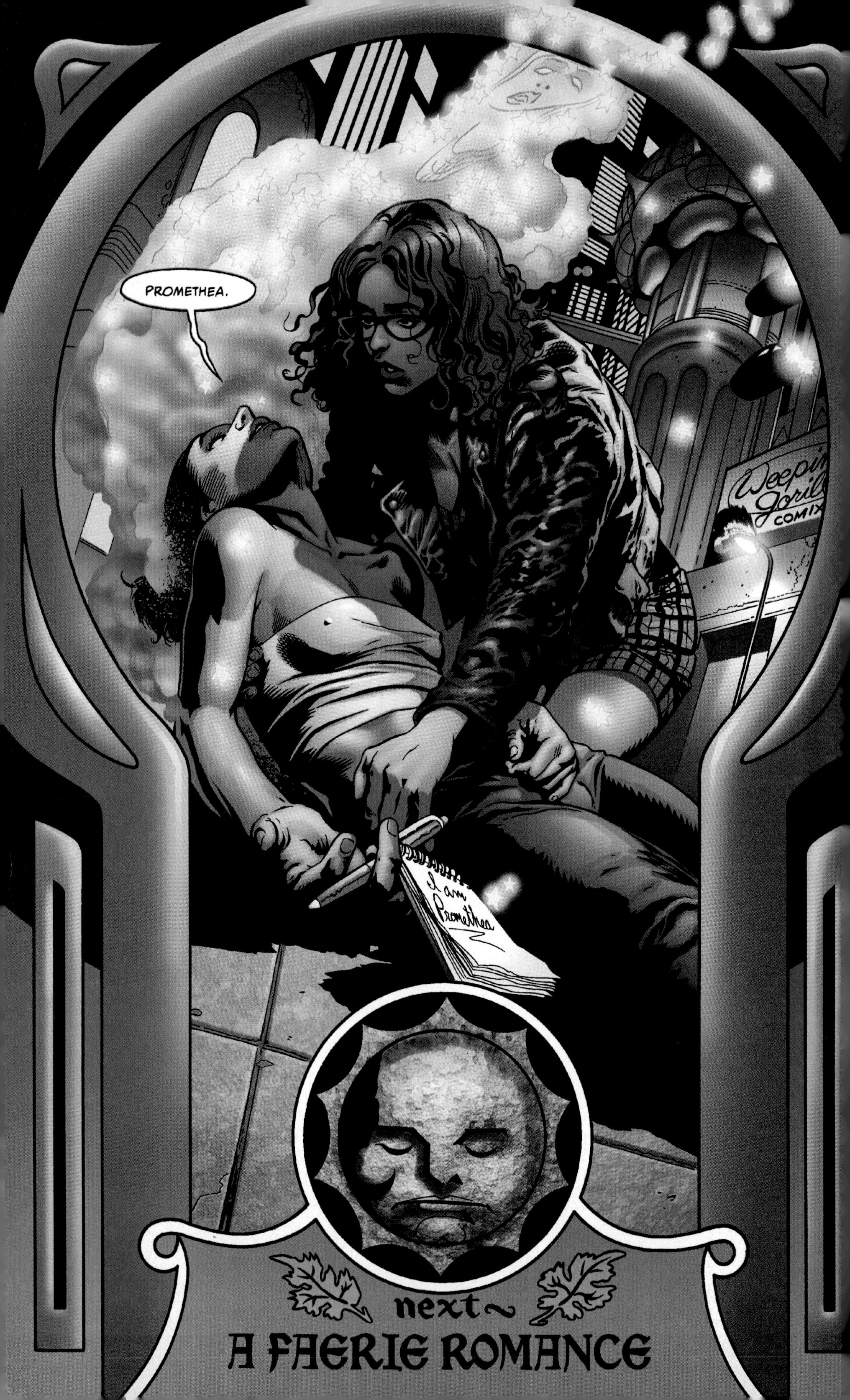
PROMETHEA.
Weepin
Gorill
COMIX
I am Promethea
next~
A FAERIE ROMANCE

CHAPTER FOUR

An old epic is illuminated,
A sly mage encountered,
A search for answers begins.

Cover art:
J.H. Williams III
& Mick Gray

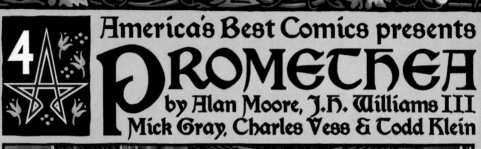

America's Best Comics presents
PROMETHEA

by Alan Moore, J.H. Williams III
Mick Gray, Charles Vess & Todd Klein

4

Being an Epicke on the Realms of Fantasie
in the wordes of Charlton Sennet, privately
imprinted in the City of Boston, entytled

A FAERIE ROMANCE

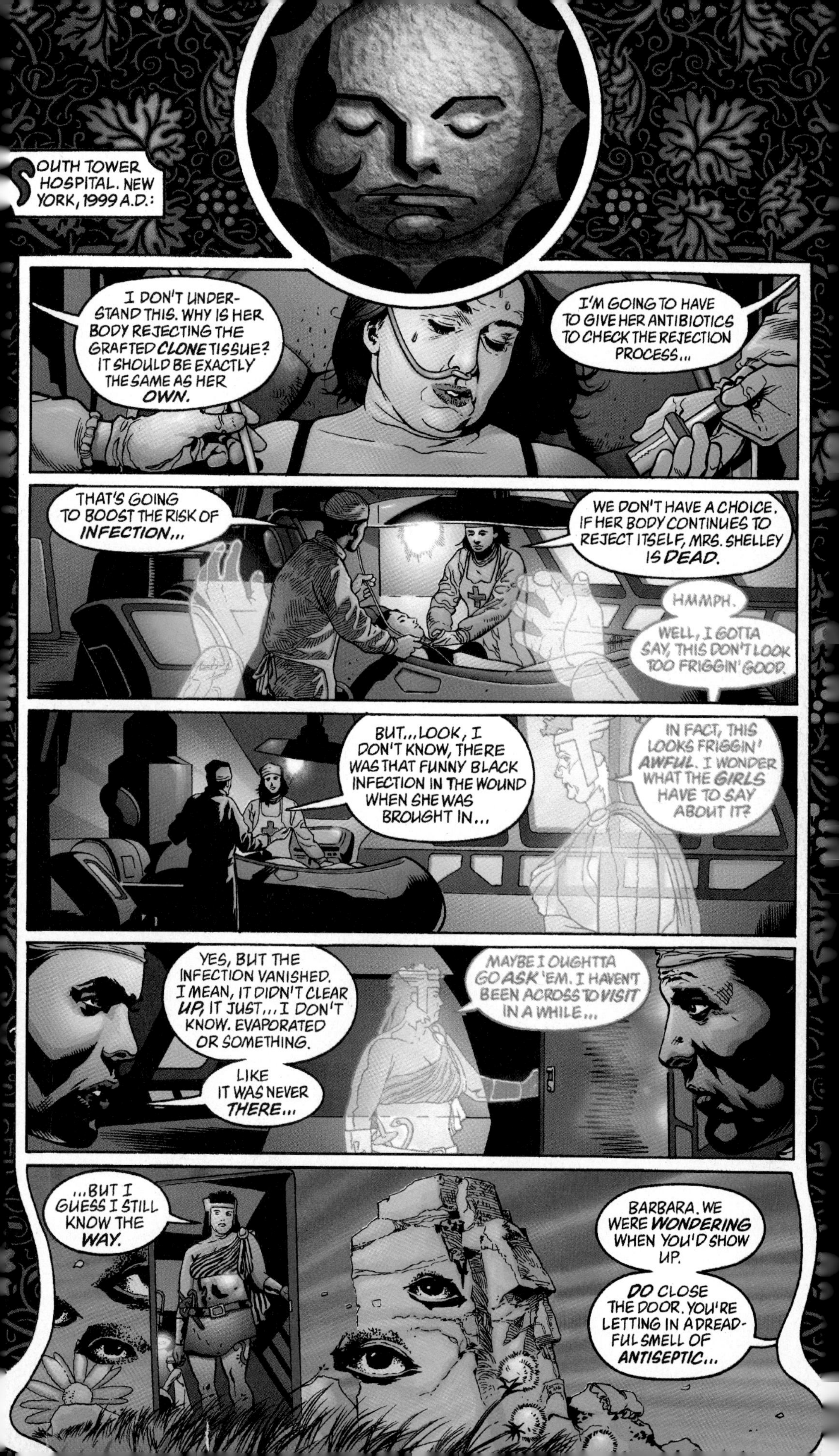
SOUTH TOWER HOSPITAL. NEW YORK, 1999 A.D.:
I DON'T UNDERSTAND THIS. WHY IS HER BODY REJECTING THE GRAFTED CLONE TISSUE? IT SHOULD BE EXACTLY THE SAME AS HER OWN.
I'M GOING TO HAVE TO GIVE HER ANTIBIOTICS TO CHECK THE REJECTION PROCESS...
THAT'S GOING TO BOOST THE RISK OF INFECTION...
WE DON'T HAVE A CHOICE. IF HER BODY CONTINUES TO REJECT ITSELF, MRS. SHELLEY IS DEAD.
HMMPH.
WELL, I GOTTA SAY, THIS DON'T LOOK TOO FRIGGIN' GOOD.
BUT...LOOK, I DON'T KNOW, THERE WAS THAT FUNNY BLACK INFECTION IN THE WOUND WHEN SHE WAS BROUGHT IN...
IN FACT, THIS LOOKS FRIGGIN' AWFUL. I WONDER WHAT THE GIRLS HAVE TO SAY ABOUT IT?
YES, BUT THE INFECTION VANISHED. I MEAN, IT DIDN'T CLEAR UP, IT JUST... I DON'T KNOW. EVAPORATED OR SOMETHING.
LIKE IT WAS NEVER THERE...
MAYBE I OUGHTTA GO ASK 'EM. I HAVEN'T BEEN ACROSS TO VISIT IN A WHILE...
...BUT I GUESS I STILL KNOW THE WAY.
BARBARA. WE WERE WONDERING WHEN YOU'D SHOW UP.
DO CLOSE THE DOOR. YOU'RE LETTING IN A DREADFUL SMELL OF ANTISEPTIC...

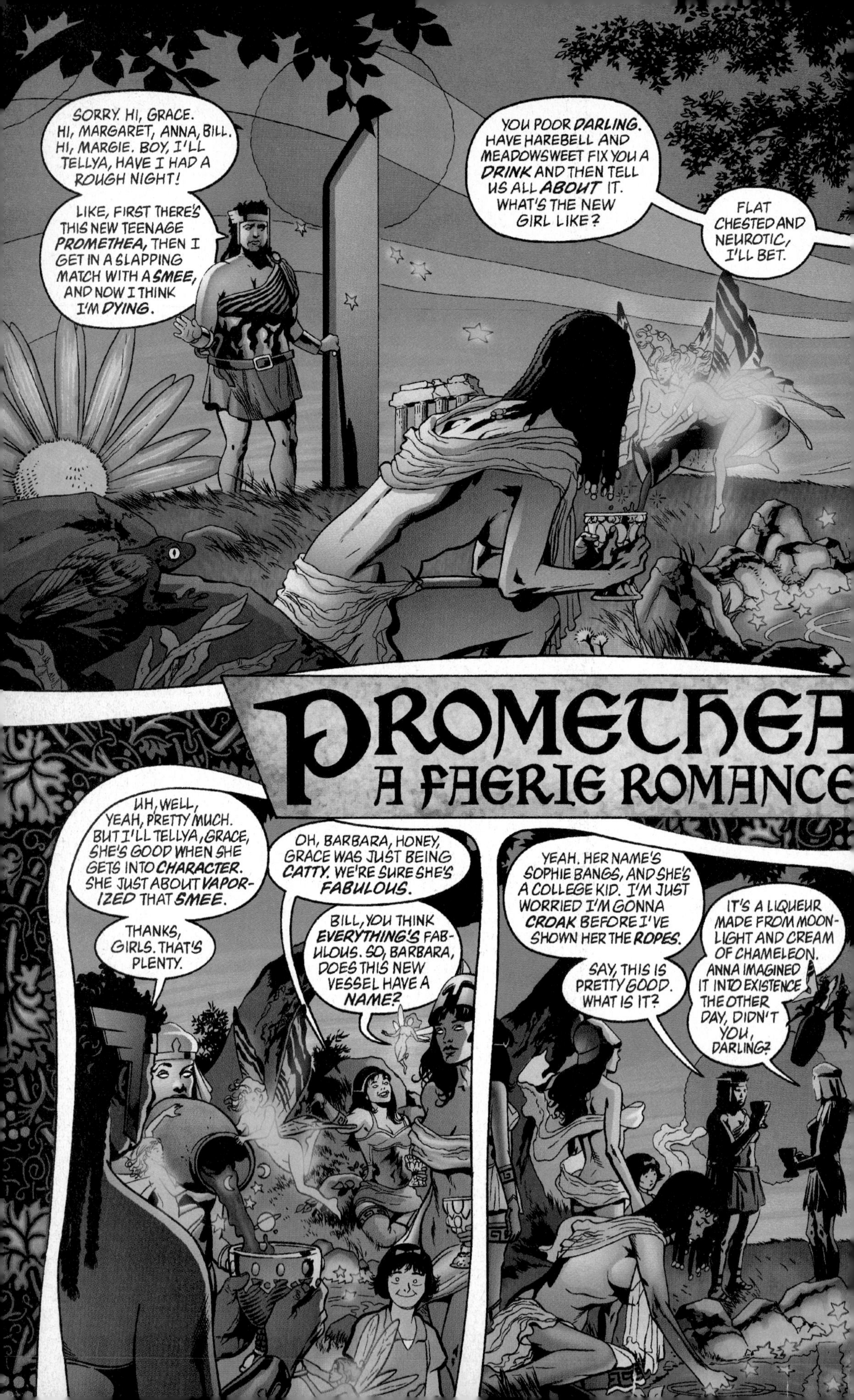
SORRY. HI, GRACE. HI, MARGARET, ANNA, BILL. HI, MARGIE. BOY, I'LL TELLYA, HAVE I HAD A ROUGH NIGHT!
LIKE, FIRST THERE'S THIS NEW TEENAGE PROMETHEA, THEN I GET IN A SLAPPING MATCH WITH A SMEE, AND NOW I THINK I'M DYING.
YOU POOR DARLING. HAVE HAREBELL AND MEADOWSWEET FIX YOU A DRINK AND THEN TELL US ALL ABOUT IT. WHAT'S THE NEW GIRL LIKE?
FLAT CHESTED AND NEUROTIC, I'LL BET.
PROMETHEA
A FAERIE ROMANCE
UH, WELL, YEAH, PRETTY MUCH. BUT I'LL TELLYA, GRACE, SHE'S GOOD WHEN SHE GETS INTO CHARACTER. SHE JUST ABOUT VAPORIZED THAT SMEE.
THANKS, GIRLS. THAT'S PLENTY.
OH, BARBARA, HONEY, GRACE WAS JUST BEING CATTY. WE'RE SURE SHE'S FABULOUS.
BILL, YOU THINK EVERYTHING'S FABULOUS. SO, BARBARA, DOES THIS NEW VESSEL HAVE A NAME?
YEAH. HER NAME'S SOPHIE BANGS, AND SHE'S A COLLEGE KID. I'M JUST WORRIED I'M GONNA CROAK BEFORE I'VE SHOWN HER THE ROPES.
SAY, THIS IS PRETTY GOOD. WHAT IS IT?
IT'S A LIQUEUR MADE FROM MOONLIGHT AND CREAM OF CHAMELEON. ANNA IMAGINED IT INTO EXISTENCE THE OTHER DAY, DIDN'T YOU, DARLING?

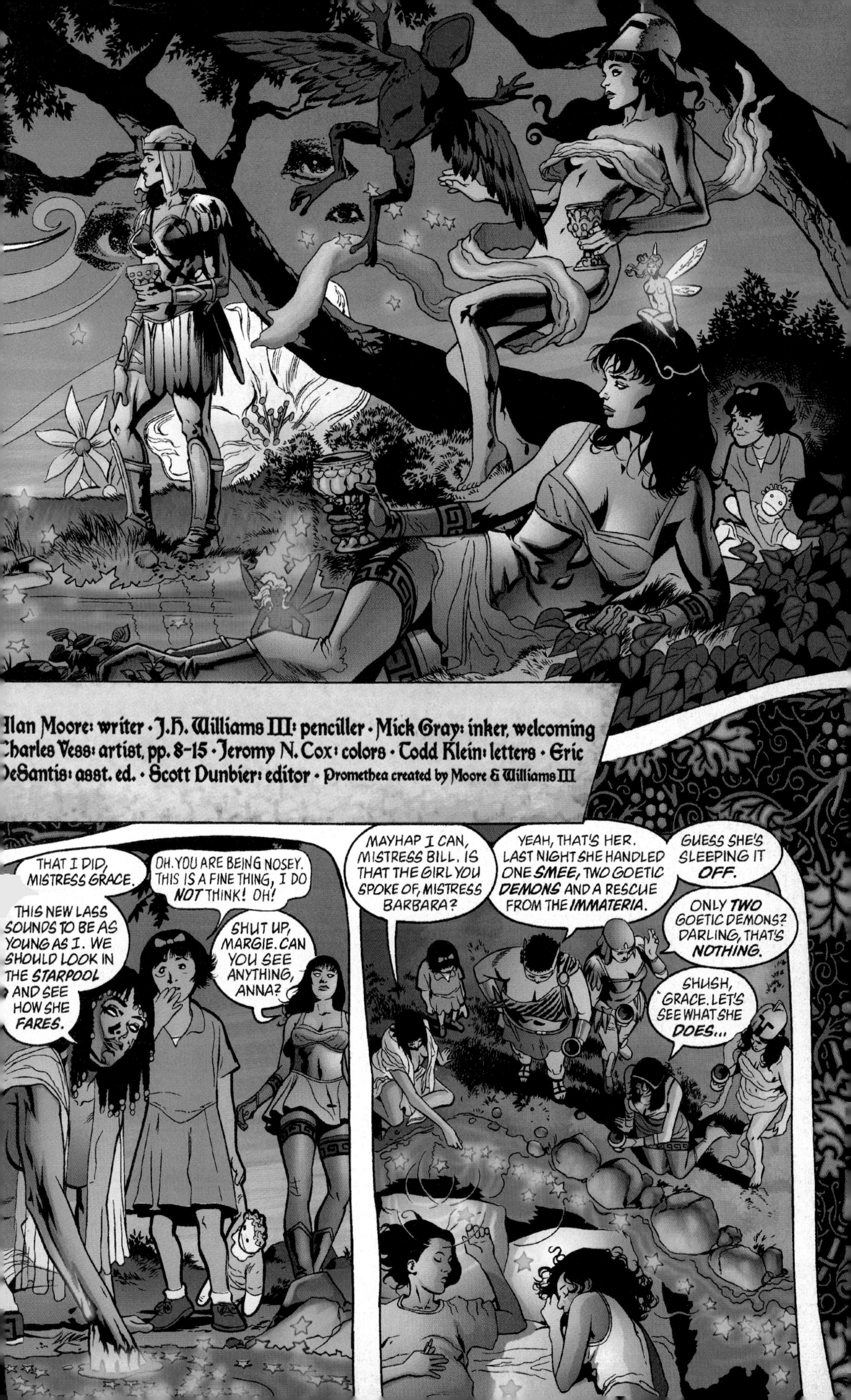
llan Moore: writer • J.H. Williams III: penciller • Mick Gray: inker, welcoming
Charles Vess: artist, pp. 8-15 • Jeromy N. Cox: colors • Todd Klein: letters • Eric
DeSantis: asst. ed. • Scott Dunbier: editor • Promethea created by Moore & Williams III
THAT I DID, MISTRESS GRACE.
THIS NEW LASS SOUNDS TO BE AS YOUNG AS I. WE SHOULD LOOK IN THE STARPOOL AND SEE HOW SHE FARES.
OH. YOU ARE BEING NOSEY. THIS IS A FINE THING, I DO NOT THINK! OH!
SHUT UP, MARGIE. CAN YOU SEE ANYTHING, ANNA?
MAYHAP I CAN, MISTRESS BILL. IS THAT THE GIRL YOU SPOKE OF, MISTRESS BARBARA?
YEAH, THAT'S HER. LAST NIGHT SHE HANDLED ONE SMEE, TWO GOETIC DEMONS AND A RESCUE FROM THE IMMATERIA.
GUESS SHE'S SLEEPING IT OFF.
ONLY TWO GOETIC DEMONS? DARLING, THAT'S NOTHING.
SHUSH, GRACE. LET'S SEE WHAT SHE DOES...

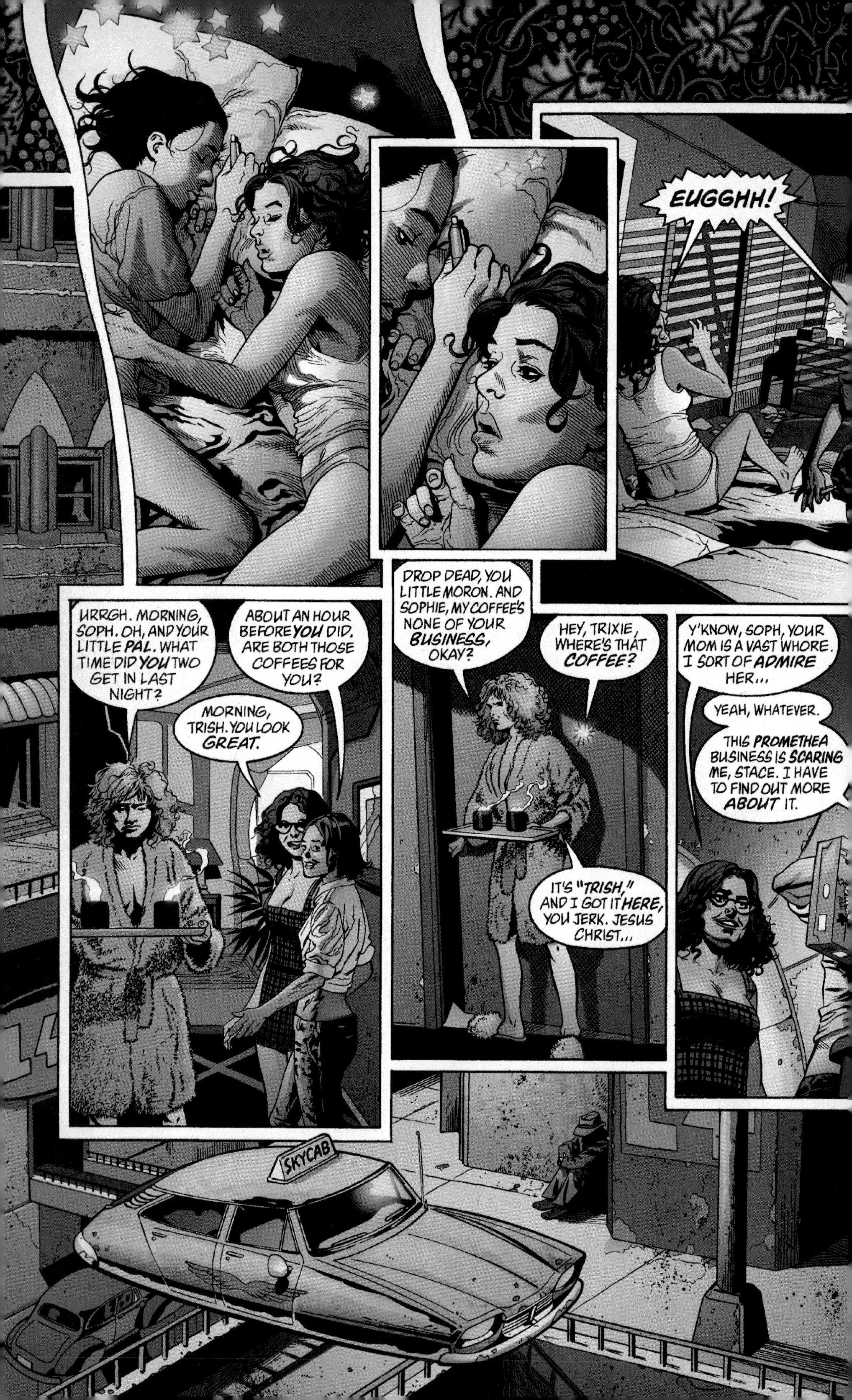
EUGGHH!
URRGH. MORNING, SOPH. OH, AND YOUR LITTLE PAL. WHAT TIME DID YOU TWO GET IN LAST NIGHT?
ABOUT AN HOUR BEFORE YOU DID. ARE BOTH THOSE COFFEES FOR YOU?
MORNING, TRISH. YOU LOOK GREAT.
DROP DEAD, YOU LITTLE MORON. AND SOPHIE, MY COFFEE'S NONE OF YOUR BUSINESS, OKAY?
HEY, TRIXIE, WHERE'S THAT COFFEE?
IT'S "TRISH," AND I GOT IT HERE, YOU JERK. JESUS CHRIST...
Y'KNOW, SOPH, YOUR MOM IS A VAST WHORE. I SORT OF ADMIRE HER...
YEAH, WHATEVER.
THIS PROMETHEA BUSINESS IS SCARING ME, STACE. I HAVE TO FIND OUT MORE ABOUT IT.
SKYCAB

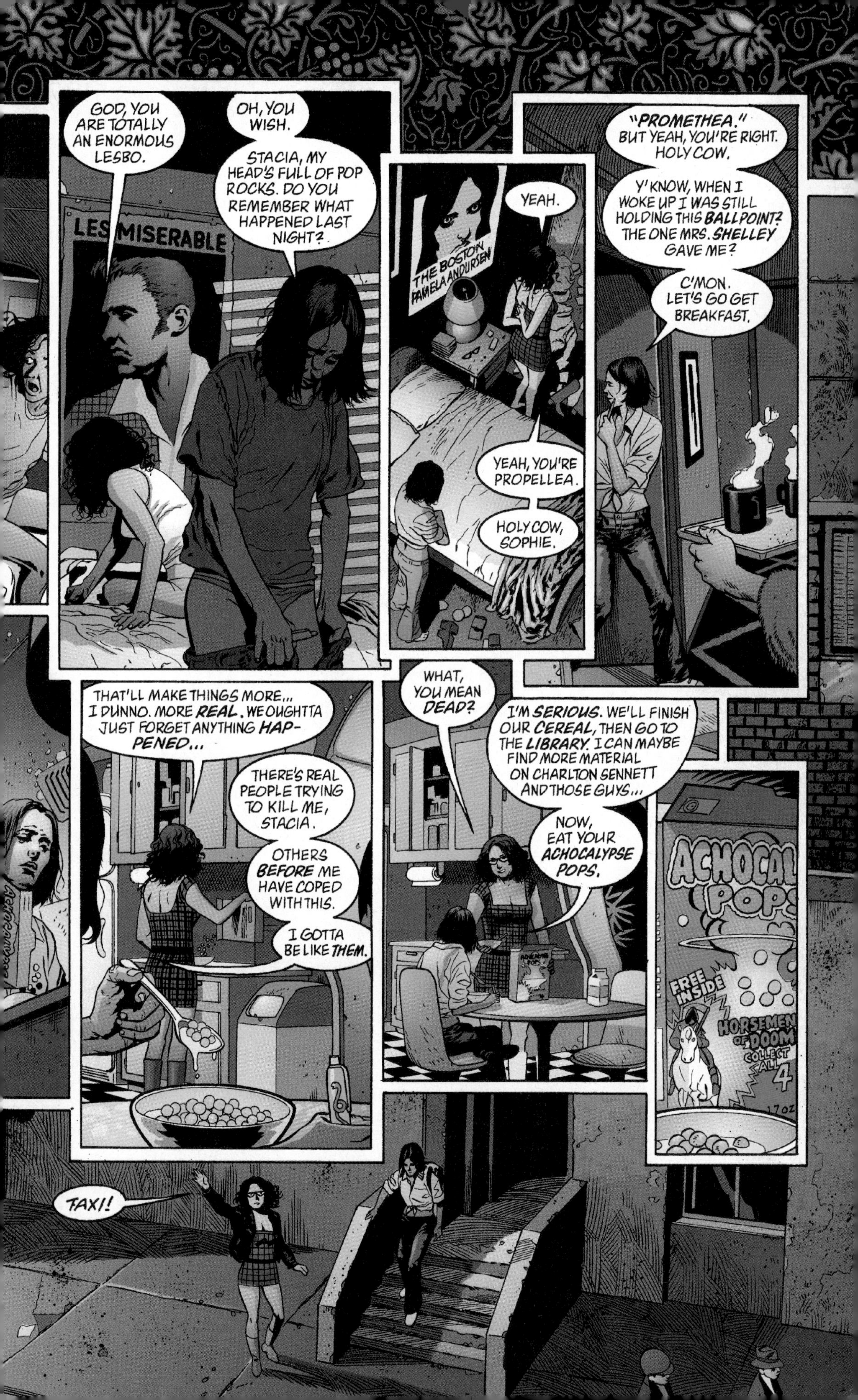
GOD, YOU ARE TOTALLY AN ENORMOUS LESBO.
OH, YOU WISH.
STACIA, MY HEAD'S FULL OF POP ROCKS. DO YOU REMEMBER WHAT HAPPENED LAST NIGHT?
LES MISERABLE
THE BOSTON PAMELA ANDURSEN
YEAH.
YEAH, YOU'RE PROPELLEA.
HOLY COW, SOPHIE.
"PROMETHEA." BUT YEAH, YOU'RE RIGHT. HOLY COW.
Y'KNOW, WHEN I WOKE UP I WAS STILL HOLDING THIS BALLPOINT? THE ONE MRS. SHELLEY GAVE ME?
C'MON. LET'S GO GET BREAKFAST.
THAT'LL MAKE THINGS MORE... I DUNNO. MORE REAL. WE OUGHTTA JUST FORGET ANYTHING HAPPENED...
THERE'S REAL PEOPLE TRYING TO KILL ME, STACIA.
OTHERS BEFORE ME HAVE COPED WITH THIS.
I GOTTA BE LIKE THEM.
WHAT, YOU MEAN DEAD?
I'M SERIOUS. WE'LL FINISH OUR CEREAL, THEN GO TO THE LIBRARY. I CAN MAYBE FIND MORE MATERIAL ON CHARLTON SENNETT AND THOSE GUYS...
NOW, EAT YOUR ACHOCALYPSE POPS.
ACHOCAL POPS
FREE INSIDE
HORSEMEN OF DOOM
COLLECT ALL 4
TAXI!

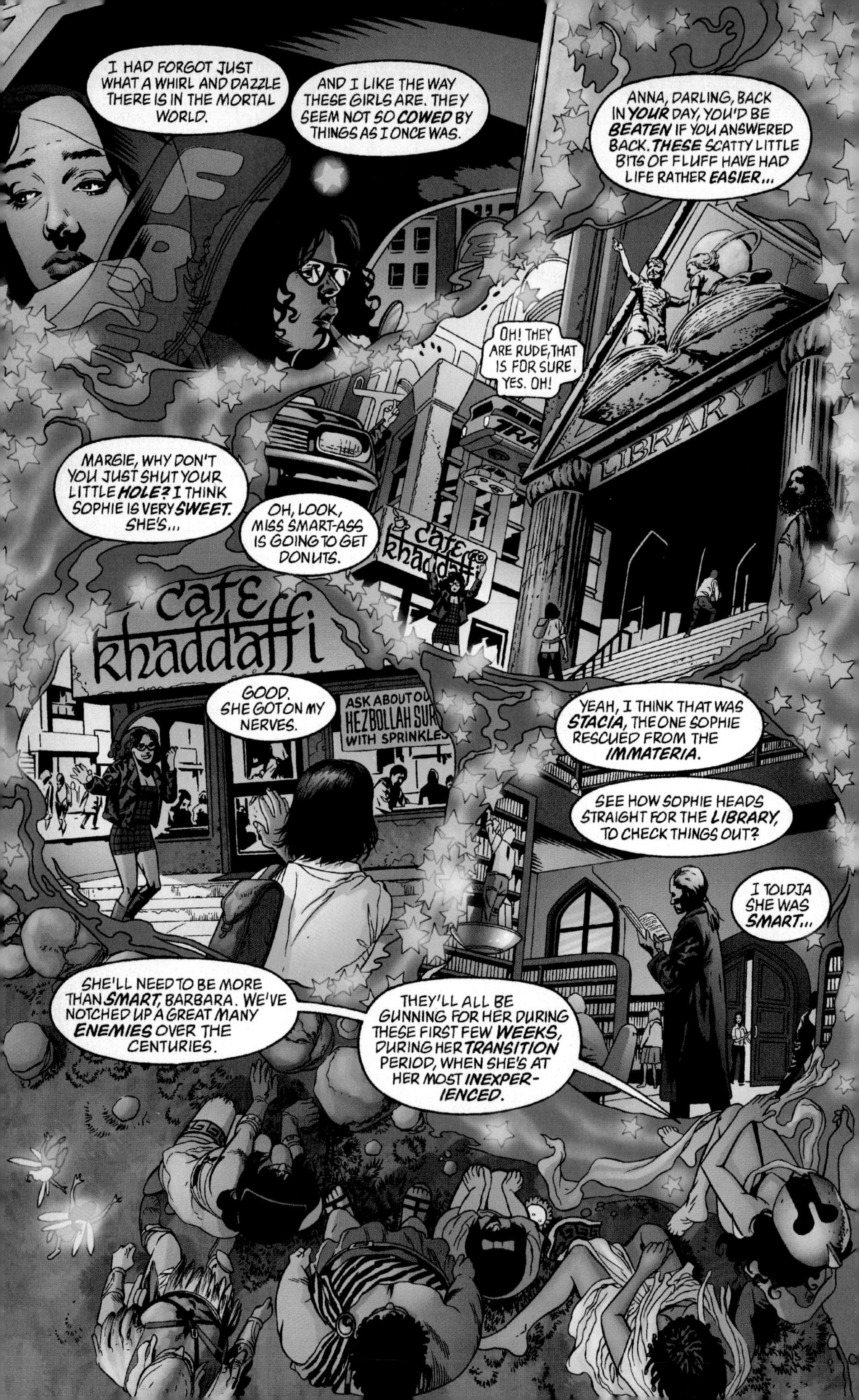
I HAD FORGOT JUST WHAT A WHIRL AND DAZZLE THERE IS IN THE MORTAL WORLD.
AND I LIKE THE WAY THESE GIRLS ARE. THEY SEEM NOT SO COWED BY THINGS AS I ONCE WAS.
ANNA, DARLING, BACK IN YOUR DAY, YOU'D BE BEATEN IF YOU ANSWERED BACK. THESE SCATTY LITTLE BITS OF FLUFF HAVE HAD LIFE RATHER EASIER...
OH! THEY ARE RUDE, THAT IS FOR SURE. YES. OH!
LIBRARY
MARGIE, WHY DON'T YOU JUST SHUT YOUR LITTLE HOLE? I THINK SOPHIE IS VERY SWEET. SHE'S...
OH, LOOK, MISS SMART-ASS IS GOING TO GET DONUTS.
cafe khaddaffi
cafe khaddaffi
GOOD. SHE GOT ON MY NERVES.
ASK ABOUT OU HEZBOLLAH SUR WITH SPRINKLE
YEAH, I THINK THAT WAS STACIA, THE ONE SOPHIE RESCUED FROM THE IMMATERIA.
SEE HOW SOPHIE HEADS STRAIGHT FOR THE LIBRARY, TO CHECK THINGS OUT?
I TOLDJA SHE WAS SMART...
SHE'LL NEED TO BE MORE THAN SMART, BARBARA. WE'VE NOTCHED UP A GREAT MANY ENEMIES OVER THE CENTURIES.
THEY'LL ALL BE GUNNING FOR HER DURING THESE FIRST FEW WEEKS, DURING HER TRANSITION PERIOD, WHEN SHE'S AT HER MOST INEXPERIENCED.

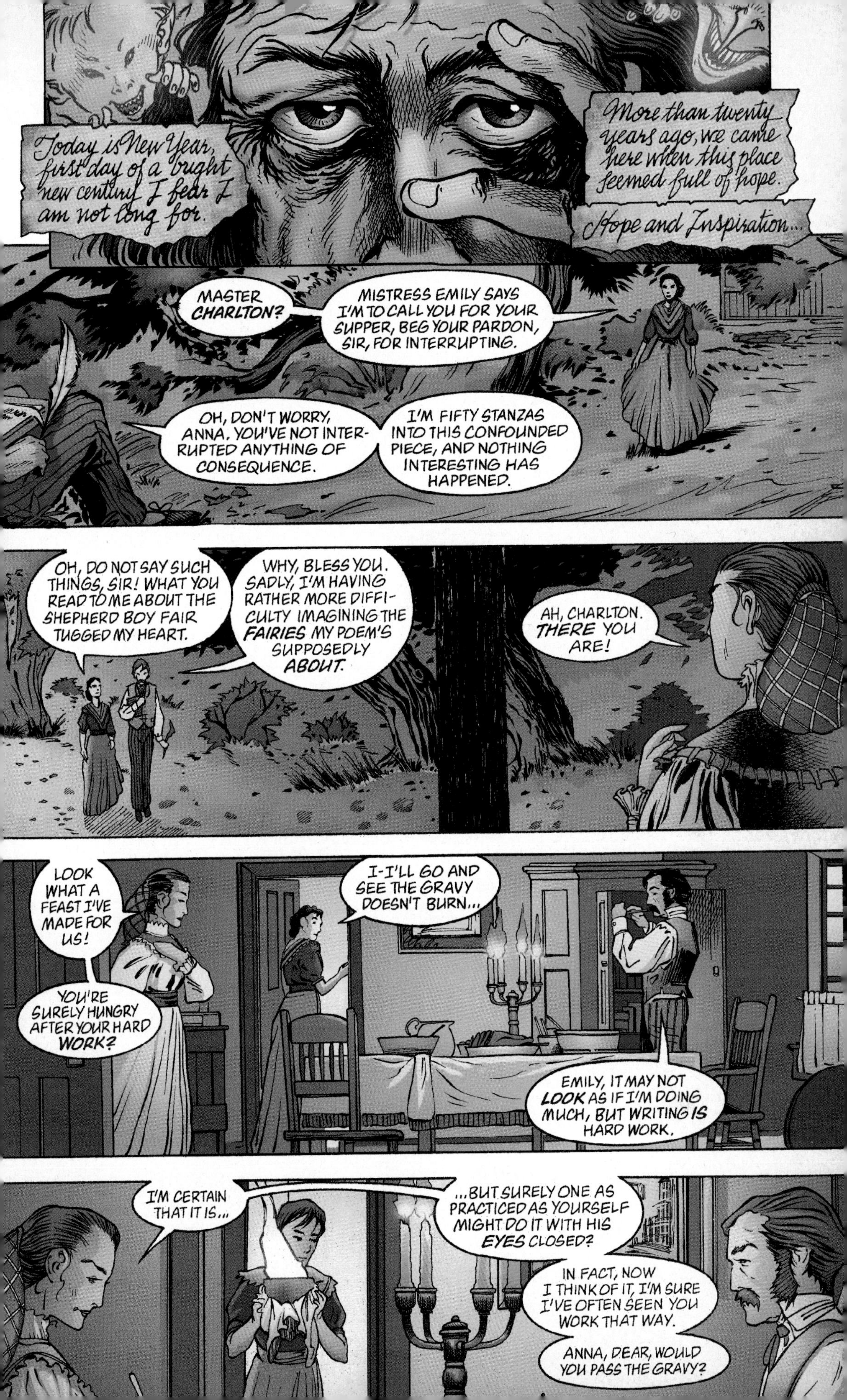

Today is New Year, first day of a bright new century I fear I am not long for.
More than twenty years ago, we came here when this place seemed full of hope.
Hope and Inspiration...
MASTER CHARLTON?
MISTRESS EMILY SAYS I'M TO CALL YOU FOR YOUR SUPPER, BEG YOUR PARDON, SIR, FOR INTERRUPTING.
OH, DON'T WORRY, ANNA. YOU'VE NOT INTERRUPTED ANYTHING OF CONSEQUENCE.
I'M FIFTY STANZAS INTO THIS CONFOUNDED PIECE, AND NOTHING INTERESTING HAS HAPPENED.
OH, DO NOT SAY SUCH THINGS, SIR! WHAT YOU READ TO ME ABOUT THE SHEPHERD BOY FAIR TUGGED MY HEART.
WHY, BLESS YOU. SADLY, I'M HAVING RATHER MORE DIFFICULTY IMAGINING THE FAIRIES MY POEM'S SUPPOSEDLY ABOUT.
AH, CHARLTON. THERE YOU ARE!
LOOK WHAT A FEAST I'VE MADE FOR US!
YOU'RE SURELY HUNGRY AFTER YOUR HARD WORK?
I-I'LL GO AND SEE THE GRAVY DOESN'T BURN...
EMILY, IT MAY NOT LOOK AS IF I'M DOING MUCH, BUT WRITING IS HARD WORK.
I'M CERTAIN THAT IT IS...
...BUT SURELY ONE AS PRACTICED AS YOURSELF MIGHT DO IT WITH HIS EYES CLOSED?
IN FACT, NOW I THINK OF IT, I'M SURE I'VE OFTEN SEEN YOU WORK THAT WAY.
ANNA, DEAR, WOULD YOU PASS THE GRAVY?

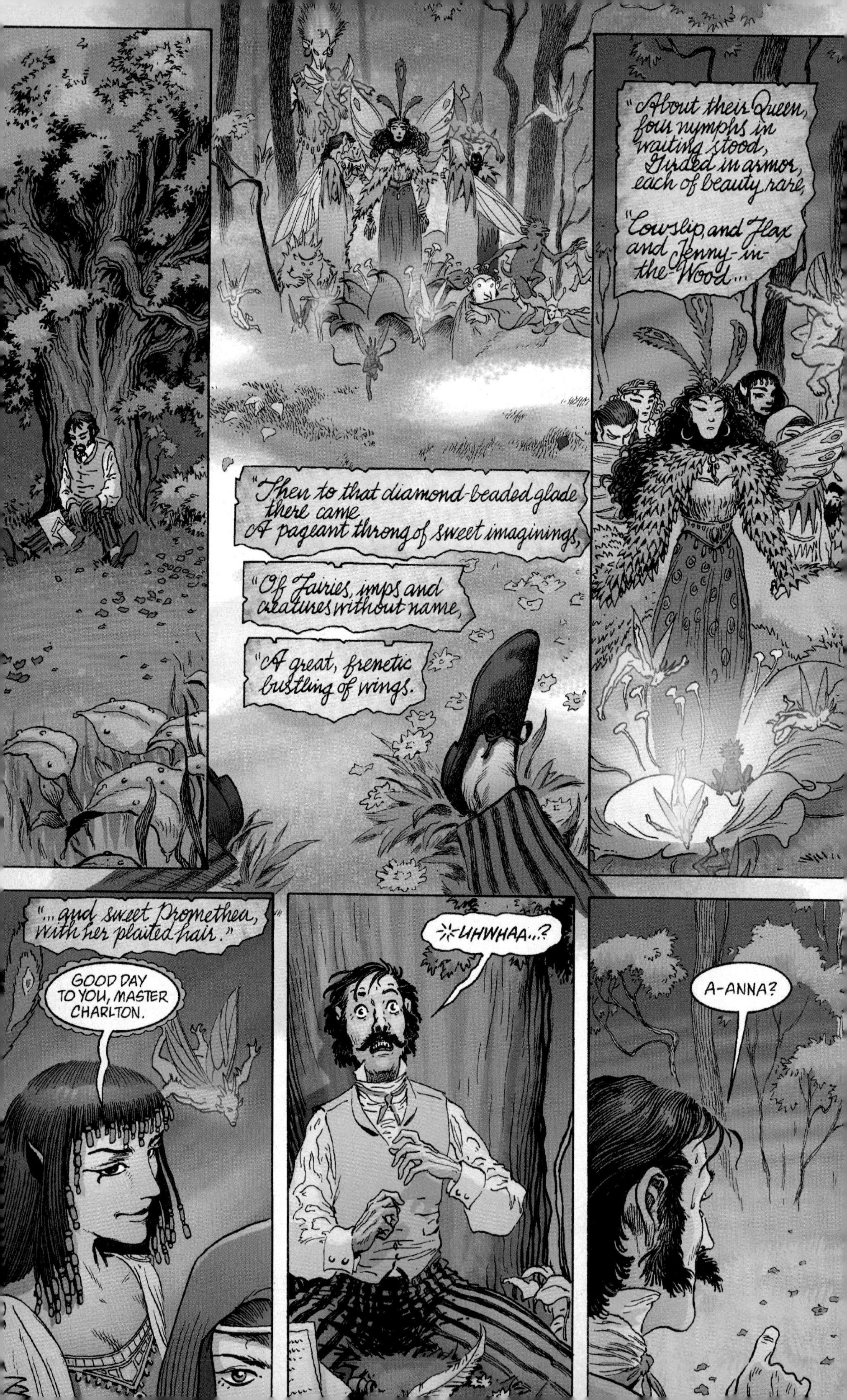
"Then to that diamond-beaded glade there came
A pageant throng of sweet imaginings,
"Of Fairies, imps and creatures without name,
"A great, frenetic bustling of wings.
"About their Queen, four nymphs in waiting stood,
Girded in armor, each of beauty rare,
"Cowslip, and Flax and Jenny-in-the-Wood...
"...and sweet Promethea, with her plaited hair."
GOOD DAY TO YOU, MASTER CHARLTON.
UHWHAA..?
A-ANNA?

June 7th, 1779:

WELL, MASTER CHARLTON, WITH MISS EMILY AWAY TO SEE HER PARENTS IN NEW HAMPSHIRE THIS NEXT WEEK, PERHAPS YOU'LL GET SOME WORK DONE.

ACTUALLY, ANNA, I'VE ALREADY MADE GREAT PROGRESS... AND IT'S THANKS TO YOU.

T-TO ME? WHY, SIR, WHATEVER DO YOU MEAN?

WELL, I'VE PARTLY BASED THE LEADING FAERIE UPON YOU, AFTER THIS SORT OF DAYDREAM THAT I HAD.

HERE, IF YOU LIKE, I'LL READ SOME TO YOU.

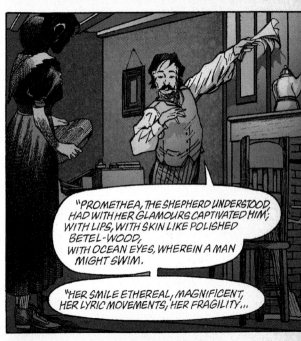

"PROMETHEA, THE SHEPHERD UNDERSTOOD, HAD WITH HER GLAMOURS CAPTIVATED HIM; WITH LIPS, WITH SKIN LIKE POLISHED BETEL-WOOD, WITH OCEAN EYES, WHEREIN A MAN MIGHT SWIM.

"HER SMILE ETHEREAL, MAGNIFICENT, HER LYRIC MOVEMENTS; HER FRAGILITY...

"HER GENTLENESS, HER ORCHIDACEOUS SCENT ENRAPTURED HIM, ENSLAVED HIM UTTERLY.

"PHANTASMAGORIA, MADE SOMEHOW REAL, YET DELICATE, PERHAPS TO DISAPPEAR AT HIS IMPETUOUS TOUCH, HIS NEED TO FEEL HER SUMMER-JASMINE BREATH CLOSE TO HIS EAR."

CHARLTON...

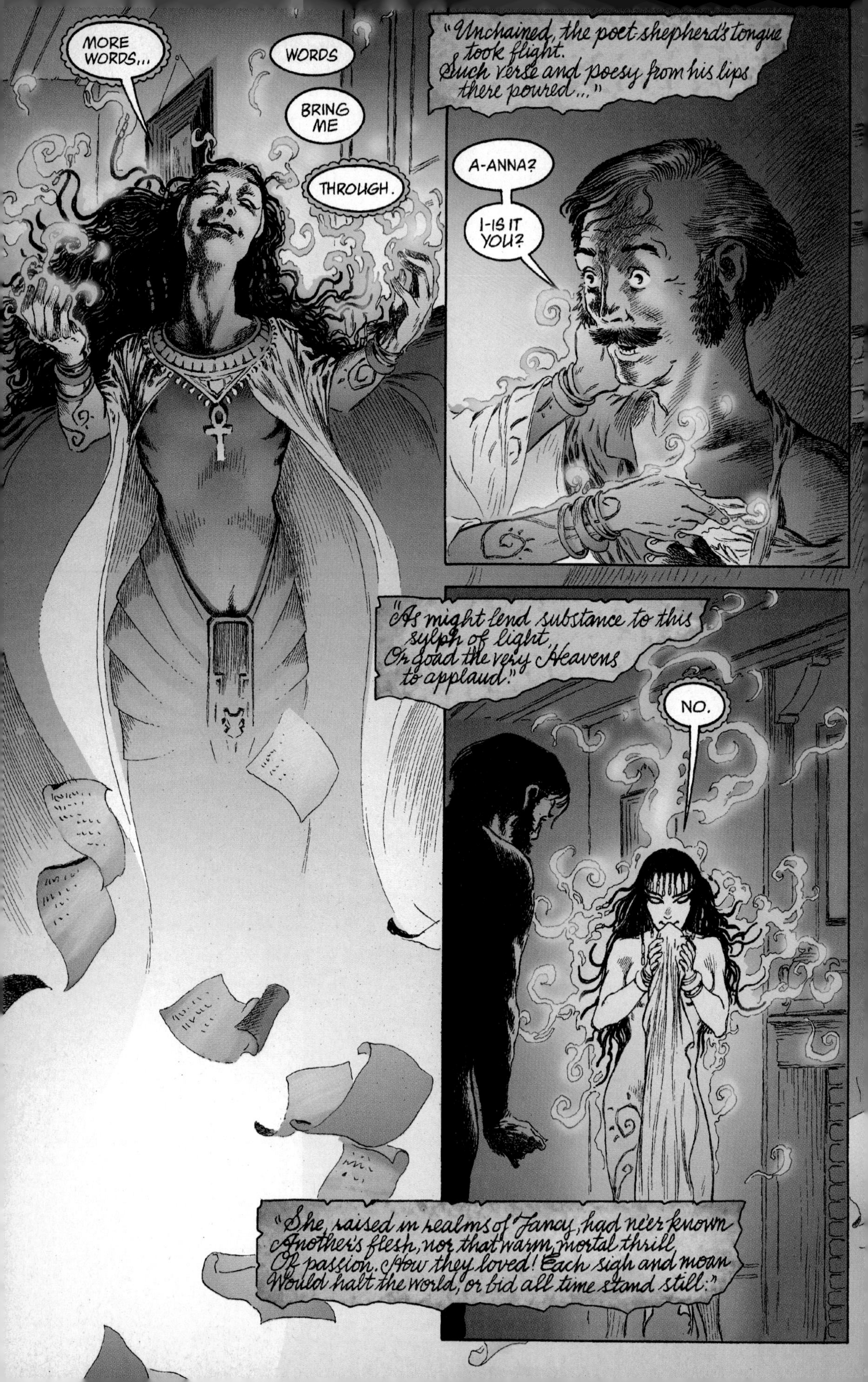
MORE WORDS...
WORDS
BRING ME
THROUGH.
"Unchained, the poet-shepherd's tongue took flight.
Such verse and poesy from his lips there poured..."
A-ANNA?
I-IS IT YOU?
"As might lend substance to this sylph of light,
Or goad the very Heavens to applaud."
NO.
"She, raised in realms of Fancy, had ne'er known
Another's flesh, nor that warm mortal thrill
Of passion. How they loved! Each sigh and moan
Would halt the world, or bid all time stand still."

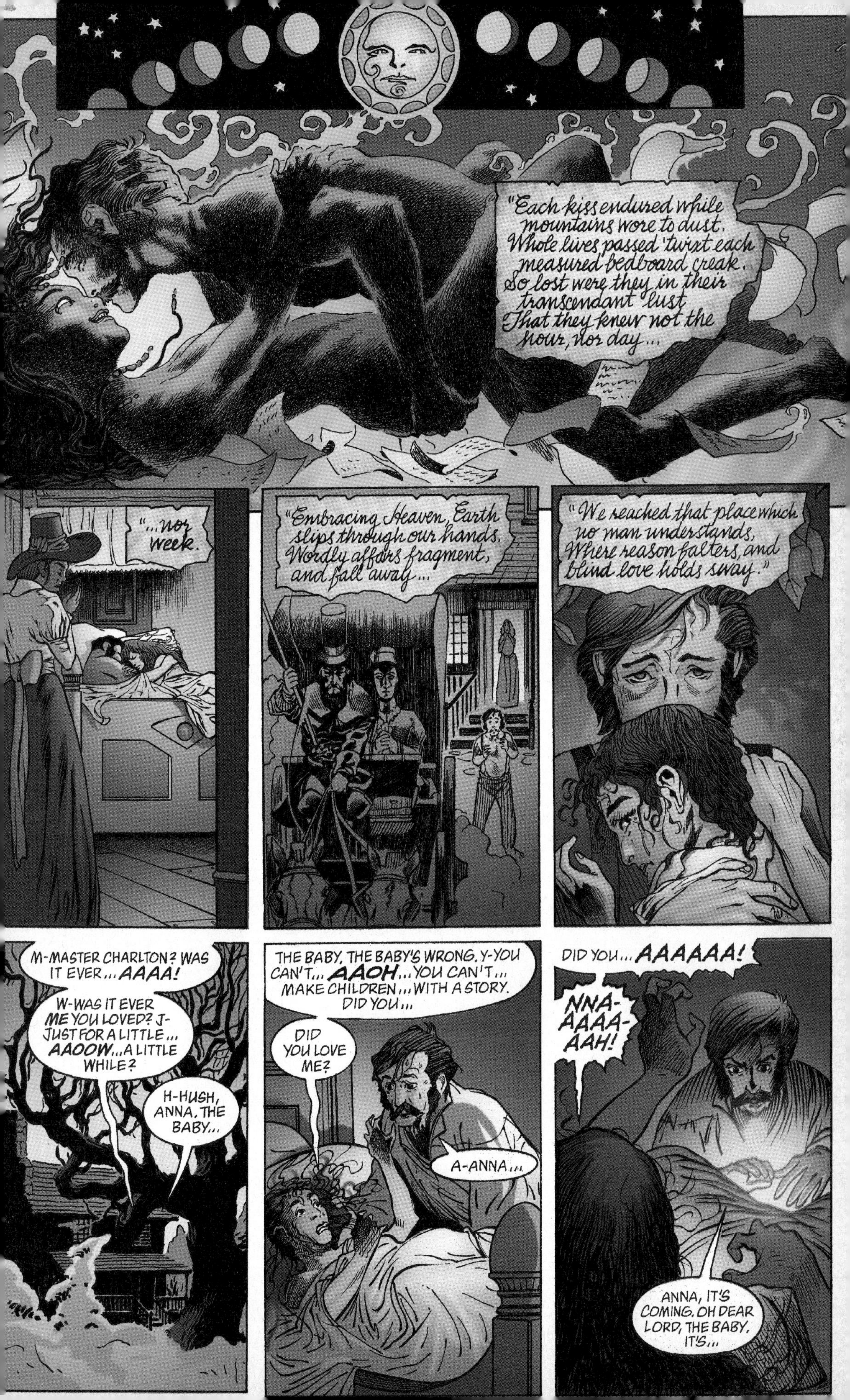
"Each kiss endured while mountains wore to dust. Whole lives passed 'twixt each measured bedboard creak. So lost were they in their transcendant lust That they knew not the hour, nor day...
"...nor week.
"Embracing Heaven, Earth slips through our hands. Wordly affairs fragment, and fall away...
"We reached that place which no man understands, Where reason falters, and blind love holds sway."
M-MASTER CHARLTON? WAS IT EVER... AAAA!
W-WAS IT EVER ME YOU LOVED? J-JUST FOR A LITTLE... AAOOW... A LITTLE WHILE?
H-HUSH, ANNA. THE BABY...
THE BABY. THE BABY'S WRONG. Y-YOU CAN'T... AAOH... YOU CAN'T... MAKE CHILDREN... WITH A STORY. DID YOU...
DID YOU LOVE ME?
A-ANNA...
DID YOU... AAAAAA!
NNA-AAAA-AAH!
ANNA, IT'S COMING. OH DEAR LORD, THE BABY. IT'S...

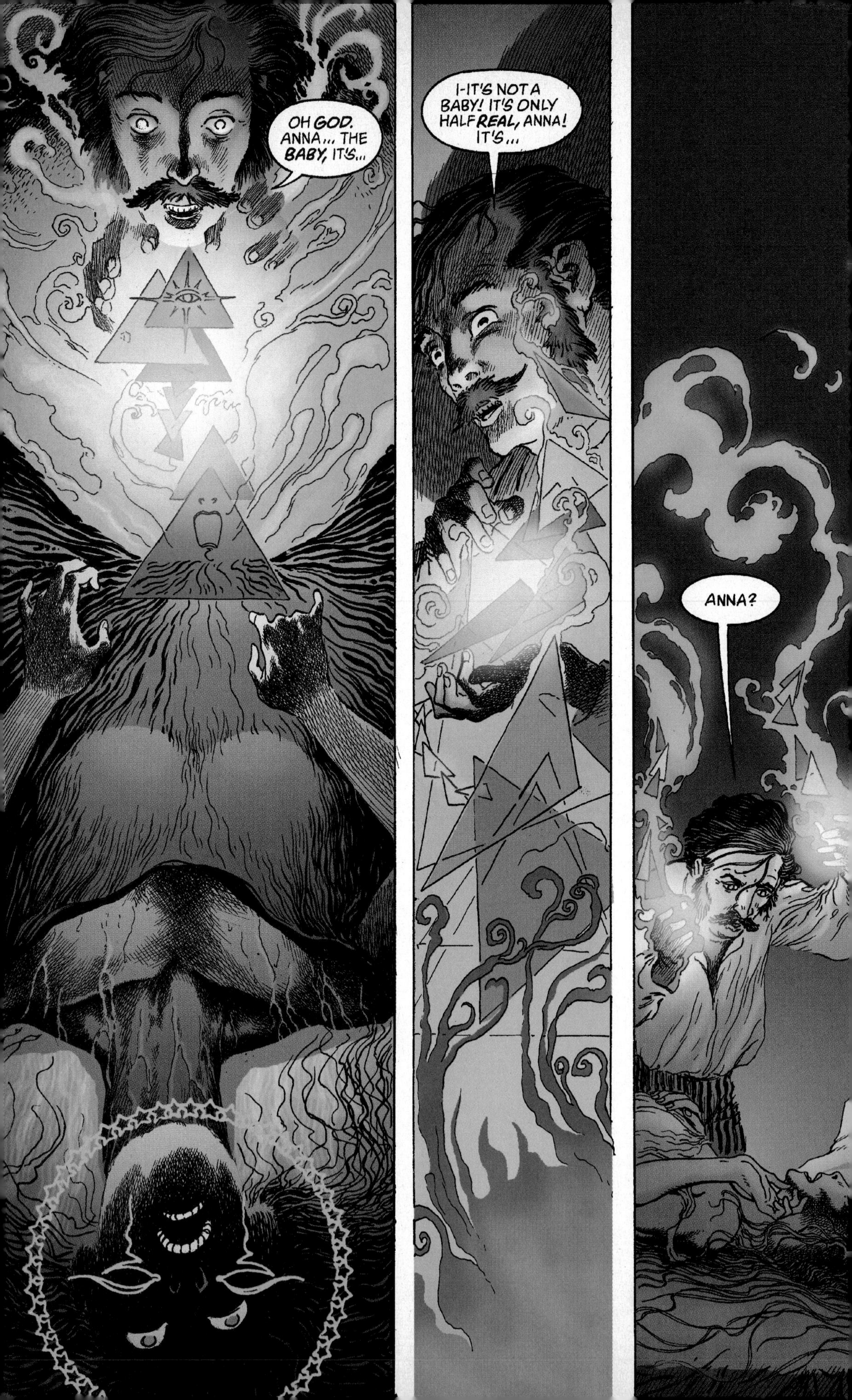
OH GOD. ANNA... THE BABY, IT'S...
I-IT'S NOT A BABY! IT'S ONLY HALF REAL, ANNA! IT'S...
ANNA?

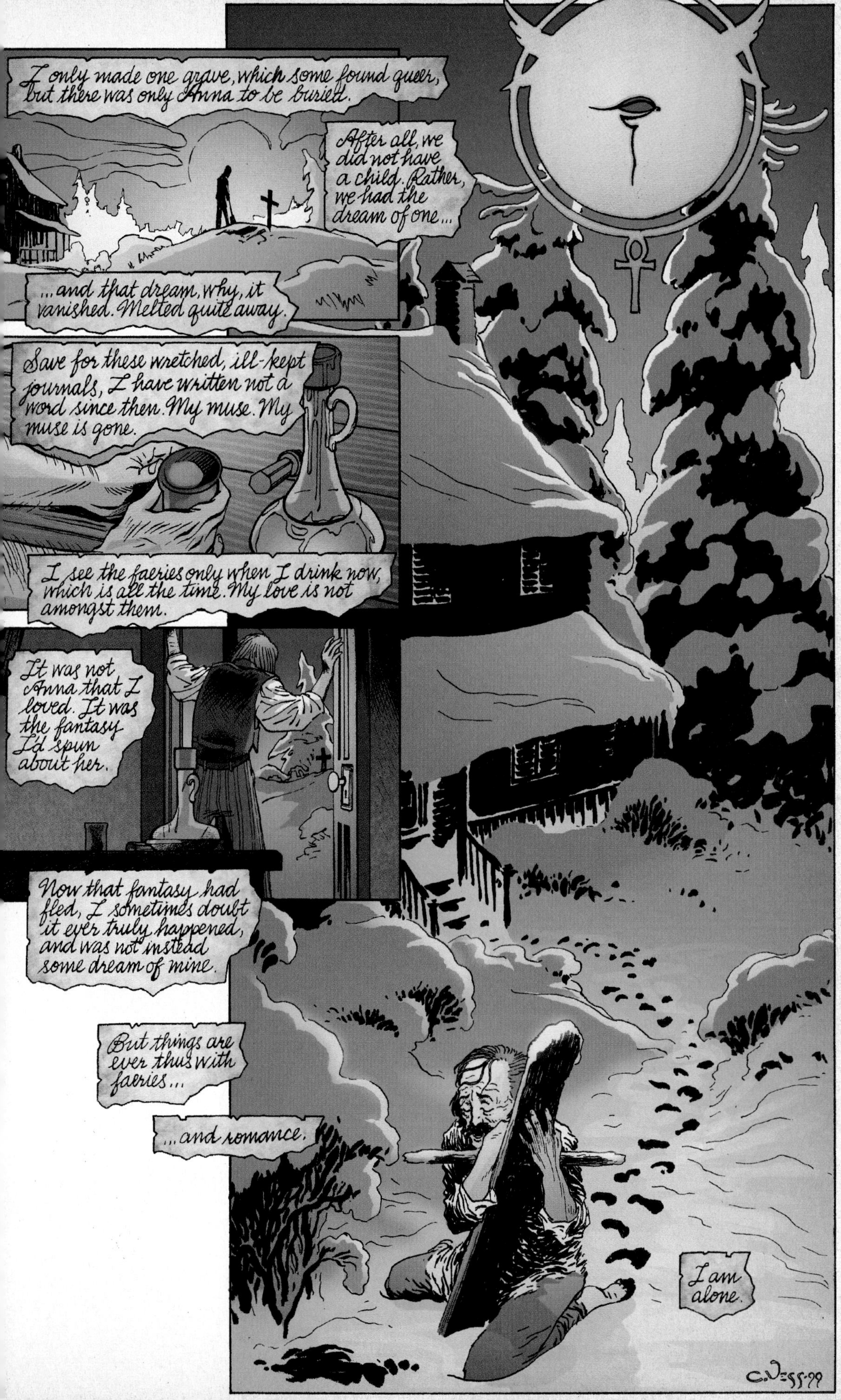

I only made one grave, which some found queer, but there was only Anna to be buried.
After all, we did not have a child. Rather, we had the dream of one...
...and that dream, why, it vanished. Melted quite away.
Save for these wretched, ill-kept journals, I have written not a word since then. My muse. My muse is gone.
I see the faeries only when I drink now, which is all the time. My love is not amongst them.
It was not Anna that I loved. It was the fantasy I'd spun about her.
Now that fantasy had fled, I sometimes doubt it ever truly happened, and was not instead some dream of mine.
But things are ever thus with faeries...
...and romance.
I am alone.
C. Vess '99

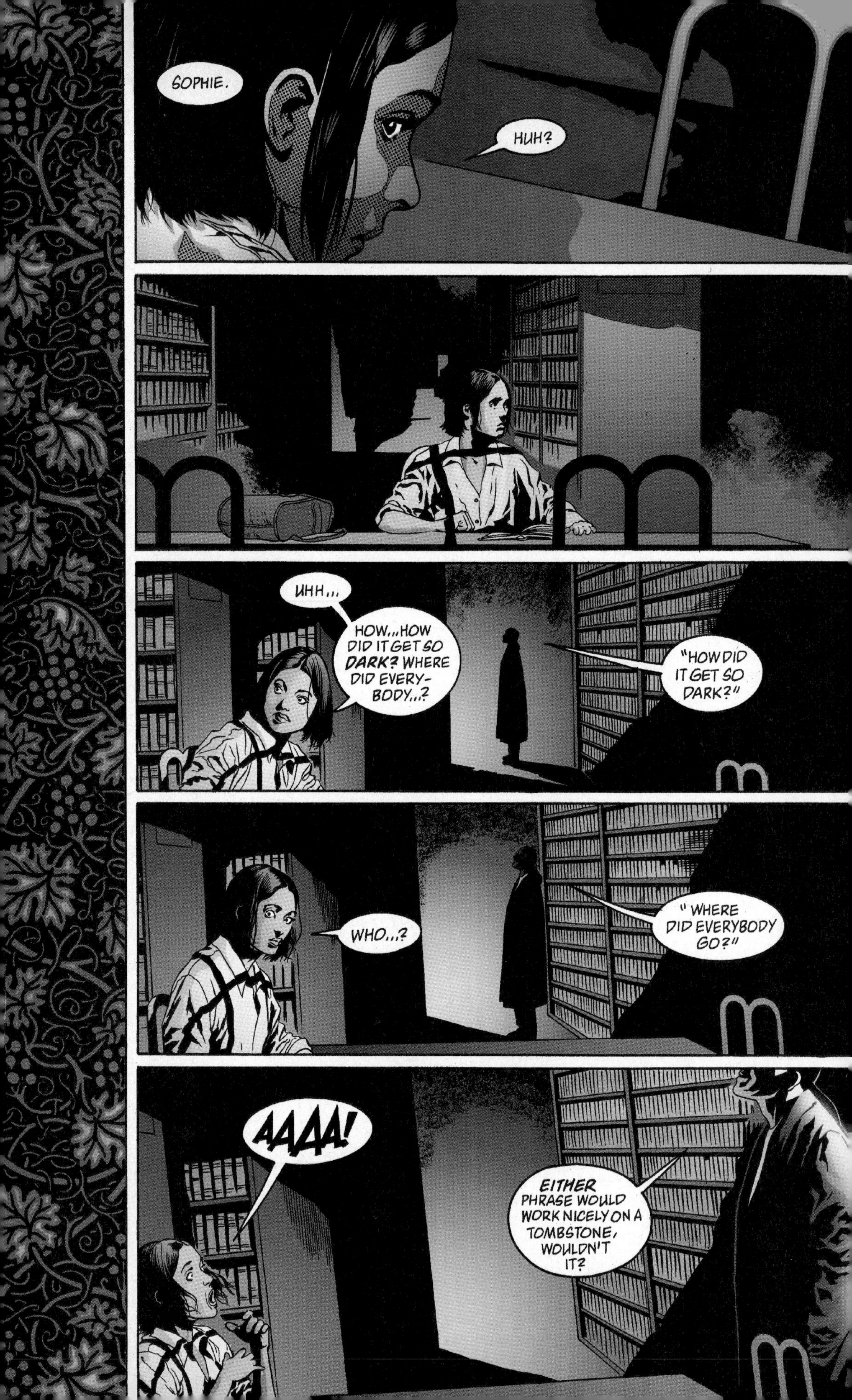
SOPHIE.
HUH?
UHH...
HOW...HOW DID IT GET SO DARK? WHERE DID EVERY-BODY...?
"HOW DID IT GET SO DARK?"
WHO...?
"WHERE DID EVERYBODY GO?"
AAAA!
EITHER PHRASE WOULD WORK NICELY ON A TOMBSTONE, WOULDN'T IT?

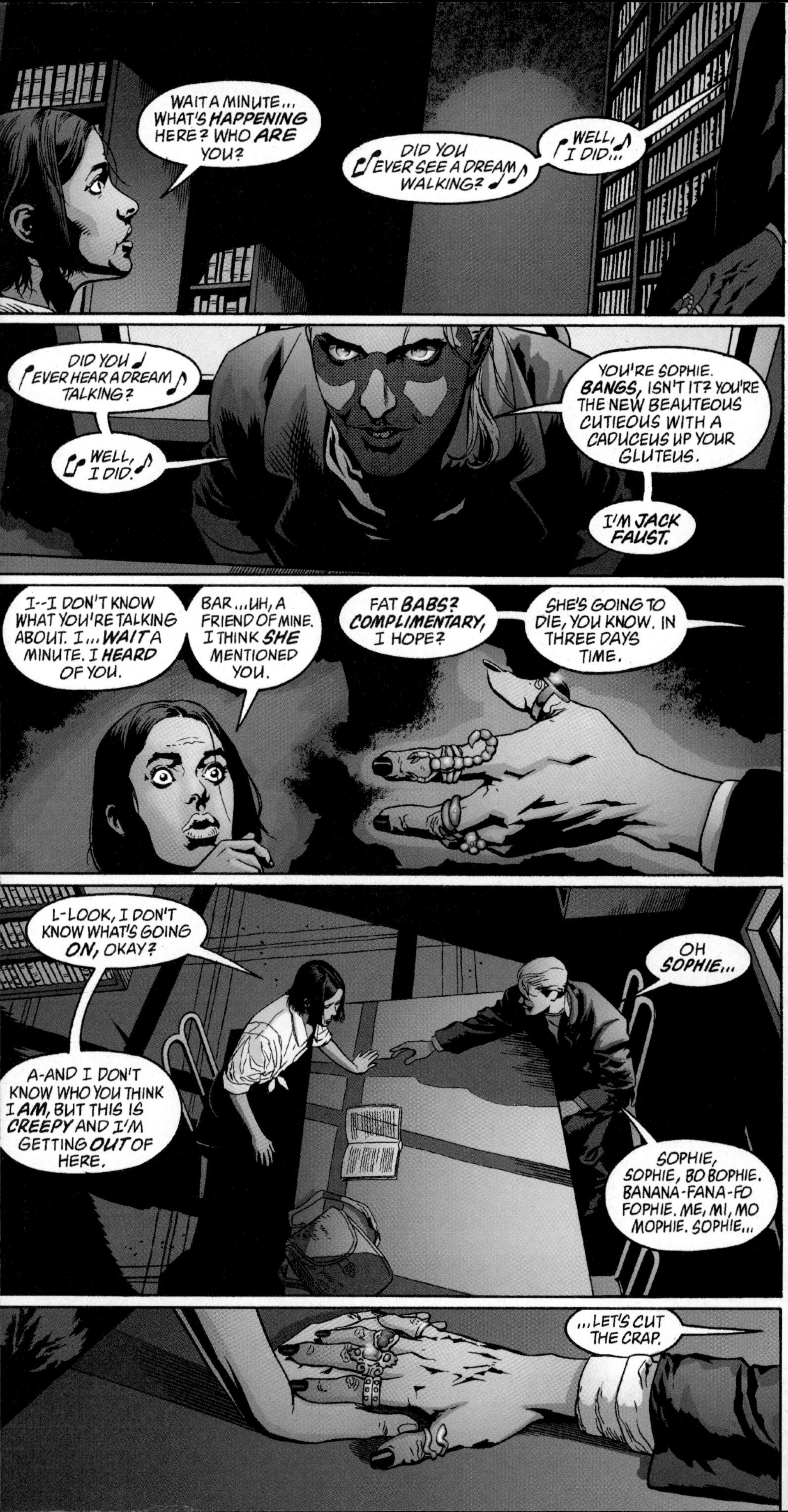
WAIT A MINUTE... WHAT'S HAPPENING HERE? WHO ARE YOU?
DID YOU EVER SEE A DREAM WALKING?
WELL, I DID...
DID YOU EVER HEAR A DREAM TALKING?
WELL, I DID.
YOU'RE SOPHIE. BANGS, ISN'T IT? YOU'RE THE NEW BEAUTEOUS CUTIEOUS WITH A CADUCEUS UP YOUR GLUTEUS.
I'M JACK FAUST.
I--I DON'T KNOW WHAT YOU'RE TALKING ABOUT. I... WAIT A MINUTE. I HEARD OF YOU.
BAR...UH, A FRIEND OF MINE. I THINK SHE MENTIONED YOU.
FAT BABS? COMPLIMENTARY, I HOPE?
SHE'S GOING TO DIE, YOU KNOW. IN THREE DAYS TIME.
L-LOOK, I DON'T KNOW WHAT'S GOING ON, OKAY?
A-AND I DON'T KNOW WHO YOU THINK I AM, BUT THIS IS CREEPY AND I'M GETTING OUT OF HERE.
OH SOPHIE...
SOPHIE, SOPHIE, BO BOPHIE. BANANA-FANA-FO FOPHIE. ME, MI, MO MOPHIE. SOPHIE...
...LET'S CUT THE CRAP.

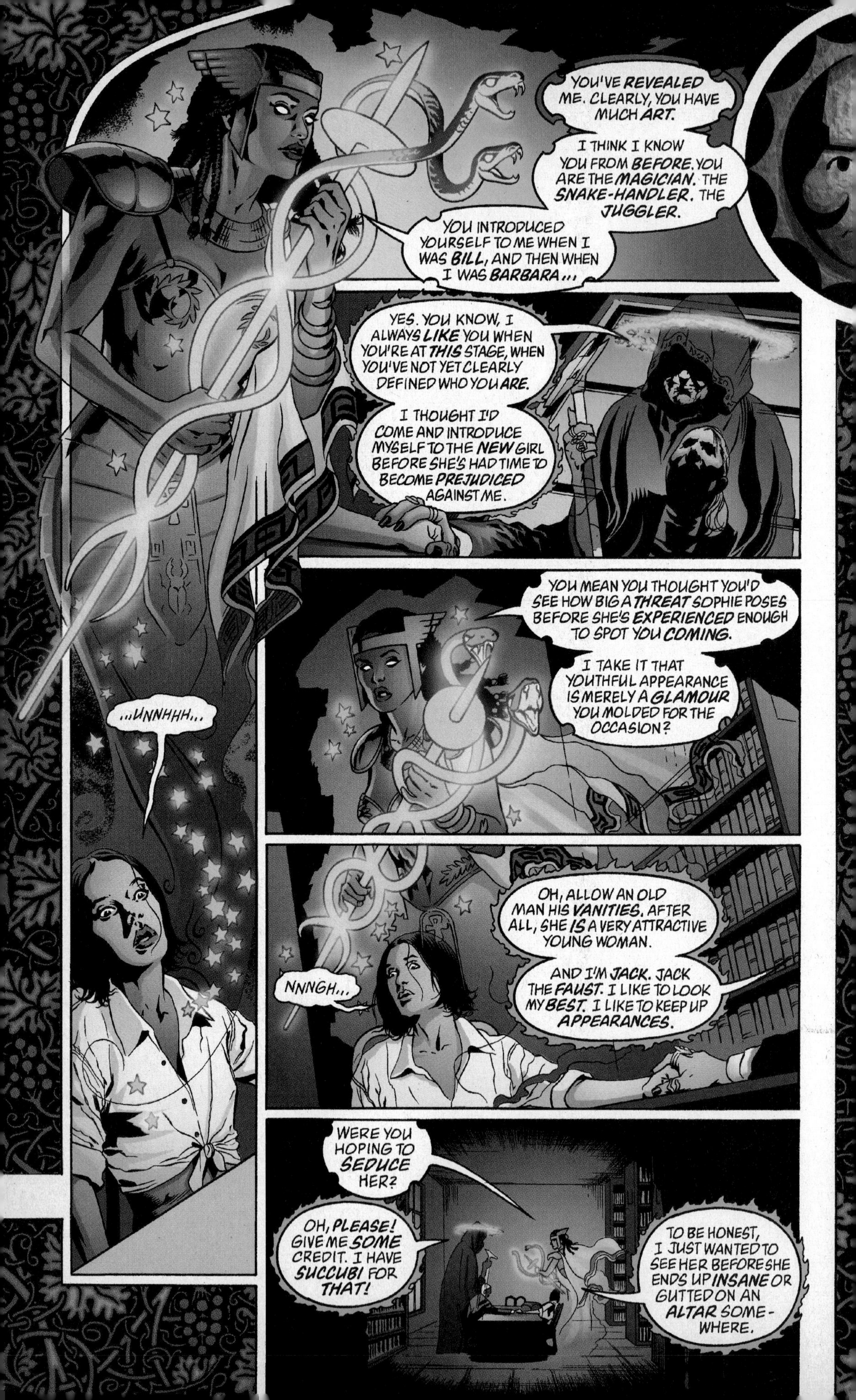

YOU'VE REVEALED ME. CLEARLY, YOU HAVE MUCH ART.
I THINK I KNOW YOU FROM BEFORE. YOU ARE THE MAGICIAN. THE SNAKE-HANDLER. THE JUGGLER.
YOU INTRODUCED YOURSELF TO ME WHEN I WAS BILL, AND THEN WHEN I WAS BARBARA...
YES. YOU KNOW, I ALWAYS LIKE YOU WHEN YOU'RE AT THIS STAGE, WHEN YOU'VE NOT YET CLEARLY DEFINED WHO YOU ARE.
I THOUGHT I'D COME AND INTRODUCE MYSELF TO THE NEW GIRL BEFORE SHE'S HAD TIME TO BECOME PREJUDICED AGAINST ME.
...UNNHHH...
YOU MEAN YOU THOUGHT YOU'D SEE HOW BIG A THREAT SOPHIE POSES BEFORE SHE'S EXPERIENCED ENOUGH TO SPOT YOU COMING.
I TAKE IT THAT YOUTHFUL APPEARANCE IS MERELY A GLAMOUR YOU MOLDED FOR THE OCCASION?
OH, ALLOW AN OLD MAN HIS VANITIES. AFTER ALL, SHE IS A VERY ATTRACTIVE YOUNG WOMAN.
AND I'M JACK. JACK THE FAUST. I LIKE TO LOOK MY BEST. I LIKE TO KEEP UP APPEARANCES.
NNNGH...
WERE YOU HOPING TO SEDUCE HER?
OH, PLEASE! GIVE ME SOME CREDIT. I HAVE SUCCUBI FOR THAT!
TO BE HONEST, I JUST WANTED TO SEE HER BEFORE SHE ENDS UP INSANE OR GUTTED ON AN ALTAR SOME-WHERE.

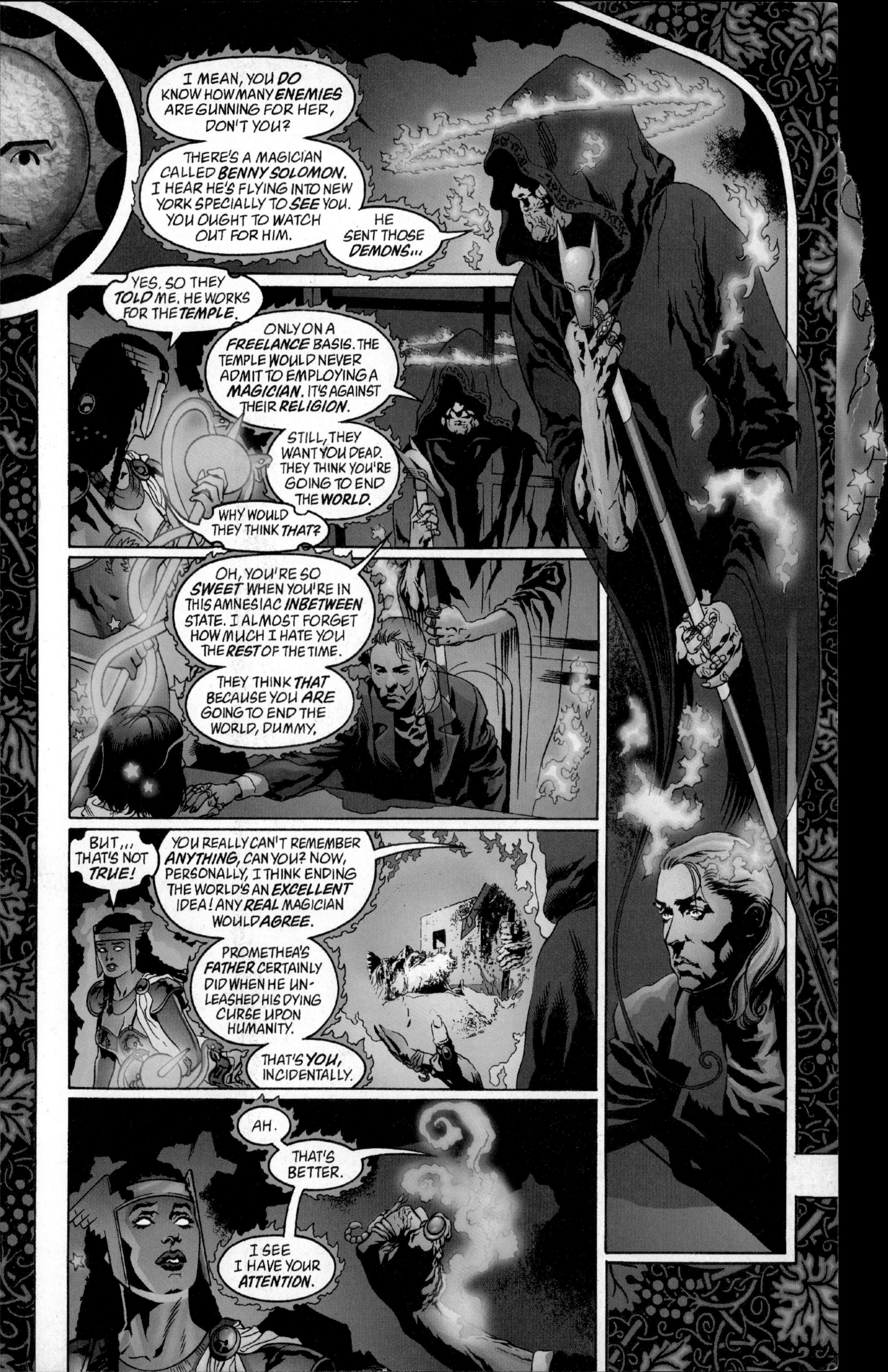
I MEAN, YOU DO KNOW HOW MANY ENEMIES ARE GUNNING FOR HER, DON'T YOU?
THERE'S A MAGICIAN CALLED BENNY SOLOMON. I HEAR HE'S FLYING INTO NEW YORK SPECIALLY TO SEE YOU. YOU OUGHT TO WATCH OUT FOR HIM.
HE SENT THOSE DEMONS...
YES, SO THEY TOLD ME. HE WORKS FOR THE TEMPLE.
ONLY ON A FREELANCE BASIS. THE TEMPLE WOULD NEVER ADMIT TO EMPLOYING A MAGICIAN. IT'S AGAINST THEIR RELIGION.
STILL, THEY WANT YOU DEAD. THEY THINK YOU'RE GOING TO END THE WORLD.
WHY WOULD THEY THINK THAT?
OH, YOU'RE SO SWEET WHEN YOU'RE IN THIS AMNESIAC INBETWEEN STATE. I ALMOST FORGET HOW MUCH I HATE YOU THE REST OF THE TIME.
THEY THINK THAT BECAUSE YOU ARE GOING TO END THE WORLD, DUMMY.
BUT... THAT'S NOT TRUE!
YOU REALLY CAN'T REMEMBER ANYTHING, CAN YOU? NOW, PERSONALLY, I THINK ENDING THE WORLD'S AN EXCELLENT IDEA! ANY REAL MAGICIAN WOULD AGREE.
PROMETHEA'S FATHER CERTAINLY DID WHEN HE UNLEASHED HIS DYING CURSE UPON HUMANITY.
THAT'S YOU, INCIDENTALLY.
AH.
THAT'S BETTER.
I SEE I HAVE YOUR ATTENTION.

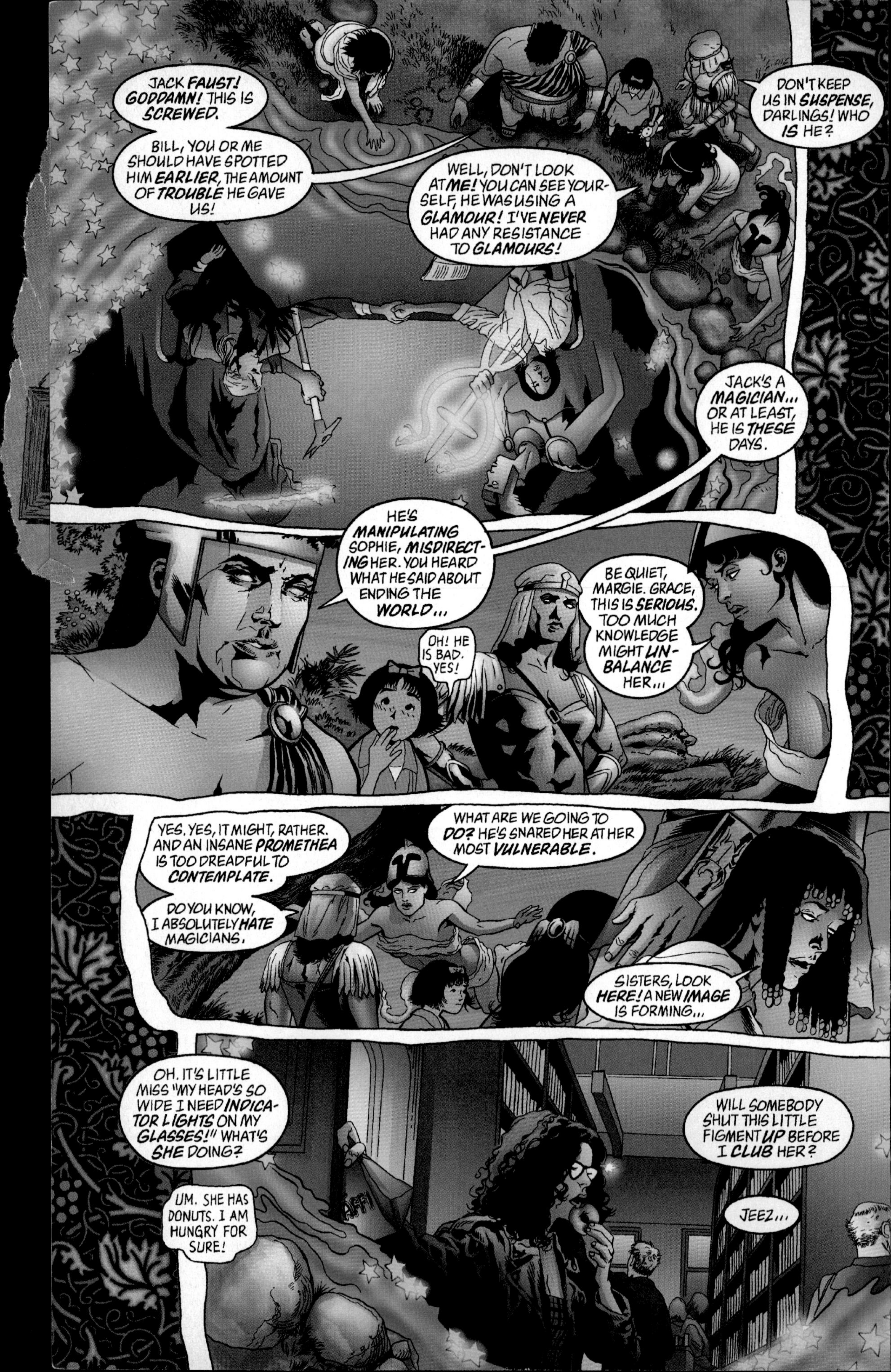
JACK FAUST! GODDAMN! THIS IS SCREWED.
BILL, YOU OR ME SHOULD HAVE SPOTTED HIM EARLIER, THE AMOUNT OF TROUBLE HE GAVE US!
WELL, DON'T LOOK AT ME! YOU CAN SEE YOURSELF, HE WAS USING A GLAMOUR! I'VE NEVER HAD ANY RESISTANCE TO GLAMOURS!
DON'T KEEP US IN SUSPENSE, DARLINGS! WHO IS HE?
JACK'S A MAGICIAN... OR AT LEAST, HE IS THESE DAYS.
HE'S MANIPULATING SOPHIE, MISDIRECTING HER. YOU HEARD WHAT HE SAID ABOUT ENDING THE WORLD...
OH! HE IS BAD. YES!
BE QUIET, MARGIE. GRACE, THIS IS SERIOUS. TOO MUCH KNOWLEDGE MIGHT UNBALANCE HER...
YES. YES, IT MIGHT, RATHER. AND AN INSANE PROMETHEA IS TOO DREADFUL TO CONTEMPLATE.
DO YOU KNOW, I ABSOLUTELY HATE MAGICIANS.
WHAT ARE WE GOING TO DO? HE'S SNARED HER AT HER MOST VULNERABLE.
SISTERS, LOOK HERE! A NEW IMAGE IS FORMING...
OH. IT'S LITTLE MISS "MY HEAD'S SO WIDE I NEED INDICATOR LIGHTS ON MY GLASSES!" WHAT'S SHE DOING?
UM. SHE HAS DONUTS. I AM HUNGRY FOR SURE!
WILL SOMEBODY SHUT THIS LITTLE FIGMENT UP BEFORE I CLUB HER?
JEEZ...

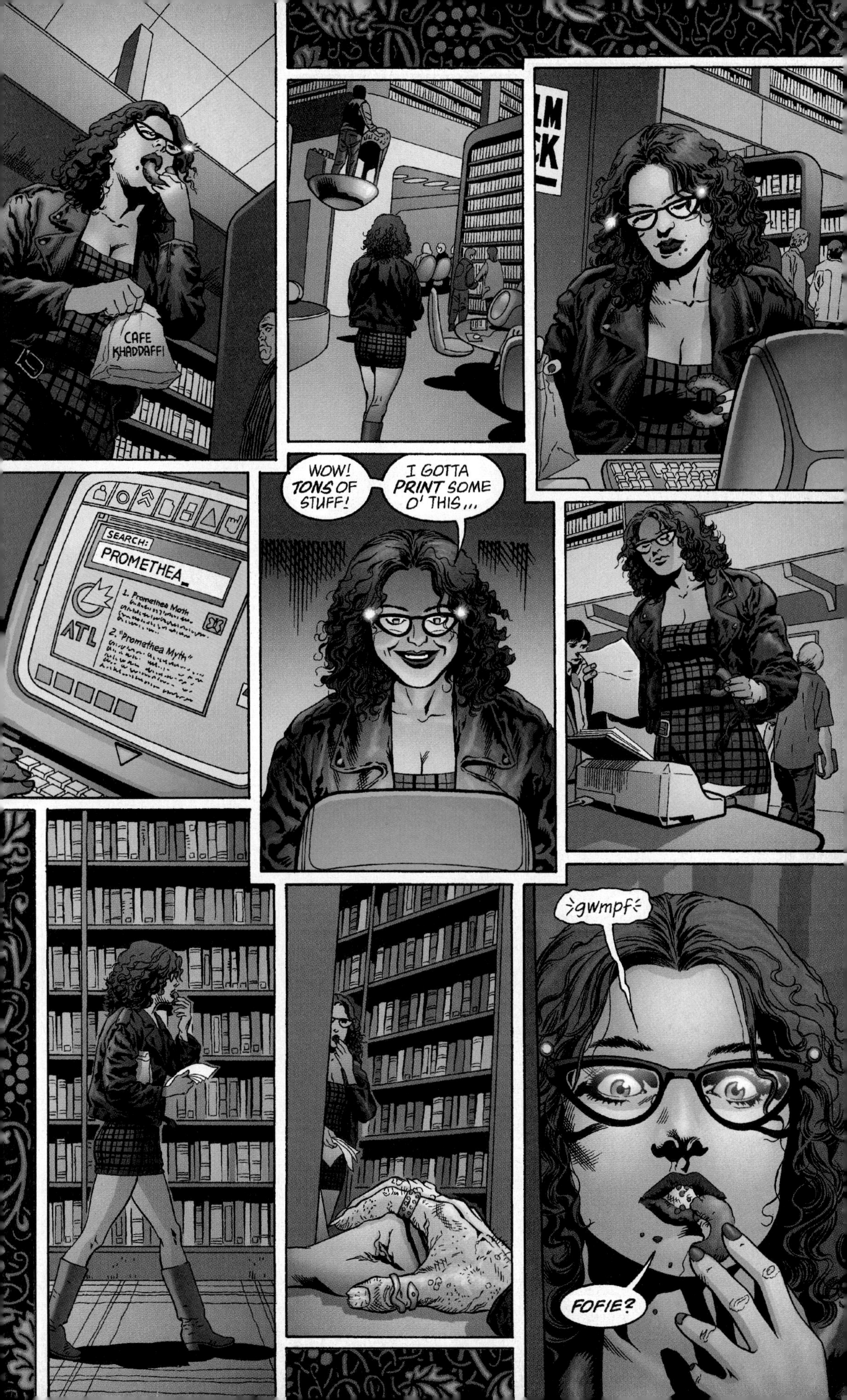
CAFE KHADDAFFI
SEARCH:
PROMETHEA_
1. Promethea Myth
ATL
2. "Promethea Myth"
WOW! TONS OF STUFF!
I GOTTA PRINT SOME O' THIS...
gwmpf
FOFIE?

OH, FOR SET'S SAKE...

UHHH...

WHAT?

WHAT... WHAT DID YOU DO? WH-WHAT HAPPENED TO THE *OTHER* GUY...?

HE WAS A *GLAMOUR*, YOU VACUOUS LITTLE *BIMBO*.

THIS WHOLE THING WAS A WASTE OF MY *TIME*. I HOPE BENNY SOLOMON'S BOYS CUT YOU TO *PIECES!*

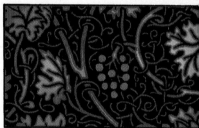

WELL, *HE* SUCKED.

GOD, WHEN I WALKED IN, HE WAS, LIKE, TOTALLY HAVING *SEX* WITH YOU!

HE WAS *NOT*. HE WAS JUST TOUCHING MY *HAND*. I-IT WAS SOME KIND OF *MIND* THING HE WAS DOING.

H-HE SAID A *LOT* OF STUFF, AND IT WAS ALL SORT OF *SCARY* AND *UPSETTING*.

EVERYTHING WAS *DARK*, LIKE THE LIBRARY WAS *DESERTED*...

AW, HE WAS JUST SOME MANIAC *WINO*.

HEY, LOOK WHAT *I* GOT!

THERE'S ALL KIND OF STUFF ABOUT *PROMETHEA* THAT I FOUND ON THE *NET*.

THERE'S THIS FRENCH *LESBIAN* WRITER DID THIS THING, "THE BOOK OF PROMETHEA," AND THERE'S THIS *BLACK METAL* BAND CALLED *HECATE ENTHRONED*...

STACIA...

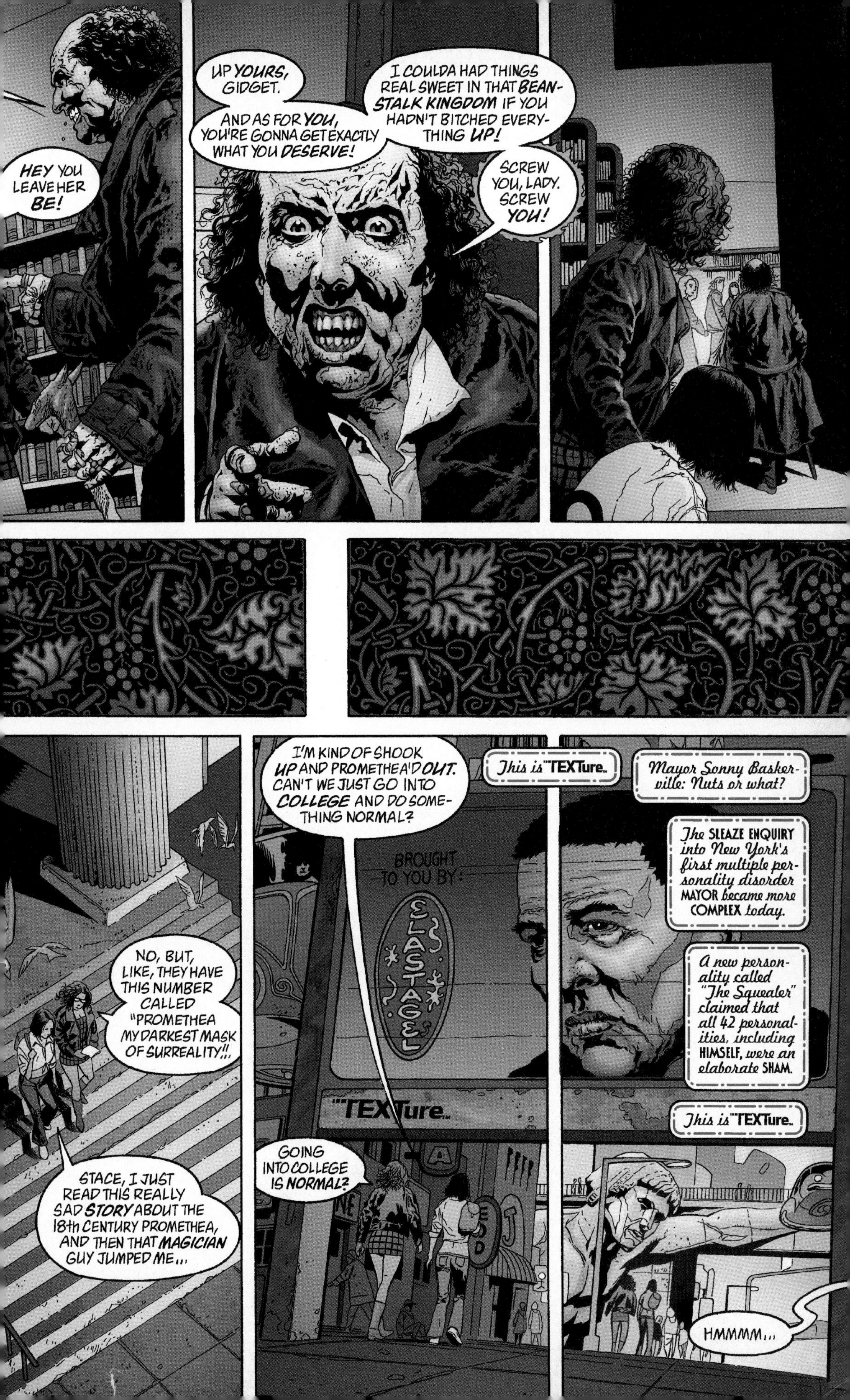
HEY YOU LEAVE HER BE!
UP YOURS, GIDGET.
AND AS FOR YOU, YOU'RE GONNA GET EXACTLY WHAT YOU DESERVE!
I COULDA HAD THINGS REAL SWEET IN THAT BEAN-STALK KINGDOM IF YOU HADN'T BITCHED EVERY-THING UP!
SCREW YOU, LADY. SCREW YOU!
NO, BUT, LIKE, THEY HAVE THIS NUMBER CALLED "PROMETHEA MY DARKEST MASK OF SURREALITY"!...
STACE, I JUST READ THIS REALLY SAD STORY ABOUT THE 18th CENTURY PROMETHEA, AND THEN THAT MAGICIAN GUY JUMPED ME...
I'M KIND OF SHOOK UP AND PROMETHEA'D OUT. CAN'T WE JUST GO INTO COLLEGE AND DO SOME-THING NORMAL?
BROUGHT TO YOU BY:
ELASTAGEL
TEXTure
GOING INTO COLLEGE IS NORMAL?
This is TEXTure
Mayor Sonny Basker-ville: Nuts or what?
The SLEAZE ENQUIRY into New York's first multiple per-sonality disorder MAYOR became more COMPLEX today.
A new person-ality called "The Squealer" claimed that all 42 personal-ities, including HIMSELF, were an elaborate SHAM.
This is TEXTure
HMMMM...

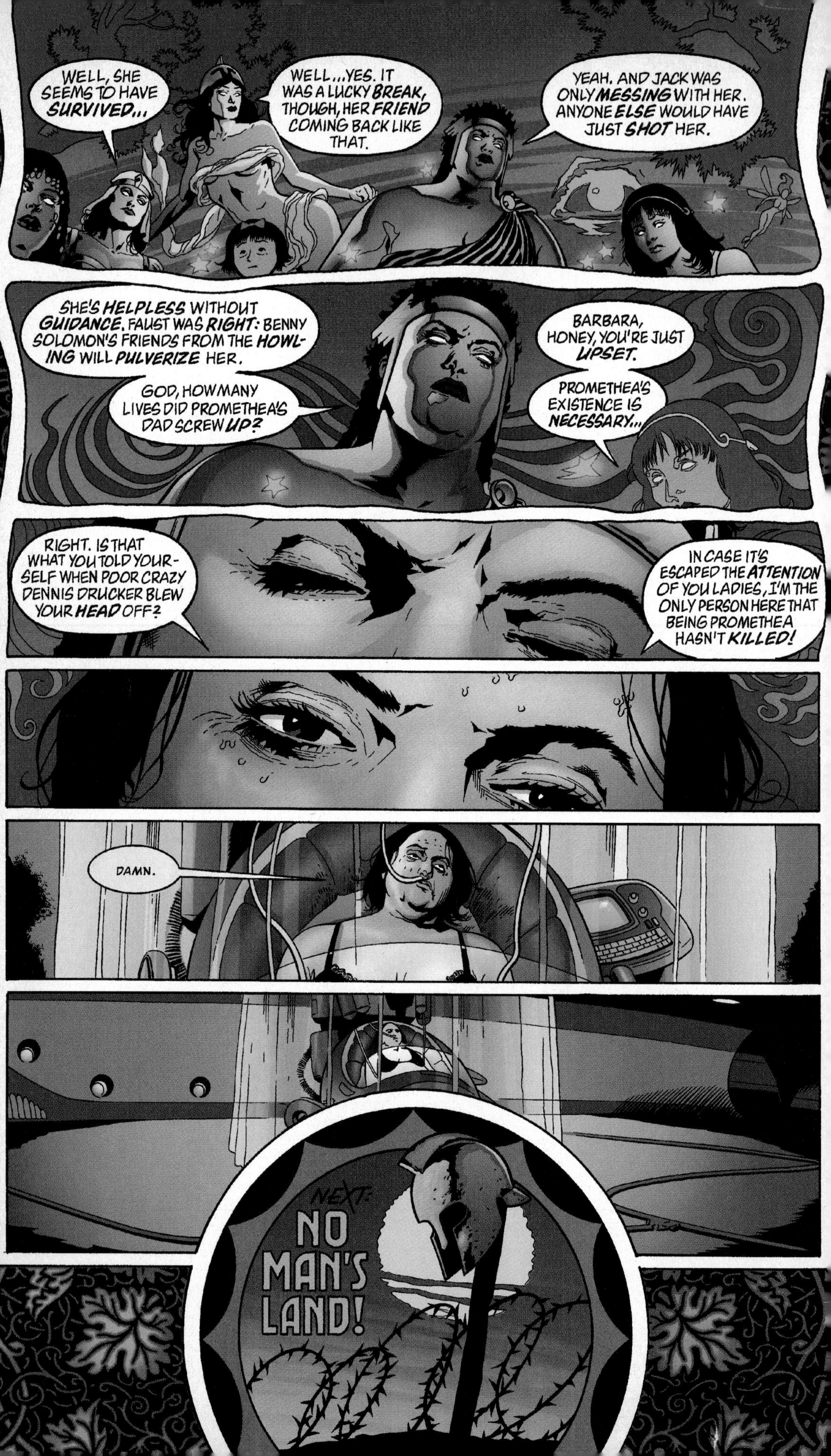
WELL, SHE SEEMS TO HAVE SURVIVED...
WELL...YES. IT WAS A LUCKY BREAK, THOUGH, HER FRIEND COMING BACK LIKE THAT.
YEAH. AND JACK WAS ONLY MESSING WITH HER. ANYONE ELSE WOULD HAVE JUST SHOT HER.
SHE'S HELPLESS WITHOUT GUIDANCE. FAUST WAS RIGHT: BENNY SOLOMON'S FRIENDS FROM THE HOWLING WILL PULVERIZE HER.
GOD, HOW MANY LIVES DID PROMETHEA'S DAD SCREW UP?
BARBARA, HONEY, YOU'RE JUST UPSET.
PROMETHEA'S EXISTENCE IS NECESSARY...
RIGHT. IS THAT WHAT YOU TOLD YOURSELF WHEN POOR CRAZY DENNIS DRUCKER BLEW YOUR HEAD OFF?
IN CASE IT'S ESCAPED THE ATTENTION OF YOU LADIES, I'M THE ONLY PERSON HERE THAT BEING PROMETHEA HASN'T KILLED!
DAMN.
NEXT:
NO MAN'S LAND!

CHAPTER FIVE

A past Promethea arrives,
A symbolic landscape explored,
A spiritual journey continues.

Cover art:
J.H. Williams III
& Mick Gray

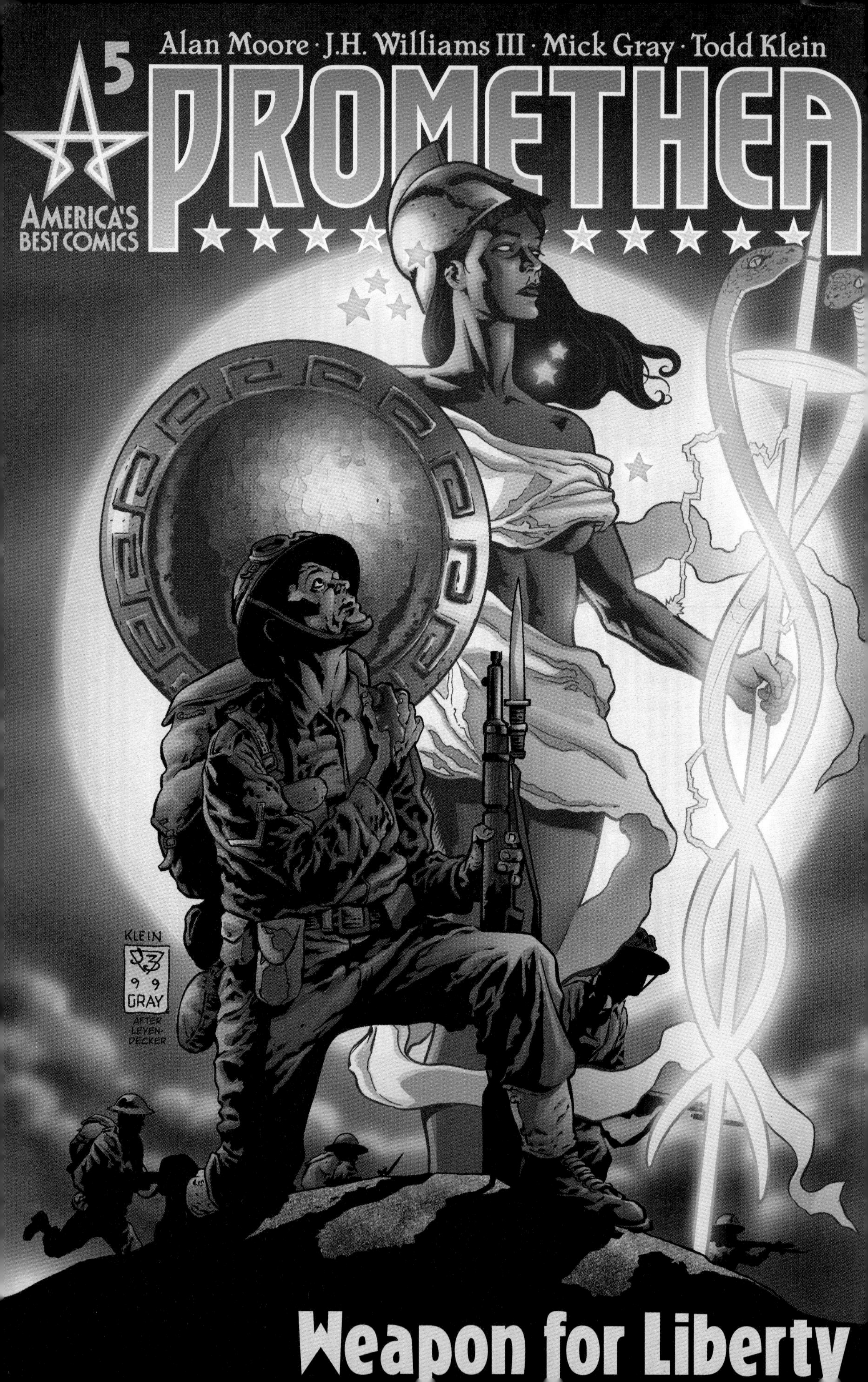

Alan Moore · J.H. Williams III · Mick Gray · Todd Klein
5
AMERICA'S BEST COMICS
PROMETHEA
KLEIN
99
GRAY
AFTER LEYEN-DECKER
Weapon for Liberty

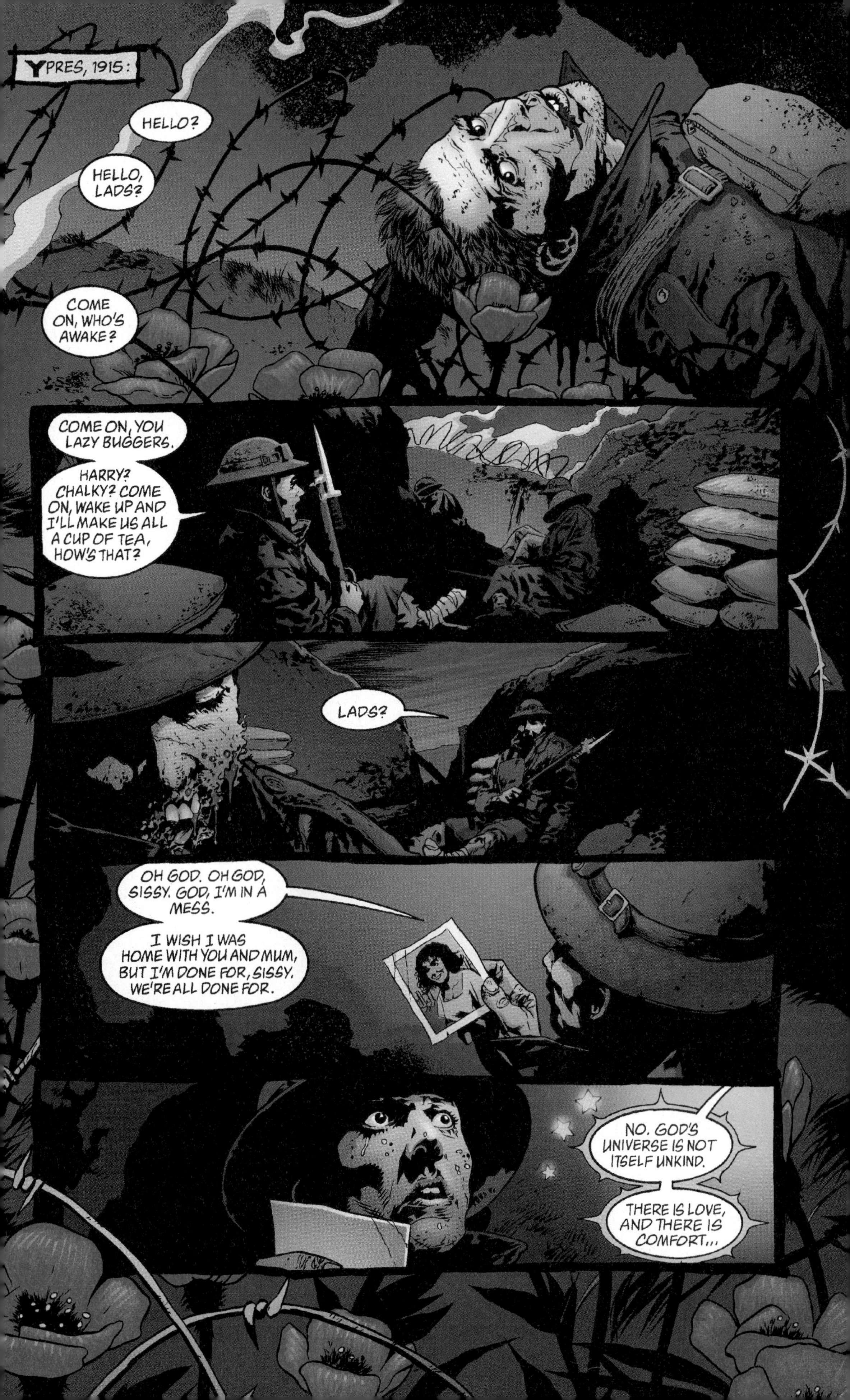
YPRES, 1915:
HELLO?
HELLO, LADS?
COME ON, WHO'S AWAKE?
COME ON, YOU LAZY BUGGERS.
HARRY? CHALKY? COME ON, WAKE UP AND I'LL MAKE US ALL A CUP OF TEA, HOW'S THAT?
LADS?
OH GOD. OH GOD, SISSY. GOD, I'M IN A MESS.
I WISH I WAS HOME WITH YOU AND MUM, BUT I'M DONE FOR, SISSY. WE'RE ALL DONE FOR.
NO. GOD'S UNIVERSE IS NOT ITSELF UNKIND.
THERE IS LOVE, AND THERE IS COMFORT...

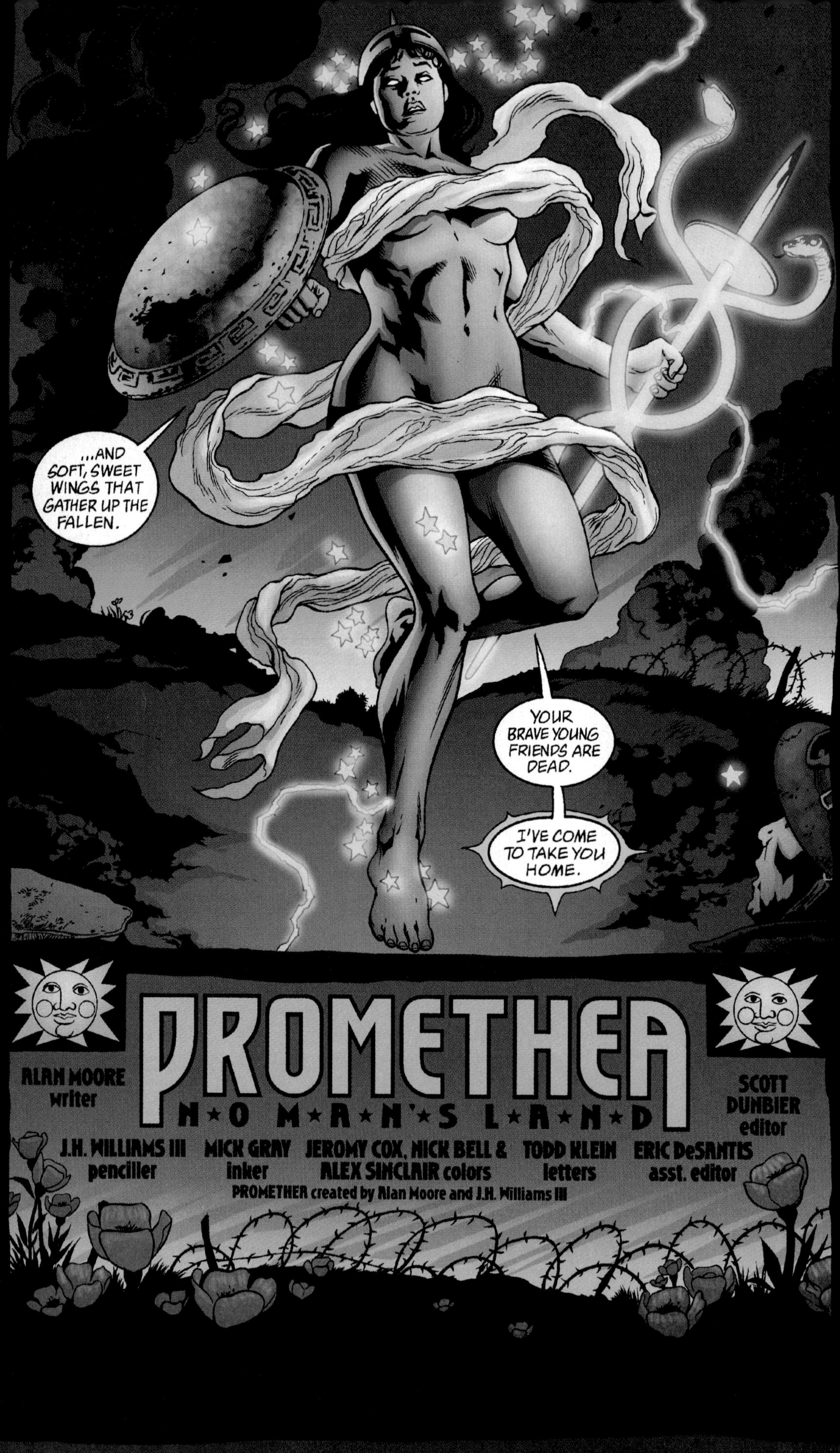
...AND SOFT, SWEET WINGS THAT GATHER UP THE FALLEN.
YOUR BRAVE YOUNG FRIENDS ARE DEAD.
I'VE COME TO TAKE YOU HOME.
PROMETHEA
N·O·M·A·N'S·L·A·N·D
ALAN MOORE writer
SCOTT DUNBIER editor
J.H. WILLIAMS III penciller
MICK GRAY inker
JEROMY COX, NICK BELL & ALEX SINCLAIR colors
TODD KLEIN letters
ERIC DeSANTIS asst. editor
PROMETHEA created by Alan Moore and J.H. Williams III

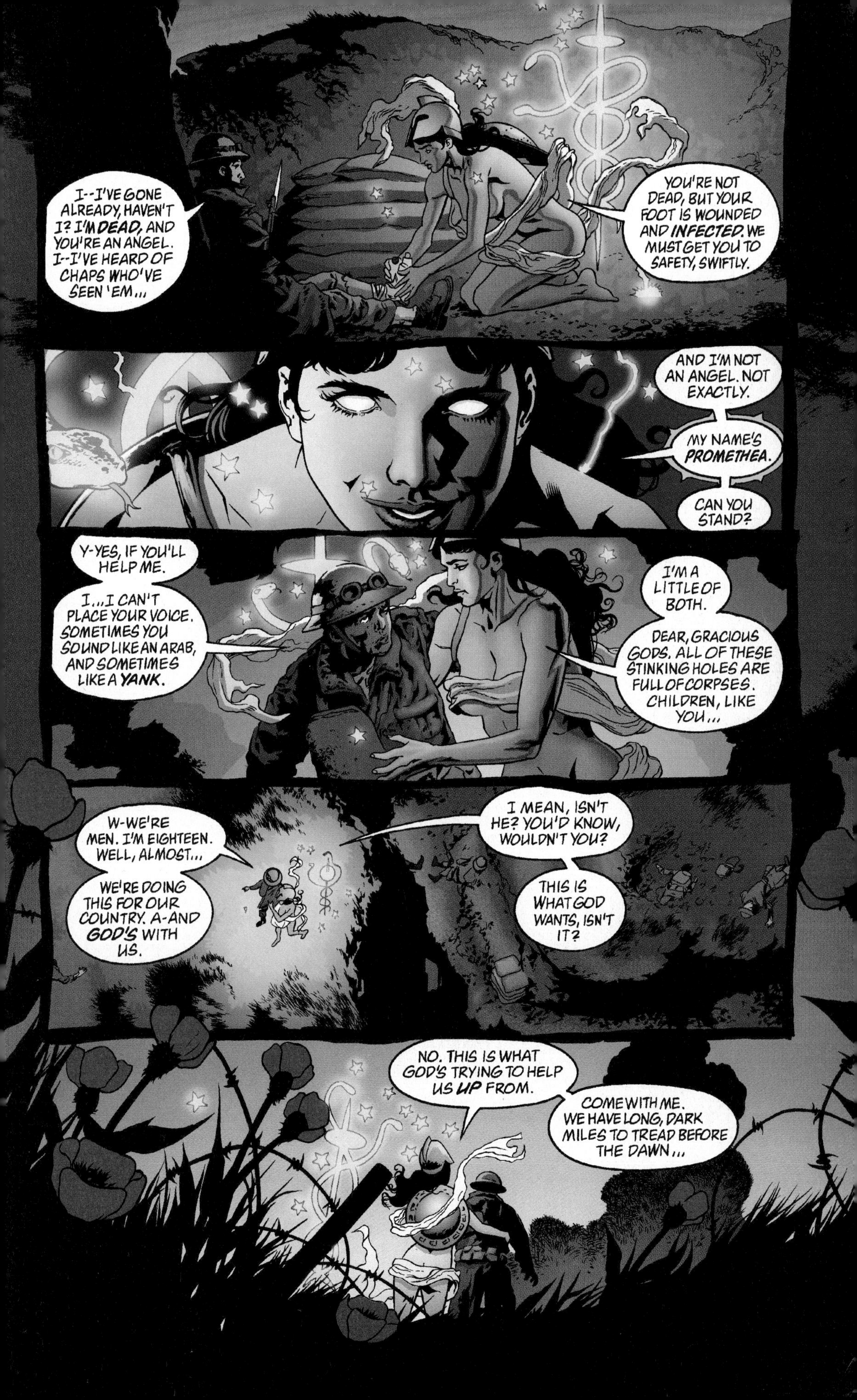
I--I'VE GONE ALREADY, HAVEN'T I? I'M DEAD, AND YOU'RE AN ANGEL. I--I'VE HEARD OF CHAPS WHO'VE SEEN 'EM...
YOU'RE NOT DEAD, BUT YOUR FOOT IS WOUNDED AND INFECTED. WE MUST GET YOU TO SAFETY, SWIFTLY.
AND I'M NOT AN ANGEL. NOT EXACTLY.
MY NAME'S PROMETHEA.
CAN YOU STAND?
Y-YES, IF YOU'LL HELP ME.
I...I CAN'T PLACE YOUR VOICE. SOMETIMES YOU SOUND LIKE AN ARAB, AND SOMETIMES LIKE A YANK.
I'M A LITTLE OF BOTH.
DEAR, GRACIOUS GODS. ALL OF THESE STINKING HOLES ARE FULL OF CORPSES. CHILDREN, LIKE YOU...
W-WE'RE MEN. I'M EIGHTEEN. WELL, ALMOST...
WE'RE DOING THIS FOR OUR COUNTRY. A-AND GOD'S WITH US.
I MEAN, ISN'T HE? YOU'D KNOW, WOULDN'T YOU?
THIS IS WHAT GOD WANTS, ISN'T IT?
NO. THIS IS WHAT GOD'S TRYING TO HELP US UP FROM.
COME WITH ME. WE HAVE LONG, DARK MILES TO TREAD BEFORE THE DAWN...

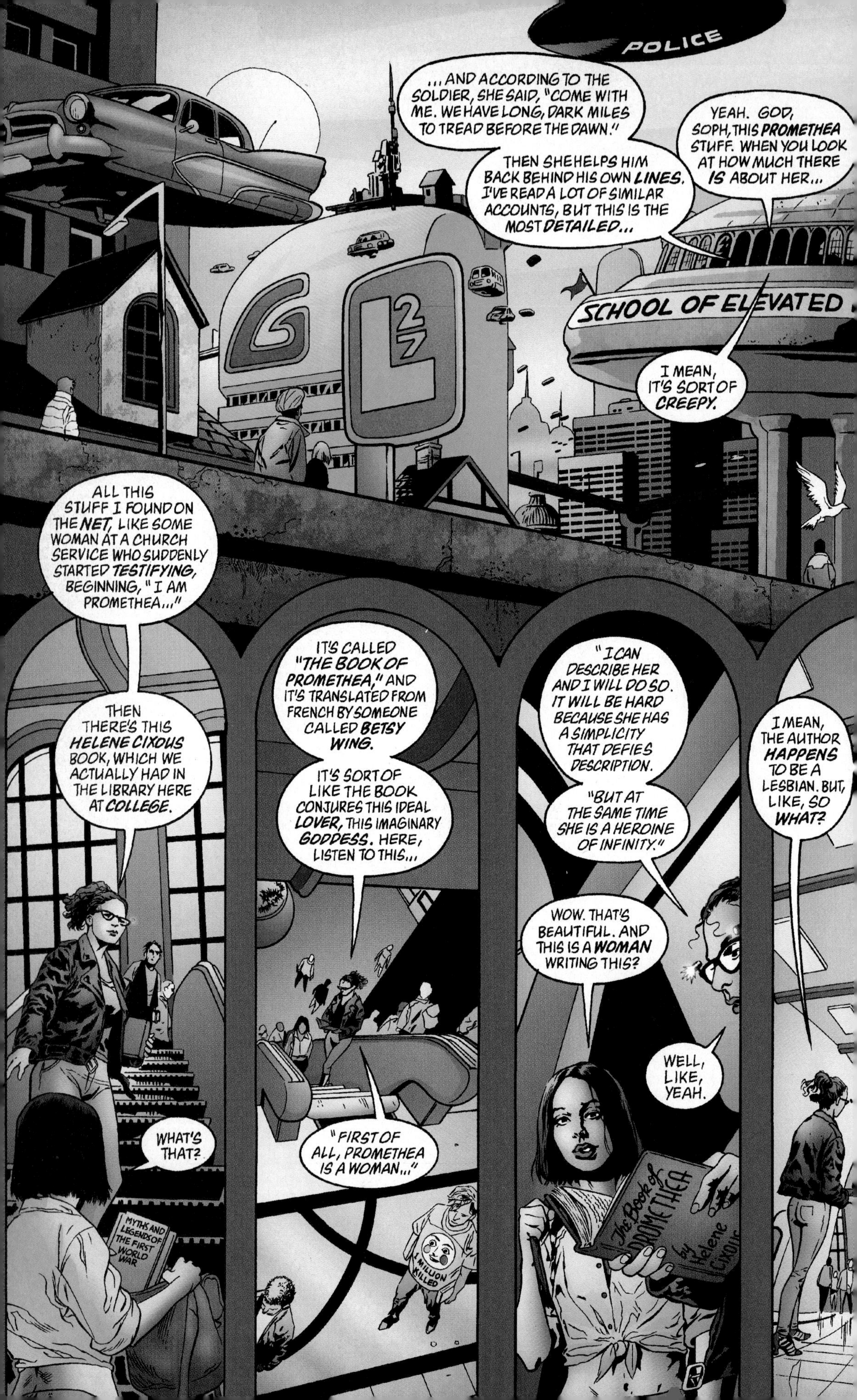
POLICE
...AND ACCORDING TO THE SOLDIER, SHE SAID, "COME WITH ME. WE HAVE LONG, DARK MILES TO TREAD BEFORE THE DAWN."
THEN SHE HELPS HIM BACK BEHIND HIS OWN LINES. I'VE READ A LOT OF SIMILAR ACCOUNTS, BUT THIS IS THE MOST DETAILED...
YEAH. GOD, SOPH, THIS PROMETHEA STUFF. WHEN YOU LOOK AT HOW MUCH THERE IS ABOUT HER...
SCHOOL OF ELEVATED
I MEAN, IT'S SORT OF CREEPY.
ALL THIS STUFF I FOUND ON THE NET, LIKE SOME WOMAN AT A CHURCH SERVICE WHO SUDDENLY STARTED TESTIFYING, BEGINNING, "I AM PROMETHEA..."
THEN THERE'S THIS HELENE CIXOUS BOOK, WHICH WE ACTUALLY HAD IN THE LIBRARY HERE AT COLLEGE.
WHAT'S THAT?
MYTHS AND LEGENDS OF THE FIRST WORLD WAR
IT'S CALLED "THE BOOK OF PROMETHEA," AND IT'S TRANSLATED FROM FRENCH BY SOMEONE CALLED BETSY WING.
IT'S SORT OF LIKE THE BOOK CONJURES THIS IDEAL LOVER, THIS IMAGINARY GODDESS. HERE, LISTEN TO THIS...
"FIRST OF ALL, PROMETHEA IS A WOMAN..."
1 MILLION KILLED
"I CAN DESCRIBE HER AND I WILL DO SO. IT WILL BE HARD BECAUSE SHE HAS A SIMPLICITY THAT DEFIES DESCRIPTION.
"BUT AT THE SAME TIME SHE IS A HEROINE OF INFINITY."
WOW. THAT'S BEAUTIFUL. AND THIS IS A WOMAN WRITING THIS?
WELL, LIKE, YEAH.
The Book of PROMETHEA by Helene Cixous
I MEAN, THE AUTHOR HAPPENS TO BE A LESBIAN. BUT, LIKE, SO WHAT?

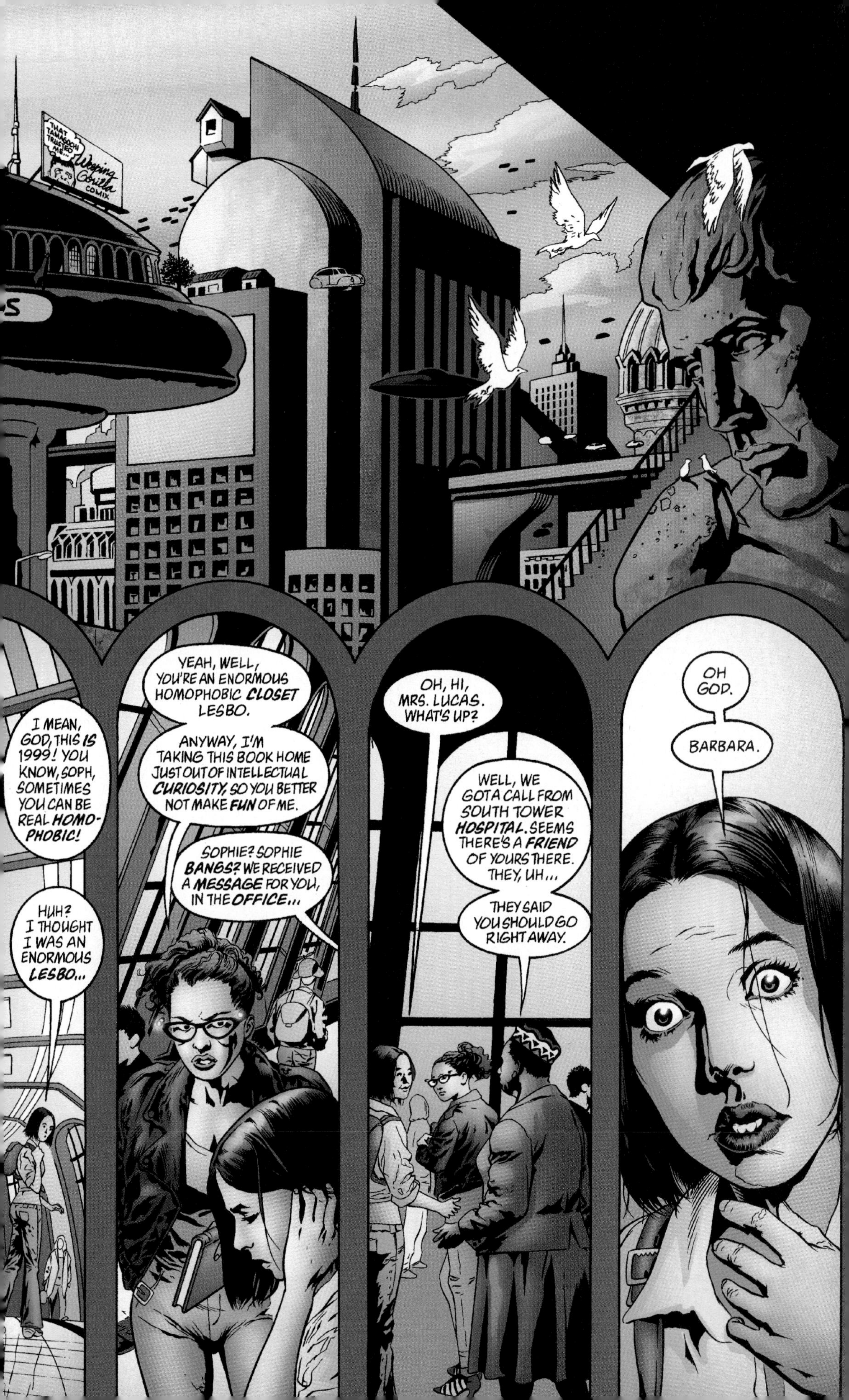
THAT TAMAGOCHI TRUSTED ME...
Weeping Gorilla COMIX
I MEAN, GOD, THIS IS 1999! YOU KNOW, SOPH, SOMETIMES YOU CAN BE REAL HOMOPHOBIC!
HUH? I THOUGHT I WAS AN ENORMOUS LESBO...
YEAH, WELL, YOU'RE AN ENORMOUS HOMOPHOBIC CLOSET LESBO.
ANYWAY, I'M TAKING THIS BOOK HOME JUST OUT OF INTELLECTUAL CURIOSITY, SO YOU BETTER NOT MAKE FUN OF ME.
SOPHIE? SOPHIE BANGS? WE RECEIVED A MESSAGE FOR YOU, IN THE OFFICE...
OH, HI, MRS. LUCAS. WHAT'S UP?
WELL, WE GOT A CALL FROM SOUTH TOWER HOSPITAL. SEEMS THERE'S A FRIEND OF YOURS THERE. THEY, UH...
THEY SAID YOU SHOULD GO RIGHT AWAY.
OH GOD.
BARBARA.

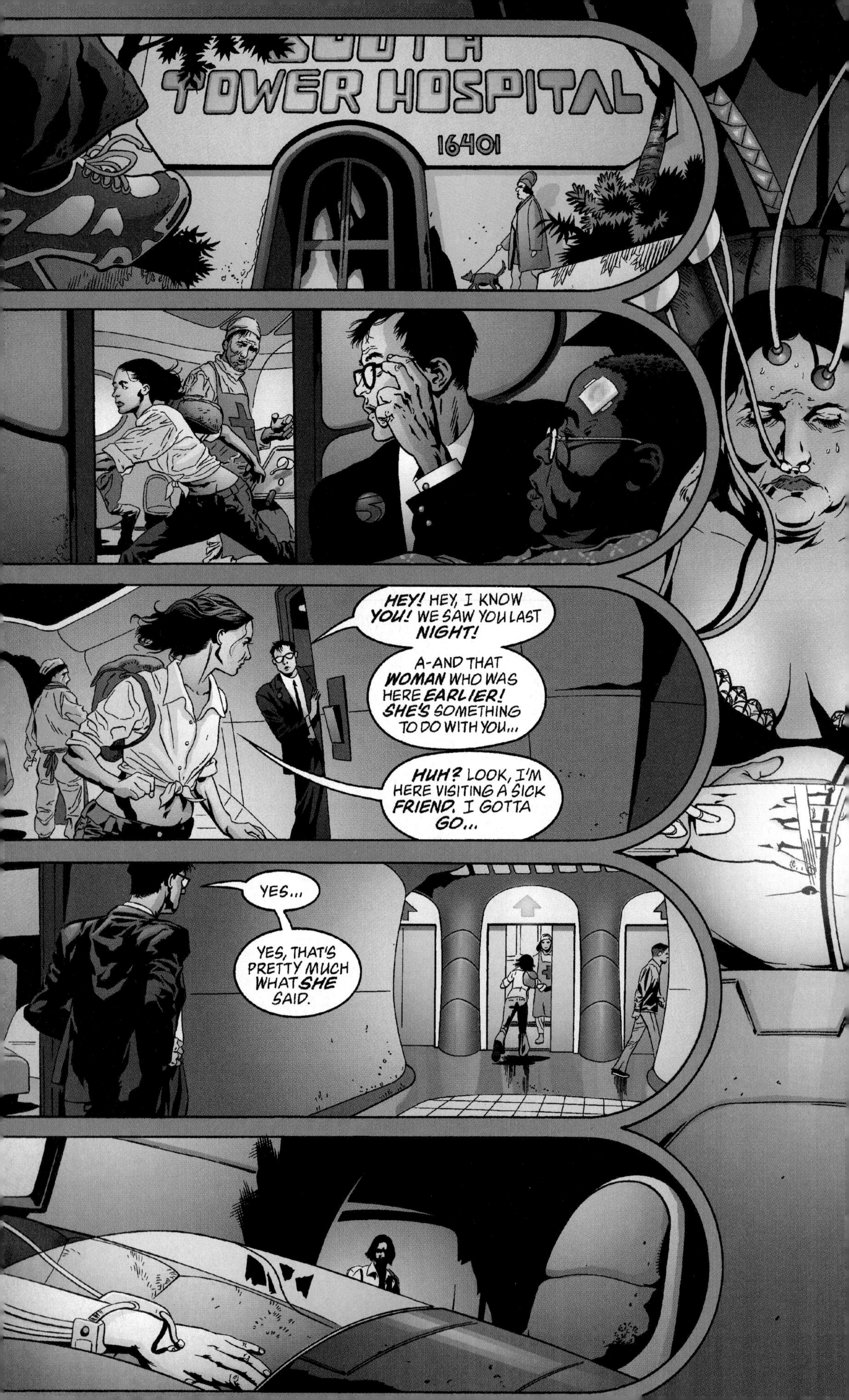
SOUTH
TOWER HOSPITAL
16401
HEY! HEY, I KNOW YOU! WE SAW YOU LAST NIGHT!
A-AND THAT WOMAN WHO WAS HERE EARLIER! SHE'S SOMETHING TO DO WITH YOU...
HUH? LOOK, I'M HERE VISITING A SICK FRIEND. I GOTTA GO...
YES...
YES, THAT'S PRETTY MUCH WHAT SHE SAID.

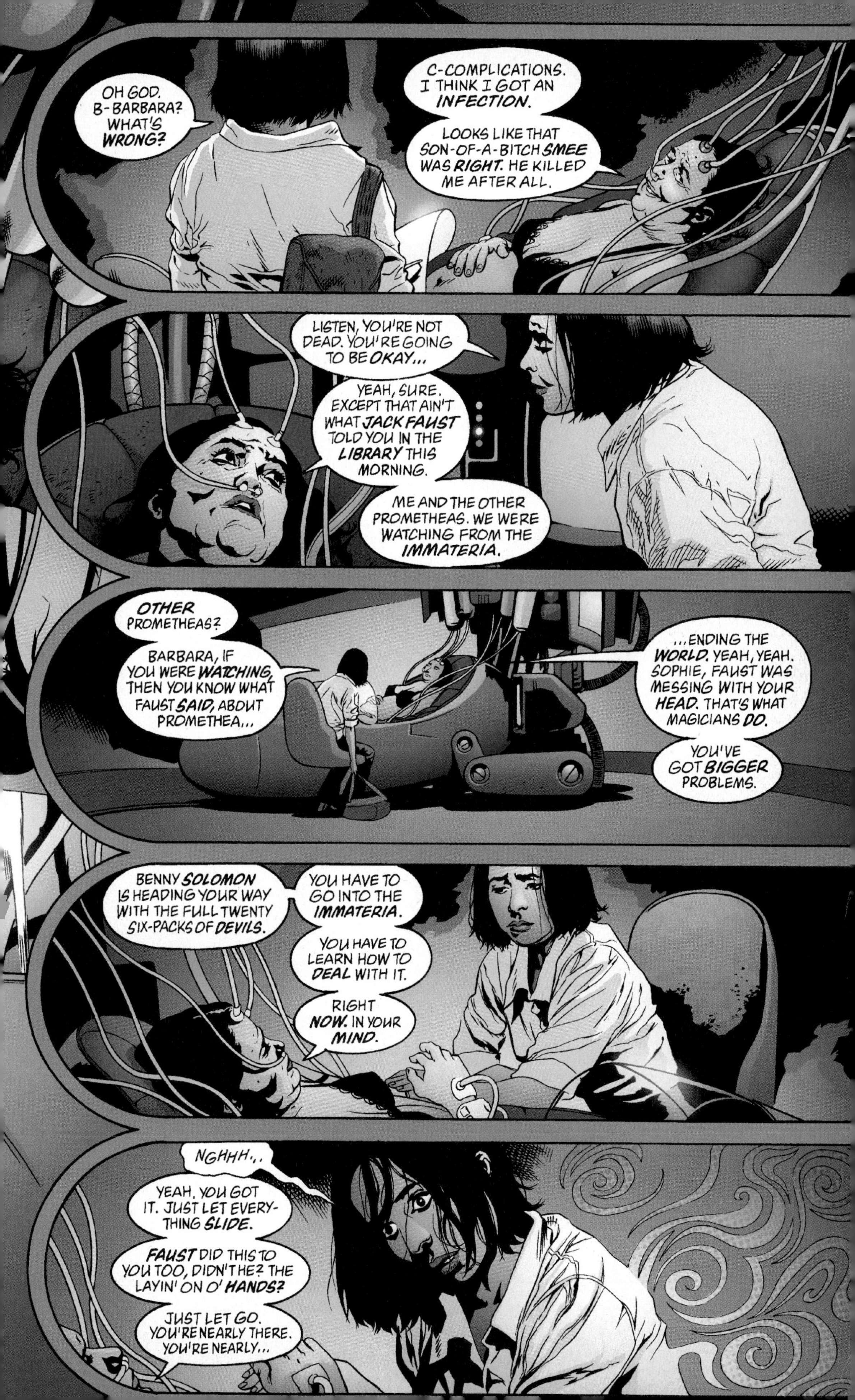
OH GOD. B-BARBARA? WHAT'S WRONG?
C-COMPLICATIONS. I THINK I GOT AN INFECTION.
LOOKS LIKE THAT SON-OF-A-BITCH SMEE WAS RIGHT. HE KILLED ME AFTER ALL.
LISTEN, YOU'RE NOT DEAD. YOU'RE GOING TO BE OKAY...
YEAH, SURE. EXCEPT THAT AIN'T WHAT JACK FAUST TOLD YOU IN THE LIBRARY THIS MORNING.
ME AND THE OTHER PROMETHEAS. WE WERE WATCHING FROM THE IMMATERIA.
OTHER PROMETHEAS?
BARBARA, IF YOU WERE WATCHING, THEN YOU KNOW WHAT FAUST SAID, ABOUT PROMETHEA...
...ENDING THE WORLD. YEAH, YEAH. SOPHIE, FAUST WAS MESSING WITH YOUR HEAD. THAT'S WHAT MAGICIANS DO.
YOU'VE GOT BIGGER PROBLEMS.
BENNY SOLOMON IS HEADING YOUR WAY WITH THE FULL TWENTY SIX-PACKS OF DEVILS.
YOU HAVE TO GO INTO THE IMMATERIA.
YOU HAVE TO LEARN HOW TO DEAL WITH IT.
RIGHT NOW. IN YOUR MIND.
NGHHH..
YEAH, YOU GOT IT. JUST LET EVERY-THING SLIDE.
FAUST DID THIS TO YOU TOO, DIDN'T HE? THE LAYIN' ON O' HANDS?
JUST LET GO. YOU'RE NEARLY THERE. YOU'RE NEARLY...

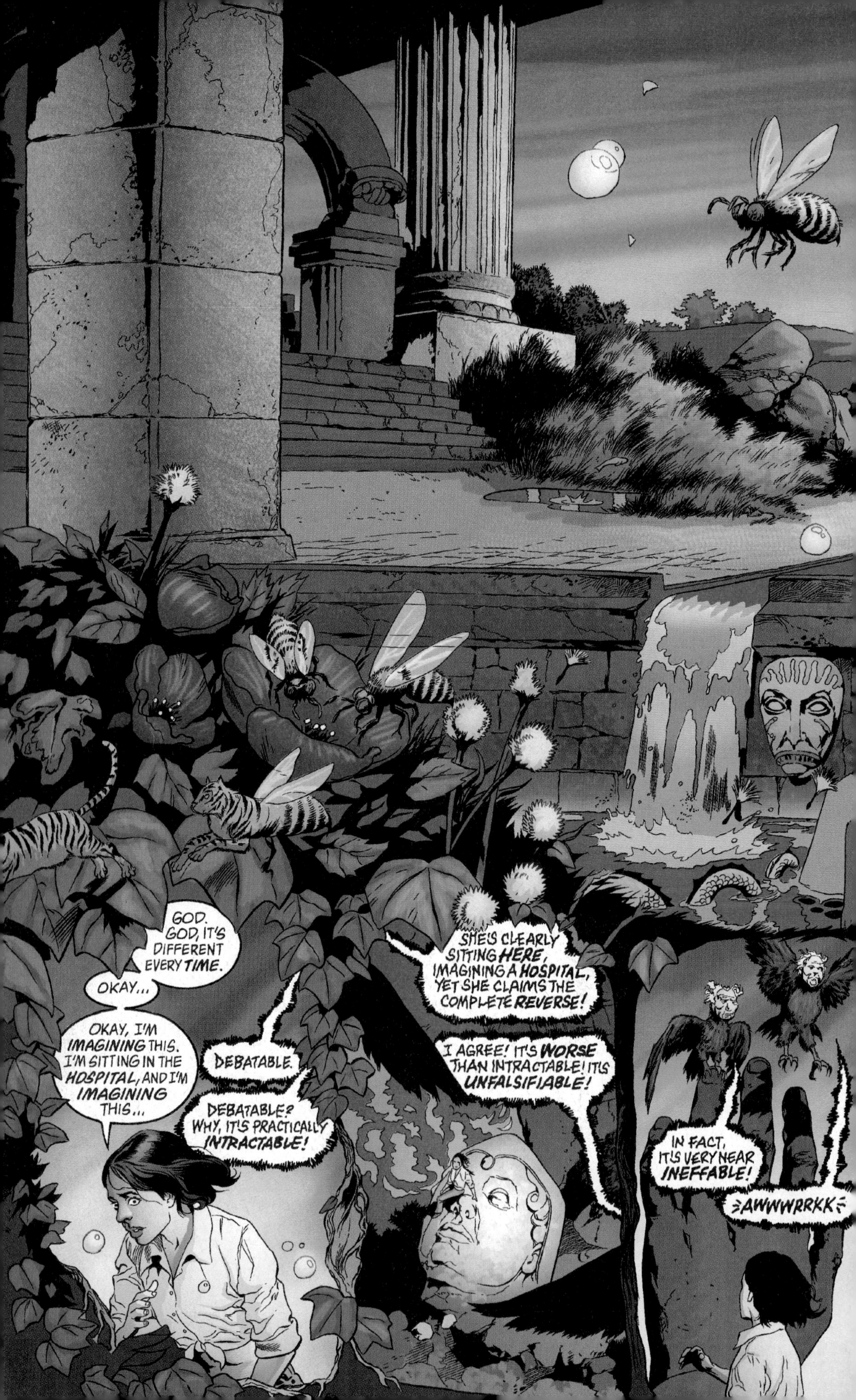
GOD. GOD, IT'S DIFFERENT EVERY TIME.
OKAY...
OKAY, I'M IMAGINING THIS. I'M SITTING IN THE HOSPITAL, AND I'M IMAGINING THIS...
DEBATABLE.
DEBATABLE? WHY, IT'S PRACTICALLY INTRACTABLE!
SHE'S CLEARLY SITTING HERE, IMAGINING A HOSPITAL, YET SHE CLAIMS THE COMPLETE REVERSE!
I AGREE! IT'S WORSE THAN INTRACTABLE! IT'S UNFALSIFIABLE!
IN FACT, IT'S VERY NEAR INEFFABLE!
AWWWRRKK

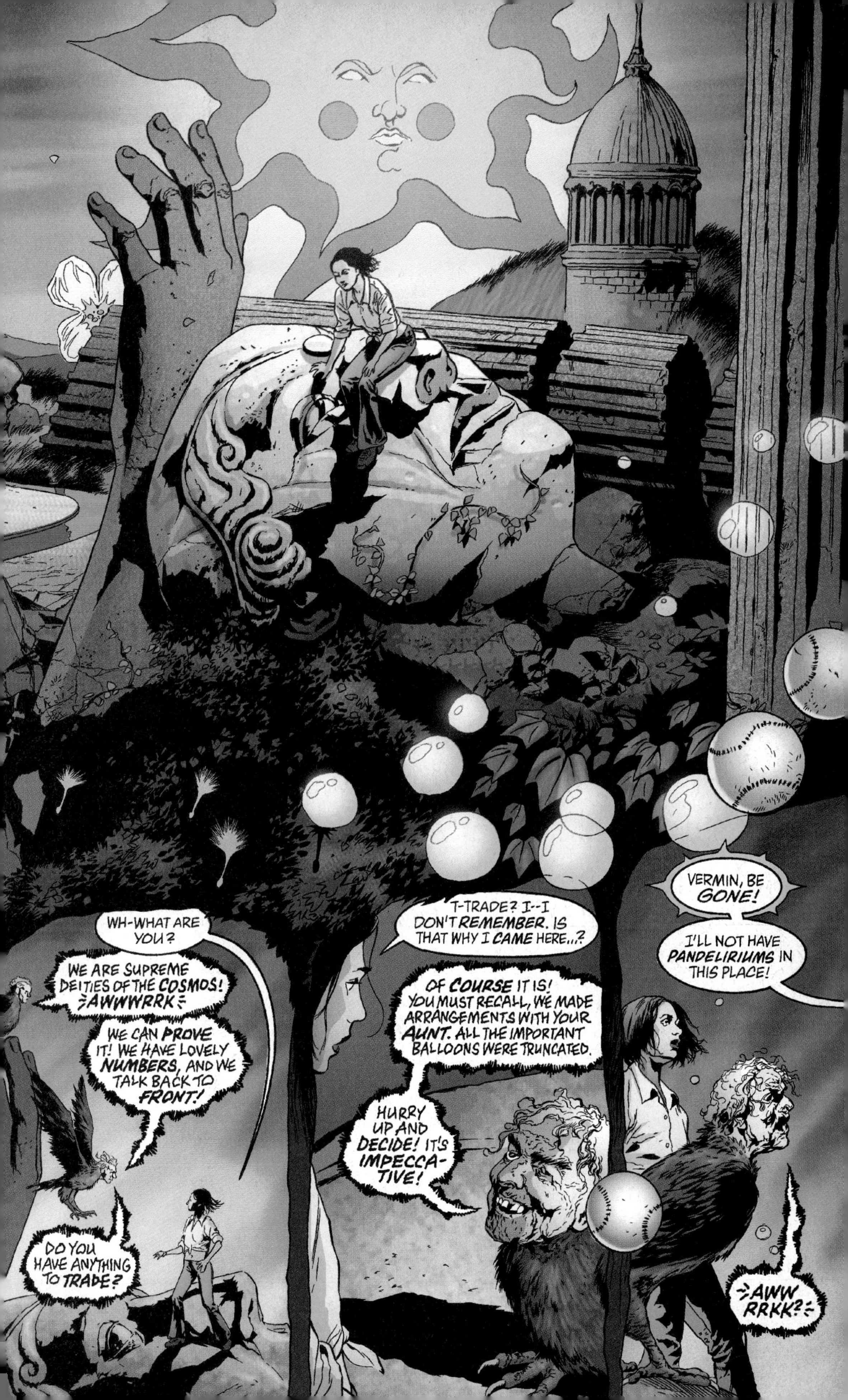
WH-WHAT ARE YOU?
WE ARE SUPREME DEITIES OF THE COSMOS! AWWWRRK
WE CAN PROVE IT! WE HAVE LOVELY NUMBERS, AND WE TALK BACK TO FRONT!
DO YOU HAVE ANYTHING TO TRADE?
T-TRADE? I--I DON'T REMEMBER. IS THAT WHY I CAME HERE...?
OF COURSE IT IS! YOU MUST RECALL, WE MADE ARRANGEMENTS WITH YOUR AUNT. ALL THE IMPORTANT BALLOONS WERE TRUNCATED.
HURRY UP AND DECIDE! IT'S IMPECCATIVE!
VERMIN, BE GONE!
I'LL NOT HAVE PANDELIRIUMS IN THIS PLACE!
AWW RRKK?

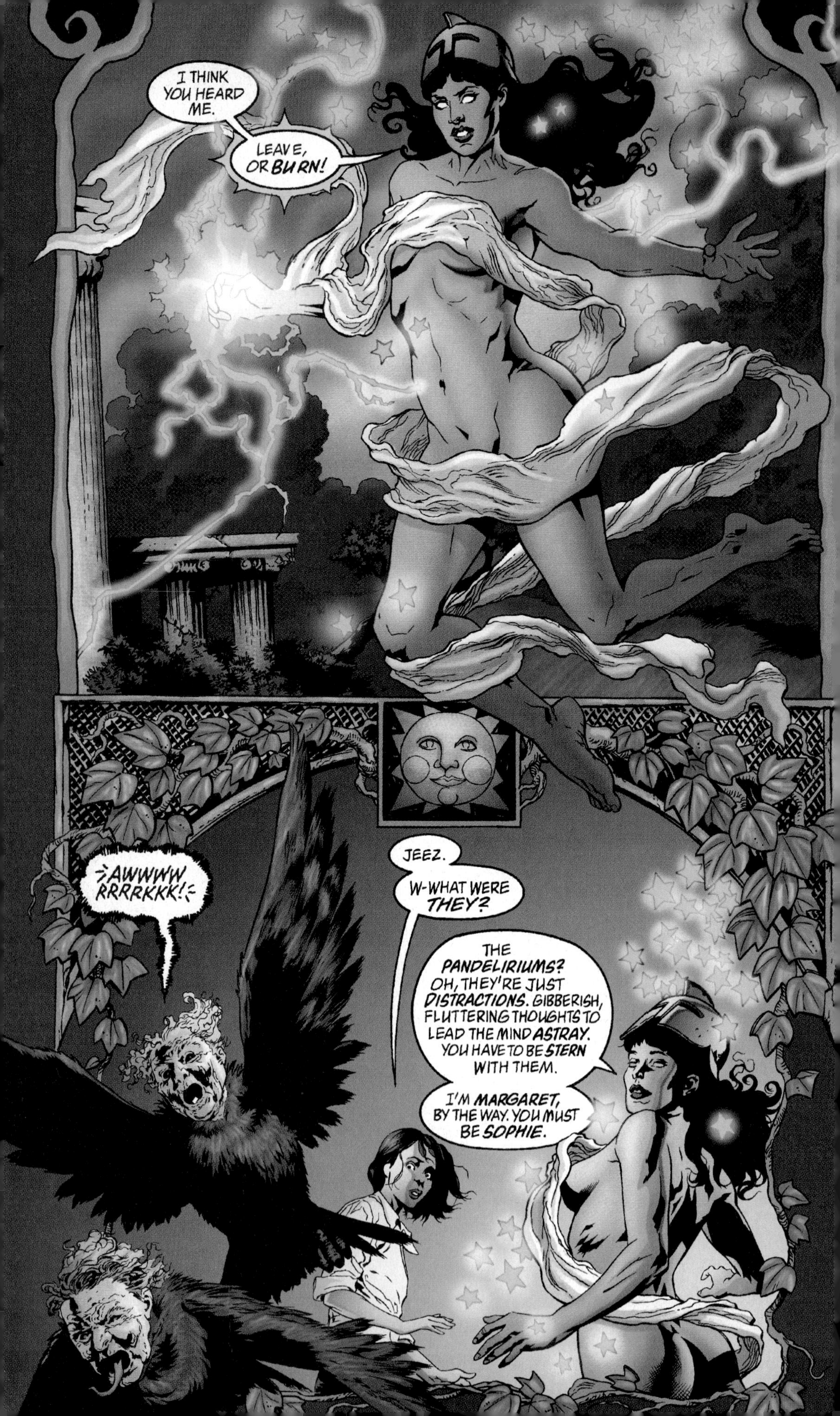
I THINK YOU HEARD ME.
LEAVE, OR BURN!
AWWWW RRRRKKK!
JEEZ.
W-WHAT WERE THEY?
THE PANDELIRIUMS? OH, THEY'RE JUST DISTRACTIONS. GIBBERISH, FLUTTERING THOUGHTS TO LEAD THE MIND ASTRAY. YOU HAVE TO BE STERN WITH THEM.
I'M MARGARET, BY THE WAY. YOU MUST BE SOPHIE.

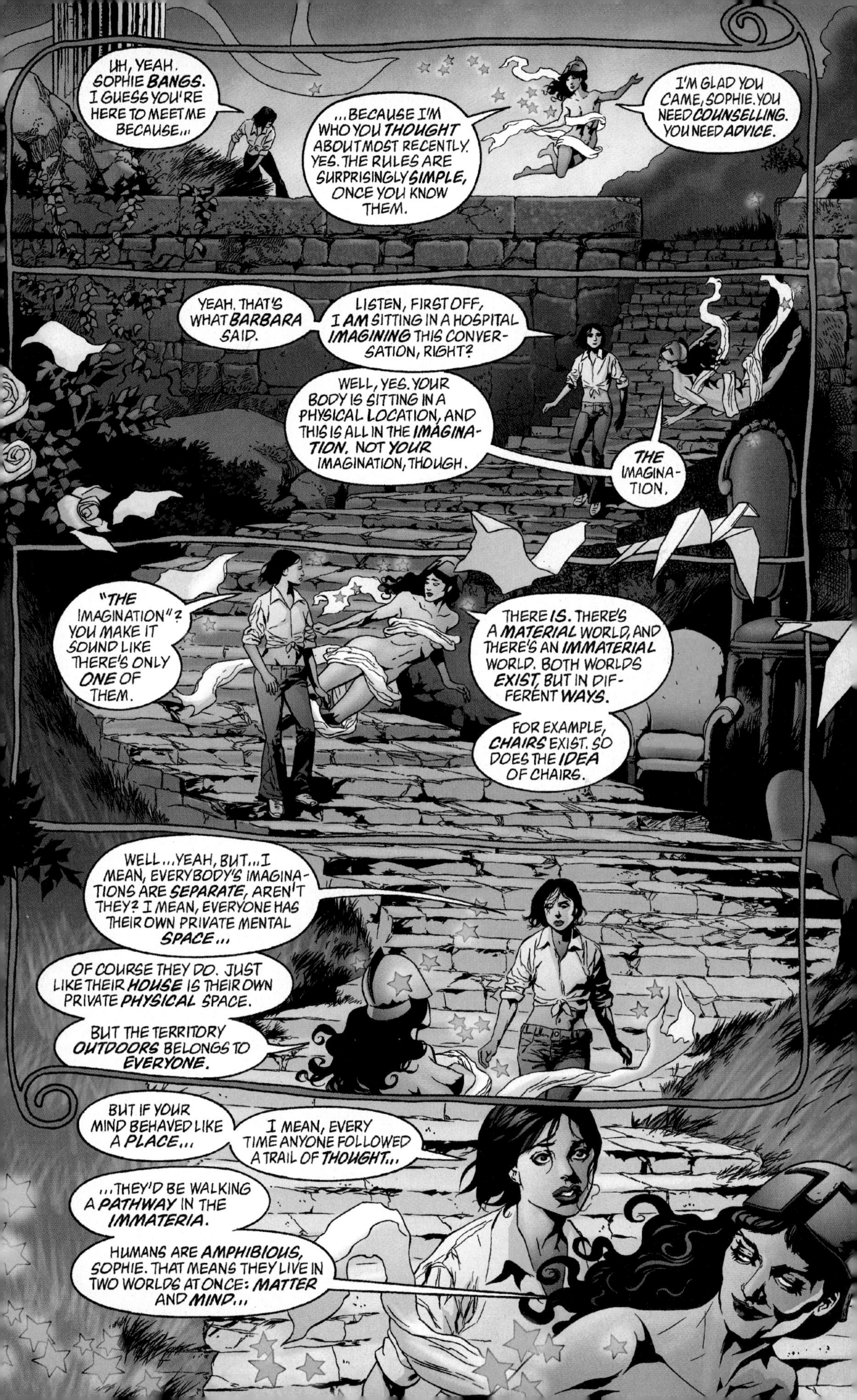
UH, YEAH. SOPHIE BANGS. I GUESS YOU'RE HERE TO MEET ME BECAUSE...
...BECAUSE I'M WHO YOU THOUGHT ABOUT MOST RECENTLY. YES. THE RULES ARE SURPRISINGLY SIMPLE, ONCE YOU KNOW THEM.
I'M GLAD YOU CAME, SOPHIE. YOU NEED COUNSELLING. YOU NEED ADVICE.
YEAH. THAT'S WHAT BARBARA SAID.
LISTEN, FIRST OFF, I AM SITTING IN A HOSPITAL IMAGINING THIS CONVERSATION, RIGHT?
WELL, YES. YOUR BODY IS SITTING IN A PHYSICAL LOCATION, AND THIS IS ALL IN THE IMAGINATION. NOT YOUR IMAGINATION, THOUGH.
THE IMAGINATION.
"THE IMAGINATION"? YOU MAKE IT SOUND LIKE THERE'S ONLY ONE OF THEM.
THERE IS. THERE'S A MATERIAL WORLD, AND THERE'S AN IMMATERIAL WORLD. BOTH WORLDS EXIST, BUT IN DIFFERENT WAYS.
FOR EXAMPLE, CHAIRS EXIST. SO DOES THE IDEA OF CHAIRS.
WELL... YEAH, BUT... I MEAN, EVERYBODY'S IMAGINATIONS ARE SEPARATE, AREN'T THEY? I MEAN, EVERYONE HAS THEIR OWN PRIVATE MENTAL SPACE...
OF COURSE THEY DO. JUST LIKE THEIR HOUSE IS THEIR OWN PRIVATE PHYSICAL SPACE.
BUT THE TERRITORY OUTDOORS BELONGS TO EVERYONE.
BUT IF YOUR MIND BEHAVED LIKE A PLACE...
I MEAN, EVERY TIME ANYONE FOLLOWED A TRAIL OF THOUGHT...
...THEY'D BE WALKING A PATHWAY IN THE IMMATERIA.
HUMANS ARE AMPHIBIOUS, SOPHIE. THAT MEANS THEY LIVE IN TWO WORLDS AT ONCE: MATTER AND MIND...

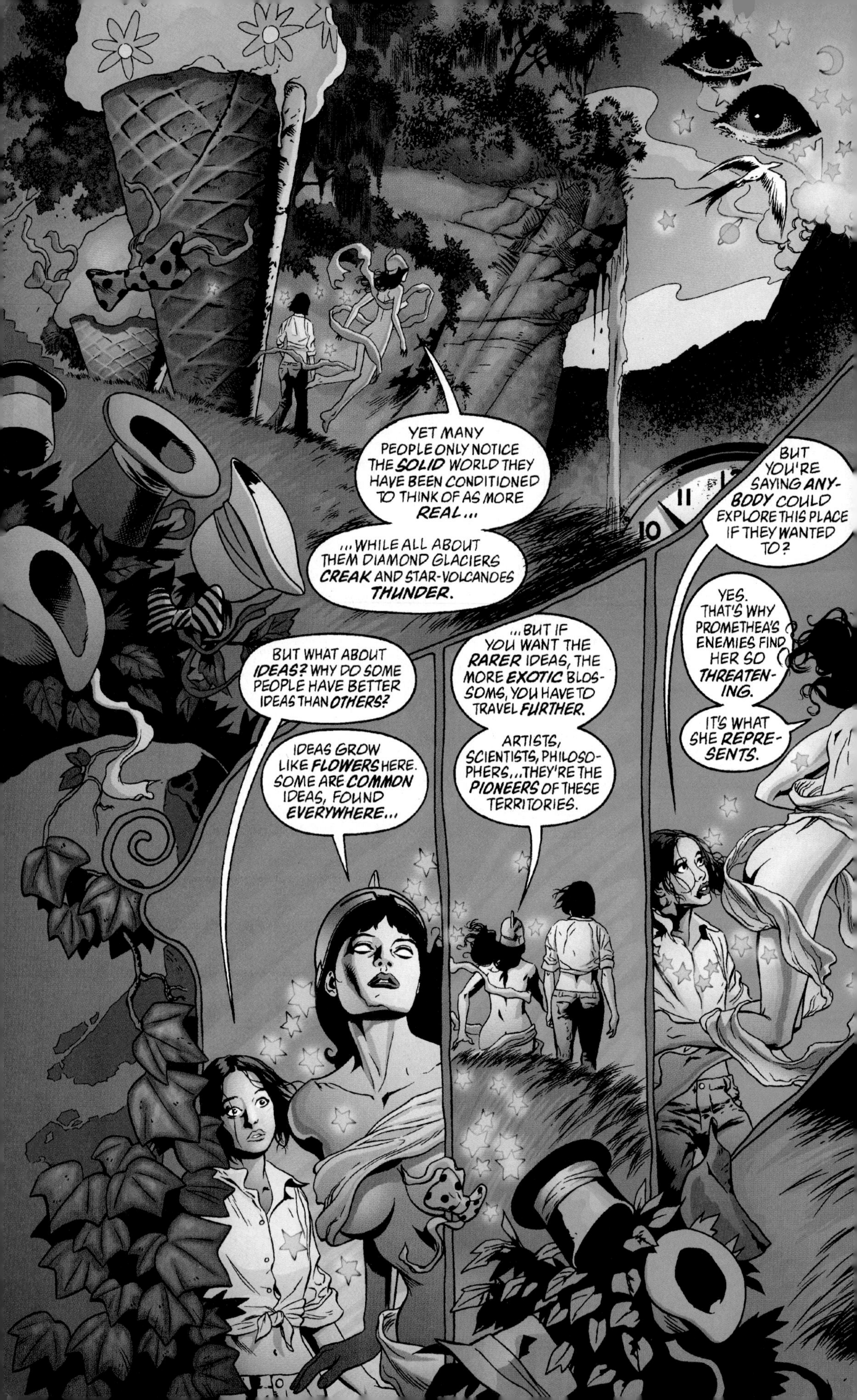
YET MANY PEOPLE ONLY NOTICE THE SOLID WORLD THEY HAVE BEEN CONDITIONED TO THINK OF AS MORE REAL...
...WHILE ALL ABOUT THEM DIAMOND GLACIERS CREAK AND STAR-VOLCANOES THUNDER.
BUT WHAT ABOUT IDEAS? WHY DO SOME PEOPLE HAVE BETTER IDEAS THAN OTHERS?
IDEAS GROW LIKE FLOWERS HERE. SOME ARE COMMON IDEAS, FOUND EVERYWHERE...
...BUT IF YOU WANT THE RARER IDEAS, THE MORE EXOTIC BLOSSOMS, YOU HAVE TO TRAVEL FURTHER.
ARTISTS, SCIENTISTS, PHILOSOPHERS... THEY'RE THE PIONEERS OF THESE TERRITORIES.
BUT YOU'RE SAYING ANYBODY COULD EXPLORE THIS PLACE IF THEY WANTED TO?
YES. THAT'S WHY PROMETHEA'S ENEMIES FIND HER SO THREATENING.
IT'S WHAT SHE REPRESENTS.

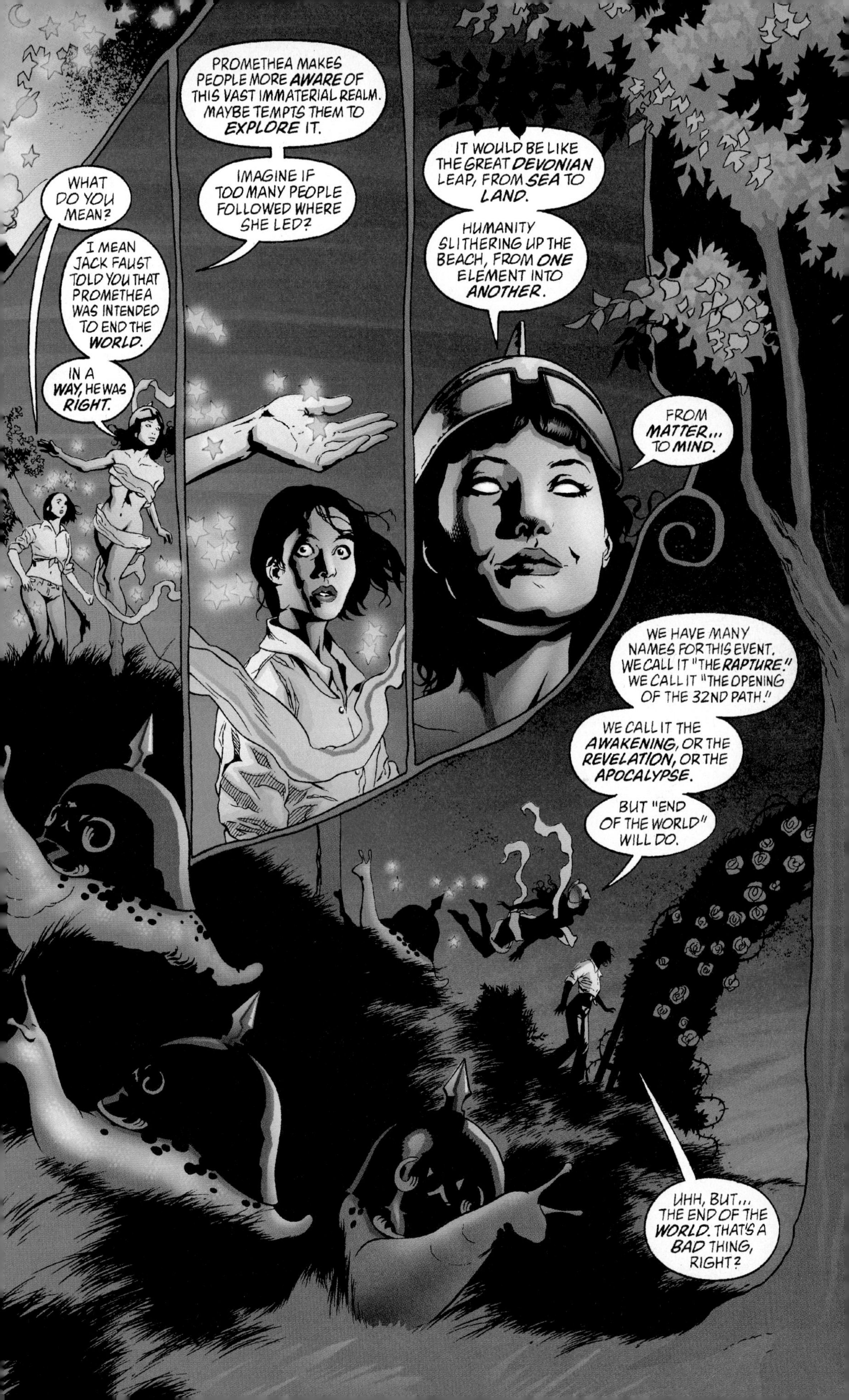
WHAT DO YOU MEAN?
I MEAN JACK FAUST TOLD YOU THAT PROMETHEA WAS INTENDED TO END THE WORLD.
IN A WAY, HE WAS RIGHT.
PROMETHEA MAKES PEOPLE MORE AWARE OF THIS VAST IMMATERIAL REALM. MAYBE TEMPTS THEM TO EXPLORE IT.
IMAGINE IF TOO MANY PEOPLE FOLLOWED WHERE SHE LED?
IT WOULD BE LIKE THE GREAT DEVONIAN LEAP, FROM SEA TO LAND.
HUMANITY SLITHERING UP THE BEACH, FROM ONE ELEMENT INTO ANOTHER.
FROM MATTER... TO MIND.
WE HAVE MANY NAMES FOR THIS EVENT. WE CALL IT "THE RAPTURE." WE CALL IT "THE OPENING OF THE 32ND PATH."
WE CALL IT THE AWAKENING, OR THE REVELATION, OR THE APOCALYPSE.
BUT "END OF THE WORLD" WILL DO.
UHH, BUT... THE END OF THE WORLD. THAT'S A BAD THING, RIGHT?

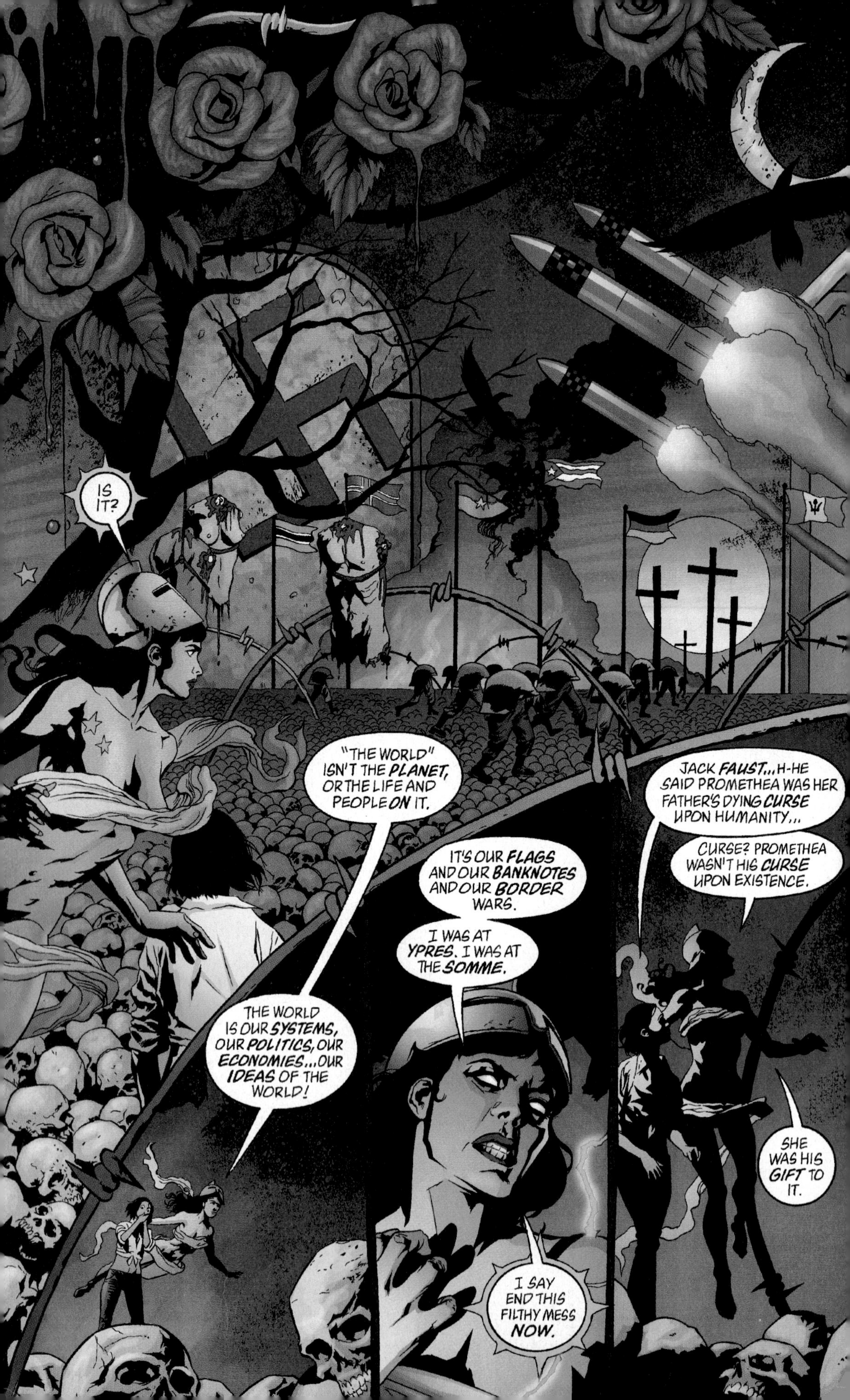
IS IT?
"THE WORLD" ISN'T THE PLANET, OR THE LIFE AND PEOPLE ON IT.
THE WORLD IS OUR SYSTEMS, OUR POLITICS, OUR ECONOMIES...OUR IDEAS OF THE WORLD!
IT'S OUR FLAGS AND OUR BANKNOTES AND OUR BORDER WARS.
I WAS AT YPRES. I WAS AT THE SOMME.
I SAY END THIS FILTHY MESS NOW.
JACK FAUST...H-HE SAID PROMETHEA WAS HER FATHER'S DYING CURSE UPON HUMANITY...
CURSE? PROMETHEA WASN'T HIS CURSE UPON EXISTENCE.
SHE WAS HIS GIFT TO IT.

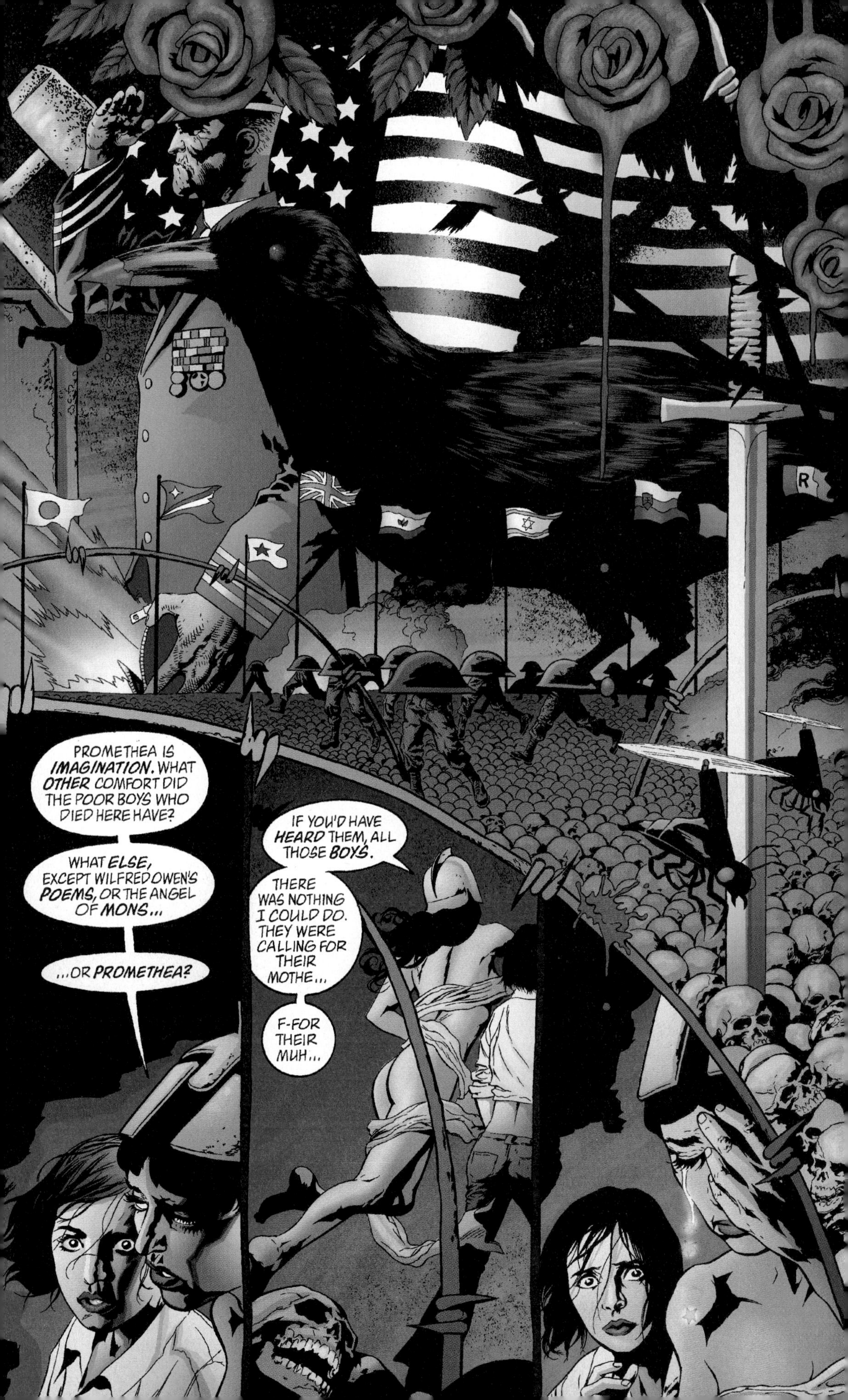

R
PROMETHEA IS IMAGINATION. WHAT OTHER COMFORT DID THE POOR BOYS WHO DIED HERE HAVE?
WHAT ELSE, EXCEPT WILFRED OWEN'S POEMS, OR THE ANGEL OF MONS...
...OR PROMETHEA?
IF YOU'D HAVE HEARD THEM, ALL THOSE BOYS.
THERE WAS NOTHING I COULD DO. THEY WERE CALLING FOR THEIR MOTHE...
F-FOR THEIR MUH...

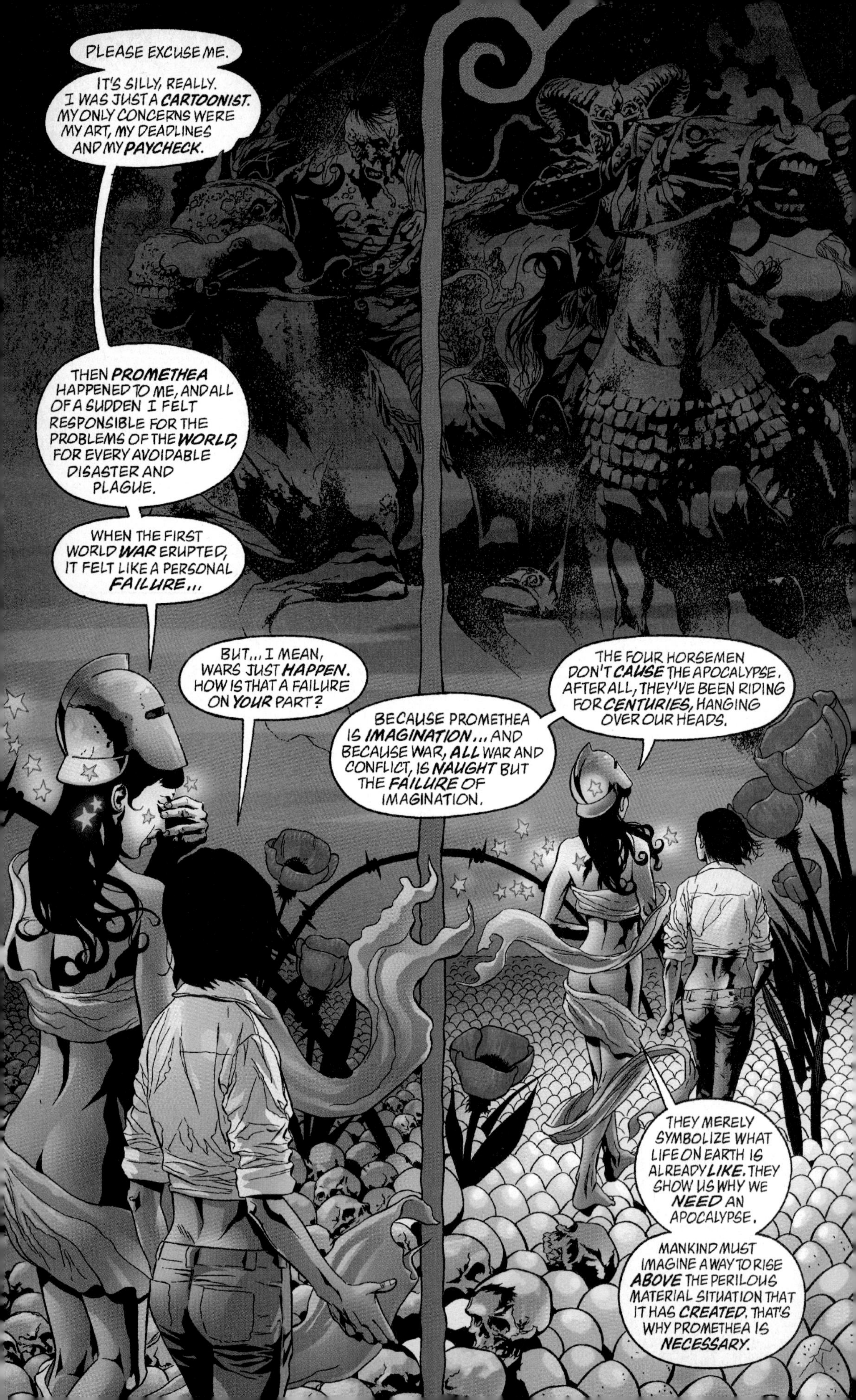
PLEASE EXCUSE ME.
IT'S SILLY, REALLY. I WAS JUST A CARTOONIST. MY ONLY CONCERNS WERE MY ART, MY DEADLINES AND MY PAYCHECK.
THEN PROMETHEA HAPPENED TO ME, AND ALL OF A SUDDEN I FELT RESPONSIBLE FOR THE PROBLEMS OF THE WORLD, FOR EVERY AVOIDABLE DISASTER AND PLAGUE.
WHEN THE FIRST WORLD WAR ERUPTED, IT FELT LIKE A PERSONAL FAILURE...
BUT... I MEAN, WARS JUST HAPPEN. HOW IS THAT A FAILURE ON YOUR PART?
BECAUSE PROMETHEA IS IMAGINATION... AND BECAUSE WAR, ALL WAR AND CONFLICT, IS NAUGHT BUT THE FAILURE OF IMAGINATION.
THE FOUR HORSEMEN DON'T CAUSE THE APOCALYPSE. AFTER ALL, THEY'VE BEEN RIDING FOR CENTURIES, HANGING OVER OUR HEADS.
THEY MERELY SYMBOLIZE WHAT LIFE ON EARTH IS ALREADY LIKE. THEY SHOW US WHY WE NEED AN APOCALYPSE.
MANKIND MUST IMAGINE A WAY TO RISE ABOVE THE PERILOUS MATERIAL SITUATION THAT IT HAS CREATED. THAT'S WHY PROMETHEA IS NECESSARY.

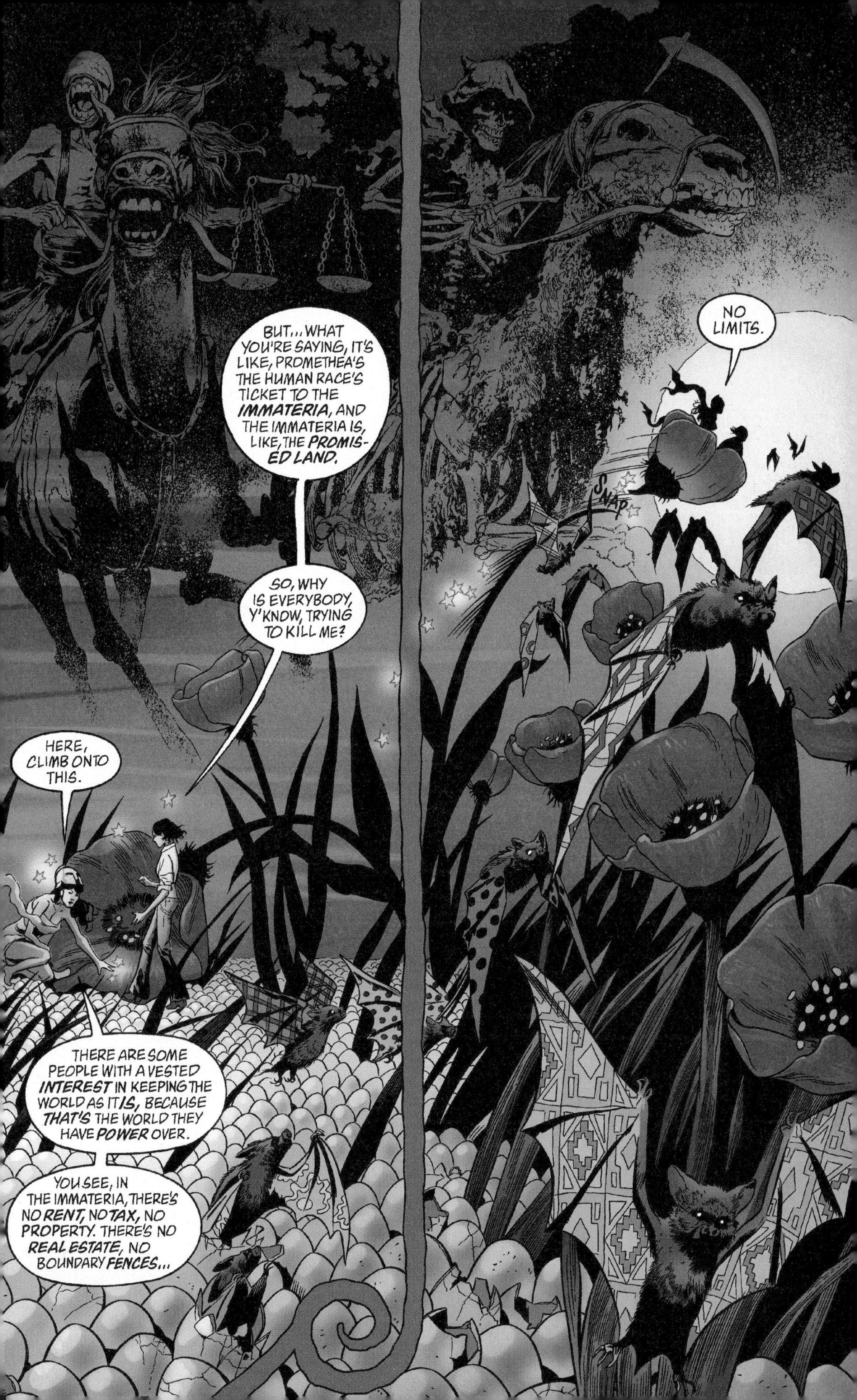
BUT... WHAT YOU'RE SAYING, IT'S LIKE, PROMETHEA'S THE HUMAN RACE'S TICKET TO THE IMMATERIA, AND THE IMMATERIA IS, LIKE, THE PROMISED LAND.
SO, WHY IS EVERYBODY, Y'KNOW, TRYING TO KILL ME?
NO LIMITS.
SNAP
HERE, CLIMB ONTO THIS.
THERE ARE SOME PEOPLE WITH A VESTED INTEREST IN KEEPING THE WORLD AS IT IS, BECAUSE THAT'S THE WORLD THEY HAVE POWER OVER.
YOU SEE, IN THE IMMATERIA, THERE'S NO RENT, NO TAX, NO PROPERTY. THERE'S NO REAL ESTATE, NO BOUNDARY FENCES...

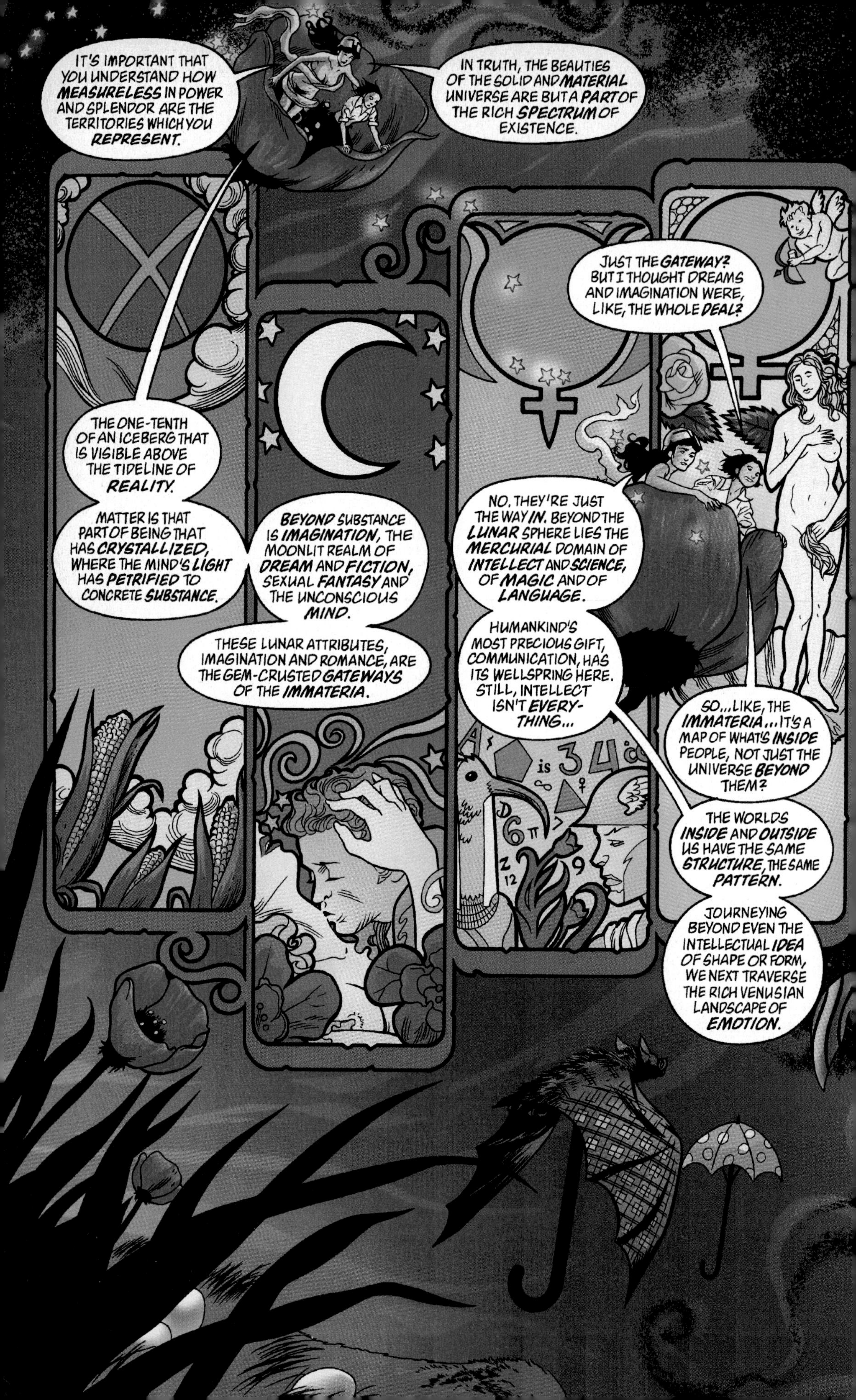
IT'S IMPORTANT THAT YOU UNDERSTAND HOW MEASURELESS IN POWER AND SPLENDOR ARE THE TERRITORIES WHICH YOU REPRESENT.
IN TRUTH, THE BEAUTIES OF THE SOLID AND MATERIAL UNIVERSE ARE BUT A PART OF THE RICH SPECTRUM OF EXISTENCE.
THE ONE-TENTH OF AN ICEBERG THAT IS VISIBLE ABOVE THE TIDELINE OF REALITY.
MATTER IS THAT PART OF BEING THAT HAS CRYSTALLIZED, WHERE THE MIND'S LIGHT HAS PETRIFIED TO CONCRETE SUBSTANCE.
BEYOND SUBSTANCE IS IMAGINATION, THE MOONLIT REALM OF DREAM AND FICTION, SEXUAL FANTASY AND THE UNCONSCIOUS MIND.
THESE LUNAR ATTRIBUTES, IMAGINATION AND ROMANCE, ARE THE GEM-CRUSTED GATEWAYS OF THE IMMATERIA.
JUST THE GATEWAY? BUT I THOUGHT DREAMS AND IMAGINATION WERE, LIKE, THE WHOLE DEAL?
NO. THEY'RE JUST THE WAY IN. BEYOND THE LUNAR SPHERE LIES THE MERCURIAL DOMAIN OF INTELLECT AND SCIENCE, OF MAGIC AND OF LANGUAGE.
HUMANKIND'S MOST PRECIOUS GIFT, COMMUNICATION, HAS ITS WELLSPRING HERE. STILL, INTELLECT ISN'T EVERY-THING...
SO...LIKE, THE IMMATERIA...IT'S A MAP OF WHAT'S INSIDE PEOPLE, NOT JUST THE UNIVERSE BEYOND THEM?
THE WORLDS INSIDE AND OUTSIDE US HAVE THE SAME STRUCTURE, THE SAME PATTERN.
JOURNEYING BEYOND EVEN THE INTELLECTUAL IDEA OF SHAPE OR FORM, WE NEXT TRAVERSE THE RICH VENUSIAN LANDSCAPE OF EMOTION.

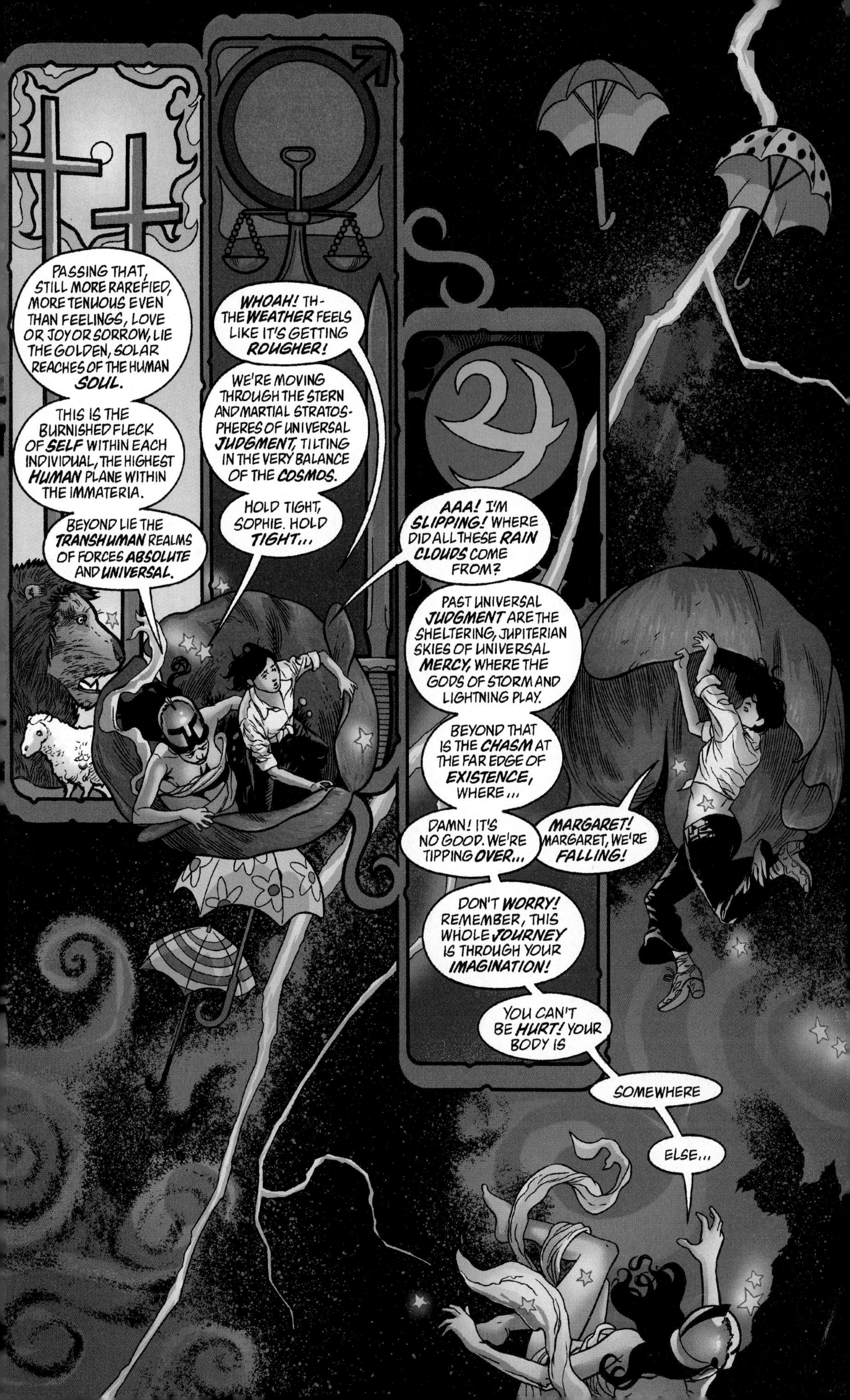
PASSING THAT, STILL MORE RAREFIED, MORE TENUOUS EVEN THAN FEELINGS, LOVE OR JOY OR SORROW, LIE THE GOLDEN, SOLAR REACHES OF THE HUMAN SOUL.
THIS IS THE BURNISHED FLECK OF SELF WITHIN EACH INDIVIDUAL, THE HIGHEST HUMAN PLANE WITHIN THE IMMATERIA.
BEYOND LIE THE TRANSHUMAN REALMS OF FORCES ABSOLUTE AND UNIVERSAL.
WHOAH! TH- THE WEATHER FEELS LIKE IT'S GETTING ROUGHER!
WE'RE MOVING THROUGH THE STERN AND MARTIAL STRATOSPHERES OF UNIVERSAL JUDGMENT, TILTING IN THE VERY BALANCE OF THE COSMOS.
HOLD TIGHT, SOPHIE. HOLD TIGHT...
AAA! I'M SLIPPING! WHERE DID ALL THESE RAIN CLOUDS COME FROM?
PAST UNIVERSAL JUDGMENT ARE THE SHELTERING, JUPITERIAN SKIES OF UNIVERSAL MERCY, WHERE THE GODS OF STORM AND LIGHTNING PLAY.
BEYOND THAT IS THE CHASM AT THE FAR EDGE OF EXISTENCE, WHERE...
DAMN! IT'S NO GOOD. WE'RE TIPPING OVER...
MARGARET! MARGARET, WE'RE FALLING!
DON'T WORRY! REMEMBER, THIS WHOLE JOURNEY IS THROUGH YOUR IMAGINATION!
YOU CAN'T BE HURT! YOUR BODY IS
SOMEWHERE
ELSE...

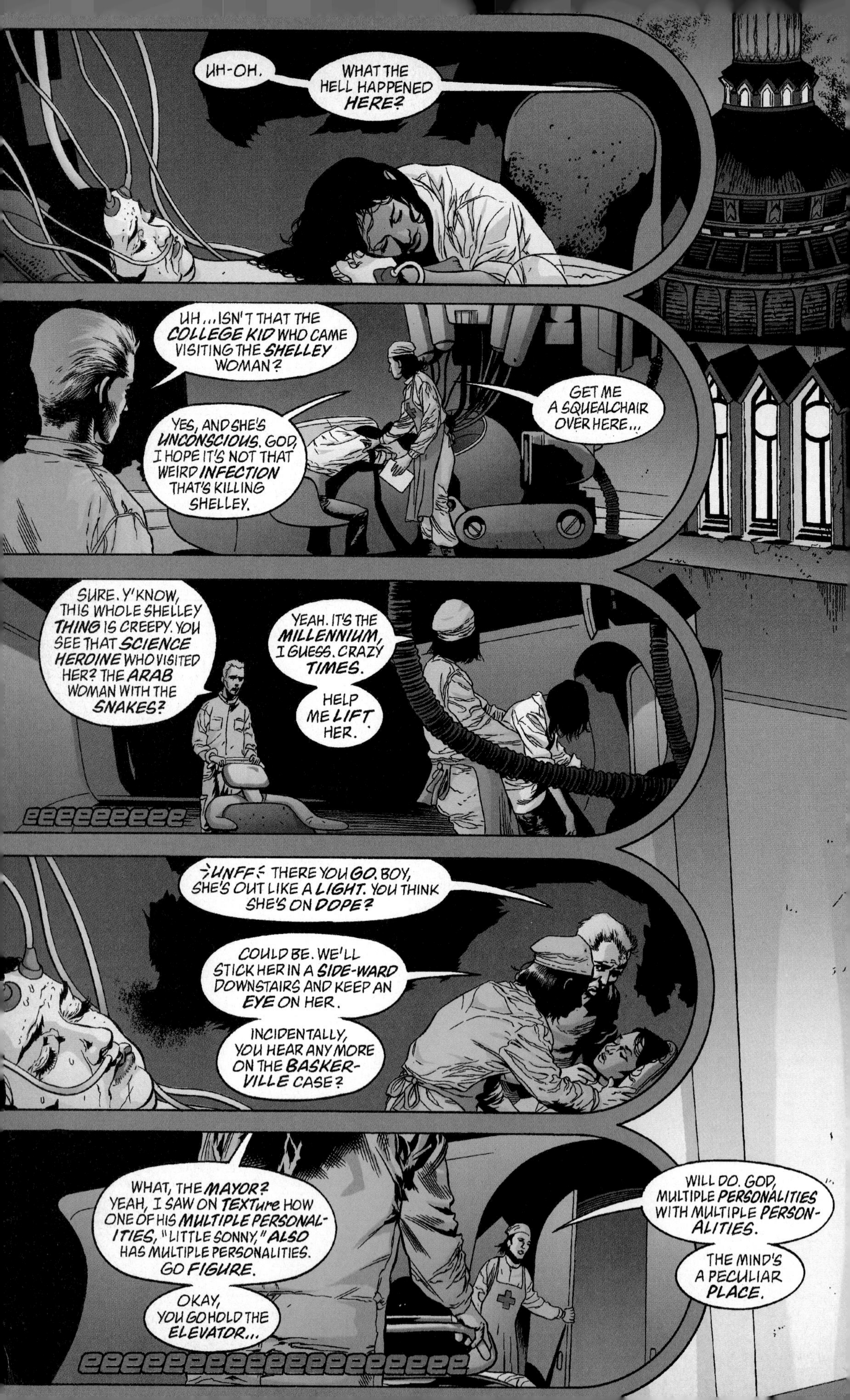
UH-OH.
WHAT THE HELL HAPPENED HERE?
UH...ISN'T THAT THE COLLEGE KID WHO CAME VISITING THE SHELLEY WOMAN?
YES, AND SHE'S UNCONSCIOUS. GOD, I HOPE IT'S NOT THAT WEIRD INFECTION THAT'S KILLING SHELLEY.
GET ME A SQUEALCHAIR OVER HERE...
SURE. Y'KNOW, THIS WHOLE SHELLEY THING IS CREEPY. YOU SEE THAT SCIENCE HEROINE WHO VISITED HER? THE ARAB WOMAN WITH THE SNAKES?
YEAH. IT'S THE MILLENNIUM, I GUESS. CRAZY TIMES.
HELP ME LIFT HER.
EEEEEEEEEE
UNFF. THERE YOU GO. BOY, SHE'S OUT LIKE A LIGHT. YOU THINK SHE'S ON DOPE?
COULD BE. WE'LL STICK HER IN A SIDE-WARD DOWNSTAIRS AND KEEP AN EYE ON HER.
INCIDENTALLY, YOU HEAR ANY MORE ON THE BASKER-VILLE CASE?
WHAT, THE MAYOR? YEAH, I SAW ON TEXTure HOW ONE OF HIS MULTIPLE PERSONAL-ITIES, "LITTLE SONNY," ALSO HAS MULTIPLE PERSONALITIES. GO FIGURE.
OKAY, YOU GO HOLD THE ELEVATOR...
WILL DO. GOD, MULTIPLE PERSONALITIES WITH MULTIPLE PERSON-ALITIES.
THE MIND'S A PECULIAR PLACE.
EEEEEEEEEEEEEEEEEEEE

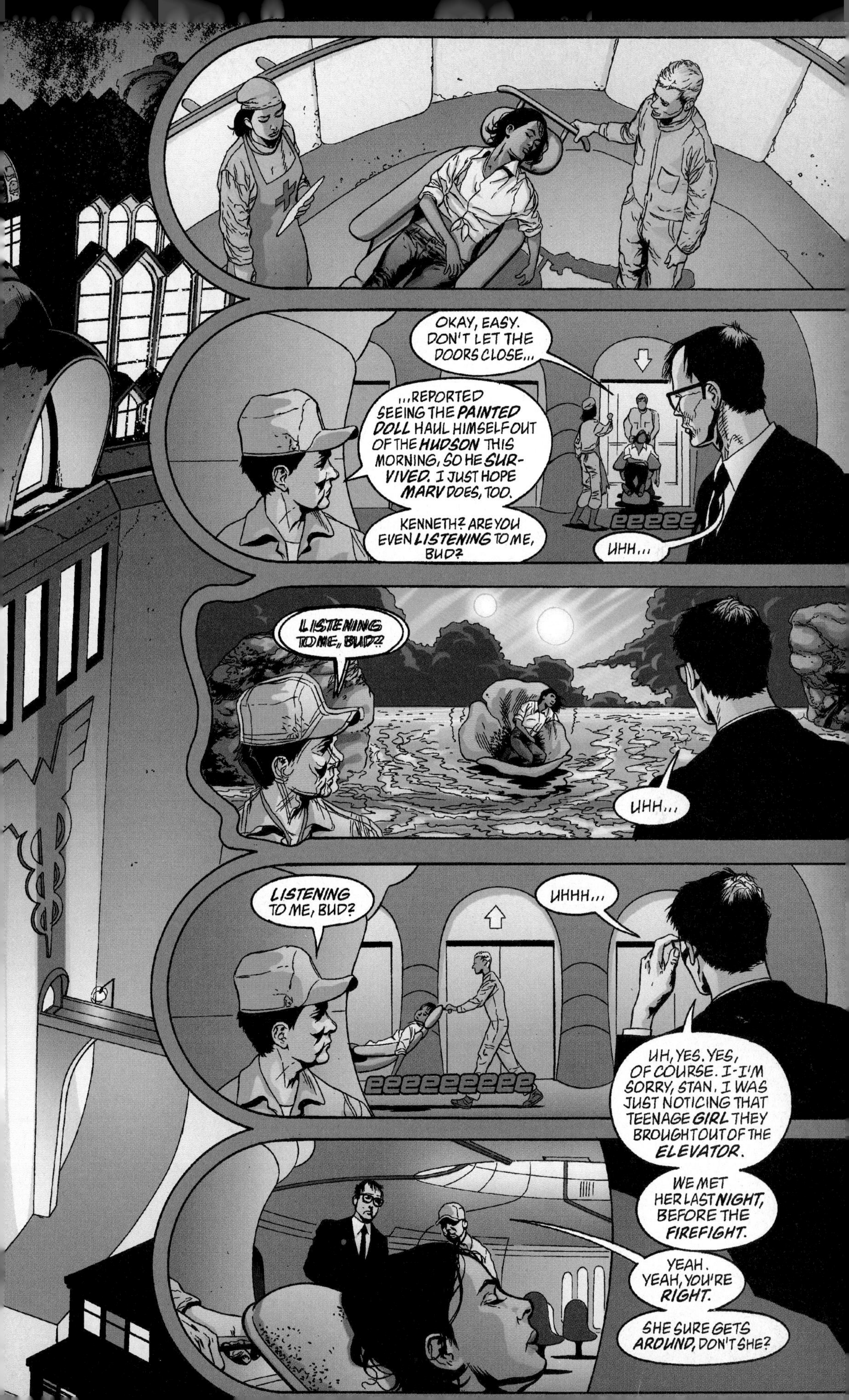
OKAY, EASY. DON'T LET THE DOORS CLOSE...
...REPORTED SEEING THE PAINTED DOLL HAUL HIMSELF OUT OF THE HUDSON THIS MORNING, SO HE SUR-VIVED. I JUST HOPE MARV DOES, TOO.
KENNETH? ARE YOU EVEN LISTENING TO ME, BUD?
eeeee
UHH...
LISTENING TO ME, BUD??
UHH...
LISTENING TO ME, BUD?
UHHH...
eeeeeeeeee
UH, YES. YES, OF COURSE. I-I'M SORRY, STAN. I WAS JUST NOTICING THAT TEENAGE GIRL THEY BROUGHT OUT OF THE ELEVATOR.
WE MET HER LAST NIGHT, BEFORE THE FIREFIGHT.
YEAH. YEAH, YOU'RE RIGHT.
SHE SURE GETS AROUND, DON'T SHE?

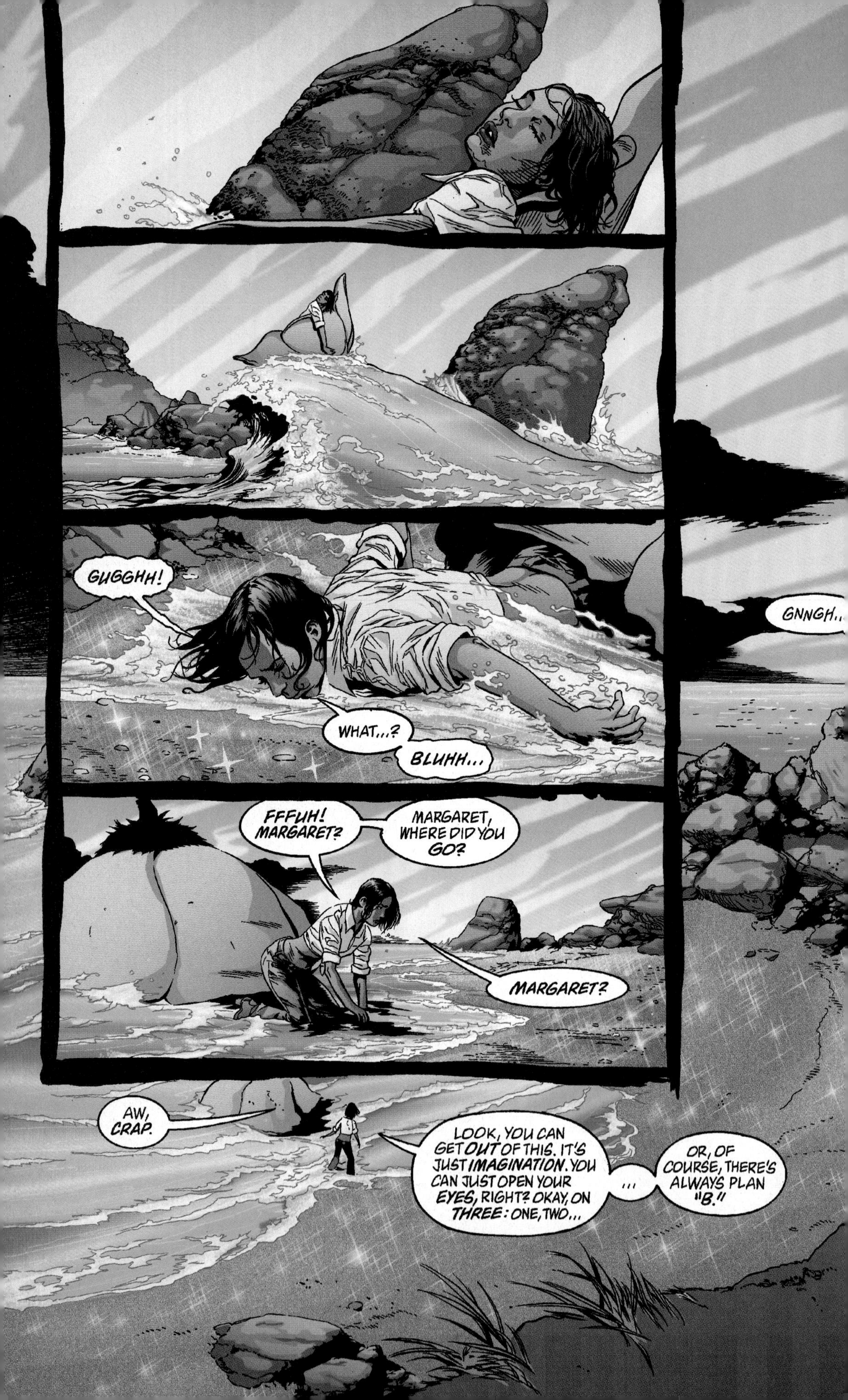
GUGGHH!
GNNGH...
WHAT...?
BLUHH...
FFFUH! MARGARET?
MARGARET, WHERE DID YOU GO?
MARGARET?
AW, CRAP.
LOOK, YOU CAN GET OUT OF THIS. IT'S JUST IMAGINATION. YOU CAN JUST OPEN YOUR EYES, RIGHT? OKAY, ON THREE: ONE, TWO...
...
OR, OF COURSE, THERE'S ALWAYS PLAN "B."

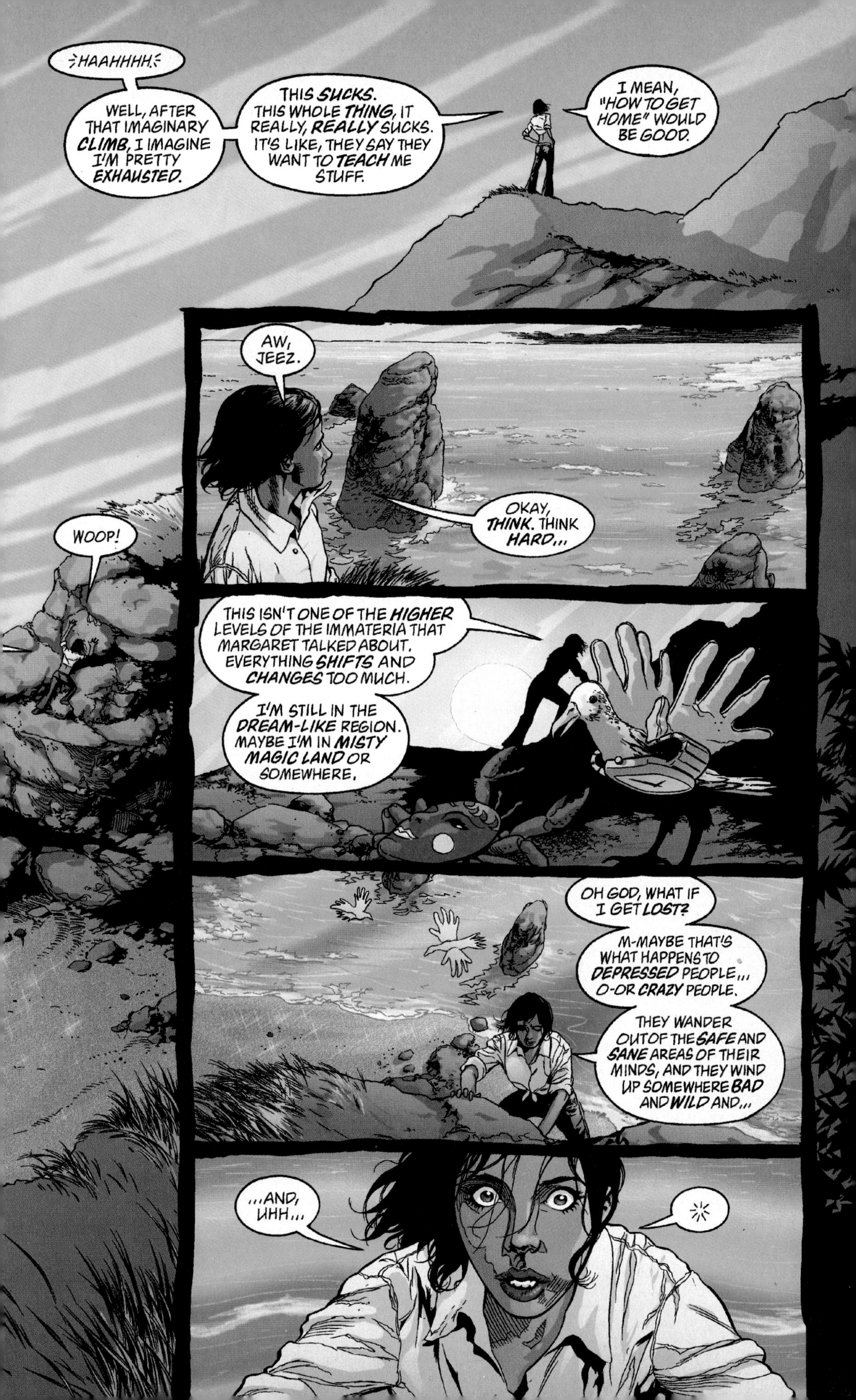

HAAHHHH.
WELL, AFTER THAT IMAGINARY CLIMB, I IMAGINE I'M PRETTY EXHAUSTED.
THIS SUCKS. THIS WHOLE THING, IT REALLY, REALLY SUCKS. IT'S LIKE, THEY SAY THEY WANT TO TEACH ME STUFF.
I MEAN, "HOW TO GET HOME" WOULD BE GOOD.
AW, JEEZ.
OKAY, THINK. THINK HARD...
WOOP!
THIS ISN'T ONE OF THE HIGHER LEVELS OF THE IMMATERIA THAT MARGARET TALKED ABOUT. EVERYTHING SHIFTS AND CHANGES TOO MUCH.
I'M STILL IN THE DREAM-LIKE REGION. MAYBE I'M IN MISTY MAGIC LAND OR SOMEWHERE.
OH GOD, WHAT IF I GET LOST?
M-MAYBE THAT'S WHAT HAPPENS TO DEPRESSED PEOPLE... O-OR CRAZY PEOPLE.
THEY WANDER OUT OF THE SAFE AND SANE AREAS OF THEIR MINDS, AND THEY WIND UP SOMEWHERE BAD AND WILD AND...
...AND, UHH...

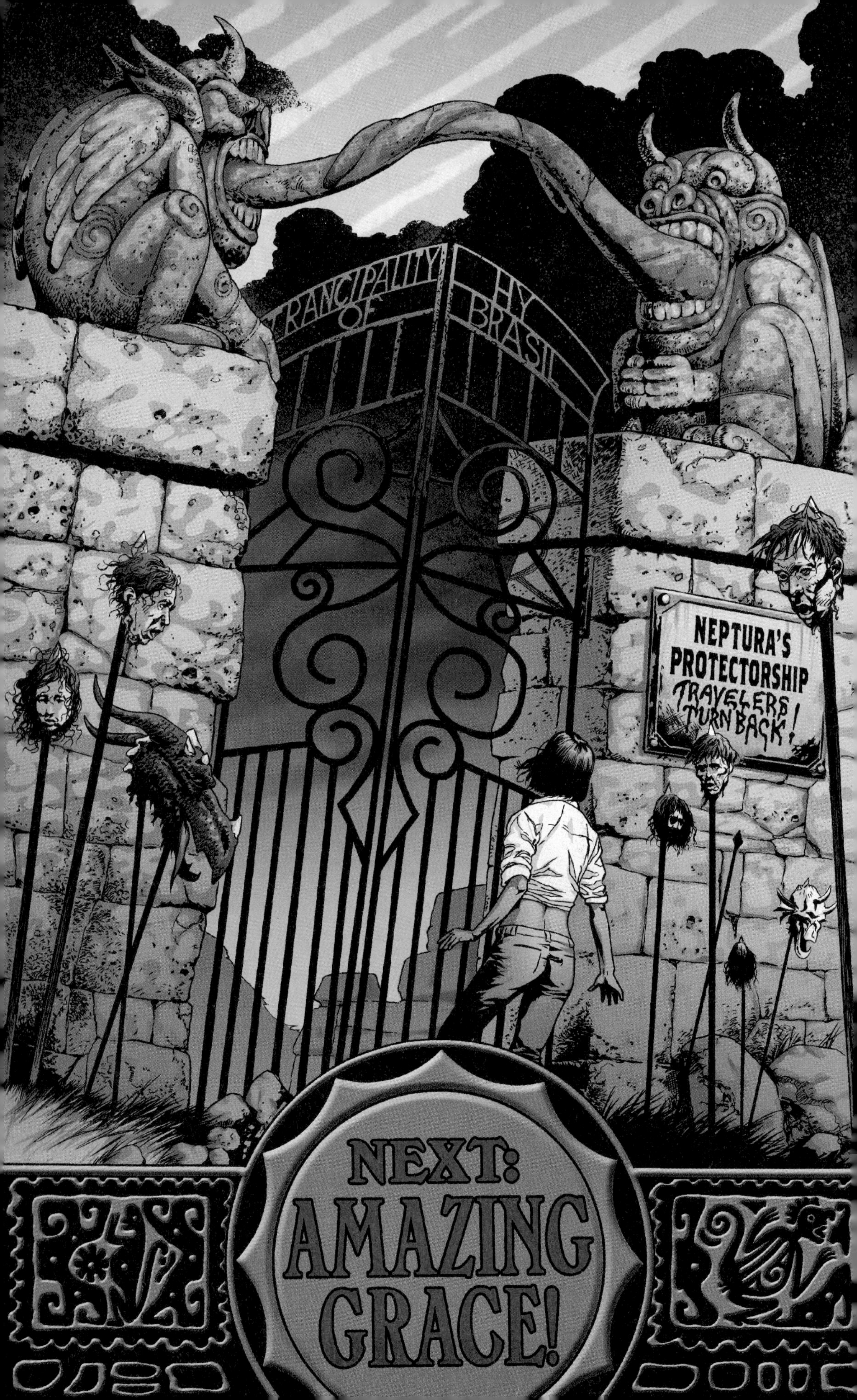

PRINCIPALITY OF HY BRASIL
NEPTURA'S PROTECTORSHIP
TRAVELERS TURN BACK!
NEXT: AMAZING GRACE!

CHAPTER SIX

A wry warrior to the rescue,
A young woman lies dreaming,
An ominous company gathers.

Cover art:
J.H. Williams III

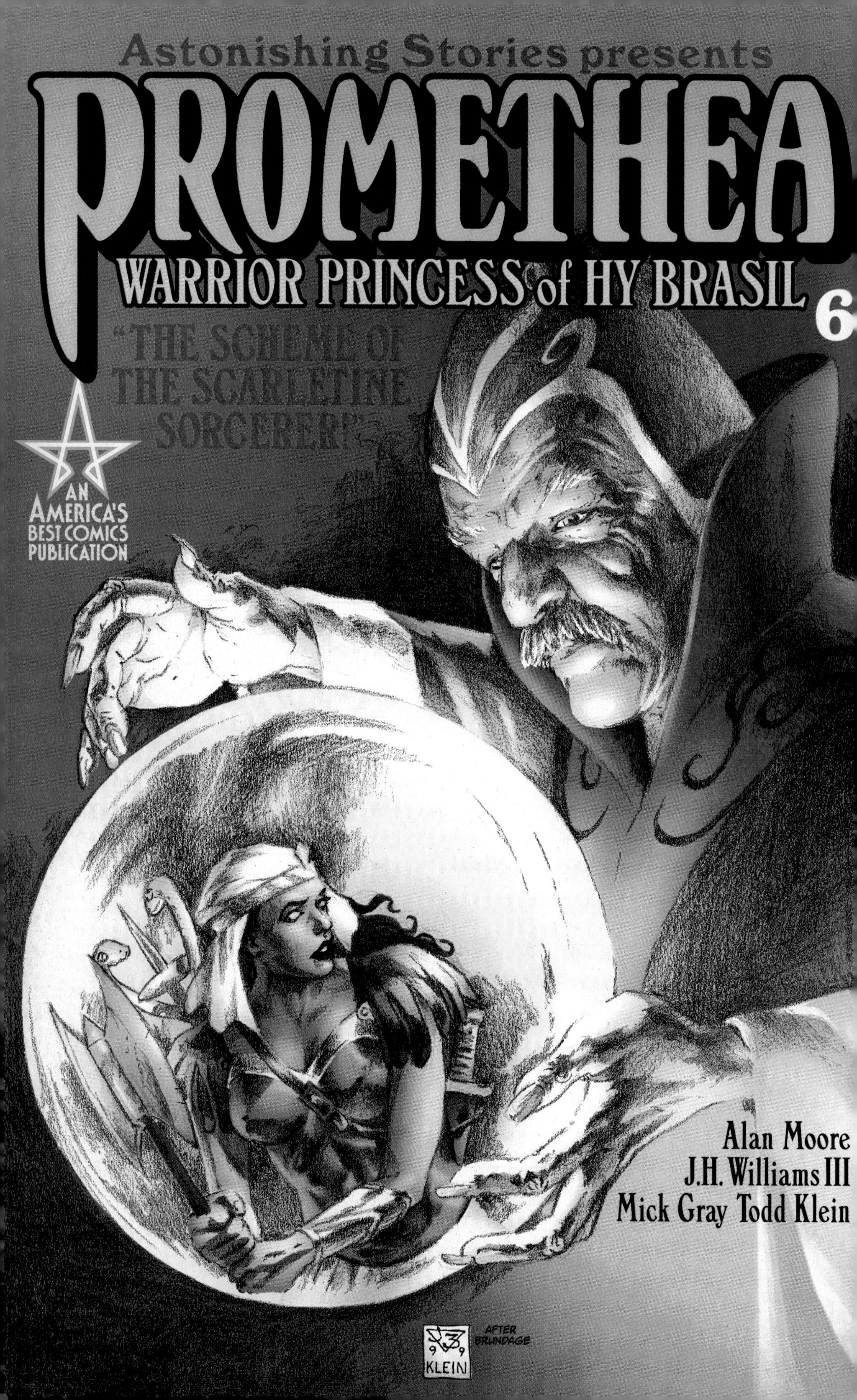

Astonishing Stories presents
PROMETHEA
WARRIOR PRINCESS of HY BRASIL
6
"THE SCHEME OF THE SCARLETINE SORCERER!"
AN AMERICA'S BEST COMICS PUBLICATION
Alan Moore
J.H. Williams III
Mick Gray Todd Klein
99
KLEIN
AFTER BRUNDAGE

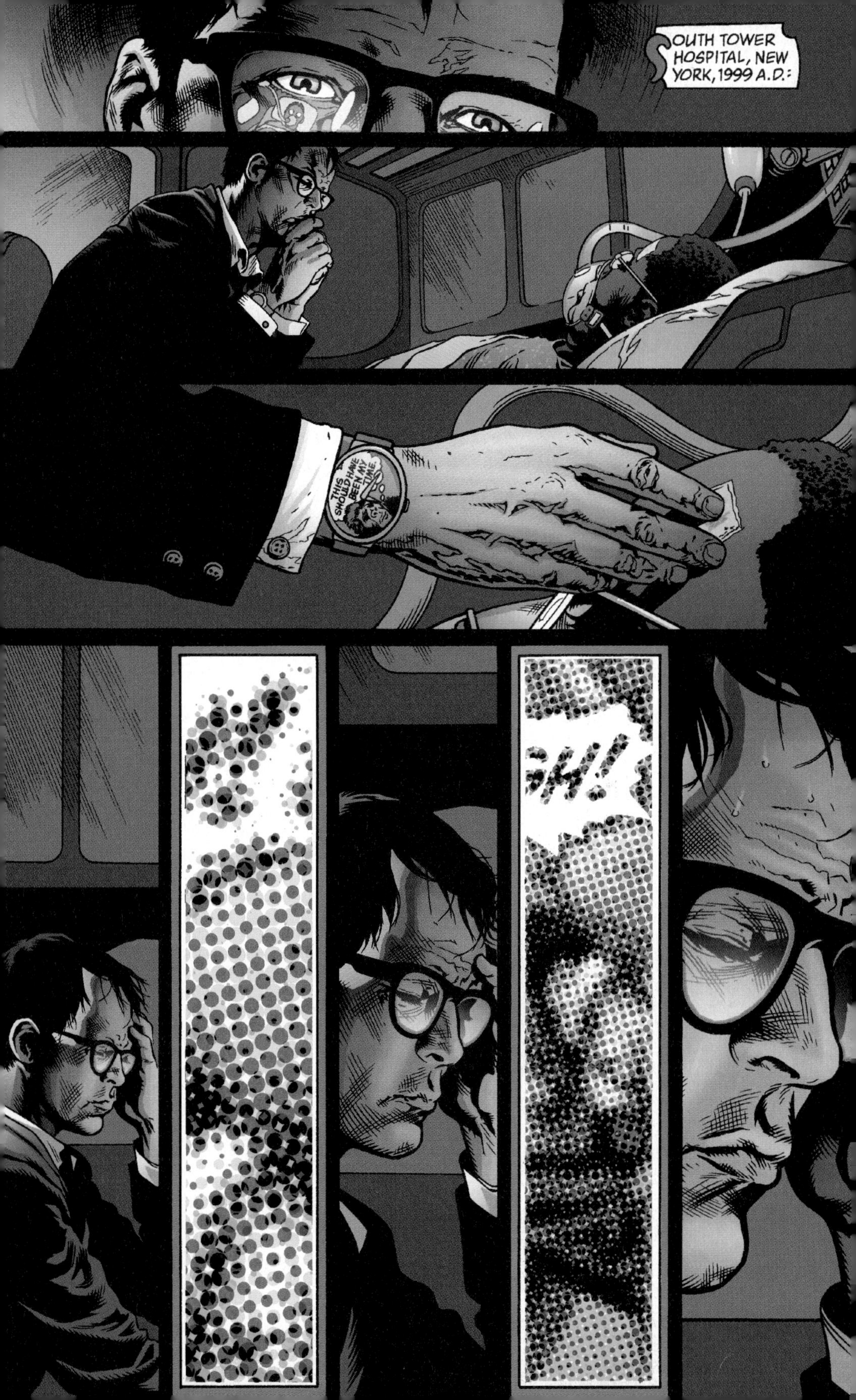

SOUTH TOWER HOSPITAL, NEW YORK, 1999 A.D.:
THIS SHOULD HAVE BEEN MY TIME

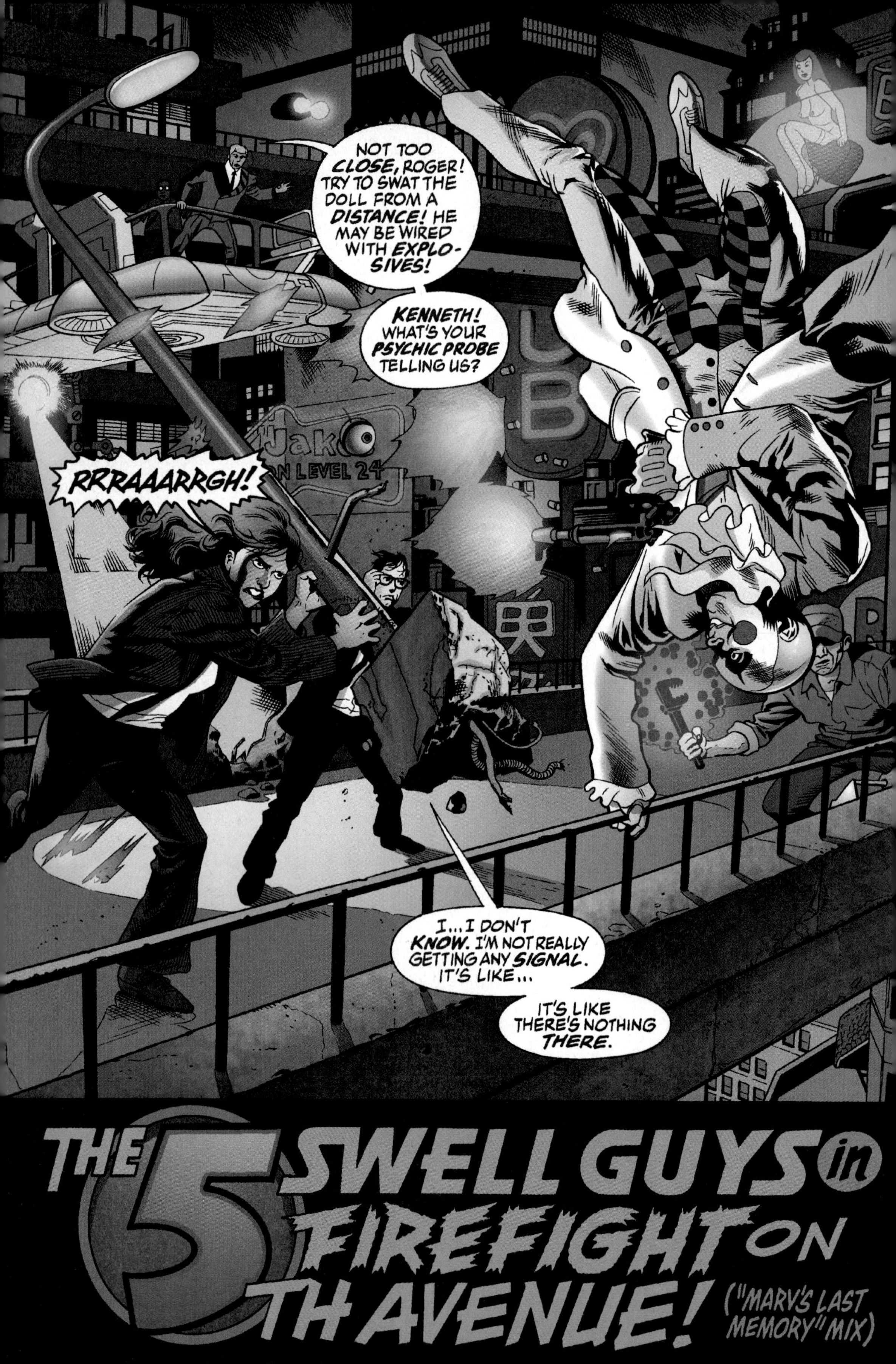
NOT TOO CLOSE, ROGER! TRY TO SWAT THE DOLL FROM A DISTANCE! HE MAY BE WIRED WITH EXPLOSIVES!
KENNETH! WHAT'S YOUR PSYCHIC PROBE TELLING US?
Jak ON LEVEL 24
RRRAAARRGH!
I... I DON'T KNOW. I'M NOT REALLY GETTING ANY SIGNAL. IT'S LIKE...
IT'S LIKE THERE'S NOTHING THERE.
THE 5 SWELL GUYS in FIREFIGHT ON 5TH AVENUE!
("MARV'S LAST MEMORY" MIX)

ALAN MOORE, WRITER; J.H. WILLIAMS III, PENCILLER; MICK GRAY, INKER; JEROMY N. COX, COLORIST; TODD KLEIN, LETTERER; ERIC DESANTIS, ASSISTANT ED; SCOTT DUNBIER, EDITOR

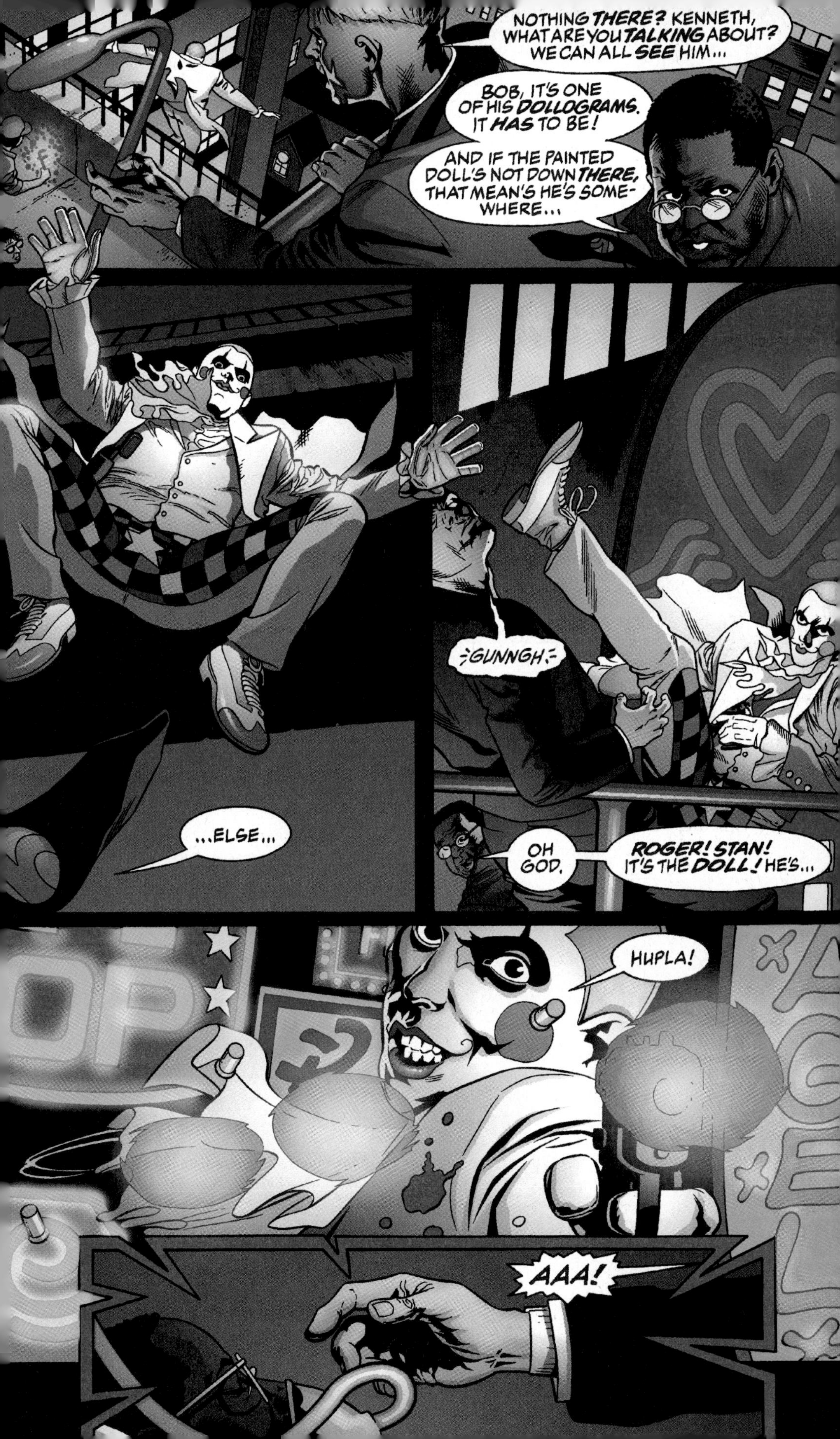

NOTHING THERE? KENNETH, WHAT ARE YOU TALKING ABOUT? WE CAN ALL SEE HIM...
BOB, IT'S ONE OF HIS DOLLOGRAMS. IT HAS TO BE!
AND IF THE PAINTED DOLL'S NOT DOWN THERE, THAT MEAN'S HE'S SOME-WHERE...
...ELSE...
GUNNGH
OH GOD.
ROGER! STAN! IT'S THE DOLL! HE'S...
HUPLA!
AAA!

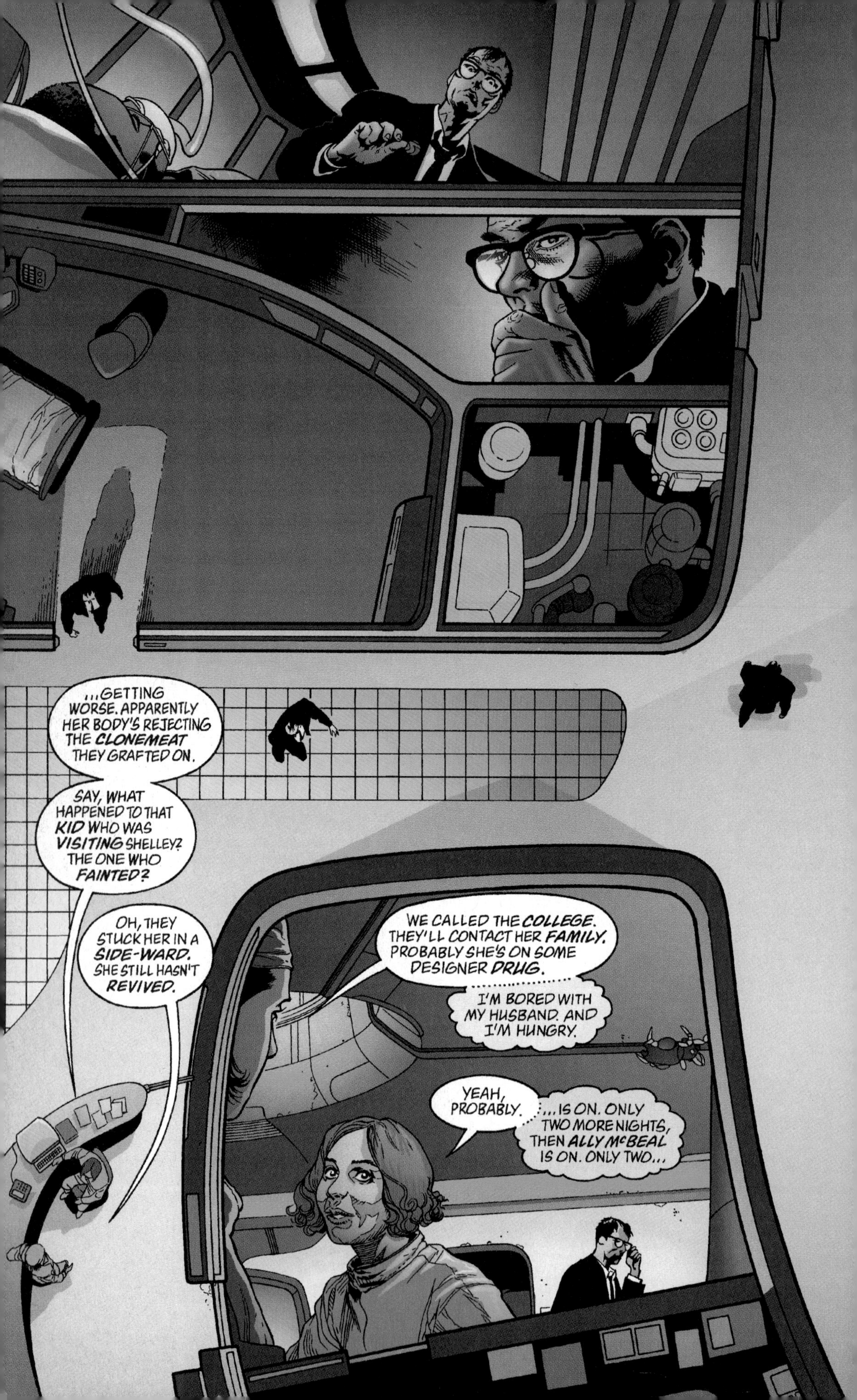
...GETTING WORSE. APPARENTLY HER BODY'S REJECTING THE CLONEMEAT THEY GRAFTED ON.
SAY, WHAT HAPPENED TO THAT KID WHO WAS VISITING SHELLEY? THE ONE WHO FAINTED?
OH, THEY STUCK HER IN A SIDE-WARD. SHE STILL HASN'T REVIVED.
WE CALLED THE COLLEGE. THEY'LL CONTACT HER FAMILY. PROBABLY SHE'S ON SOME DESIGNER DRUG.
I'M BORED WITH MY HUSBAND. AND I'M HUNGRY.
YEAH, PROBABLY.
...IS ON. ONLY TWO MORE NIGHTS, THEN ALLY McBEAL IS ON. ONLY TWO...

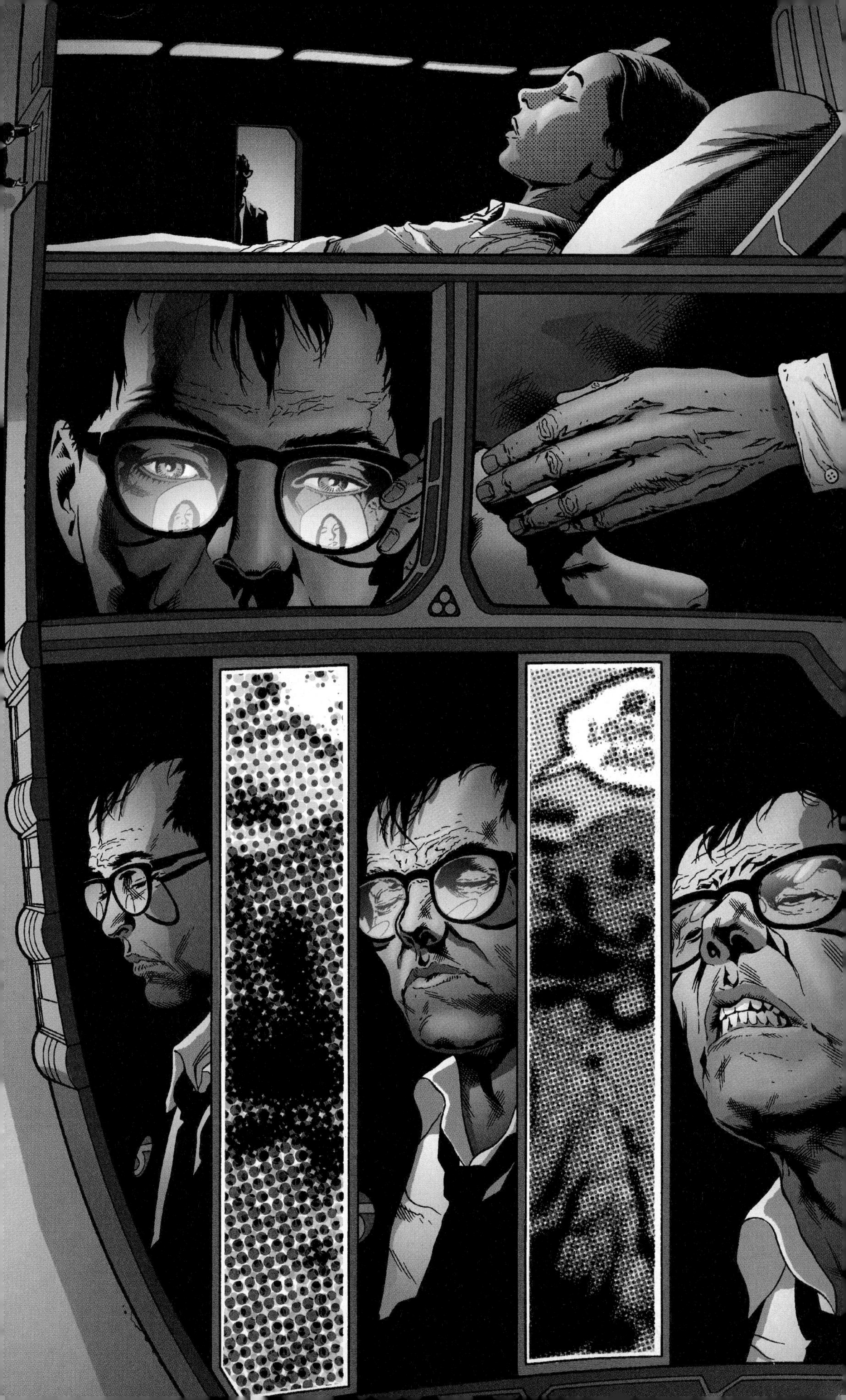

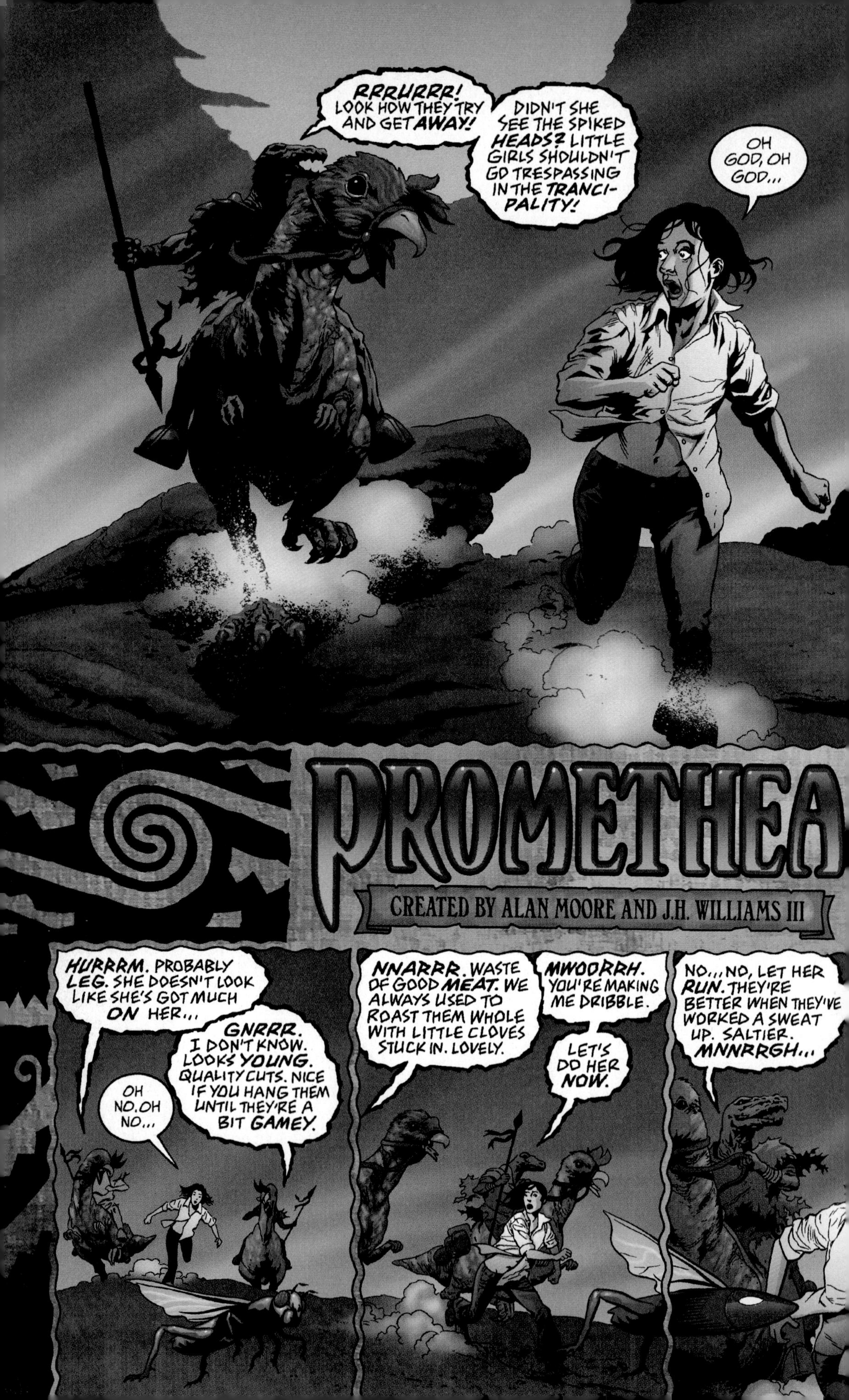

RRRURRR! LOOK HOW THEY TRY AND GET AWAY!
DIDN'T SHE SEE THE SPIKED HEADS? LITTLE GIRLS SHOULDN'T GO TRESPASSING IN THE TRANCI-PALITY!
OH GOD, OH GOD...
PROMETHEA
CREATED BY ALAN MOORE AND J.H. WILLIAMS III
HURRRM. PROBABLY LEG. SHE DOESN'T LOOK LIKE SHE'S GOT MUCH ON HER...
OH NO. OH NO...
GNRRR. I DON'T KNOW. LOOKS YOUNG. QUALITY CUTS. NICE IF YOU HANG THEM UNTIL THEY'RE A BIT GAMEY.
NNARRR. WASTE OF GOOD MEAT. WE ALWAYS USED TO ROAST THEM WHOLE WITH LITTLE CLOVES STUCK IN. LOVELY.
MWOORRH. YOU'RE MAKING ME DRIBBLE.
LET'S DO HER NOW.
NO... NO, LET HER RUN. THEY'RE BETTER WHEN THEY'VE WORKED A SWEAT UP. SALTIER. MNNRRGH...

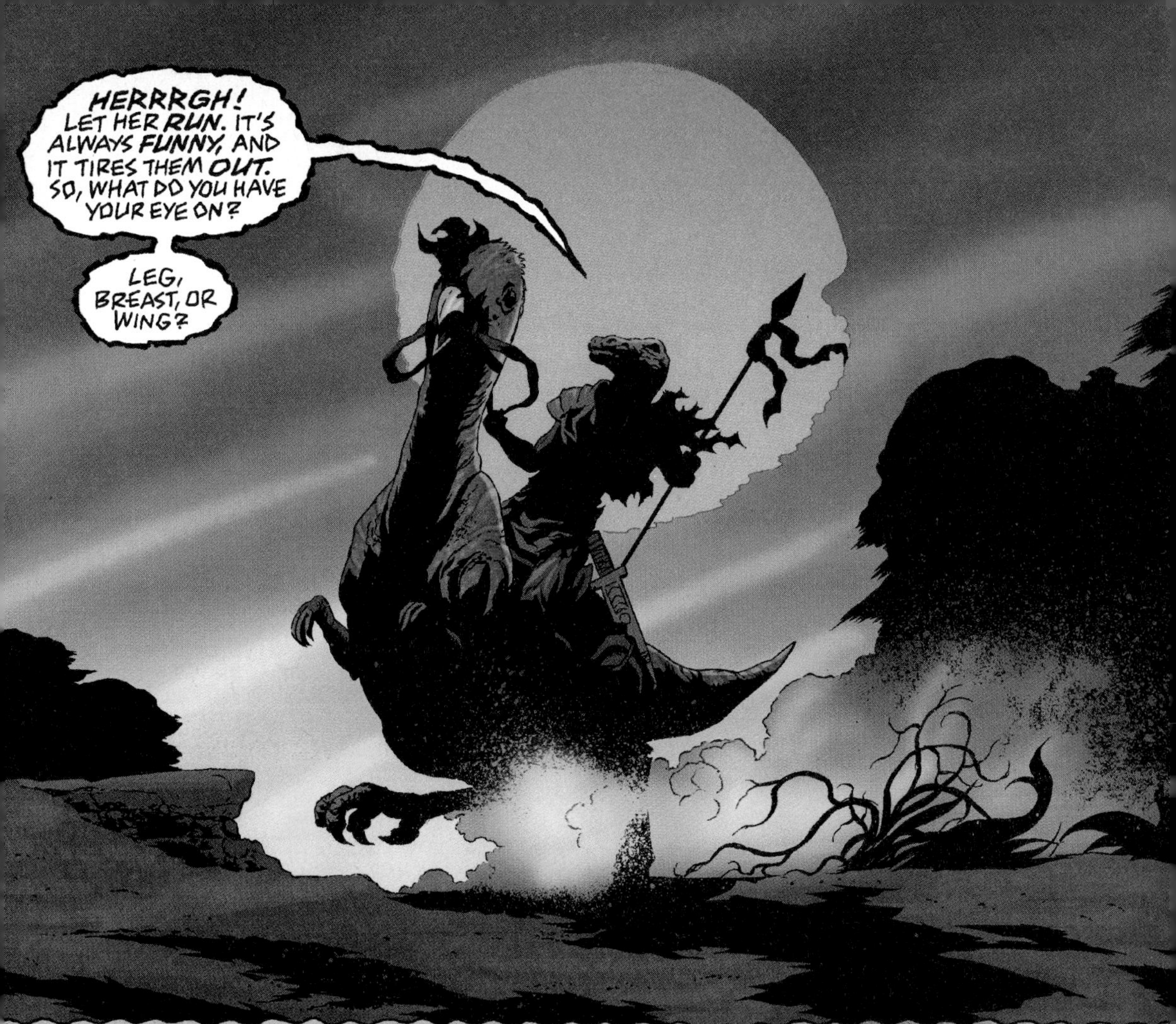
HERRRGH! LET HER RUN. IT'S ALWAYS FUNNY, AND IT TIRES THEM OUT. SO, WHAT DO YOU HAVE YOUR EYE ON?
LEG, BREAST, OR WING?

A WARRIOR PRINCESS of HY BRASIL

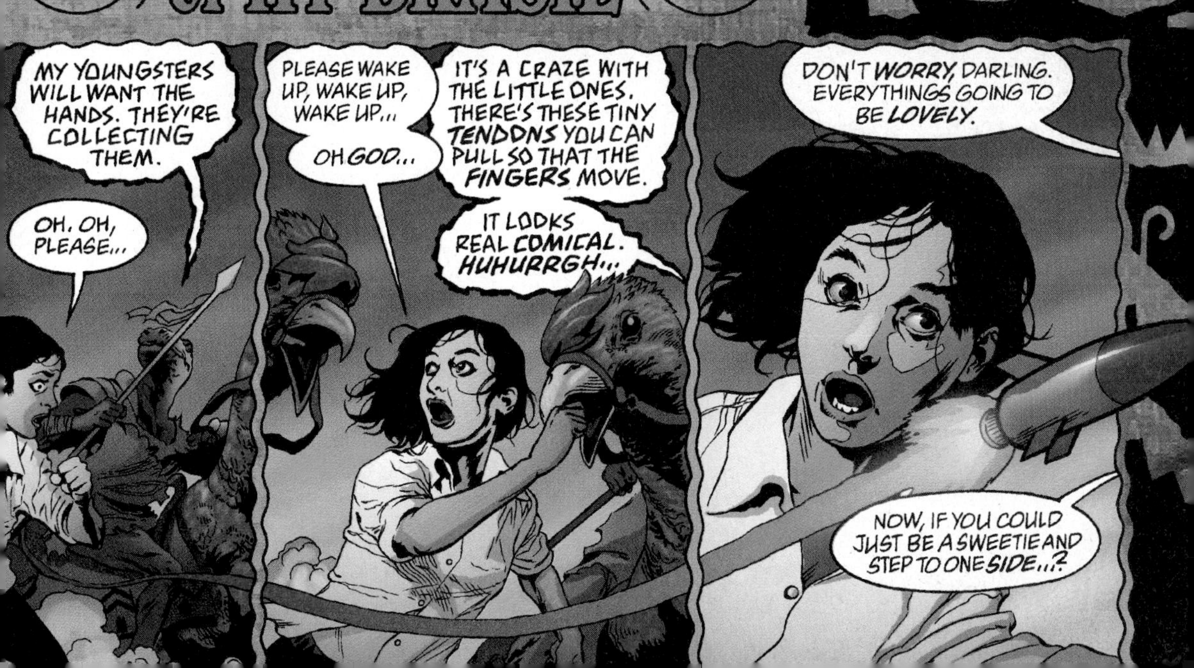
MY YOUNGSTERS WILL WANT THE HANDS. THEY'RE COLLECTING THEM.
OH. OH, PLEASE...
PLEASE WAKE UP, WAKE UP, WAKE UP...
OH GOD...
IT'S A CRAZE WITH THE LITTLE ONES. THERE'S THESE TINY TENDONS YOU CAN PULL SO THAT THE FINGERS MOVE.
IT LOOKS REAL COMICAL. HUHURRGH...
DON'T WORRY, DARLING. EVERYTHINGS GOING TO BE LOVELY.
NOW, IF YOU COULD JUST BE A SWEETIE AND STEP TO ONE SIDE...?

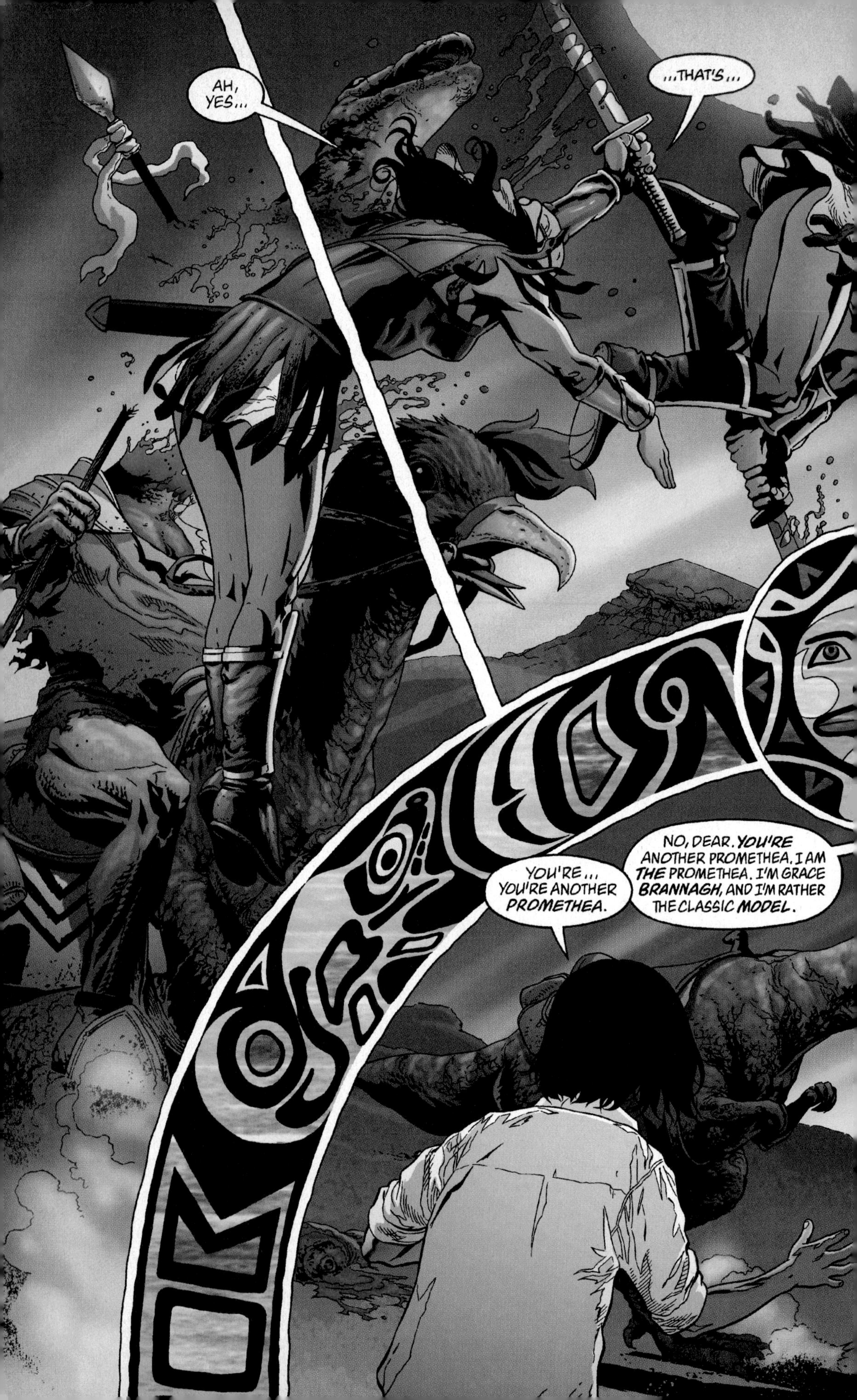
AH, YES...
...THAT'S...
YOU'RE... YOU'RE ANOTHER PROMETHEA.
NO, DEAR. YOU'RE ANOTHER PROMETHEA. I AM THE PROMETHEA. I'M GRACE BRANNAGH, AND I'M RATHER THE CLASSIC MODEL.

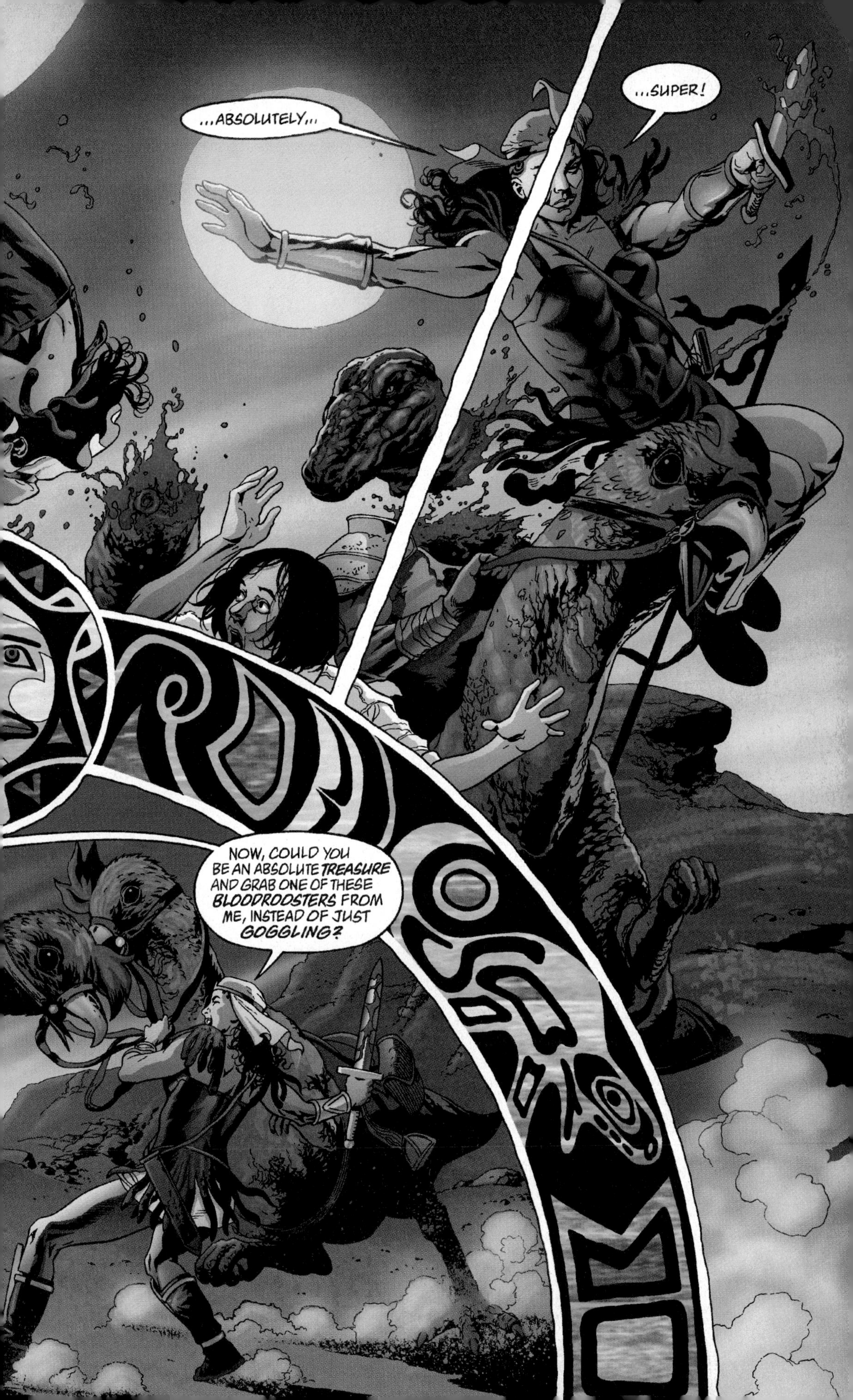
...ABSOLUTELY...
...SUPER!
NOW, COULD YOU BE AN ABSOLUTE TREASURE AND GRAB ONE OF THESE BLOODROOSTERS FROM ME, INSTEAD OF JUST GOGGLING?

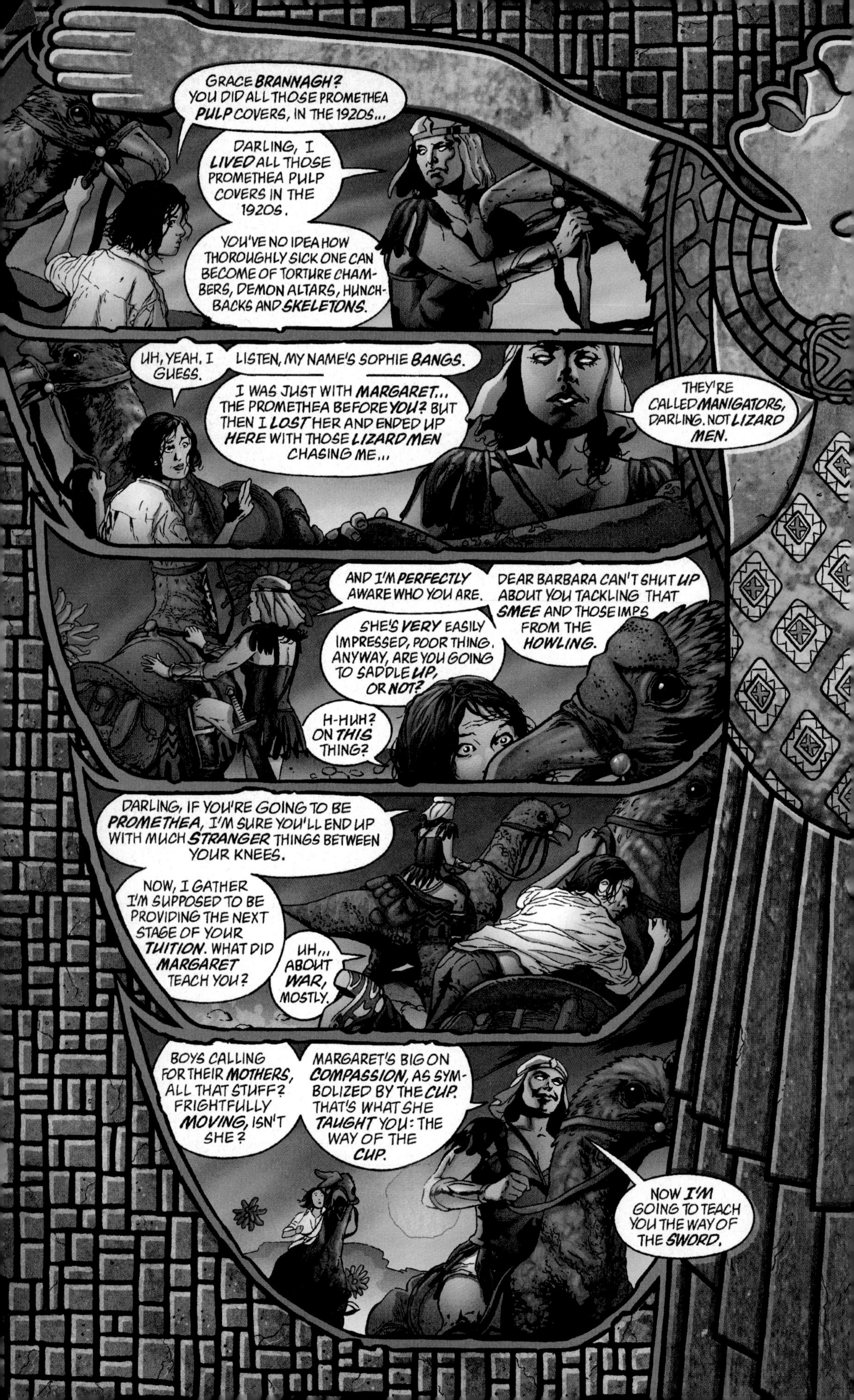
GRACE BRANNAGH? YOU DID ALL THOSE PROMETHEA PULP COVERS, IN THE 1920S...
DARLING, I LIVED ALL THOSE PROMETHEA PULP COVERS IN THE 1920S.
YOU'VE NO IDEA HOW THOROUGHLY SICK ONE CAN BECOME OF TORTURE CHAMBERS, DEMON ALTARS, HUNCHBACKS AND SKELETONS.
UH, YEAH. I GUESS.
LISTEN, MY NAME'S SOPHIE BANGS.
I WAS JUST WITH MARGARET... THE PROMETHEA BEFORE YOU? BUT THEN I LOST HER AND ENDED UP HERE WITH THOSE LIZARD MEN CHASING ME...
THEY'RE CALLED MANIGATORS, DARLING. NOT LIZARD MEN.
AND I'M PERFECTLY AWARE WHO YOU ARE.
DEAR BARBARA CAN'T SHUT UP ABOUT YOU TACKLING THAT SMEE AND THOSE IMPS FROM THE HOWLING.
SHE'S VERY EASILY IMPRESSED, POOR THING. ANYWAY, ARE YOU GOING TO SADDLE UP, OR NOT?
H-HUH? ON THIS THING?
DARLING, IF YOU'RE GOING TO BE PROMETHEA, I'M SURE YOU'LL END UP WITH MUCH STRANGER THINGS BETWEEN YOUR KNEES.
NOW, I GATHER I'M SUPPOSED TO BE PROVIDING THE NEXT STAGE OF YOUR TUITION. WHAT DID MARGARET TEACH YOU?
UH... ABOUT WAR, MOSTLY.
BOYS CALLING FOR THEIR MOTHERS, ALL THAT STUFF? FRIGHTFULLY MOVING, ISN'T SHE?
MARGARET'S BIG ON COMPASSION, AS SYMBOLIZED BY THE CUP. THAT'S WHAT SHE TAUGHT YOU: THE WAY OF THE CUP.
NOW I'M GOING TO TEACH YOU THE WAY OF THE SWORD.

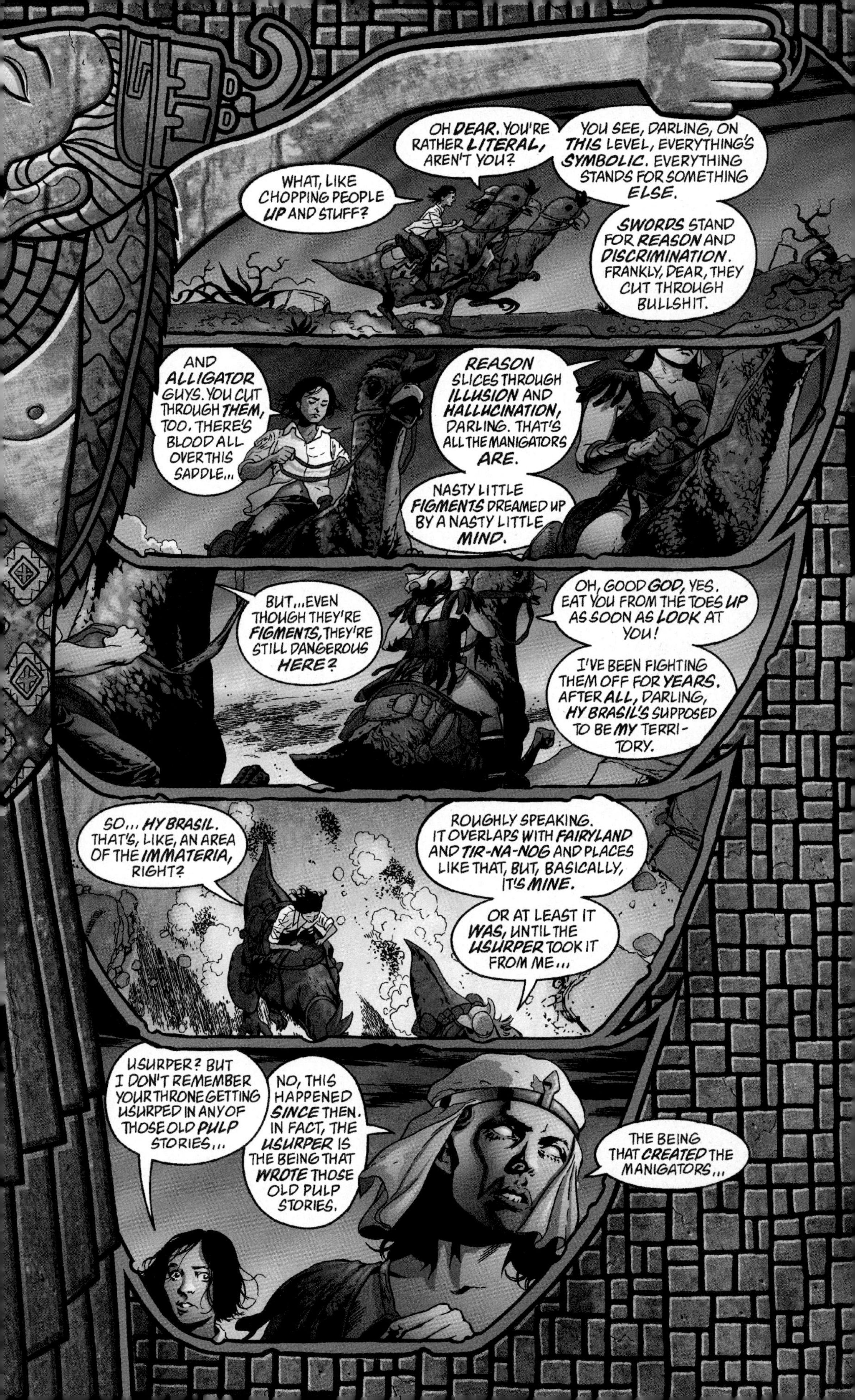
OH DEAR. YOU'RE RATHER LITERAL, AREN'T YOU?
WHAT, LIKE CHOPPING PEOPLE UP AND STUFF?
YOU SEE, DARLING, ON THIS LEVEL, EVERYTHING'S SYMBOLIC. EVERYTHING STANDS FOR SOMETHING ELSE.
SWORDS STAND FOR REASON AND DISCRIMINATION. FRANKLY, DEAR, THEY CUT THROUGH BULLSHIT.
AND ALLIGATOR GUYS. YOU CUT THROUGH THEM, TOO. THERE'S BLOOD ALL OVER THIS SADDLE...
REASON SLICES THROUGH ILLUSION AND HALLUCINATION, DARLING. THAT'S ALL THE MANIGATORS ARE.
NASTY LITTLE FIGMENTS DREAMED UP BY A NASTY LITTLE MIND.
BUT... EVEN THOUGH THEY'RE FIGMENTS, THEY'RE STILL DANGEROUS HERE?
OH, GOOD GOD, YES. EAT YOU FROM THE TOES UP AS SOON AS LOOK AT YOU!
I'VE BEEN FIGHTING THEM OFF FOR YEARS. AFTER ALL, DARLING, HY BRASIL'S SUPPOSED TO BE MY TERRI-TORY.
SO... HY BRASIL. THAT'S, LIKE, AN AREA OF THE IMMATERIA, RIGHT?
ROUGHLY SPEAKING. IT OVERLAPS WITH FAIRYLAND AND TIR-NA-NOG AND PLACES LIKE THAT, BUT, BASICALLY, IT'S MINE.
OR AT LEAST IT WAS, UNTIL THE USURPER TOOK IT FROM ME...
USURPER? BUT I DON'T REMEMBER YOUR THRONE GETTING USURPED IN ANY OF THOSE OLD PULP STORIES...
NO, THIS HAPPENED SINCE THEN. IN FACT, THE USURPER IS THE BEING THAT WROTE THOSE OLD PULP STORIES.
THE BEING THAT CREATED THE MANIGATORS...

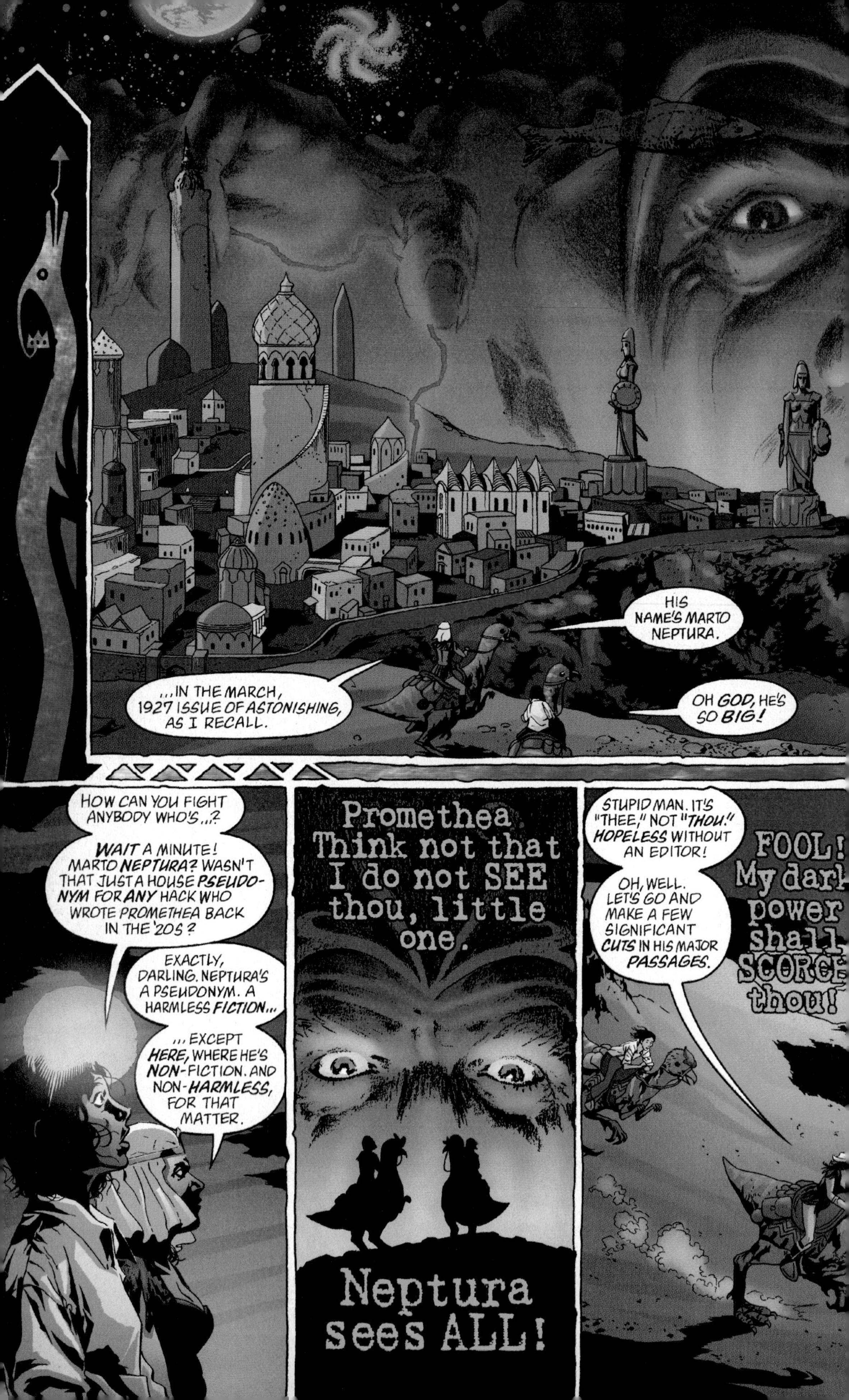

HIS NAME'S MARTO NEPTURA.
...IN THE MARCH, 1927 ISSUE OF ASTONISHING, AS I RECALL.
OH GOD, HE'S SO BIG!
HOW CAN YOU FIGHT ANYBODY WHO'S...?
WAIT A MINUTE! MARTO NEPTURA? WASN'T THAT JUST A HOUSE PSEUDONYM FOR ANY HACK WHO WROTE PROMETHEA BACK IN THE '20S?
EXACTLY, DARLING. NEPTURA'S A PSEUDONYM. A HARMLESS FICTION...
...EXCEPT HERE, WHERE HE'S NON-FICTION. AND NON-HARMLESS, FOR THAT MATTER.
Promethea. Think not that I do not SEE thou, little one.
Neptura sees ALL!
STUPID MAN. IT'S "THEE," NOT "THOU." HOPELESS WITHOUT AN EDITOR!
OH, WELL. LET'S GO AND MAKE A FEW SIGNIFICANT CUTS IN HIS MAJOR PASSAGES.
FOOL! My dark power shall SCORCH thou!

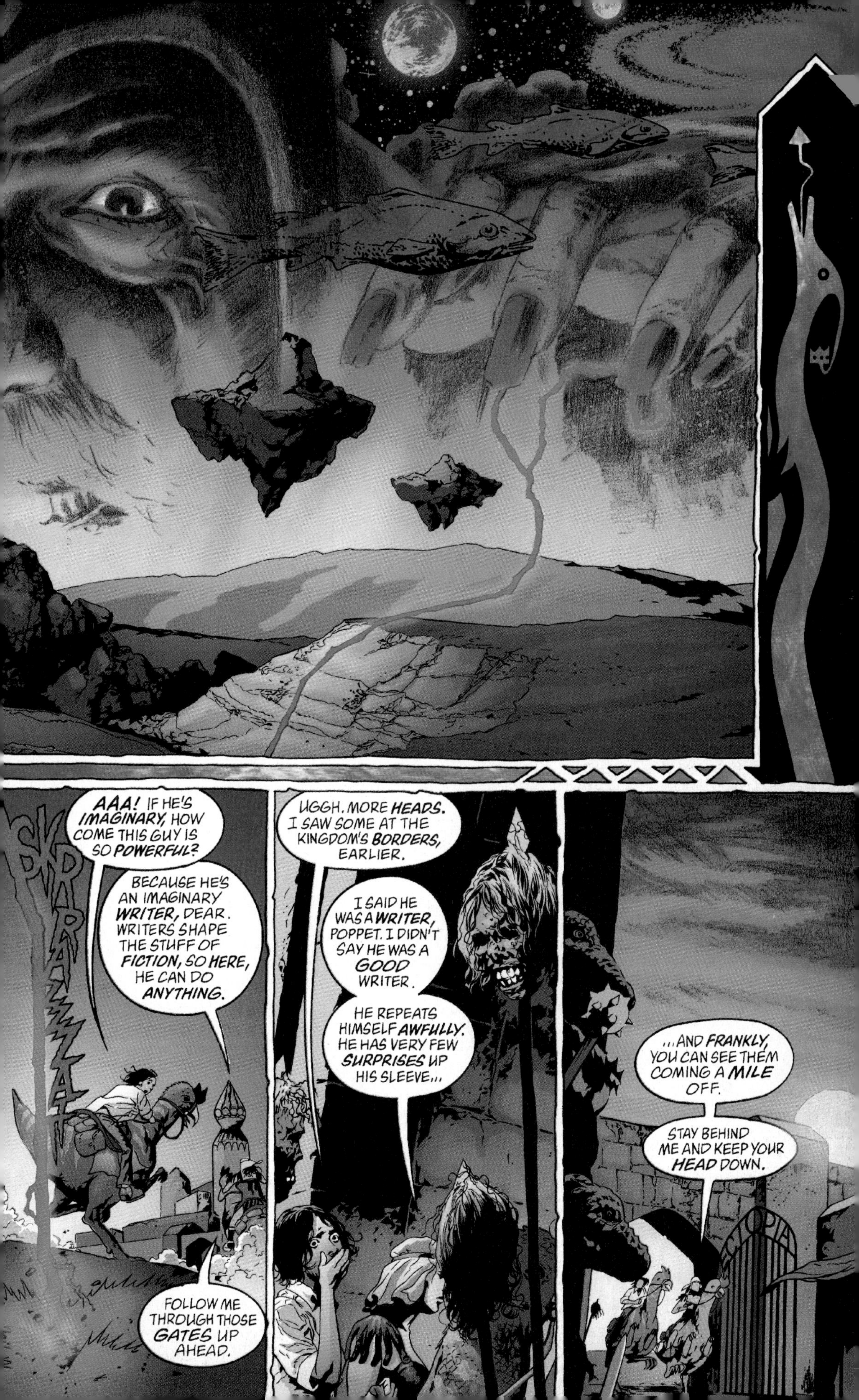
AAA! IF HE'S IMAGINARY, HOW COME THIS GUY IS SO POWERFUL?
BECAUSE HE'S AN IMAGINARY WRITER, DEAR. WRITERS SHAPE THE STUFF OF FICTION, SO HERE, HE CAN DO ANYTHING.
FOLLOW ME THROUGH THOSE GATES UP AHEAD.
UGGH. MORE HEADS. I SAW SOME AT THE KINGDOM'S BORDERS, EARLIER.
I SAID HE WAS A WRITER, POPPET. I DIDN'T SAY HE WAS A GOOD WRITER.
HE REPEATS HIMSELF AWFULLY. HE HAS VERY FEW SURPRISES UP HIS SLEEVE...
...AND FRANKLY, YOU CAN SEE THEM COMING A MILE OFF.
STAY BEHIND ME AND KEEP YOUR HEAD DOWN.

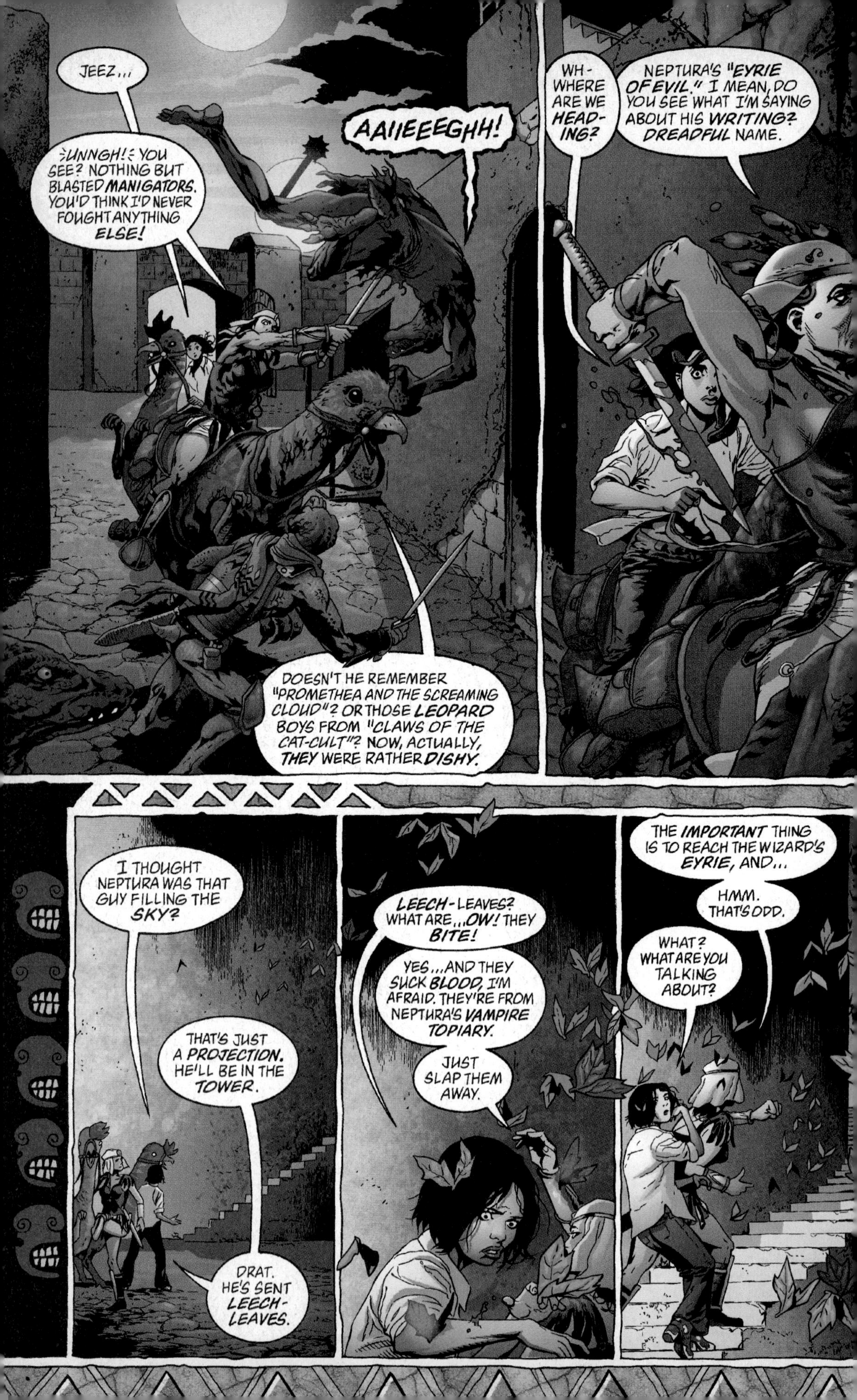
JEEZ...
-UNNGH!- YOU SEE? NOTHING BUT BLASTED MANIGATORS. YOU'D THINK I'D NEVER FOUGHT ANYTHING ELSE!
AAIIEEEGHH!
DOESN'T HE REMEMBER "PROMETHEA AND THE SCREAMING CLOUD"? OR THOSE LEOPARD BOYS FROM "CLAWS OF THE CAT-CULT"? NOW, ACTUALLY, THEY WERE RATHER DISHY.
WH- WHERE ARE WE HEADING?
NEPTURA'S "EYRIE OF EVIL." I MEAN, DO YOU SEE WHAT I'M SAYING ABOUT HIS WRITING? DREADFUL NAME.
I THOUGHT NEPTURA WAS THAT GUY FILLING THE SKY?
THAT'S JUST A PROJECTION. HE'LL BE IN THE TOWER.
DRAT. HE'S SENT LEECH-LEAVES.
LEECH-LEAVES? WHAT ARE... OW! THEY BITE!
YES... AND THEY SUCK BLOOD, I'M AFRAID. THEY'RE FROM NEPTURA'S VAMPIRE TOPIARY.
JUST SLAP THEM AWAY.
THE IMPORTANT THING IS TO REACH THE WIZARD'S EYRIE, AND...
HMM. THAT'S ODD.
WHAT? WHAT ARE YOU TALKING ABOUT?

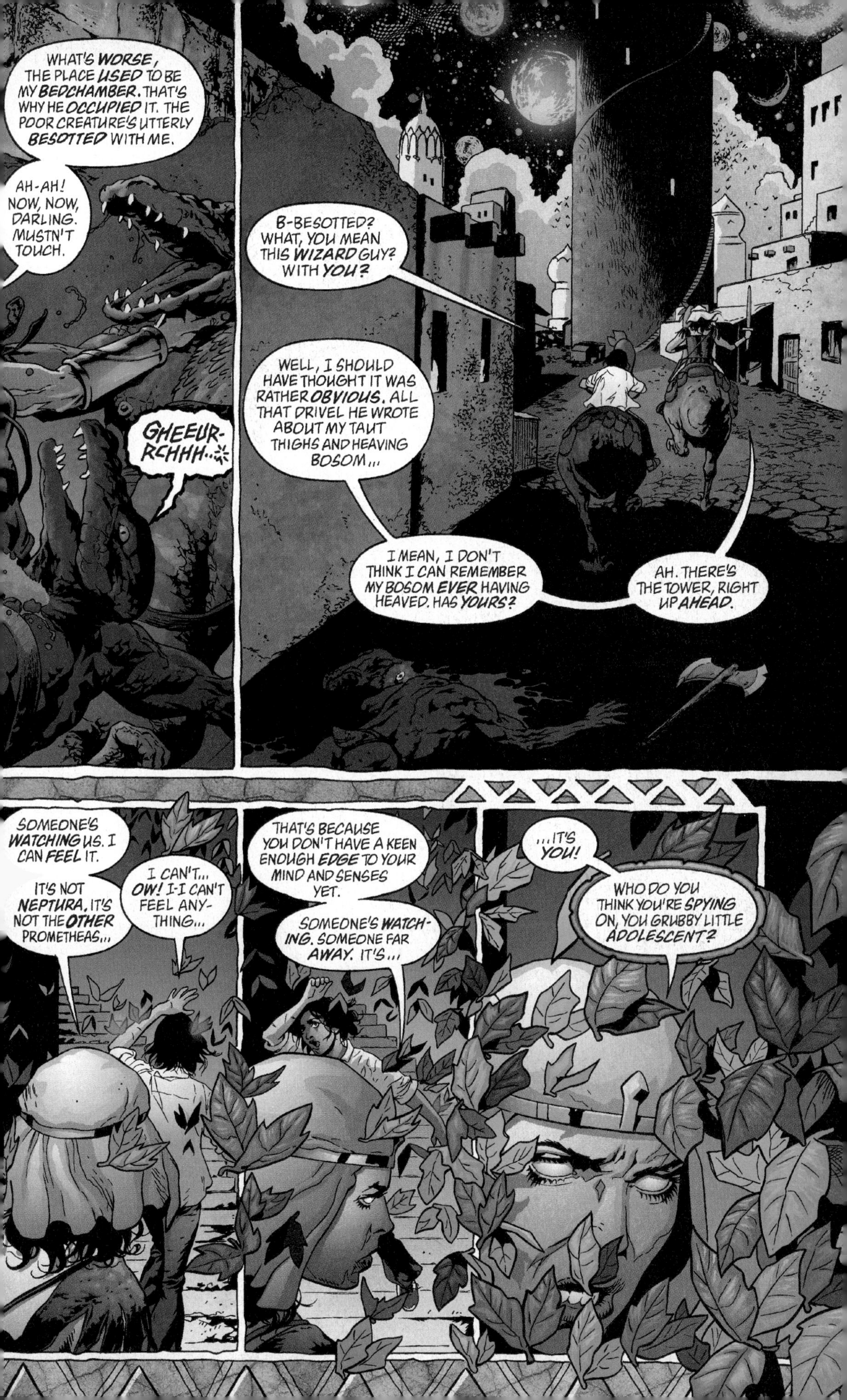
WHAT'S WORSE, THE PLACE USED TO BE MY BEDCHAMBER. THAT'S WHY HE OCCUPIED IT. THE POOR CREATURE'S UTTERLY BESOTTED WITH ME.
AH-AH! NOW, NOW, DARLING. MUSTN'T TOUCH.
GHEEUR-RCHHH...
B-BESOTTED? WHAT, YOU MEAN THIS WIZARD GUY? WITH YOU?
WELL, I SHOULD HAVE THOUGHT IT WAS RATHER OBVIOUS. ALL THAT DRIVEL HE WROTE ABOUT MY TAUT THIGHS AND HEAVING BOSOM...
I MEAN, I DON'T THINK I CAN REMEMBER MY BOSOM EVER HAVING HEAVED. HAS YOURS?
AH. THERE'S THE TOWER, RIGHT UP AHEAD.
SOMEONE'S WATCHING US. I CAN FEEL IT.
IT'S NOT NEPTURA. IT'S NOT THE OTHER PROMETHEAS...
I CAN'T... OW! I-I CAN'T FEEL ANY-THING...
THAT'S BECAUSE YOU DON'T HAVE A KEEN ENOUGH EDGE TO YOUR MIND AND SENSES YET.
SOMEONE'S WATCH-ING. SOMEONE FAR AWAY. IT'S...
...IT'S YOU!
WHO DO YOU THINK YOU'RE SPYING ON, YOU GRUBBY LITTLE ADOLESCENT?

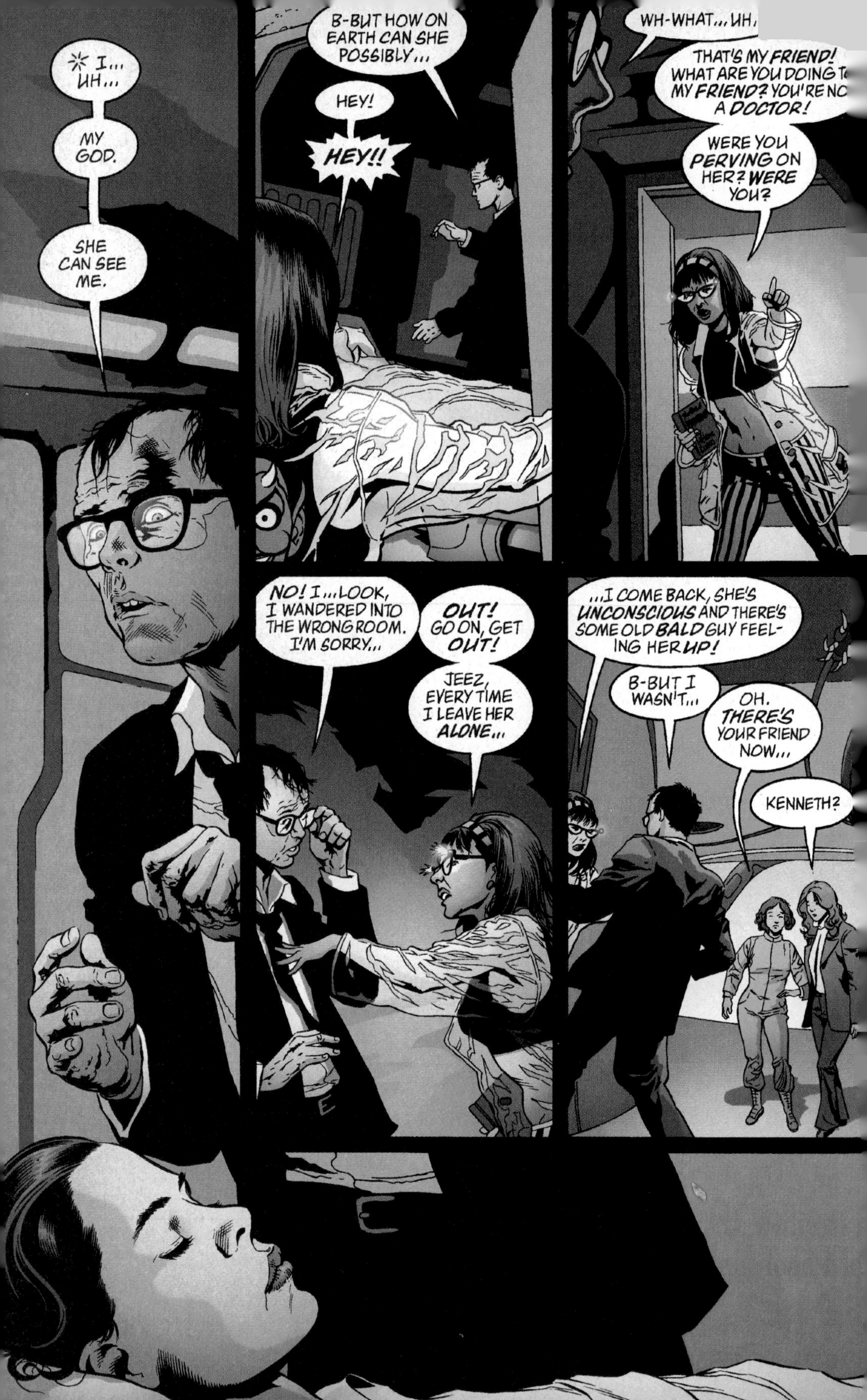

* I... UH...
MY GOD.
SHE CAN SEE ME.
B-BUT HOW ON EARTH CAN SHE POSSIBLY...
HEY!
HEY!!
WH-WHAT... UH,
THAT'S MY FRIEND! WHAT ARE YOU DOING TO MY FRIEND? YOU'RE NOT A DOCTOR!
WERE YOU PERVING ON HER? WERE YOU?
NO! I...LOOK, I WANDERED INTO THE WRONG ROOM. I'M SORRY...
OUT! GO ON, GET OUT!
JEEZ, EVERY TIME I LEAVE HER ALONE...
...I COME BACK, SHE'S UNCONSCIOUS AND THERE'S SOME OLD BALD GUY FEEL-ING HER UP!
B-BUT I WASN'T...
OH. THERE'S YOUR FRIEND NOW...
KENNETH?

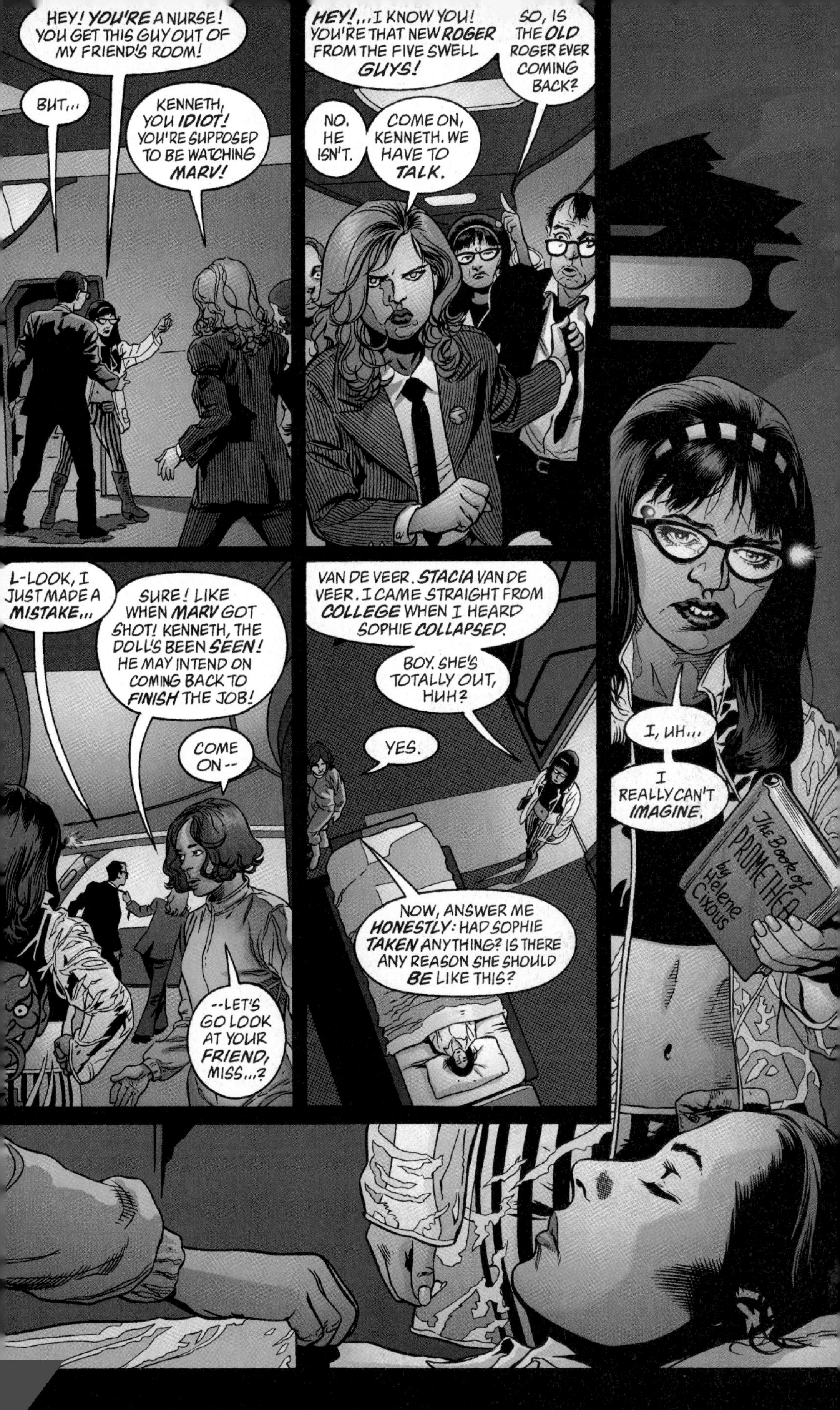
HEY! YOU'RE A NURSE! YOU GET THIS GUY OUT OF MY FRIEND'S ROOM!
BUT,..
KENNETH, YOU IDIOT! YOU'RE SUPPOSED TO BE WATCHING MARV!
HEY!... I KNOW YOU! YOU'RE THAT NEW ROGER FROM THE FIVE SWELL GUYS!
SO, IS THE OLD ROGER EVER COMING BACK?
NO. HE ISN'T.
COME ON, KENNETH. WE HAVE TO TALK.
L-LOOK, I JUST MADE A MISTAKE...
SURE! LIKE WHEN MARV GOT SHOT! KENNETH, THE DOLL'S BEEN SEEN! HE MAY INTEND ON COMING BACK TO FINISH THE JOB!
COME ON --
--LET'S GO LOOK AT YOUR FRIEND, MISS...?
VAN DE VEER. STACIA VAN DE VEER. I CAME STRAIGHT FROM COLLEGE WHEN I HEARD SOPHIE COLLAPSED.
BOY. SHE'S TOTALLY OUT, HUH?
YES.
NOW, ANSWER ME HONESTLY: HAD SOPHIE TAKEN ANYTHING? IS THERE ANY REASON SHE SHOULD BE LIKE THIS?
I, UH...
I REALLY CAN'T IMAGINE.
The Book of PROMETHEA by Helene Cixous

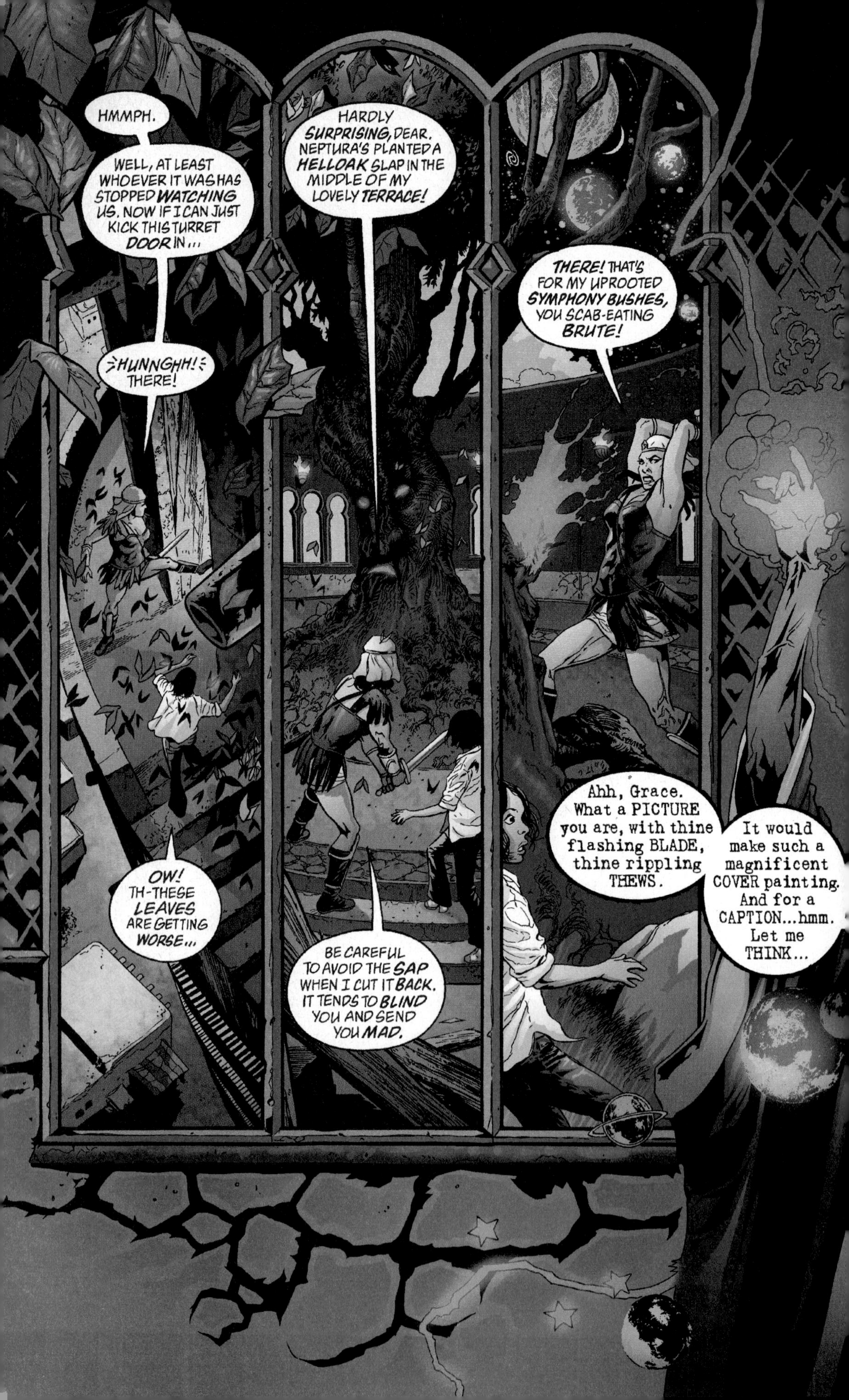

HMMPH.
WELL, AT LEAST WHOEVER IT WAS HAS STOPPED WATCHING US. NOW IF I CAN JUST KICK THIS TURRET DOOR IN...
HUNNGHH! THERE!
HARDLY SURPRISING, DEAR. NEPTURA'S PLANTED A HELLOAK SLAP IN THE MIDDLE OF MY LOVELY TERRACE!
THERE! THAT'S FOR MY UPROOTED SYMPHONY BUSHES, YOU SCAB-EATING BRUTE!
OW! TH-THESE LEAVES ARE GETTING WORSE...
BE CAREFUL TO AVOID THE SAP WHEN I CUT IT BACK. IT TENDS TO BLIND YOU AND SEND YOU MAD.
Ahh, Grace. What a PICTURE you are, with thine flashing BLADE, thine rippling THEWS.
It would make such a magnificent COVER painting. And for a CAPTION...hmm. Let me THINK...

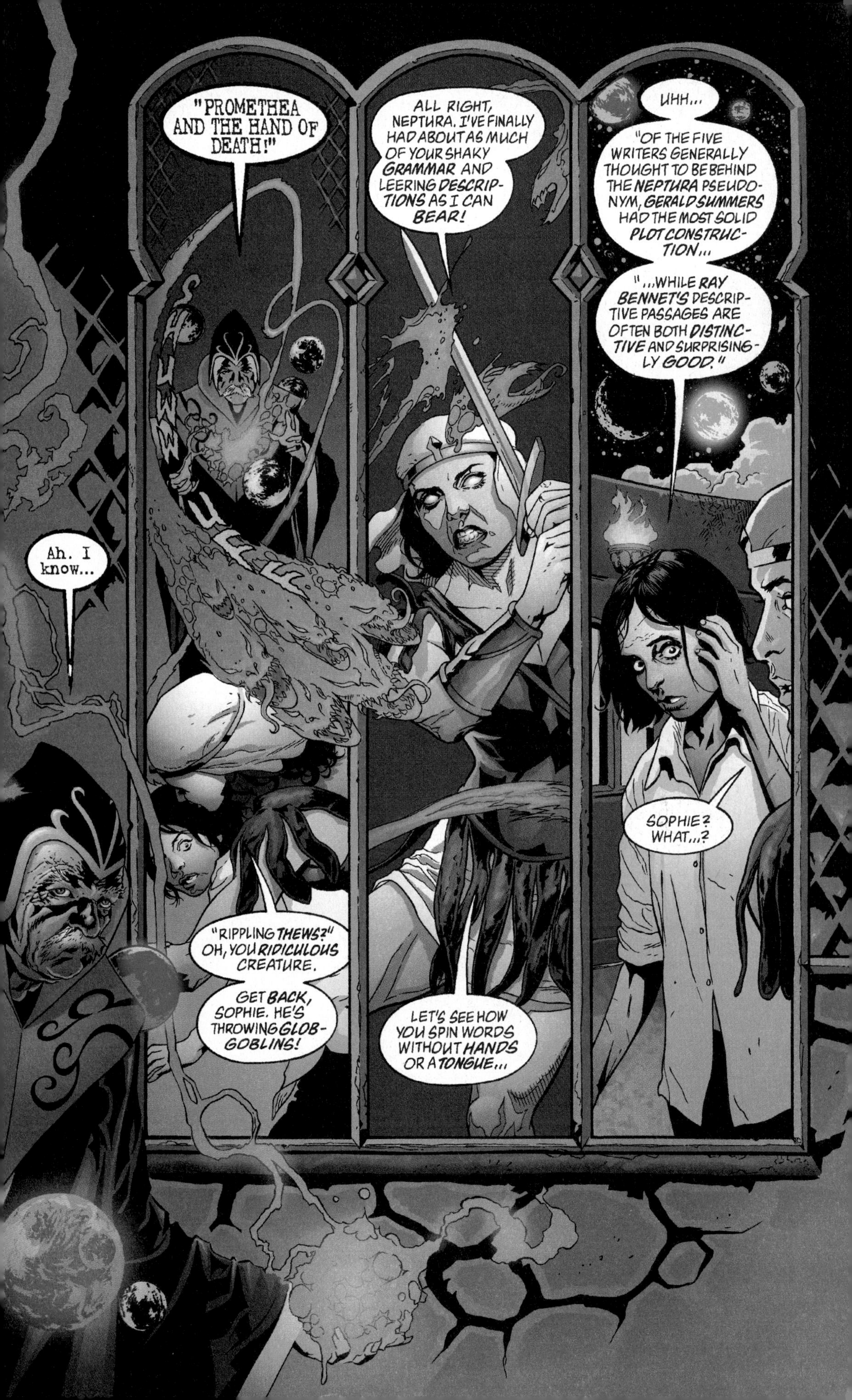
"PROMETHEA AND THE HAND OF DEATH!"
ALL RIGHT, NEPTURA. I'VE FINALLY HAD ABOUT AS MUCH OF YOUR SHAKY GRAMMAR AND LEERING DESCRIPTIONS AS I CAN BEAR!
UHH...
"OF THE FIVE WRITERS GENERALLY THOUGHT TO BE BEHIND THE NEPTURA PSEUDONYM, GERALD SUMMERS HAD THE MOST SOLID PLOT CONSTRUCTION...
"...WHILE RAY BENNET'S DESCRIPTIVE PASSAGES ARE OFTEN BOTH DISTINCTIVE AND SURPRISINGLY GOOD."
Ah. I know...
SOPHIE? WHAT...?
"RIPPLING THEWS?" OH, YOU RIDICULOUS CREATURE.
GET BACK, SOPHIE. HE'S THROWING GLOB-GOBLINS!
LET'S SEE HOW YOU SPIN WORDS WITHOUT HANDS OR A TONGUE...

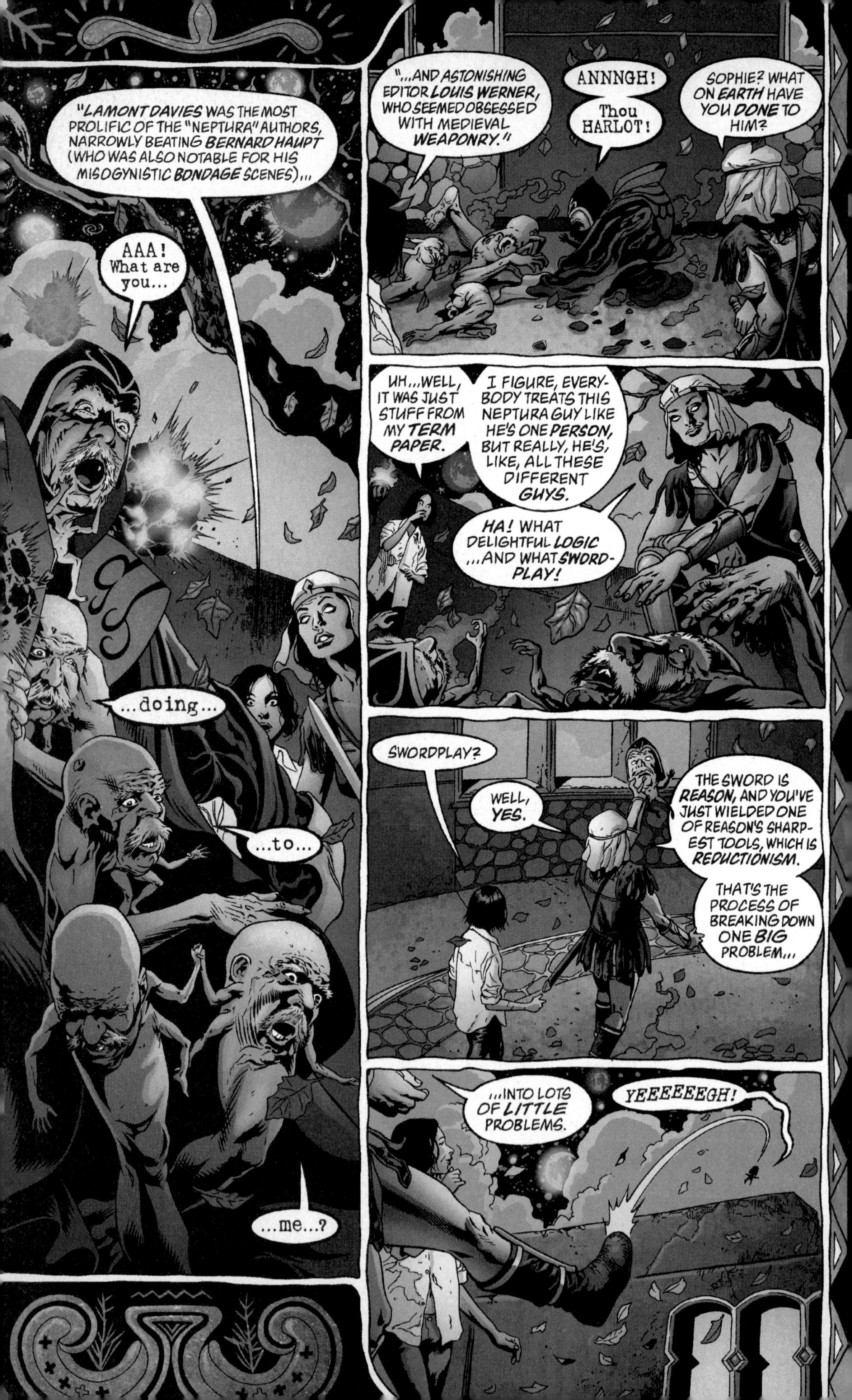
"LAMONT DAVIES WAS THE MOST PROLIFIC OF THE "NEPTURA" AUTHORS, NARROWLY BEATING BERNARD HAUPT (WHO WAS ALSO NOTABLE FOR HIS MISOGYNISTIC BONDAGE SCENES)...
AAA! What are you...
...doing...
...to...
...me...?
"...AND ASTONISHING EDITOR LOUIS WERNER, WHO SEEMED OBSESSED WITH MEDIEVAL WEAPONRY."
ANNNGH!
Thou HARLOT!
SOPHIE? WHAT ON EARTH HAVE YOU DONE TO HIM?
UH...WELL, IT WAS JUST STUFF FROM MY TERM PAPER.
I FIGURE, EVERYBODY TREATS THIS NEPTURA GUY LIKE HE'S ONE PERSON, BUT REALLY, HE'S, LIKE, ALL THESE DIFFERENT GUYS.
HA! WHAT DELIGHTFUL LOGIC ...AND WHAT SWORDPLAY!
SWORDPLAY?
WELL, YES.
THE SWORD IS REASON, AND YOU'VE JUST WIELDED ONE OF REASON'S SHARPEST TOOLS, WHICH IS REDUCTIONISM.
THAT'S THE PROCESS OF BREAKING DOWN ONE BIG PROBLEM...
...INTO LOTS OF LITTLE PROBLEMS.
YEEEEEEGH!

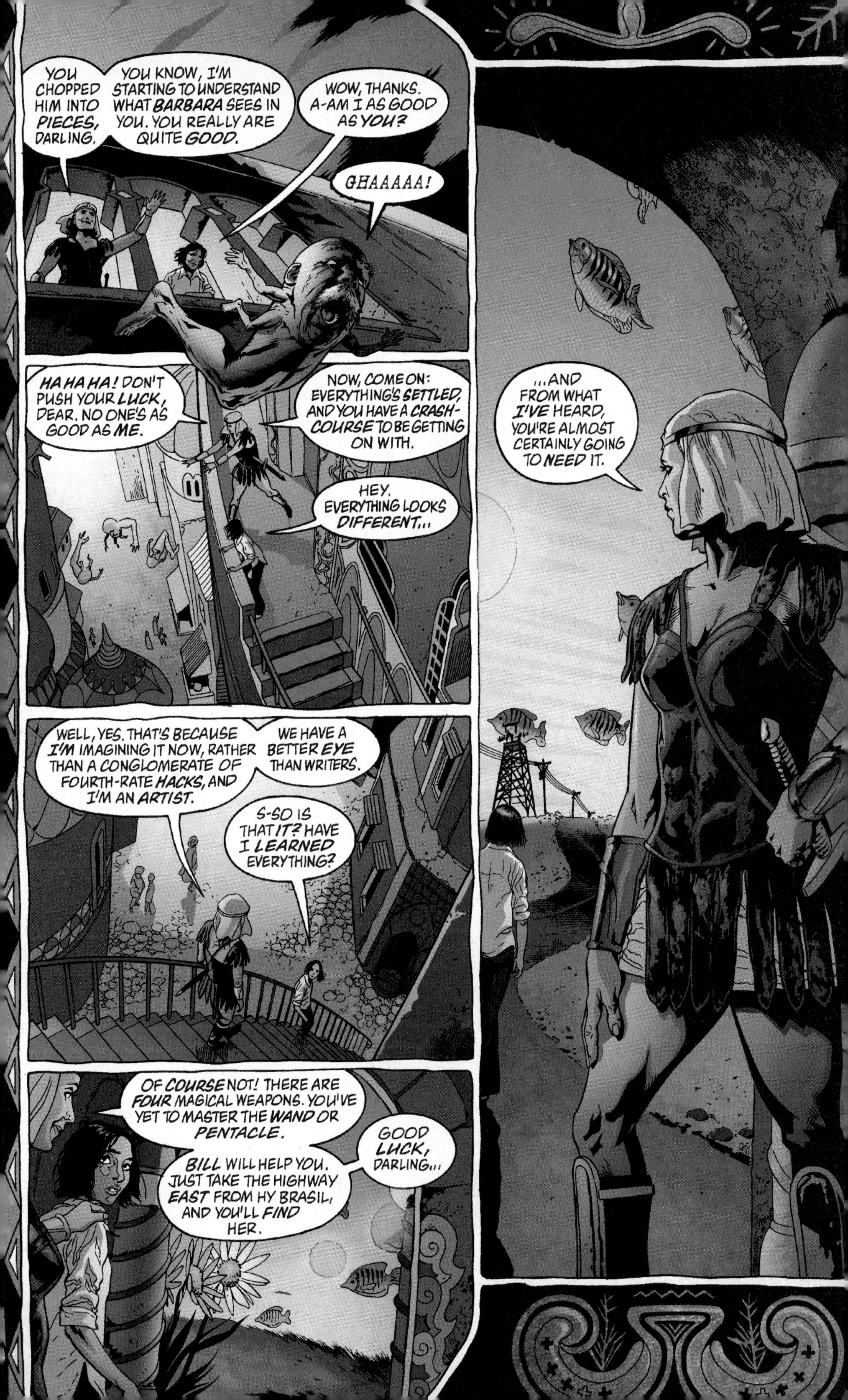
YOU CHOPPED HIM INTO PIECES, DARLING.
YOU KNOW, I'M STARTING TO UNDERSTAND WHAT BARBARA SEES IN YOU. YOU REALLY ARE QUITE GOOD.
WOW, THANKS. A-AM I AS GOOD AS YOU?
GHAAAAA!
HA HA HA! DON'T PUSH YOUR LUCK, DEAR. NO ONE'S AS GOOD AS ME.
NOW, COME ON: EVERYTHING'S SETTLED, AND YOU HAVE A CRASH-COURSE TO BE GETTING ON WITH.
HEY. EVERYTHING LOOKS DIFFERENT...
WELL, YES. THAT'S BECAUSE I'M IMAGINING IT NOW, RATHER THAN A CONGLOMERATE OF FOURTH-RATE HACKS, AND I'M AN ARTIST.
WE HAVE A BETTER EYE THAN WRITERS.
S-SO IS THAT IT? HAVE I LEARNED EVERYTHING?
OF COURSE NOT! THERE ARE FOUR MAGICAL WEAPONS. YOU'VE YET TO MASTER THE WAND OR PENTACLE.
BILL WILL HELP YOU. JUST TAKE THE HIGHWAY EAST FROM HY BRASIL, AND YOU'LL FIND HER.
GOOD LUCK, DARLING...
...AND FROM WHAT I'VE HEARD, YOU'RE ALMOST CERTAINLY GOING TO NEED IT.

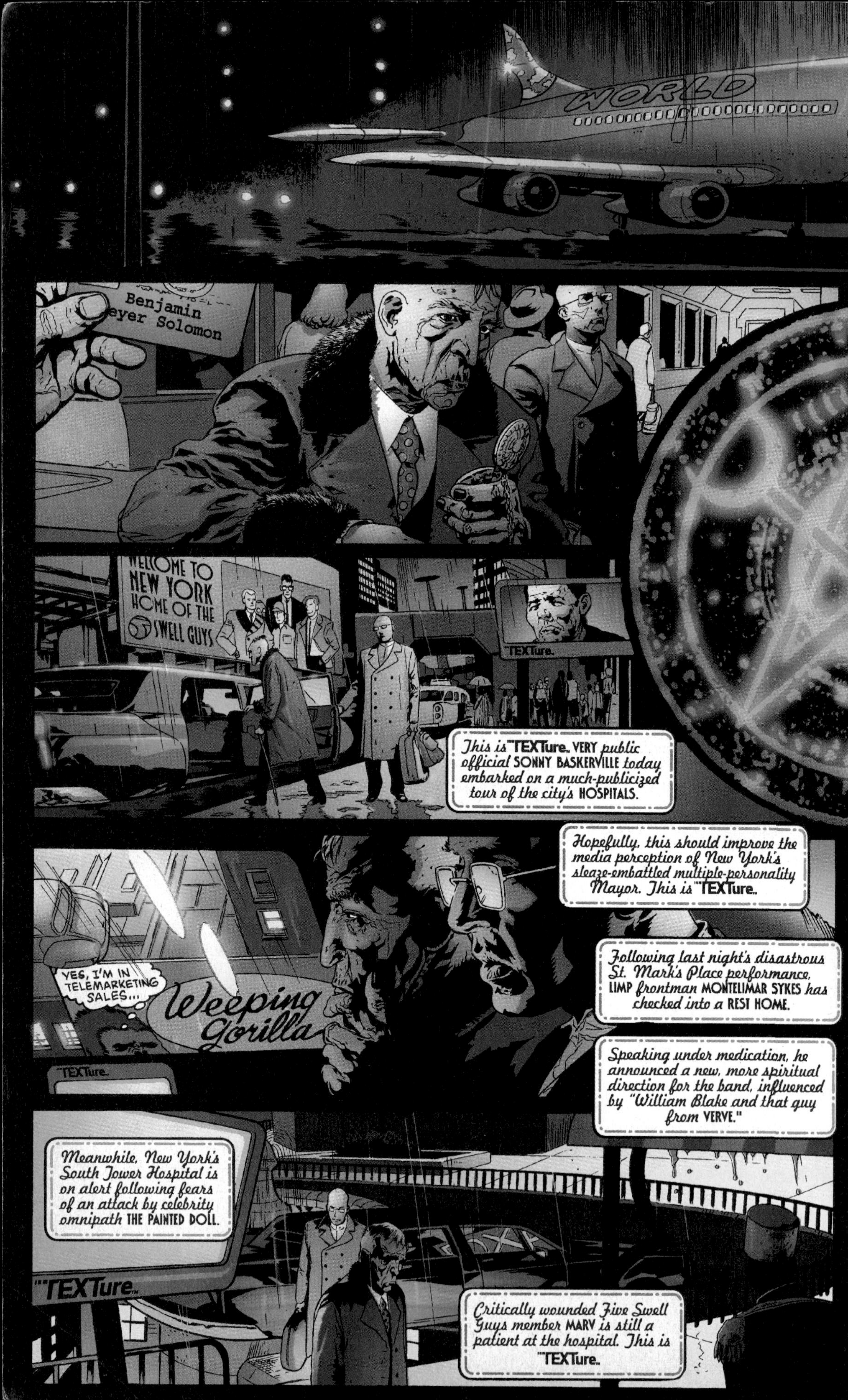
WORLD
Benjamin
eyer Solomon
WELCOME TO
NEW YORK
HOME OF THE
SWELL GUYS
TEXTure
This is TEXTure. VERY public official SONNY BASKERVILLE today embarked on a much-publicized tour of the city's HOSPITALS.
Hopefully, this should improve the media perception of New York's sleaze-embattled multiple-personality Mayor. This is TEXTure.
YES, I'M IN TELEMARKETING SALES...
Weeping Gorilla
TEXTure
Following last night's disastrous St. Mark's Place performance, LIMP frontman MONTELIMAR SYKES has checked into a REST HOME.
Speaking under medication, he announced a new, more spiritual direction for the band, influenced by "William Blake and that guy from VERVE."
Meanwhile, New York's South Tower Hospital is on alert following fears of an attack by celebrity omnipath THE PAINTED DOLL.
TEXTure
Critically wounded Five Swell Guys member MARV is still a patient at the hospital. This is TEXTure.

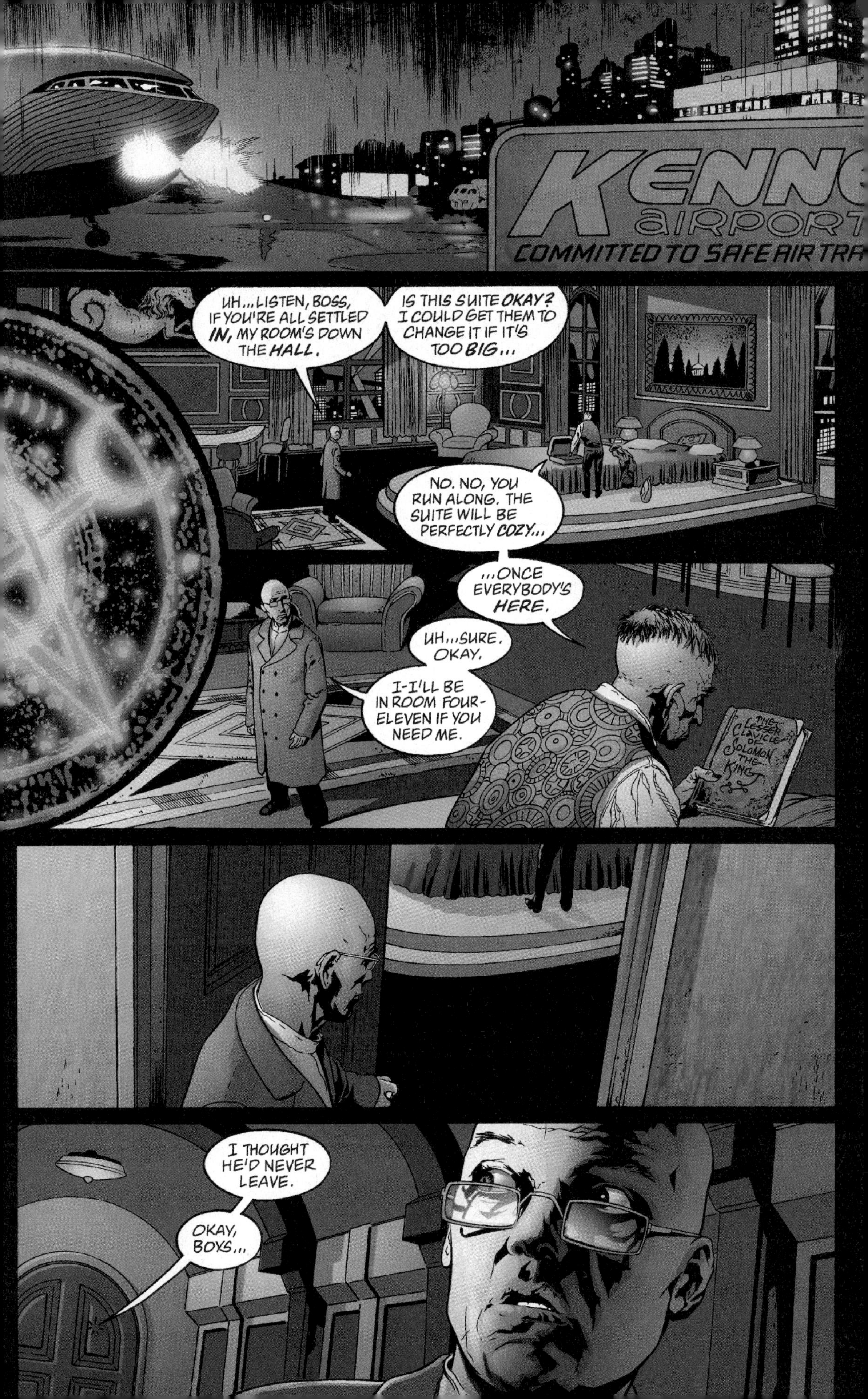
KENN
AIRPORT
COMMITTED TO SAFE AIR TRA
UH... LISTEN, BOSS, IF YOU'RE ALL SETTLED IN, MY ROOM'S DOWN THE HALL.
IS THIS SUITE OKAY? I COULD GET THEM TO CHANGE IT IF IT'S TOO BIG...
NO. NO, YOU RUN ALONG. THE SUITE WILL BE PERFECTLY COZY...
...ONCE EVERYBODY'S HERE.
UH...SURE. OKAY.
I-I'LL BE IN ROOM FOUR-ELEVEN IF YOU NEED ME.
THE LESSER CLAVICLE OF SOLOMON THE KING
I THOUGHT HE'D NEVER LEAVE.
OKAY, BOYS...

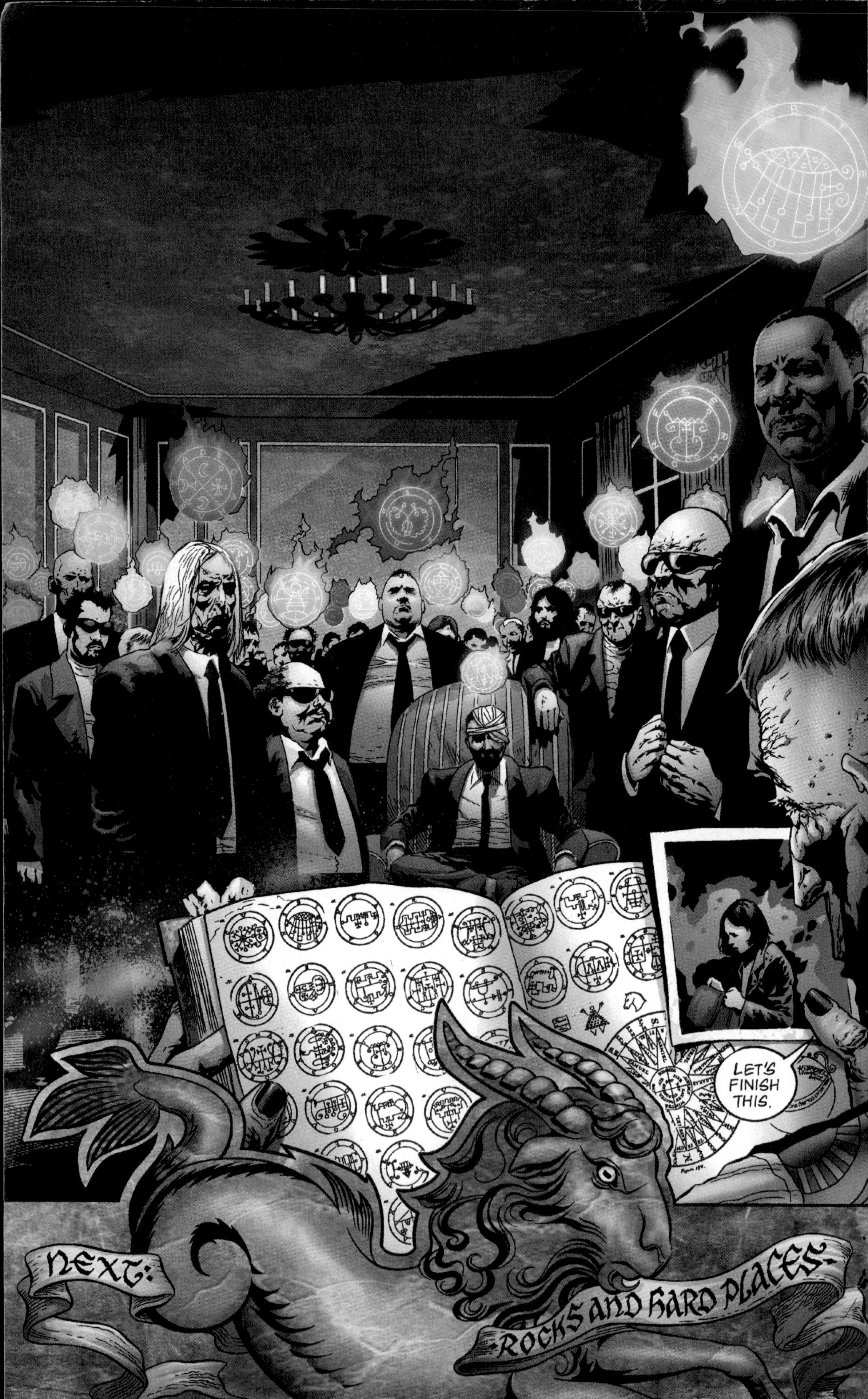
LET'S FINISH THIS.
NEXT:
ROCKS AND HARD PLACES.

PROMETHEA GALLERY

Designs by J.H. WILLIAMS III based on concepts by ALAN MOORE. Original costume sketches on this page designed by J.H. and Wendy Williams.

NOTES: STAFF SHOULD BE GLOWING PURE-WHITE WITH FAINT BLUE EDGING
ALSO SNAKES AT TOP WILL BE MOVING AROUND WITH LIFE -
STAFF SHOULD APPEAR AS IF WERE MADE OF LIGHT BECOMING SOLID AT TOP - LOADED WITH ENERGY
COSTUMING IS AN ELABORATE COMBINATION OF GREEK (HERMES) + EGYPTIAN (THOTH) STYLINGS
ARMORING SHOULD BE IN GOLD TONES (VERY METALLIC) ALL ROBING IS PURE WHITE WITH RED EDGES AND GREEK KEY DESIGNS

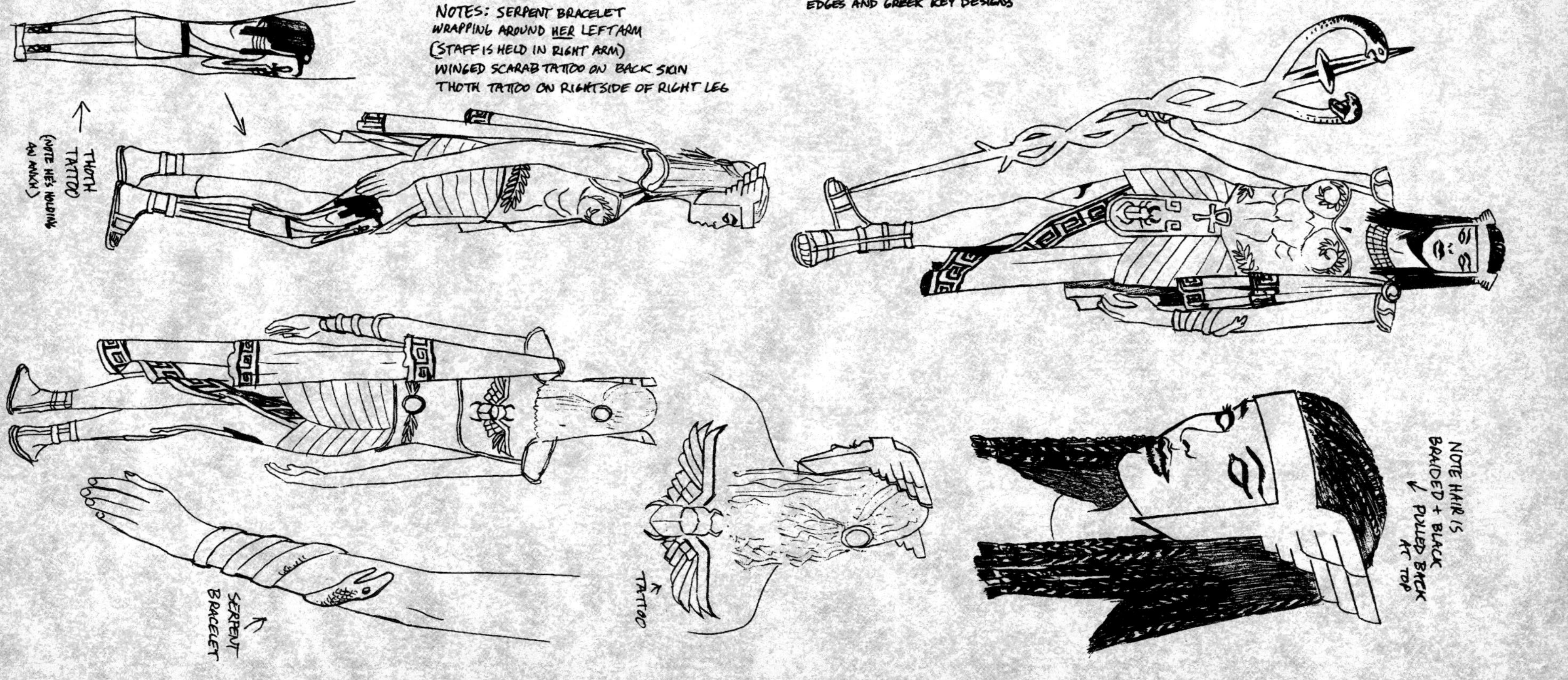

NOTES: SERPENT BRACELET
WRAPPING AROUND HER LEFT ARM
(STAFF IS HELD IN RIGHT ARM)
WINGED SCARAB TATTOO ON BACK SKIN
THOTH TATTOO ON RIGHTSIDE OF RIGHT LEG
THOTH TATTOO
(NOTE HE'S HOLDING AN ANKH)
NOTE HAIR IS BRAIDED + BLACK
PULLED BACK AT TOP
TATTOO
SERPENT BRACELET

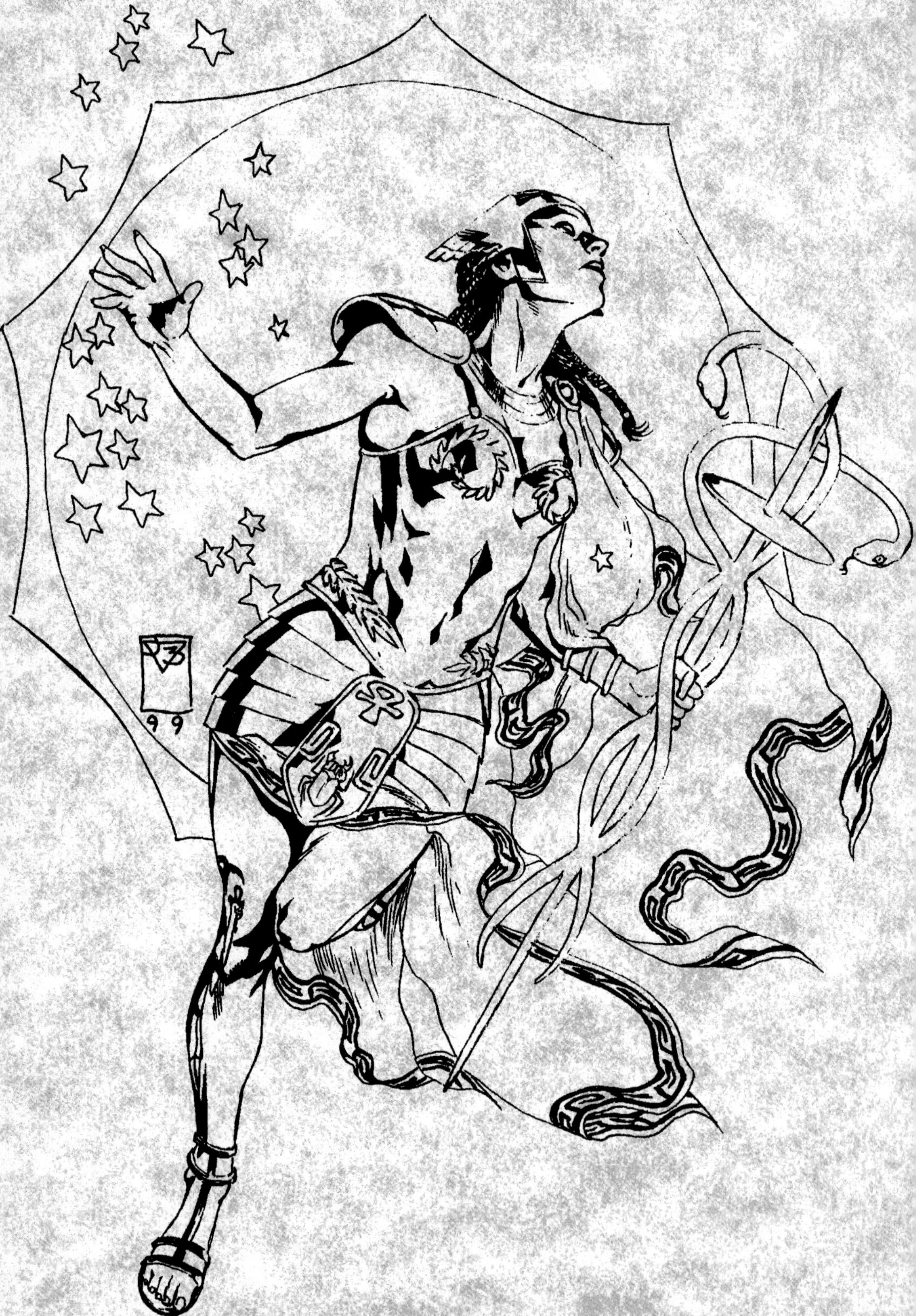

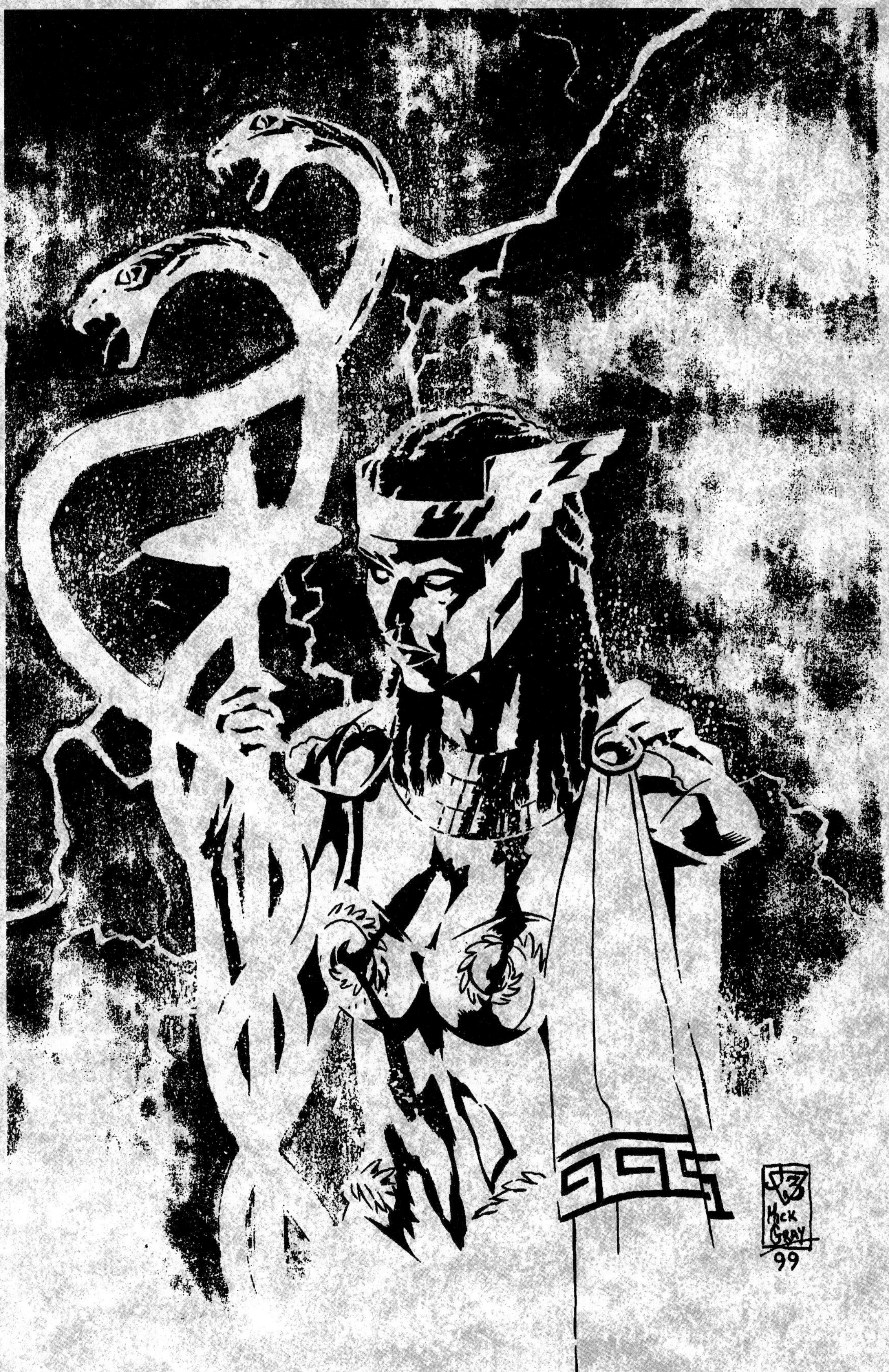
MACK
GRAY
99

Here's the original art from the cover of issue six, highlighting the lithographic effect meant to recall old pulp illustrations.

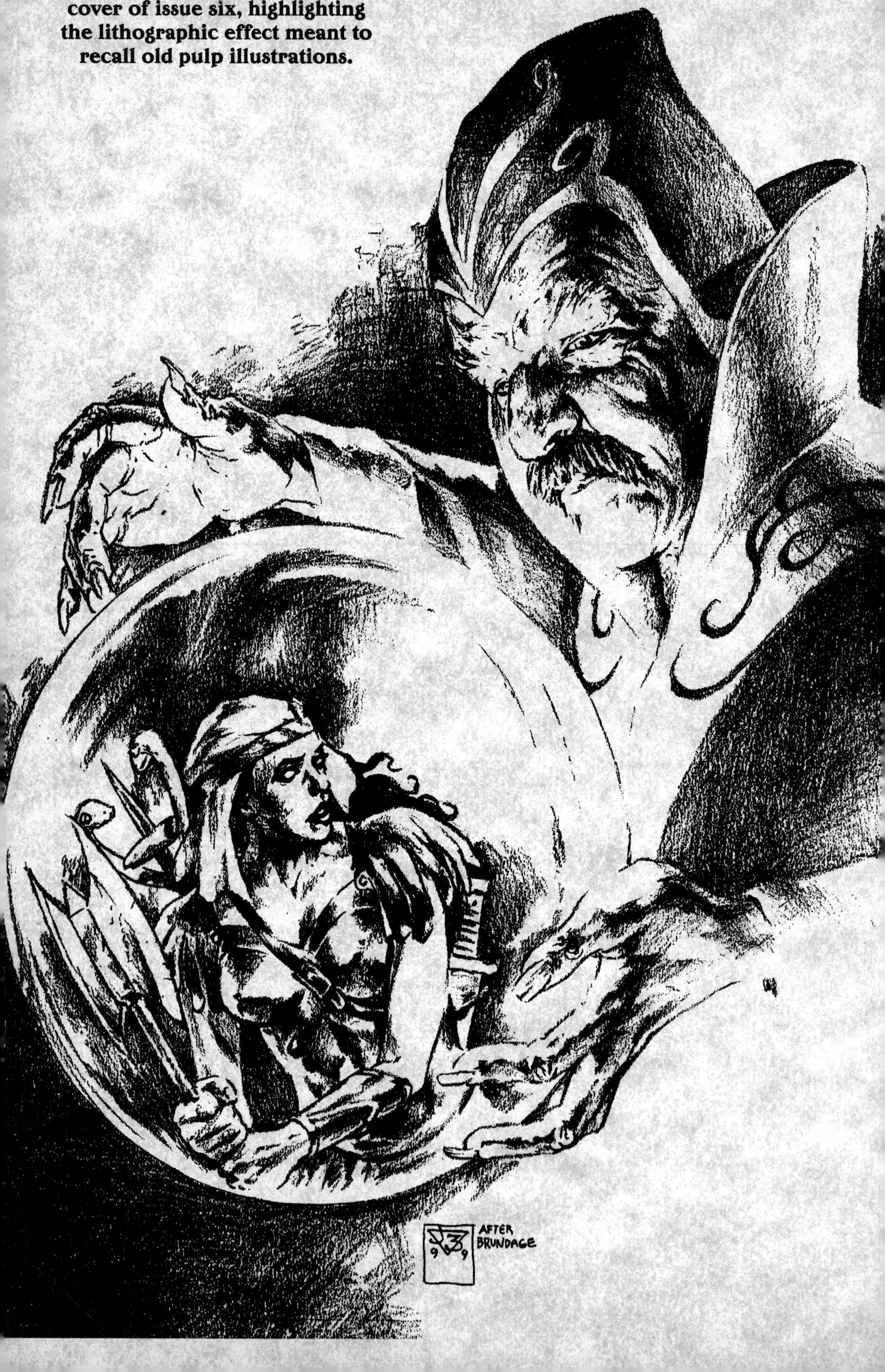
AFTER BRUNDAGE

DEDICATIONS

To Leah, Amber, and Melinda;

To all my family, all my friends.

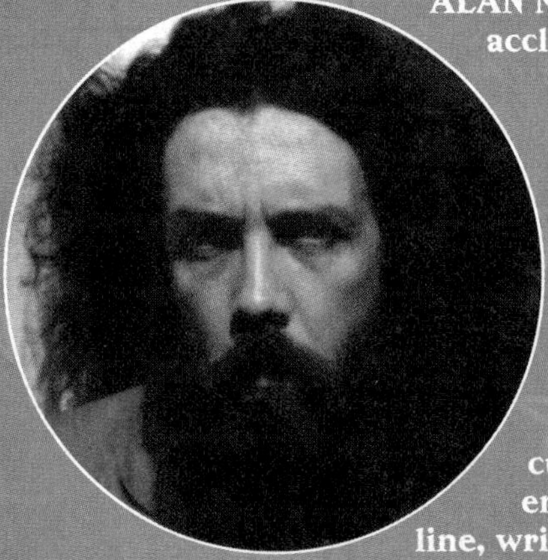

ALAN MOORE is perhaps the most acclaimed writer in the graphic story medium, having garnered many awards for such works as WATCHMEN, V FOR VENDETTA, FROM HELL, MIRACLEMAN, SWAMP THING and SUPREME, among others, along with the many fine artists he has collaborated with on those works. He is currently masterminding the entire America's Best Comics line, writing TOM STRONG, TOP 10 and TOMORROW STORIES in addition to PROMETHEA, with more in the planning stages. He resides in central England.

To my wife, Wendy, for all her everloving support, inspiration and insightful help in the design of Promethea. The art and my life wouldn't be as good without her. Oh, and for her cookies, I must not forget the cookies! Also to Mick Gray, my friend and colleague, and to the power of the imagination.

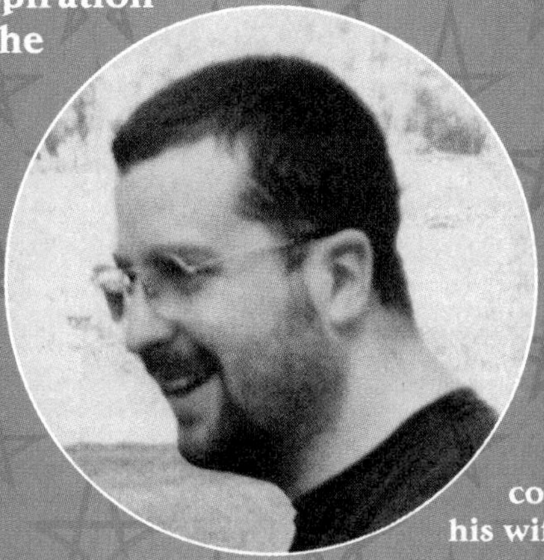

J.H. WILLIAMS III, penciller and co-creator of PROMETHEA, entered the comics field in 1991 and immediately began getting attention for his finely crafted work on such titles as BATMAN and STARMAN. More recently he's been praised for SON OF SUPERMAN and another co-creation, CHASE. J.H. and his wife Wendy live in California.

The ink that I slapped around on this book is dedicated to all the people who made it possible for me to slap around ink on comic books: J.H. Williams III, Mark McKenna, Dan Vado, Chuck Austen, Frank Cirocco, and the rest of you...you know who you are. To my favorite comic book writer, Alan Moore -- THANK YOU! Also, I can't forget my wonderful wife, and assistant, Holly...the greatest gal in the world.

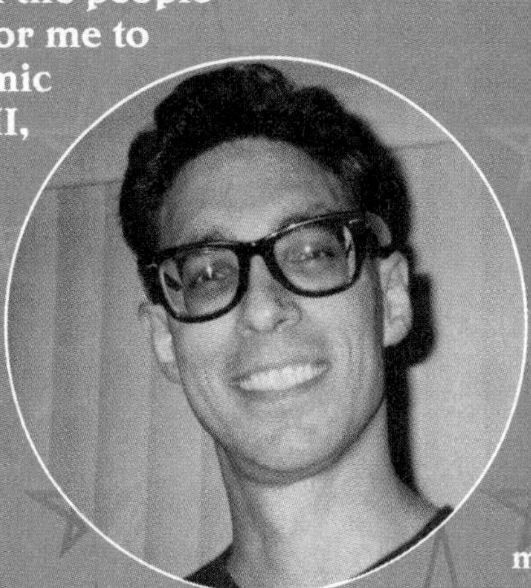

MICK GRAY, a longtime comics inker, began his collaboration with Williams in 1995, and his accurate attention to every detail and nuance on such titles as BATMAN, CHASE and SON OF SUPERMAN, not to mention PROMETHEA, continue to make this an exclusive team. Mick and his wife Holly also live in California.

AMERICA'S BEST COMICS COLLECTED EDITIONS

TOM STRONG BOOK 1
Alan Moore, Chris Sprouse & Alan Gordon

PROMETHEA BOOK 1
Alan Moore, J. H. Williams III & Mick Gray

Forthcoming:

TOP 10 BOOK 1
Alan Moore, Gene Ha & Zander Cannon

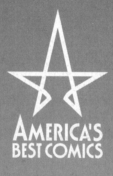